Down in the Dumps

Down in the Dumps

Administration of the Unfair Trade Laws

Richard Boltuck and
Robert E. Litan

editors

The Brookings Institution
Washington, D.C.

Copyright © 1991 by

THE BROOKINGS INSTITUTION

1775 Massachusetts Avenue, N.W., Washington, D.C. 20036

All rights reserved

Library of Congress Cataloging-in-Publication data:

Down in the dumps: administration of the unfair trade laws /
  Richard Boltuck and Robert E. Litan, editors.
    p.   cm.
    Includes bibliographical references and index.
    ISBN 0-8157-1020-8 (alk. paper)—ISBN 0-8157-1019-4
    (alk. paper)
    1. Antidumping duties—Law and legislation—United
States. 2. Competition, Unfair—United States. 3. Foreign
trade regulation—United States. I. Boltuck, Richard,
1955– . II. Litan, Robert E., 1950– .
KF6708.D8D68   1991
343.73'072—dc20
[347.30372]   91-28538
                                      CIP

9 8 7 6 5 4 3 2 1

₿ THE BROOKINGS INSTITUTION

The Brookings Institution is an independent organization devoted to nonpartisan research, education, and publication in economics, government, foreign policy, and the social sciences generally. Its principal purposes are to aid in the development of sound public policies and to promote public understanding of issues of national importance.

The Institution was founded on December 8, 1927, to merge the activities of the Institute for Government Research, founded in 1916, the Institute of Economics, founded in 1922, and the Robert Brookings Graduate School of Economics and Government, founded in 1924.

The Board of Trustees is responsible for the general administration of the Institution, while the immediate direction of the policies, program, and staff is vested in the President, assisted by an advisory committee of the officers and staff. The by-laws of the Institution state: "It is the function of the Trustees to make possible the conduct of scientific research, and publication, under the most favorable conditions, and to safeguard the independence of the research staff in the pursuit of their studies and in the publication of the results of such studies. It is not a part of their function to determine, control, or influence the conduct of particular investigations or the conclusions reached."

The President bears final responsibility for the decision to publish a manuscript as a Brookings book. In reaching his judgment on the competence, accuracy, and objectivity of each study, the President is advised by the director of the appropriate research program and weighs the views of a panel of expert outside readers who report to him in confidence on the quality of the work. Publication of a work signifies that it is deemed a competent treatment worthy of public consideration but does not imply endorsement of conclusions or recommendations.

The Institution maintains its position of neutrality on issues of public policy in order to safeguard the intellectual freedom of the staff. Hence interpretations or conclusions in Brookings publications should be understood to be solely those of the authors and should not be attributed to the Institution, to its trustees, officers, or other staff members, or to the organizations that support its research.

Foreword

W ITH THE increasing integration of the major economies of the world, trade frictions have also increased. The Uruguay Round of multilateral trade negotiations, once scheduled for completion in December 1990, has been slowed over the issue of agricultural subsidies. U.S.-Japanese trade relations have continued to be a source of friction between the two countries. At issue in all these disputes is whether the United States and other countries are playing "fairly" in the international trade arena.

The General Agreement on Tariffs and Trade outlines a variety of rules designed to ensure fairness. The United States, like other GATT signatories, has enacted statutes designed, for the most part, to be consistent with the GATT requirements.

In this book, Richard Boltuck and Robert E. Litan, joined by a team of attorneys and economists with direct experience in "unfair trade" practice investigations, provide the first study of how one of the U.S. governmental agencies charged with implementing the U.S. laws governing unfair trade—the Department of Commerce—has actually discharged its statutory mission. In particular, the book focuses on the antidumping and countervailing duty statutes, provisions allowing the United States to impose offsetting duties on imports that are sold here at prices below those charged by the producers in their home countries or that benefit from subsidies provided by foreign governments to encourage exports. Although these provisions may have once been obscure parts of the U.S. trade laws, they have figured importantly in many recent celebrated trade disputes, including those involving the sale here of foreign-made semiconductors, steel, lumber, screen displays for laptop computers, word processors, and minivan automobiles.

All but one of the authors in the volume are highly critical of the procedures used by the Department of Commerce to calculate margins of dumping and export subsidization. Specifically, they find that at many points in the investigations, both through substantive and procedural requirements, there is a bias toward higher margins, and therefore higher import duties, than is warranted by economic theory, and in some cases by the GATT antidumping and subsidy codes themselves. Significantly, these authors contend that most of the biases can be removed without legislative change, through changes in administrative practice.

Richard Boltuck is an economist with the Special Studies Division of the Office of Management and Budget. He formerly served as a senior economist with the U.S. International Trade Commission. Robert E. Litan is a senior fellow in the Economic Studies program at Brookings, where he is also the director of the Center for Economic Progress and Employment and the new Center for Law, Economics, and Politics. While at Brookings, he has consulted privately for foreign respondents in two antidumping investigations at the Department of Commerce, and on several occasions has testified on behalf of foreign respondents in antidumping investigations at the International Trade Commission.

The essays in this volume were presented in draft form to a conference at the Brookings Institution in November 1990, which was attended by approximately 100 private and government attorneys and economists with expertise in antidumping and subsidy investigations, as well as by interested corporate representatives. The authors incorporated responses to comments made at this conference where appropriate. In addition, a summary of the comments appears at the end of the volume. All the authors in this volume who are employees of the U.S. government, or were employees at the time their papers were written, have presented their own personal views and not those of the agencies or departments where they are or were employed.

Caroline Lalire edited the manuscript, Roshna M. Kapadia verified its factual content, and Susan L. Woollen prepared it for typesetting. Anita G. Whitlock provided valuable secretarial assistance. The index was prepared by Florence Robinson.

Funding for this project was provided by Archer-Daniels-Midland Foundation; Caterpillar Foundation; Dayton Hudson Foundation; and the General Electric Foundation.

The views expressed here are those of the authors and should not be attributed to the trustees, officers, or staff members of the Brookings Institution.

BRUCE K. MAC LAURY
President

November 1991
Washington, D.C.

Contents

Figures

Down in the Dumps

CHAPTER ONE

America's "Unfair" Trade Laws

Richard Boltuck and Robert E. Litan

"UNFAIR TRADE ." The term itself invites condemnation. Certainly many nations think so. The more than ninety signatories to the General Agreement on Tariffs and Trade (GATT) allow member countries to offset the trade effects of dumping by imposing import duties. The Subsidies Code to the GATT, signed in 1979 by fewer countries, authorizes similar offsetting duties against imports that benefit from certain "countervailable" subsidies. Consistent with these international rules, the United States has enacted a series of statutory provisions and constructed a major administrative program to root out unfair dumping and subsidization and apply remedial penalties.

For years these provisions and their enforcement wallowed in the backwaters of trade policymaking. Investigations are carried out by relatively obscure technicians operating in corners of the federal bureaucracy. Industry specialists, accountants, and computer programmers, initially belonging to a small unit within the Treasury Department and more recently occupying an office in the Commerce Department, determine whether and to what extent an unfair practice exists. If the decision is affirmative, then the International Trade Commission (ITC)—a six-member independent agency—determines whether the practice is a cause of "material injury" to an American industry. If both decisions are affirmative, the offsetting duties are imposed. The calculations are then repeated every year when requested by interested parties in "administrative reviews" until the practice stops (for three years) or, as is more often the case, the foreign exporter moves its operations to the United States and manufactures here what it used to but can no longer export here profitably.

In fact, the unfair practice investigations were *designed* to ensure their

Table 1-1. *Numbers of Antidumping and Countervailing Duty Investigations in the United States, 1980–89*

Year	Antidumping	CVD	Year	Antidumping	CVD
1980	37	69	1986	71	20
1981	15	17	1987	15	3
1982	65	116	1988	42	8
1983	46	8	1989	23	3
1984	74	26	Total,		
1985	63	31	1980–89	451	301

Sources: Robert E. Baldwin and Jeffrey W. Steagall, "An Analysis of Factors Influencing ITC Decisions in Antidumping, Countervailing Duty and Safeguards Cases," paper presented at University of Wisconsin–Free University of Brussels Conference on Trade Policy, Washington, May 14, 1991; and U.S. International Trade Commission Annual Reports, 1980–89.

obscurity and thus to insulate them from the highly charged political atmosphere that surrounds trade disputes. The thinking was, and remains, that the investigation of unfair trade practices is more like a judicial contest than a political event. Either the imports are or are not "fairly traded" according to well-established statutory standards. Let some impartial government agency make that decision, and let the consequences flowing from the decision be automatic. That way politicians can say trade matters are "out of their hands" and thus out of the political arena. If foreigners complain about the outcomes, it must be because they're guilty of offending internationally accepted rules of the game.

For many years the whole process worked pretty much as designed. Unfair trade investigations *were* obscure. Their results did not usually hit the front pages of the newspapers or the nightly television news programs. The big trade developments were to be found instead at the highly visible United States Trade Representative (USTR), the small and highly prestigious trade policy office found in the Executive Office of the President—a long way up from the technicians at the Treasury or Commerce departments or from the commissioners at the ITC.

But much has changed in recent years. In the 1980s, 451 antidumping investigations were launched in the United States (table 1-1), of which 327 were completed. More than half of these (54 percent) resulted in affirmative dumping orders or were settled.[1] A lower but still substantial number (301) of countervailing duty (CVD) cases were also filed during the decade. Clearly, unfair trade investigations have been a booming phenomenon, deserving of further study.

The bare statistics, however, conceal the much higher visibility of certain individual unfair trade cases, which triggered some of the most

1. The data on affirmative decisions were provided by I. M. Destler and Paul Baker.

Table 1-2. *Target Industries of U.S. Antidumping and CVD Investigations, 1980–89*

Industry	Antidumping	CVD
Chemicals	58	37
Food	16	45
Iron and steel	201	149
Leather	. . .	6
Machinery	8	6
Nonferrous metals	16	5
Oil country tubular goods	12	8
Textiles and apparel	15	6
Lumber	. . .	4
Other	125	34
All products	451	300

Sources: See table 1-1.

important trade policy decisions of the 1980s. The "voluntary restraint agreement" limiting steel imports from eighteen nations in 1982 was the price the exporting countries paid to settle a massive number of dumping and CVD cases brought by U.S. steel producers (as shown in table 1-2, which breaks down unfair trade practice cases by industry). A controversial CVD filing by the U.S. lumber industry in 1985 resulted in import restraints on Canadian lumber. And the well-known semiconductor accord reached with Japan in 1986, which set floor prices for Japanese semiconductors around the world, was greatly facilitated by a dumping suit filed by American companies.[2]

More recently, unfair trade investigations have targeted everyday products known to American consumers. In 1989 dumping orders were entered against computer diskettes and cellular mobile telephones. In 1991 word processors and display screens for computer displays were subjected to dumping duties and, in perhaps the most highly publicized case of all, dumping proceedings were launched against the main Japanese producers of minivans and threatened against Japanese luxury automobiles.

In short, unfair trade investigations have been brought out of the closet. They now are and will continue to be a major element of trade policymaking not only in the United States but abroad. Indeed, GATT-legal trade remedies against "unfair" practices are in part a *product* of GATT's success in outlawing other forms of protection that the United States considered more discretionary or arbitrary. Thus, unfair trade investi-

2. See table 1-A for a list of products on which dumping or countervailing duties were imposed between 1985 and 1989.

Table 1-3. *Target Countries of U.S. Antidumping and CVD Investigations, 1980–89*

Country	Antidumping	CVD	Country	Antidumping	CVD
Belgium	10	17	India	3	3
Canada	25	18	Indonesia	...	1
Denmark	...	7	Malaysia	1	1
France	22	28	Pakistan	...	3
Greece	2	1	Philippines	1	1
			Thailand	3	...
Ireland	1	6			
Italy	26	24	Argentina	6	...
Luxembourg	6	13	Brazil	24	36
Netherlands	9	13	Chile	2	1
Portugal	3	1	Colombia	4	...
			Costa Rica	1	...
Spain	15	21	Ecuador	1	...
United Kingdom	18	18			
West Germany	29	18	El Salvador	1	1
Economic	...	3	Mexico	8	2
Community			Peru	1	...
			Trinidad and Tobago	1	...
Austria	5	5	Uruguay	...	1
Finland	4	...	Venezuela	13	10
Norway	1	1			
Sweden	6	4	Iran	1	...
Switzerland	4	...	Israel	5	4
Turkey	2	4	Kenya	1	...
Australia	3	1	Czechoslovakia	2	...
New Zealand	2	3	East Germany	7	...
South Africa	7	...	Hungary	4	...
			Poland	6	...
Hong Kong	3	...	Romania	9	...
Japan	58	6	Soviet Union	2	...
Korea	27	17	Yugoslavia	5	...
Singapore	6	1			
Taiwan	28	7			
China	17	...	All countries	451	301

Sources: See table 1-1.

gations today provide substantial and growing income to a small army of trade lawyers and their consultants who are hired to represent both petitioner firms and respondent importers and exporters.

But along with the growing importance of the trade remedy cases there has come growing controversy. The U.S. investigations have targeted not just one or a few countries but many (see table 1-3). And increasingly, a number of commentators have wondered aloud whether the investigations are "fair" themselves. Do the procedures punish truly unfair trade,

Table 1-4. *Trade Investigations around the World, 1980–88*

Investigation	1980	1981	1982	1983	1984	1985	1986	1987	1988	All years
					Number of actions					
					United States					
Antidumping	24	15	63	47	73	65	70	14	40	411
CVD	11	22	145	22	52	38	26	5	3	332
GATT safeguard	...	...	...	2	...	...	...	...	...	2
Escape clause	2	6	1	5	6	3	3	2	2	30
Other	...	10	7	7	2	1	3	4	5	39
					European Community					
Antidumping	26	47	55	43	42	35	31	34	40	353
CVD	...	1	4	3	1	...	...	2	...	11
GATT safeguard	...	...	1	...	1	1	2	1	...	6
Escape clause	...	...	2	5	1	8	4	11	...	31
Other	...	...	...	...	...	...	...	2	...	2
					Australia					
Antidumping	58	49	77	80	56	63	62	17	16	478
CVD	...	...	3	7	6	3	3	...	...	22
GATT safeguard	...	...	...	1	...	...	...	...	...	1
					Canada					
Antidumping	25	23	72	36	31	36	85	86	53	447
CVD	3	...	1	3	2	2	4	6	2	23
GATT safeguard	...	1	1	...	...	...	...	...	...	2
					Developing countries					
Antidumping	...	...	...	...	...	...	5	23	47	75
CVD	...	...	...	...	...	...	...	...	...	0
GATT safeguard	...	...	...	...	...	...	...	...	...	0

Source: Patrick A. Messerlin, "Antidumping," in Jeffrey J. Schott, ed., *Completing the Uruguay Round: A Results-Oriented Approach to the GATT Trade Negotiations* (Washington: Institute for International Economics, 1990), chap. 6. The table is found on pp. 110–11.

or do they punish trade that Americans—and only Americans—deem to be unfair?

The question is important not just for abstract reasons. Thus far the United States has been the world's leading prosecutor of unfair trade practices. But other nations are catching up (see table 1-4). Australia, Canada, and the members of the European Community—all industrialized countries like the United States—have been particularly active. Indeed, the table shows that in the latter part of the 1980s these other countries were even more aggressive than the United States. And perhaps most significant, such developing countries as Brazil, Korea, and Mexico—in the past major *targets* of trade complaints in industrialized countries—have been rapidly attempting to turn the tables by stepping up their own case filings against firms in other countries, including those headquartered here.

Indeed, wittingly or unwittingly, U.S. enthusiasm for identifying pervasive unfair trade practices and the U.S. "technology" (the rules Americans have developed to measure dumping and subsidization) for doing so have been transferred abroad. Yet just as the transfer of industrial technologies to other countries has come back to haunt those firms that willingly sold them (or gave them away), so too will the United States reap the consequences of its own practices in rooting out unfair trade when they are copied by other countries, as is now happening.

Indeed, U.S. laws need not be exported to be used by foreign parties. Here at home, where foreign-owned firms operate under the principles of national treatment, foreign enterprises with U.S. manufacturing facilities have begun to take advantage of the trade remedy laws. Witness the antidumping complaint brought in 1991 by a Japanese-owned manufacturer of typewriters in the United States against an American-owned competitor with plants in Southeast Asia exporting typewriters. Probably more foreign companies will try to take advantage of similar opportunities when their U.S. lawyers advise them it would be in their interests.

The way the United States administers its trade laws matters to American citizens generally as well. Any biases systematically built into the administration of the trade laws hurt either consumers, who may be forced to pay excessive prices for imported goods and their domestically produced counterparts, or producers of downstream products, who may be irreparably damaged or even run out of business.

For all these reasons, the time is ripe for a thorough examination of exactly how American trade investigators and administrators go about discharging their responsibilities under the U.S. trade laws. Do they arrive at decisions that truly offset the consequences of "unfair trade," or of trade that is truly harmful to U.S. economic welfare? Do they fail to find unfair trade where they should? Or do they consistently tilt in a protectionist direction, finding practices to be unfair that aren't and recommending "remedies" that go beyond what is necessary to offset the unfairness and thus wrongly penalize importers, consumers, and downstream producers?

These are the questions that the following chapters address. Collectively, the authors bring a broad range of economic and legal expertise to their subject. All have been active in the field, as private attorneys or economists representing domestic and foreign parties in trade investigations, or as government officials involved in making decisions in these cases. In many instances, the authors have worked both inside and outside the government during their careers.

Preliminary versions of the chapters were presented at a conference held at Brookings in November 1990 and attended by an even wider range of trade experts from inside and outside the government. Also included in the volume are the formal remarks of those who were asked to comment on the papers and a final chapter summarizing the remarks made by conference participants.[3]

Although, as noted at the outset, the investigation of dumping and CVD cases is split between the Commerce Department and the ITC, the authors were asked to focus primarily on the methods used by Commerce to estimate the amount of dumping and subsidization. The reason for this choice is not that the injury determinations of the ITC are unimportant. Rather, we decided to concentrate on the procedures and methods used by the Commerce Department because those issues have until now attracted much less attention in scholarly journals and other publications than the questions typically decided by the ITC. Moreover, it is our judgment that the decisions by Commerce about the presence and magnitude of unfair trade practices ultimately have a more important impact than injury determinations, since the ITC renders only "up or down" decisions, whereas the often esoteric and complex methods used by the Commerce Department to measure the magnitude of unfair trade practices affect the amounts of any offsetting penalties.

As discussed in more detail below, the chapters that follow, with one exception, are highly critical of many of the current practices used by the International Trade Administration (ITA) within the Commerce Department to make dumping and CVD findings.[4] On balance, the authors argue, both types of investigations are tilted systematically against importers. The results are difficult to square with economic theory or with the interests of American consumers, although they *do* serve some American industries competing against imports, at the expense of other U.S. industries. And to the extent that other nations copy them, U.S. procedures ultimately will not serve the interests of American exporters

---

3. We originally invited a representative of the Commerce Department to prepare a paper for presentation at the conference. In lieu of contributing a formal paper, the department was represented at the conference by a number of officials within the Office of Import and Trade Administration, who delivered comments during general discussion.

4. A strong dissent comes from Terence Stewart, who was originally a discussant of one of the papers at the conference. But he later expanded his discussion into an essay-length critique, which is included as the last chapter in this volume.

either, whose products will face new forms of trade hurdles in the years ahead.

Many of the criticisms voiced here are widely recognized among those who have dealt and continue to deal with this area of law and policy. And U.S. trade negotiators have attempted to discuss some of the issues during the Uruguay Round of trade negotiations. However, most of the issues raised here are not currently on the international trade negotiating agenda. At the end of this chapter we consider the merits and prospects of putting them there or, alternatively, of changing them unilaterally.

Unfair Trade Defined and Its Prohibitions "Justified"

It is important first to define our terms, for there is much confusion about the meaning of both dumping and unfair subsidization. It is also essential to know why, if at all, the laws against unfair trade should exist and be enforced.

Contrary to the popular notion that dumping is "selling below cost," both in law and in economic theory dumping is defined as international price discrimination, or the practice of charging a higher price for sales in a foreign producer's home market than for export to the United States.[5] Under current U.S. law, when comparisons to home market or other third-market prices are not possible or when U.S. investigators find that a large part of the home market sales are made "below cost," export prices to the United States are compared to a measure of production cost constructed from accounting data, through the use of statutory guidelines. In principle, all price comparisons are made at the "factory gate," or at the point when the goods leave their plants, and thus before any transportation or selling costs are incurred that would result in legitimate price differences among international markets. Once dumping has been found, U.S. law grants producers of a "like product" relief in the form of an antidumping duty if they then can prove to the ITC that they have been materially injured "by reason of the subject imports."

In contrast to the clear legal and economic definition of dumping, there

---

5. The legal penalties for dumping are found in article 6 of the GATT and the Trade Act of 1979 (19 U.S.C. 1673). For an early and now classic economic treatment of dumping, see Jacob Viner, *Dumping: A Problem in International Trade* (University of Chicago Press, 1923).

is much less agreement about the appropriate definition of *undesirable* and therefore *unlawful* subsidization. Under both the GATT Subsidies Code and U.S. trade law, countervailable subsidies include direct export subsidies, production subsidies, and subsidies to factors of production, *when they distort international trade*. Trade restrictions on upstream inputs, such as product components, have also been deemed to be countervailable in some instances because they reduce the cost of production in much the same way as a production factor subsidy. GATT recognizes that domestic subsidies may serve valid national purposes but permits them to be countervailed by offsetting duties *to the extent* that trade is affected. U.S. law has interpreted this permission to countervail domestic subsidies that effectively, de jure or de facto, benefit specific industries, as opposed to generalized subsidies that benefit many or all industries in the economy. This principle recognizes that it is economically impossible to subsidize everything.

Many economists have opposed the unfair trade laws, arguing that if firms from other nations want to sell their products at cheap prices in the United States—whether because of price discrimination or because of home country subsidies—then Americans as consumers ought to take advantage of their generosity. That argument has never been a majority view among non-economists, however. Even the GATT, which is designed to promote freer trade, recognizes that dumping and subsidization can distort international trade by shifting production to locales that might otherwise not deserve it on the basis of comparative advantage. In that event, producers in importing countries (such as the United States) will be harmed by the offending practices. And if trade ends up being governed by factors other than comparative advantage, then truly unfair trade also detracts from global economic welfare.

It can be more difficult, however, to provide justifications of both elements of the unfair trade laws—antidumping and CVD—once an effort is made to be more specific about exactly what distortions these laws are designed to correct.

Thus, a standard defense of antidumping laws is that they are necessary to prevent international predatory pricing. But such practices make sense only if the practitioner of predatory pricing can later raise prices to recoup any profits lost during the period of low pricing. And this can occur only if there are significant barriers that prevent the firms driven out of business by the acts of predation from coming back into the market when prices have indeed been increased. Antitrust commentators have been skeptical, however, that such conditions hold in a domestic context. The same skepticism should apply in the international context as well.[6]

In any event, U.S. antidumping law does not direct government investigators to determine whether imports reflect a predatory pattern; if it did, dumping would be found only when import prices fall below the marginal or variable cost of production. But that is not the nature of the inquiry which the dumping statute mandates. The exercise instead is simply mathematical. If home country prices are higher than those in the United States, dumping occurs. And if such price comparisons cannot be made, dumping is found when U.S. import prices are below the *average* cost of production, a standard that no current U.S. court of which we are aware accepts as the test for predatory pricing.[7]

More recently, another economic justification of the antidumping law has been advanced by advocates of the "new trade theory" who point to the advantages that "first-mover" firms have when operating in industries that are highly capital intensive and when "learning by doing" allows firms to lower their operating costs as they expand production. In such instances, protection of the home market can afford a firm sufficient profits to fund the exploitation of other markets abroad. If firms in other countries do not enjoy these advantages of home market protection, they can be driven out of business and rendered unable to return because the technology has passed them by.[8]

However appropriate the new trade theory may be as a guide for actual policymaking—even one of the theory's principal authors is skeptical[9]—there is no evidence that the antidumping law in the United States or in any other country is either designed or administered in a manner to ensure

---

6. See J. A. Ordover, A. O. Sykes and R. D. Willig, "Unfair International Trade Practices," *NYU Journal of International Law and Politics*, vol. 15 (Winter 1983), pp. 323–37.

7. For a similar criticism of the antidumping laws, see Brian Hindley, "The Economics of Dumping and Antidumping Action: Is There a Baby in the Bathwater?" in P. K. M. Tharakan, ed., *Policy Implications of Antidumping Measures* (Amsterdam: North Holland, 1991), chap. 2.

8. For a guide to the new trade theory, see Paul R. Krugman, ed., *Strategic Trade Policy and the New International Economics* (MIT Press, 1986); James A. Brander and Barbara J. Spencer, "Export Subsidies and International Market Share Rivalry," *Journal of International Economics*, vol. 18 (February 1985), pp. 83–100; and Barbara J. Spencer and James A. Brander, "International R&D and Industrial Strategy," *Review of Economic Studies*, vol. 50 (1983), pp. 707–22.

9. Paul R. Krugman, "Is Free Trade Passé?" *Journal of Economic Perspectives*, vol. 1 (Fall 1987), pp. 131–44.

that its application is limited to such instances. Nor is there evidence that possibilities for such intervention are at all commonplace.[10]

Yet another argument advanced in support of both the antidumping and CVD laws is that while they do not promote *national* efficiency, they are necessary to encourage competitive practices abroad and thus *global* efficiency.[11] The trouble with this view is that the unfair trade laws in the United States and the other countries that have and enforce them are explicitly designed to serve domestic import-competing interests, not to benefit the world economy. Certainly the idea that the law is about global efficiency, particularly when it is in conflict with national efficiency, should be highly suspect when allegedly pursued as part of national law. Moreover, with respect to the CVD law in particular, no effort is made to distinguish between Pigovian subsidies—those that correct existing externalities and thus should be permitted—and subsidies that create trade distortions: both are effectively discouraged by the CVD law.

Finally, current administrative practice regarding the antidumping statute, in particular, has been described, but not actually defended, as a "baby 201," referring to the U.S. escape clause or safeguards remedy that authorizes temporary trade protection for domestic industries seriously injured by import competition (whether "fair" or not).[12] The term is apt because, at least in recent years, the statute has been administered in such a way that dumping and causation of injury can be found in many cases, and the presence of material injury refers to the health of the industry— much as in escape clause cases. Since the standards in dumping cases are otherwise easier to meet than in escape clause cases, and the relief is automatic rather than at the discretion of the president, dumping allegations have largely displaced the use of section 201 of the U.S. Trade Act. This insight suggests that dumping may also have replaced section 201 for the purpose of promoting efficient and orderly economic adjustment to external economic shocks.

If so, however, the dumping laws are too broad and would undoubtedly grant trade remedies when industries suffer ill health for purely domestic, as well as external, reasons. Moreover, dumping remedies are,

10. See Joseph Francois, "Optimal Commercial Policy with International Returns to Scale," May 1991; forthcoming in *Canadian Journal of Economics*.

11. See James D. Reitzes, "Antidumping Policy," May 1991, unpublished manuscript.

12. See Seth Kaplan, "Injury and Causation in USITC Antidumping Determinations: Five Recent Approaches," in Tharakan, ed., *Policy Implications of Antidumping Measures*, chap. 6.

effectively, forever (with rare exceptions). Thus, it is difficult to argue that they facilitate orderly adjustment. From a national perspective, both dumping and subsidies lower the price of imports and thus benefit domestic consumers more than they burden import-competing producers. Ordinarily, concern for the national welfare leads policymakers to welcome those events that, on balance, increase the real income of U.S. residents.

In reality, of course, whereas the practices that trigger dumping or CVD complaints arguably raise overall national income, they *redistribute* the way income is apportioned in an economy, from the producers of the import-competing products to their consumers. Plainly, some human practices which redistribute wealth have ethical implications that might justify policy intervention by government, even at the expense of economic efficiency. It is difficult, however, to see why dumping and subsidies are among them. Domestic subsidies distort domestic trade, and yet are not countervailed. Domestic "dumping," that is, price discrimination without predatory intent or result, occurs regularly without litigation. Consider, for example, senior citizen discounts, magazines that offer promotional discounts to new subscribers, or loss leader items sold below wholesale cost and designed to attract customers into a store.[13] It is certainly a puzzle why practices that are accepted in everyday business domestically should be prohibited as unethical internationally.

Some will answer that the puzzle is easily explained by special-interest pressures for protection. While naked protection has not been popular in the United States, at least since the end of World War II, opposition to "unfair trade" has become a political fact of life. Who, after all, is *for* unfair trade? In chapter 7, Robert Baldwin and Michael Moore suggest that domestic interests have been able to successfully exploit the popularity of punishing unfair trade in order to influence the administration of the laws consistently in their favor.

There nevertheless are also nagging doubts about this purported "justification" of the unfair trade laws, although, as we suggest below, there is ample evidence that in many ways the administration of the laws *has* been tilted in favor of domestic interests. If support for the unfair trade laws is solely grounded in protectionist sentiment, then the supporters are certainly big risk-takers. Why would import-competing industries seek protection that must be paid for through the use of an increasingly

---

13. The Robinson-Patman Act prohibits some forms of domestic price discrimination, but it has fallen into disuse in recent years.

expensive procedure the outcome of which cannot be predicted with certainty? Indeed, as already noted, only about 40 percent of all anti-dumping petitions filed in the 1980s actually resulted in the imposition of duties (although the success rate for petitioners rose well above 50 percent in the last four years of the decade).

At bottom, the imperfect success with which domestic interests have pursued unfair trade remedies suggests perhaps only the principled reason for the statutes: as a legal "safety valve" for channeling the strongest claimants for protection away from overtly supporting more transparent forms of protection. Thus, the overall effort to enforce the unfair trade practice program can be rationalized to the extent it successfully prevents more unjustified protection than it hands out. In essence, the supply of protection cannot be eliminated but only reduced and regulated—much like twisting and tying a balloon can alter its shape but cannot eliminate the air pressure within.

To be sure, it is not possible to determine whether the way the current unfair trade laws are administered provides net social benefits by this standard. But if the laws are to exist—and for political reasons we suspect they always will—society can nevertheless maximize the likelihood that they actually confer net benefits. It must ensure, first, that the enforce-ment of the laws is carefully circumscribed to practices which truly do distort international trade and, second, that the remedies it generates are carefully calibrated to the magnitude of the injury they may cause. The authors in this volume have devoted their analysis toward that end.

Findings

Whatever views they hold about the way in which the ITA has admin-istered the unfair trade laws in the past, the authors generally agree that the agency has considerable discretion under the dumping and CVD statutes. Similarly, the courts have tended to approve a wide array of administrative methodologies. Insofar as the authors find patterns in the administration of the law, they do not point to or detect political inter-ference in *individual* case outcomes. Instead, with the exception of Stew-art, they find that the ITA has adopted certain practices and procedures which tend to systematically favor higher rather than lower dumping and CVD "margins."

Without repeating all the criticisms voiced by the authors, we sum-marize here only those that are potentially the most important. In addition, we distinguish between critiques of substantive statistical methodologies and the procedures the ITA uses to collect and analyze information. Significantly, most of the complaints about the current practices—both substantive and procedural—*can be cured by administrative action alone without the need for congressional approval.*

Dumping

The most important bias built into the administration of the dumping law, according to many of the authors, is the ITA's practice of refusing to average both U.S. and foreign prices in computing dumping margins, although in 1984 Congress specifically authorized Commerce to use conceptually correct comparisons. Under the practice trade investigators have long used, foreign transaction prices are typically averaged over a six-month period to determine a benchmark "foreign market value," whereas the U.S. import prices with which they are compared are those from *individual* sales. The Department of Commerce ignores any U.S. import prices that may be *above* the foreign market average, and thus counts in its computation of the dumping margin only the U.S. import prices that are *below* the foreign average price.

The refusal to average both the foreign and the U.S. prices is traditionally justified by the desire of the ITA to prevent "spot" or "rifle shot" dumping. But as Tracy Murray and David Palmeter point out in chapters 2 and 3, producers engaged solely in domestic trade can, and often do, charge different prices at different times, depending on demand and supply fluctuations. Why should foreign producers selling their wares in this country be penalized for doing the same thing? Moreover, as Richard Boltuck, Joseph Francois, and Seth Kaplan demonstrate in chapter 5, given the current dumping methodology, the *average* price in the United States must always exceed that in the home country whenever the exporter ensures a zero dumping margin (by Commerce's methodology) by charging a higher price on *each and every* U.S. sale than its average home market price. Such a result needlessly harms U.S. consumers, especially since Congress has already granted the ITA permission to average U.S. prices.

A second criticism of current dumping methodology voiced by many of the authors relates to the ITA's tendency to exclude from the dumping comparisons home market sales that are below the full or average cost of production. This has the effect of increasing the home market or "fair value" price with which U.S. import prices are compared, and thus magnifies dumping margins. Although the ITA is instructed by the dumping statute to ignore below-cost sales made "in substantial quantities over an extended period of time," it has wide latitude in interpreting this provision. Most of the authors criticize the ITA for exercising its discretion in this regard so as to ignore the fact that many firms in a purely domestic context may sell below *average*, but not below *variable*, costs for significant parts of the year or the business cycle, when demand is below normal.

Murray and several other authors advance the related complaint that when Commerce finds it cannot use home market or third-country prices as a "fair value" benchmark (because the sales volumes either do not exist or have been thrown out under the "below cost" test), it then compares U.S. import prices to an artificial "constructed value," which essentially is average cost plus fixed statutory amounts for overhead and profit. In such a circumstance, Commerce does not determine whether price discrimination exists (for pricing comparisons have been ruled out or are impossible), but instead decides whether the import prices are simply below cost. As already suggested, economists would say that such an inquiry makes sense only if the purpose is to discover predatory pricing, or pricing below variable cost. But that is not what the dumping statute directs Commerce to do, and thus it has the effect of punishing foreigners for pricing practices—selling above variable cost but below an artificially calculated average cost—that are perfectly legal for U.S. firms to engage in when selling in the domestic market.[14]

Several authors also point to a number of technical rules, both statutory and administrative, that they believe either are economically indefensible or, as Ronald Cass and Steve Narkin claim, are clearly inconsistent with GATT. Rules in this category include a statutory mandate that 8 percent profit and 10 percent overhead margins be added in the calculation of constructed value and administrative limits on indirect selling expenses in calculating the fair value of certain exported products.

Finally, several authors suggest that the current practice of assessing dumping duties retrospectively—that is, after the imports have already entered this country, and sometimes years later—introduces needless uncertainty into the international trade environment, which is again harmful to U.S. consumers. This problem would be easily corrected if the dumping margins determined in each annual review applied prospectively to the next year's imports.

14. In his comment, Robert Feinberg also urges the ITC to be more willing to use antitrust concepts in defining the "like product" for purposes of assessing whether unfairly traded imports have been a cause of material injury.

Countervailing Duties

Joseph Francois, David Palmeter, and Jeffrey Anspacher in chapter 4 and Boltuck, Francois, and Kaplan in chapter 5 deal specifically with the administration of the CVD law. Aside from several technical criticisms of the way Commerce calculates the subsidy rate in the investigations of *export* subsidies, the authors are at least generally comfortable with the methodological approach the department uses in these cases.

They are far more critical, however, of the Commerce Department's calculations of countervailable *domestic* subsidies, or those subsidies that are provided by governments to specific sectors of the economy and are not tied to the level of exports. Under current practice, the ITA calculates these subsidies by computing the *benefits* they confer to domestic producers. But as the authors point out, domestic subsidies can benefit firms *without distorting trade*. Thus, unless the subsidy somehow lowers the *marginal cost* of production, it will benefit shareholders without influencing the output produced by the firm or the prices it is able to charge consumers. Accordingly, both sets of authors believe the only appropriate measure of a countervailable subsidy must reflect the trade-distorting *effects* caused by the subsidy—thus converting a domestic subsidy through economic theory into an equivalent export subsidy to determine the appropriate size of the countervailing duty. Furthermore, they observe that such an approach is consistent with the GATT Subsidies Code, which *requires* any countervailing duties to be lower than the amount of any subsidy if a lesser duty is sufficient to remove the injury caused by the subsidy.

In his comments on chapter 4, Gary Horlick questions whether the "effects" approach can be administered, since it requires the department to estimate the degree to which the demand and the supply of the relevant product are sensitive to price changes (or technically, the price elasticities of demand and supply). In many cases, there may be insufficient information to make such estimates. And even when the information is adequate, the statistical techniques that are commonly used to provide the estimates often entail a great deal of uncertainty. How then is the department to decide on a single estimate of the countervailing duty required to offset the effects of any domestic subsidy?

The answer, of course, is that analysts make point estimates all the time in conventional economic and statistical work, recognizing that there is a band of uncertainty around those estimates. We believe it is far more appropriate for the ITA to live with those uncertainties but at least estimate the right number than to use the wrong number—namely, the subsidy measured by the benefits approach—simply because it may be easy to compute. Indeed, the current practice reminds us of the joke about the man who says he is looking under a street lamp for his lost quarter because "that's where the light is"—even though he lost the coin across the street! Surely, there is a better and more acceptable way to countervail domestic subsidies.

Procedures

Apart from any biases built into the substantive approaches used by the ITA to calculate dumping or subsidy margins, several of the authors also point to procedural practices that they believe unjustifiably tilt the outcomes toward domestic interests. In particular, they criticize the ITA for what they think is too much willingness to reject the data submissions of foreign respondents and to substitute "best information available" (BIA), which is usually prices and costs alleged by domestic petitioners.

The Commerce Department maintains the BIA rule, of course, as a stick with which to threaten exporters and importers if they do not cooperate with the department's requests for information. Several aspects of unfair trade investigations, however, place heavy burdens on foreign respondents, especially on smaller companies, which find it very difficult and expensive (not to mention highly intrusive) to comply with the requests. In particular, not only must the lengthy questionnaires be filled out in English (requiring foreign parties to hire American law firms), but also the price and cost data the respondents are asked to submit must be supplied in a computer-readable format (another hurdle for many smaller companies). The task is further complicated by the fact that foreign companies may use different accounting conventions than those required for data submission by the Commerce Department. Finally, because of the time constraints of the statutory timetables of unfair trade investigations, all this information must be supplied quickly.

In combination, these various factors can sometimes be too much for foreign companies to fully absorb, a fact that, according to some of the authors, helps to account for the ITA's tendency to turn to BIA. Baldwin and Moore find that when the ITA uses BIA, the dumping margins are significantly higher than when BIA is not used.

It is important to note that one of the authors, Terence Stewart, does not agree with the procedural and substantive criticisms advanced by the others. Stewart disputes Palmeter's claim that the burdens of Commerce questionnaires have increased in recent years, and thus he believes the department is justified in turning to BIA as often as it does. On substantive matters, Stewart notes that the department *has* used averaging techniques at least in perishable products cases, and he asserts that Commerce is correct to determine the presence of below-cost sales by looking at average rather than variable costs. The reason, he argues, is that the dumping law is designed to provide more protection than would a statute that was limited to addressing cases of predatory pricing. Specifically, the dumping law is aimed, in his view, at protecting the interests of *producers*, not consumers. On this ground, Stewart believes that, if anything, the current U.S. antidumping law needs to be strengthened.

We respectfully disagree with much of Stewart's analysis. Although we agree that an important objective of U.S. antidumping law is to protect producers from unfair pricing practices, we also observe that the United States is a party to the GATT, whose principal objective is to further the interests of consumers. The antidumping and subsidies provisions are carefully carved out exceptions to the general principles of the GATT that favor freer rather than more restrictive trade. Thus, we find it difficult to defend practices that punish foreigners for pricing behavior that either is no different from domestic practices of U.S. firms or that does not truly distort trading patterns.

Injury Investigation

Finally, although the analysis in this book overwhelmingly focuses on the calculations of dumping and subsidy margins by the ITA, we cannot resist adding a few thoughts about the so-called injury phase of unfair trade practice investigations carried out by the ITC.

As we have noted, dumping or countervailing duties will not actually be imposed under the law—even if Commerce has found dumping or countervailable subsidization to exist—unless the ITC also determines that through these practices a domestic industry has been materially injured "by reason of the subject imports."[15] The U.S. trade law pretty much tracks article 6 of the GATT, which requires the material injury to be "through the effects of dumping."

In recent years a few ITC commissioners have faithfully followed the GATT language by requiring that dumping or subsidies must cause ma-

---

15. The law also allows the commission to find in the affirmative if a practice "threatens" injury or "materially retards" the establishment of a U.S. industry.

terial injury before an affirmative "injury" determination can be reached. In the language of the law, these commissioners have applied a "but for" test—that is, but for the unfair pricing, would the performance of the competing domestic industry have been materially better? What amount of injury is "material" under this approach must inherently be based on each commissioner's subjective judgment, though once it has been defined implicitly, each commissioner may in principle apply the definition consistently among cases.

Although this reading of the U.S. dumping law may seem self-evident, most ITC commissioners have announced a sharply contrasting interpretation of the injury test. In their view, sometimes called the bifurcated approach, the commission must first ask whether trends in financial condition and other indicators suggest that the U.S. industry which makes the like product is in poor or worsening health. If the "poor-health test" is not passed, the inquiry ends: a negative decision is reached. But if the domestic industry is deemed by some standard to be in poor health, the bifurcated approach asks whether increases in imports have contributed even minimally to the industry's poor or worsening condition; if they have, the commissioners find in the affirmative.

Here, too, the courts have provided little guidance, permitting both approaches to be consistent with the unfair trade laws. To the extent the injury methodology used by a majority of the ITC tilts in any direction, it favors *foreign* producers and not domestic industries, unlike the bias we believe the ITA procedures display in calculating the unfair pricing margins. The reason is that under the bifurcated approach, relief will be denied healthy industries even though they may be able to show that they could do materially better in the absence of dumping or foreign government subsidies.[16]

Where To from Here?

For those who agree with most of the authors here that the current practices used by the ITA in unfair trade practice cases tilt unjustifiably

16. We do not mean to suggest, however, that the commissioners who have used the bifurcated approach, in practice, have *applied* that approach in a way that shows a bias toward either respondents or petitioners. We only point out here that the *logic* of the bifurcated approach clearly favors foreign parties relative to a "but for" test. In fact, either the "but for" approach or the bifurcated approach may prove more generous to petitioners, depending on general economic conditions and the subjective level of "materiality" required by commissioners in applying each method. The two approaches favor different subsets of U.S. industries.

toward domestic interests, the natural question that arises is, how are reforms of those practices best accomplished? The question is complicated by the fact that, as documented in Brian Hindley's comment, other nations are as guilty as the United States in this regard. As we suggested at the outset, this should hardly be surprising, because other nations tend to look to the United States as a model in implementing trade policy. In particular, since the United States has at least claimed to be one of the most open economies in the world, other countries take notice when it practices protection, especially if done in the name of "fair trade." Exact emulation provides some cover against U.S. charges that the methods and procedures of other countries are unacceptable or GATT-illegal.

Two obvious paths to reform are open: either the United States changes its practices unilaterally, or it waits until it can persuade other countries to do likewise at the same time. The choices are somewhat different from the nuclear context, where opposition to unilateral disarmament is grounded in the fear that other nuclear powers could then wreak devastation on the United States without threat of retaliation. In the trade arena, any move that Americans take on their own to bring the administration of their unfair trade laws more in line with the underlying theory of the laws—to remedy only true distortions of international trade—would enhance the economic welfare of the United States without exposing it to any other threat. Indeed, unilateral change could usher in a virtuous cycle whereby other nations might be encouraged to respond in kind or limit the ability of other countries to seek cover in the sincerest form of flattery.

But as Baldwin and Moore observe in chapter 7, unilateral change in the current political climate—one that comes close to reversing the current administration of the unfair trade laws—is highly unlikely. At the same time, however, they hold out two sources of hope. First, as other nations continue to copy the worst features of our practices, U.S. exporters will gain stronger ammunition in their efforts to persuade U.S. policymakers that they ought to halt, and conceivably reverse, the spiral to the bottom. Second, U.S. manufacturers that rely on imported components hit unfairly or excessively with unfair trade penalties are also in a position to help lead a movement for unilateral reform.

There is some evidence that U.S. companies have begun to realize the risks to which they are exposed. The U.S. computer industry, for example, has felt the sting of higher semiconductor prices, triggered by the 1986 dumping complaint (that resulted in the U.S.-Japan semiconductor accord). More recently, the same manufacturers stand to be hurt by dumping penalties assessed against certain computer screen displays.

Ultimately, however, we believe that the better chances for reform of current practices lie in multilateral negotiation, if only because the United States in the past has rarely acted unilaterally to reduce other trade restrictions. To be sure, many of the issues discussed in this book are not on the negotiating agenda in the Uruguay Round, or may not be resolved in a manner consistent with the recommendations advanced here. This need not be true for future negotiations, however.

Perhaps one way to move matters along is to heed Robert Herzstein, who in his comment on chapter 6 notes that the GATT currently entertains few (if any) complaints about the enforcement of national dumping and CVD provisions. The reason is that the GATT does not permit complaints to be filed by private parties, only by their governments. Since governments can be strongly tempted to clothe their protectionist impulses in the convenient garb of popular "unfair trade" complaints, they have little reason to bring complaints in this area before the GATT. If, however, private parties could complain directly to the GATT—and if the GATT tribunals were given more effective enforcement powers— then issues like those addressed in this book could be aired in a neutral forum.

In the meantime, it is important to understand how the unfair trade laws are being administered in the country that so far has made the most use of them. This volume tells what we believe is a critical part of that story.

Table 1-A. *Affirmative Findings by Product in Antidumping and Countervailing Duty Investigations, 1985–89*

1985	1986	1987	1988	1989
Barium chloride	Cellular mobile phones	Erasable read-only memories	Stainless steel pipes and tubes	Cellular mobile phones
Choline chloride	Candles	Welded carbon steel pipes and tubes	Color picture tubes	3.5-inch microdiscs
Carbon steel wire rod	Wire stand	Porcelain cooking ware	Butt-weld pipe fittings	Antifriction bearings
Titanium sponge	Photo albums and fillers	Steel cooking ware	Forklift trucks	Electrolytic manganese dioxide
Cell-site transceivers	Bristle paint brushes	Butt-weld pipe fittings	Electrical conductor aluminum redraw rod	Light-walled rectangular pipes and tubes
Brass valves, nozzles, and connectors	Pistachio nuts	Brass sheet and strip	Brass sheet and strip	Industrial belts
Calcium hypochlorite	Low-fuming brazing copper wire	Urea	Nitrile rubber	New steel rails
Oil country tubular goods	Welded carbon steel pipes and tubes	Aspirin	Granular polytetra-fluoroethylene resin	Pork
Red raspberries	Offshore platform jackets and piles	Phosphoric acid	Forged steel crankshafts	
Dried salted codfish	Construction castings	Fresh cut flowers		
Fabric and expanded neoprene laminate	Atlantic groundfish	Forged steel crankshafts		
Carbon steel products	Tillage tools	Tubeless steel disc wheels		
	Steel wire nails	Silica filament fabric		
	64K random access memory components	Frozen concentrate orange juice		
	Oil country tubular goods	Oil country tubular goods		
	Cast-iron pipe fittings	Tapered roller bearings		
		Cast-iron pipe fittings		

Source: International Trade Commission Annual Reports.

CHAPTER TWO

The Administration of the Antidumping Duty Law by the Department of Commerce

Tracy Murray

DUMPING occurs when imports are sold at less than fair value (LTFV) and such imports cause material injury to a domestic industry in the United States. The practice of dumping violates the antidumping code of the General Agreement on Tariffs and Trade (GATT), which authorizes a contracting party to remedy dumped imports by introducing an antidumping duty in an amount up to the margin of dumping.[1]

U.S. antidumping law is contained in title VII of the Tariff Act of 1930, as amended by the Trade Agreements Act of 1979.[2] Under this law

---

I would like to thank the following people for their assistance: Jeff Anspacher, Seth Kaplan, Michael Coursey, and Eric Sims. The views expressed in this chapter are personal.

1. The various terms used in the administration of antidumping laws are defined in the appendix to this chapter.

2. The concern about dumped imports dates back to the late 1700s, when it was feared that dumped imports from Britain would stifle young American industry. Insofar as dumping was "intended" to harm domestic industry, it could be remedied under the Sherman Act of 1890. But it was also feared that the application of the Sherman Act might constitute "extraterritorial" application of U.S. law, with the result that section 73 of the Tariff Act of 1894 made illegal the "conspiracy" to sell foreign goods in the United States at prices lower than abroad. This statute has been ineffective because of the difficulty of proving that a conspiracy existed and that the conspiracy was formed within the borders of the United States and included at least one U.S. citizen. The Revenue Act of 1916, still in existence, directly addresses the problem of dumping. It holds dumping illegal when the intent is that of "destroying or injuring an industry in the United States . . . or of restraining or monopolizing any part of trade and commerce . . . in the United States." But again, enforcement was ineffective, owing to the need to establish an "intent" and "conspiracy" with respect to the domestic importer.

Section 201 of the Tariff Act of 1921 was the basic antidumping statute before the enactment of title VII of the Trade Agreements Act of 1979. This statute removed the "intent" and "conspiracy" requirements and concentrated on the remedy of injury caused by dumped imports. The focus of dumping shifted from concern for "predatory" practices to the prevention of injury. The Tariff Act remained intact until it was amended by the

the administration of antidumping duties is divided between the Department of Commerce (DOC) and the International Trade Commission (ITC). The DOC's task is to determine whether imports are being dumped, and if so, to estimate the margin of dumping; the ITC's task is to determine whether dumping causes injury.[3]

If both agencies find in the affirmative, an antidumping order is issued directing that antidumping duties be assessed in addition to the normal duties imposed on imports of the merchandise. The amount of the antidumping duty is appraised on an entry-by-entry basis; any entry of merchandise at or above its fair price will not be assessed the antidumping duty.

This chapter explains how the Department of Commerce carries out its responsibilities under the antidumping statutes and what administrative issues are in need of attention. These statutes are accepted without question, but some thought should be given to whether the remedies against dumped imports would better serve the national interest if they underwent certain revisions. The discussion does not cover dumping by state-controlled enterprises.

The Responsibility of the Department of Commerce

The DOC faces extremely complex issues in the area of dumping. To simplify, the department has two basic responsibilities: to determine whether alleged imports are dumped and, if so, to estimate the margin of dumping. The authorizing legislation specifies that the DOC must formally investigate dumping allegations, that the investigation should include specific stages with intermediate determinations, and that these stages must be completed by specified deadlines.

Customs Simplification Act of 1954; subsequent amendments are contained in section 5 of the Customs Simplification Act of 1956 and the Trade Act of 1974. All these amendments are essentially procedural.

For source material, see Harvey Kaye, Paul Plaia, Jr., and Michael A. Hertzberg, *International Trade Practice*, vol. 1 (McGraw-Hill, 1987); and Jacob Viner, *Dumping: A Problem in International Trade* (University of Chicago Press, 1923).

3. The DOC is to determine "whether a class or kind of foreign merchandise is being, or is likely to be, sold in the United States at less than fair value." The ITC is to determine whether "an industry in the United States is materially injured, or is threatened with material injury, or the establishment of an industry in the United States is materially retarded, by reason of imports of that merchandise." See 19 U.S.C. sec. 1673 and 19 U.S.C. sec. 1673(d).

In the first stage of the proceedings, a petition is filed on behalf of a domestic industry alleging that imports are entering the United States at prices below fair value and that such imports are causing injury to the domestic industry. The ITC immediately begins a preliminary investigation to determine whether there is a "reasonable indication" of injury (if not, the case is terminated). At the same time, the DOC conducts a summary investigation of the petition to determine whether it contains adequate information to support the allegation (if not, the petition is dismissed and the ITC is so notified). If the ITC preliminary determination is positive, the DOC conducts a preliminary investigation to determine whether there is a "reasonable likelihood" that imports are being sold at less than fair value. If the DOC finds in the affirmative, imports from that date are cleared through customs under "suspension of liquidation"; the DOC also reports its preliminary estimate of the margin of dumping.

The DOC issues its preliminary determination approximately halfway through the proceedings. It then completes its investigation and issues its final determination as to whether dumping exists. If negative, the case is terminated; if positive, the DOC reports its estimate of the margin of dumping. Finally, the ITC completes its investigation to determine whether imports subject to the investigation cause or threaten to cause injury to the domestic industry. If both the DOC and ITC reach positive final determinations, an antidumping duty order is issued.

"Sales at less than fair value," or dumping, are said to exist when prices charged by the foreign producer on sales to the United States (the U.S. price) are below the "foreign market value." Foreign market value may be defined in three ways: as the price charged by the foreign producer on sales in the producer's home market; as the price charged on exports to a third country; or as the costs of production, which are used if neither of those two prices is considered adequate.[4] A complication in observing the U.S. price has led to two definitions for this price. What is known as the "purchase price" is used if the imports are sold by the foreign producer or foreign exporter for importation into the United States before exportation. In some cases, however, the foreign producer or exporter is also the importer (or the importer may be an affiliate owned by the foreign producer or exporter); consequently, the purchase price would

---

4. Product costs are constructed by the DOC using cost data applicable to the particular foreign producer. This method of estimating the foreign market value is called the "constructed value method."

Table 2-1. *Time Deadlines for Antidumping Proceedings*

Day (time deadlines)	Action	If negative
1	Petition is filed	No action required
20	DOC summary investigation—if positive, DOC initiates an investigation	Petition is dismissed
45	ITC preliminary determination	Investigation terminated
80	DOC 60-day review—if positive, results are disclosed to parties	No action required
110[a]	DOC preliminary determination—if positive, suspension of liquidation is initiated	Case continues without suspension of liquidation
75[b]	DOC final determination—if positive, suspension of liquidation is initiated if not already in force	Investigation terminated
120[c]	ITC final determination—if positive, an antidumping order is issued	Investigation terminated

a. Provided the case is not "complex," and there is a waiver of verification. The deadline for "complex cases" is delayed 50 days; similarly, the deadline is delayed 50 days if verification is required. If the case is "complex" and verification is required, the deadline can be delayed 100 days. The meaning of "complex cases" and "verification" are explained in the appendix.

b. From the date of the DOC preliminary determination. The DOC final determination can be delayed 60 days upon request by the petitioner in the case of a negative DOC preliminary determination or by the respondent in the case of a positive DOC preliminary determination.

c. From the date of a positive DOC preliminary determination, and 45 days have elapsed since the positive DOC final determination; the ITC will have at least 45 days from the date of the DOC final determination. If the DOC preliminary determination was negative, the ITC will have 75 days from the date of the positive DOC final determination.

be an intrafirm transfer price rather than an arm's-length price. If the first sale to an unrelated party occurs after importation into the United States, the price used is the "exporter's sales price" (ESP).

The margin of dumping is defined as the difference between the foreign market value and the U.S. price, where the foreign market value is either (a) the price charged in the home market, (b) the price charged on sales to a third country, or (c) the constructed value; and the U.S. price is either (a) the purchase price when the first sale to an unrelated party occurs prior to importation into the United States, or (b) the exporter's sales price when the first sale to an unrelated party occurs after importation into the United States. The deadlines for each step in the proceedings are presented in table 2-1.

The administration of any law must incorporate particular circumstances, which vary from case to case. Administrators usually have certain discretionary powers with which to administer a law. They are guided by the statutes and the intent of the law as laid down in the legislative history. The range of discretionary power varies from law to law and from case to case.

The law that guides the DOC in administering antidumping duty proceedings is quite specific with respect to the criteria for positive or negative determinations, standards of evidence, definitions of the variables to be measured, and actions to be taken throughout the proceedings. From the degree of detail contained in the legislation, it is obvious that Congress received substantial technical assistance from government administrators of the law as well as from other parties that participate in antidumping proceedings.[5] As revisions and amendments were introduced and more and more specific details were included in the antidumping duty law, the range of DOC discretion became narrower.

Such specificity in the law cuts two ways. On the one hand, it limits DOC discretion in choosing methodological alternatives. On the other hand, it protects the DOC from criticism when inappropriate but legislated methods are applied in particular cases. The existing legislation also provides the DOC with significant discretion regarding the use of statistical methods and particular accounting practices. In general, the methods used by the DOC yield verifiable numbers, follow generally accepted accounting practices, and are consistent across cases.

The Administration of the Law

In this section, I discuss the principal elements of the antidumping law that affect the outcomes of its administration. As mentioned earlier, the law is extremely detailed. To avoid smothering the reader with too much detail, the discussion is organized by issue rather than section of the law.

Initiation of an Antidumping Duty Case

Who has the standing to file a petition? The law clearly states that petitions are to be filed "on behalf of an industry" in the United States. In practice, however, petitions are filed by individual firms. In some cases, additional firms in the industry will join a petition filed by one firm; in others, a group of U.S. firms in the same industry will file a petition. The question of standing should be investigated in all such cases.

The problem is complex in that some firms may use U.S. materials

5. At the time of the Trade Agreements Act of 1979, the Department of Treasury was responsible for determining whether dumping existed and, if so, for estimating the margin of dumping.

and components to produce their product whereas other firms may use imported inputs. Moreover, some U.S. firms may be subsidiaries of foreign companies or may own the foreign source company. Some firms may operate at more than one stage in the production process, being producers or importers of upstream inputs as well as producers of the subject product. With such interlocking possibilities, the different firms in an industry may have conflicting interests in an antidumping proceeding.

The law defines the term "industry" as "domestic producers as a whole of a like product, or those producers whose collective output . . . constitutes a major proportion of the total domestic production" (19 U.S.C. sec. 1677). The law further stipulates that related parties—that is, domestic producers who are related to the exporters or importers or who are themselves importers of the dumped merchandise—may be excluded from the domestic industry. A case in 1987 illustrates the complexity.[6] The petitioner was a domestic firm, a domestic firm was among the respondents, and another domestic firm declared itself a neutral party in the proceedings. Interestingly, all the firms relied to a large extent on imported components. None of the firms added much value in the United States.

In general, the DOC assumes that a petition is being submitted on behalf of the domestic industry as long as a majority of the domestic firms (unrelated parties) do not actively oppose the petition. In a recent case before the Court of International Trade (court no. 88-09-00726), however, a single firm in the United States filed a petition; no other firm in the domestic industry supported the petition. In Judge R. Kenton Musgrave's opinion, this was "a clear example of misapplication, indeed misuse, of the Trade Agreements Act by a single litigant that has sought . . . to obtain relief solely for its own benefit. The statutes involved do not contemplate such private litigation; in fact, they prohibit such actions."[7]

In this case, the opinions of other domestic firms regarding the petition were known, and not a single firm supported the petition; one domestic firm actively opposed the petition, and all other firms refused to support

6. For the preliminary determination, see ITC investigation 731-TA-377, *Internal Combustion Engine Fork-Lift Trucks from Japan*, USITC Publication 1985 (Washington, June 1987). For the final determination, see ITC investigation 731-TA-377, *Internal Combustion Engine Fork-Lift Trucks from Japan*, USITC Publication 2082 (Washington, 1988).

7. *Customs Bulletin and Decisions* (Department of the Treasury), vol. 24 (September 19, 1990), p. 3.

it. Thus, the petitioner was clearly acting alone. Judge Musgrave explicitly rejected the DOC practice of assuming that a petitioner's "claim" represents the domestic industry and indicated that the petitioner has a self-interest in so claiming. The legislative intent is clear. The petition is to be brought on behalf of "the domestic producers as a whole . . . or those producers whose collective output . . . constitutes a major proportion of the total domestic production of that product"—in other words, "all of the domestic industry by number of producers" *or* those domestic "producers whose combined output . . . constitutes a majority proportion of the total domestic production."[8]

To complicate matters, the DOC did not know the views of every member of the domestic industry in this case, whereas the ITC did obtain that information in the normal course of its investigation. Since the DOC had accepted the petition, the ITC argued, it did not have the authority to question the petitioner's standing. Commissioner Ronald A. Cass further argued that, given the separation of responsibility between the DOC and the ITC, the laws should be administered in a manner that avoids interagency conflict. Judge Musgrave refused to address the question of which agency should decide the petitioner's standing. Nevertheless, his decision did state unequivocally that the petitioner's standing must be investigated and decided.

RECOMMENDATION. Standing should be decided early in the investigation. The DOC could investigate this issue during its summary review of the adequacy of the petition. However, that would place an additional burden on the DOC, since its normal investigation concentrates on collecting information from foreign producers and exporters. In contrast, investigating standing would impose little additional work on the ITC. The ITC begins its investigation as soon as a petition is submitted. The ITC identifies and contacts members of the domestic industry to investigate the question of injury by reason of dumped imports. If standing was part of the ITC's preliminary injury determination, a decision could be made within forty-five days of the filing of the petition. Congress should provide for an explicit investigation into standing and include that investigation in the ITC's preliminary investigation.

UNITARY DETERMINATION. The DOC's responsibility is (1) to determine whether imports are being, or are likely to be, sold in the United States at less than fair value and, if so, (2) to estimate the margin of dumping. Clearly, the DOC has two separate responsibilities, as is ex-

8. *Customs Bulletin and Decisions*, p. 13.

plicitly set forth in the authorizing legislation (section 733[b] of the Trade Agreements Act of 1979). In practice, however, the DOC has combined these responsibilities. It begins the investigation by collecting the information needed to quantify the U.S. price of imports and the foreign market value of like merchandise in order to estimate the margin of dumping. If the estimated margin of dumping exceeds the threshold value, a positive dumping determination will be issued.

The DOC does not conduct an independent investigation to reveal whether the allegation makes sense from the foreign producer's point of view. For example, there have been cases in which productive capacity has been established overseas purely for sale in the United States. Furthermore, such production and exportation to the United States has been going on for a number of years. Since there are no home market sales or sales to third countries, the constructed value technique must be used. Because of the problems in allocating cost and the other legislated requirements in arriving at a constructed value, the DOC could obtain a verifiable constructed value that is higher than the U.S. price. Nevertheless, how much credence can a DOC investigation have if it is determined that the foreign firm is selling at less than the cost of production and has been for a number of years, that is, the foreign firm is losing money on exports to the United States? What motive could the foreign firm have to sell at a loss? Or is it more likely that the DOC, in using the constructed value method, erred in its estimation of the foreign market value?

RECOMMENDATION. The DOC should (1) determine whether dumping exists and, if so, (2) estimate the margin of dumping. Both questions could be investigated concurrently, but separate determinations should be made.

The investigation into the existence of dumping might reveal such motives as the exploitation of market power (that is, traditional profit-maximizing price discrimination), predation, market share objectives, and hidden subsidies. Or the investigation into the pricing policies of the foreign producer might produce evidence that the foreign firm is not engaged in dumping. For example, the foreign firm's financial statement may document healthy profits from the sale of the product alleged to be dumped.

The Low Threshold for the Existence of Dumping

The DOC determines that dumping exists whenever the estimated margin of dumping equals or exceeds one-half of 1 percent (0.005 in decimal form) of the U.S. price. There are two problems with this low threshold. First, the methodology for estimating the average margin of dumping includes an upward statistical bias that usually produces an estimated margin of dumping in excess of half of 1 percent—even if no dumping exists (see the section "The Method of Averaging" below).

Second, the antidumping duty law is a pricing law aimed at preventing injury to the competing domestic industry. A price that is only half of 1 percent below a legitimate fair price is extremely unlikely to cause injury to a domestic industry. But it must be recognized that the injury test is to be conducted by the ITC. It is certainly not legitimate for the DOC to set a threshold that usurps the ITC role.

RECOMMENDATION. Given the statistical bias inherent in the methodology the DOC uses to estimate the margin of dumping, the threshold below which the margin of dumping would be considered de minimis should be raised substantially. Since Congress has divided the responsibility for administering the antidumping law between the DOC and the ITC, the setting of the threshold level should not be the responsibility of either agency. Instead, it should be considered a matter of national policy and established by Congress in a technical amendment to the antidumping duty law.

Lower Standard for Positive Preliminary Determination

The antidumping duty law provides for two stages of decisionmaking. Preliminary determinations are rendered early in the investigation of both agencies; these determinations are subsequently sustained, revised, or reversed in the final determinations. One objective of the preliminary determination is to prevent irreparable injury to domestic industry during the course of the full investigation, which can easily take one year to complete.[9] If both the ITC and the DOC reach positive preliminary determinations, a temporary remedy is put in force. The liquidation of imports is suspended from the date of the DOC preliminary determination (which cannot be announced before the ITC's preliminary determination); imports from that date will be assessed in accordance with (1) the dumping margin estimated and reported by the DOC in its preliminary determination or (2) the antidumping duty assessed under the anti-

---

9. A second objective of the preliminary determination is to put an early end to frivolous cases. This results if the ITC renders a negative preliminary determination.

dumping order resulting from a positive final determination, *whichever is lower.*

If the ITC renders a negative preliminary determination, the case is terminated. However, Congress protects the petitioner against termination if evidence is inadequate. Consequently, Congress sets modest standards of evidence for continuing the investigation to the final stage for both the ITC and the DOC.[10] Moreover, a case is not terminated as a result of a DOC negative preliminary determination. The case continues without the suspension of liquidation.

It is no small matter to suspend liquidation on the basis of the preliminary investigation. When liquidation is suspended, imports are cleared through customs and permitted entry into the U.S. market subject to the posting of a bond or otherwise guaranteeing that tariffs and other fees, including possible antidumping duties, will be paid upon assessment. However, assessment is delayed until the final investigations have been concluded. If either the ITC or the DOC reaches a negative determination in its final investigations, no antidumping duty will ultimately be assessed. Nevertheless, the importers are at risk for the payment of antidumping duties beginning on the date of a positive preliminary determination by the DOC and continuing throughout the period of the investigation, which can last an additional six to nine months. As a consequence, it is common for importers to begin shifting orders from the alleged unfair trading partners to domestic and other foreign suppliers of competing goods. Thus, the alleged dumpers will lose sales even if they are subsequently judged to be innocent of the allegation.

What is needed at the preliminary stage is a reasonable balance between

10. The ITC is to render a positive preliminary determination if "based upon the best information available . . . there is a reasonable indication that" an industry in the United States is being materially injured by dumped imports (19 U.S.C. sec. 1673). This standard has been further specified by the Court of Appeals for the Federal Circuit (*American Lamb Company* v. *United States*, 785 F. 2d 994, Fed. Cir. 1986). The ITC standard for determining that there is no reasonable indication of material injury or threat is (a) there is clear and convincing evidence of the absence of such reasonable indication, and (b) the record shows it extremely unlikely that evidence of a "reasonable indication" would be developed in a final investigation. The ITC recognizes that there are two standards for making determinations, a lower standard for the preliminary determination and a higher standard for the final determination. To cite a recent case: "This determination reflects the lower standard used by the Commission, and approved by the Courts, in preliminary investigations." This quotation includes a reference to *American Lamb*. See *Digital Readout Systems and Subassemblies Thereof from Japan*, Investigation no. 731-TA-390 (Preliminary), USITC Publication 2081 (Washington, May 1988).

protecting domestic import-competing firms from irreparable injury caused by dumped imports and safeguarding foreign exporters and U.S. importers (and consumers or domestic firms using imported inputs) from unjustified risks caused by the suspension of liquidation. The current rules are skewed in the direction of protecting domestic import-competing firms at the expense of foreign firms and U.S. buyers. To make matters worse, the DOC often resorts to the "best information available" to reach its preliminary determination. As explained in the next section, the best information available is most often DOC terminology for the information contained in the petition; certainly, the petitioner has an incentive to select information that will result in the highest possible estimate of the margin of dumping. Using this information as the sole basis of the DOC's preliminary estimate of the margin of dumping unduly penalizes the foreign producer and U.S. importers.

RECOMMENDATION. Given the low standard of evidence, preliminary determinations are likely to be positive and liquidation suspended. In such cases, the estimated margin of dumping, which sets the maximum antidumping duty to be assessed during the remainder of the investigation, becomes critical. Using only that information contained in the petition to estimate the margin of dumping is an unreasonable trade-off between protecting domestic firms from irreparable injury caused by dumped imports and safeguarding foreign firms and buyers from unjustified risks caused by the suspension of liquidation. The DOC should estimate the margin of dumping by using evidence and methods that will enable it to obtain an unbiased estimate. If the DOC does not have adequate information, it should make the best possible estimate from the evidence that is available.

The Use of Best Information Available

The DOC "shall make a determination, based upon the best information available to it at the time of the determination, of whether there is a reasonable basis to believe or suspect that the merchandise is being sold, or is likely to be sold, at less than fair value."[11] The DOC usually bases its preliminary determination on the information collected during the first sixty days of its investigation. If the information collected from the foreign producer or exporter is inadequate, the DOC will base its

11. Trade Agreements Act of 1979, sec. 733(b)(1).

determination on the best information otherwise available, which may include information submitted by the petitioner.[12]

I wish to emphasize the word "otherwise." The implication is that if the information provided by the foreign respondent is incomplete or is not in the format desired by the DOC, it may be rejected. Instead the DOC will base its determination on the best information otherwise available, that is, the information provided by the petitioner. Clearly, the petitioner has an incentive to select evidence that will allow it to claim the highest possible margin of dumping. Although this information may not be the "worst available information," it cannot be considered objective and unbiased, and it is unlikely to be the "best information available."

Consider the problem facing the foreign respondent who receives a request for information from the DOC. It arrives in the form of a questionnaire, some 100 pages long, in English, requesting specific accounting data on individual sales in the home market (and possibly to third countries), data on sales to the United States, data needed to adjust arm's-length market prices to net ex-factory prices (that is, packaging costs, shipping costs, selling costs, distributor and other middleman costs, adjustments for taxes and duties on imported inputs, and adjustments for exporter's sales prices, international shipping costs, tariffs in the United States, distribution costs in the United States, and any costs of adding value in the United States), and a host of other details (especially if the foreign market value needs to be constructed). There must be enough information for the DOC to investigate nearly every U.S. sale (that is, every transaction) for a period of six months. All this information must be identified, retrieved, recorded, and then transmitted to the DOC in English on hard copy and in a computer-readable format within the short deadline stipulated under the U.S. antidumping statutes.

A significant number of foreign respondents would not be able to fully comply with such a request. If the DOC were to reject all of the respondent's information simply because the respondent was unable to fully comply with the DOC request, the DOC would be using its option to rely on the "best information available" to coerce the foreign respondent to fully cooperate with its investigation. Although such coercion may occasionally be warranted, in many cases the foreign respondent would

12. "Whenever information cannot be satisfactorily verified, or is not submitted in a timely fashion or in the form required, the submitter of the information will be notified and the affected determination will be made on the basis of the best information then otherwise available which may include the information submitted in support of the petition." Commerce Regulations, sec. 353.51(b).

be making good faith attempts to cooperate with the DOC, but the burden of the task would be overwhelming.

If questionnaire information is incomplete or is submitted in a computer format that is not consistent with the DOC computer system, should the DOC disregard all information that is reported in favor of information contained in the petition? If it does, the DOC will, in effect, be collecting no information of relevance during the investigation. With its experience and expertise in administering this law, the DOC can certainly do better than simply take the allegation submitted by the petitioner as fact.[13]

RECOMMENDATION. The DOC should not estimate the margin of dumping solely on the basis of information contained in the petition. Clearly, the petitioner has an incentive to submit information selected to yield the highest possible dumping margin. No penalty should be imposed if the respondents are unable to fully comply with the information requests of the DOC in the short time available. Moreover, respondents should be able to submit evidence to refute allegations reported in the petition before the DOC reaches its preliminary determination. Before each determination, the DOC should give petitioners and respondents full recourse to the rights of the adversarial process. The final determination, of course, is to be made by the officials of the DOC. But in reaching a determination, the DOC should use the best information available, including the expertise and experience of the DOC staff, any appropriate evidence submitted by the respondents, and evidence contained in the petition or subsequently submitted by the petitioners. Only in the most extreme cases should the DOC use the "best information otherwise available" based on the petition as a tool to coerce cooperation from the respondents. There may be cases in which a respondent is cooperating but is unable to fully comply with the requests of the DOC.

The Method of Averaging

The margin of dumping is the difference between the foreign market value and the U.S. price. The margin used in assessing antidumping duties is determined on the basis of each entry of merchandise. Thus, during the assessment the DOC compares the U.S. price for a given entry with

---

13. The petition does not contain information that even approximates in scope the information requested of the foreign respondent. Nor does the ITC request such detailed information from domestic producers for use in the ITC injury investigation. In fact, it is the norm rather than the exception for the ITC to use incomplete questionnaire information.

the appropriate foreign market value of sales on the closest date. Those entries with a U.S. price higher than the foreign market value are admitted without an antidumping duty. Antidumping duties are assessed on those entries with a U.S. price below the matched foreign market value; the margin of dumping is the difference between the matched prices.

However, the method used by the DOC to assess actual antidumping duties is different from the method used to estimate the margin of dumping during the investigation. During the investigation the DOC first calculates the average foreign market value of a sample of sales that occur during the period of investigation, which generally lasts six months. It then compares the U.S. price of each entry during this period with the average foreign market value; those transactions with lower U.S. prices are considered dumped, and the difference between the U.S. price and the average foreign market value is the margin of dumping for that entry. Those entries having higher U.S. prices are said to have zero margins of dumping. Finally, the DOC calculates a weighted average margin of dumping, the weights being the volume of each entry. If the resulting average margin of dumping exceeds one-half of 1 percent (0.005 in decimal form), the DOC renders a positive dumping determination and reports the calculated average as the estimated margin of dumping.

At first glance, this methodology for estimating the average margin of dumping seems consistent with Congress's intent to assess antidumping duties on an entry-by-entry basis.[14] However, it contains a statistical error that will yield a positive average margin of dumping in every real-world situation except the one that would take place if every single transaction (including both the home market and U.S. sales) during the six-month period of investigation occurred at the same price and if the exchange rate between the exporting country's currency and the U.S. dollar was constant. However, if either the foreign market price or the exchange rate fluctuates during the period of investigation, the DOC methodology will yield an upward-biased estimate of the average margin of dumping.

This point can be illustrated by a simple hypothetical example (see table 2-2). The example assumes that a foreign market sale and a U.S. sale occur on the same day and that each transaction involves the same volume of merchandise (100 units). It further assumes that prices are trending upward throughout the period of investigation, with the exchange rate being constant.[15] No dumping exists; hence the foreign market

---

14. See 19 U.S.C. sec. 1675(a).

15. Alternatively, home currency prices could be constant, with the international value of the U.S. dollar trending downward relative to the exporting country's currency.

Table 2-2. *Example of the DOC Method to Calculate the Margin of Dumping*

Transaction date (1)	Volume of dumped imports (2)	Foreign market value (3)	U.S. price (4)	True margin of dumping (col. 3 − col. 4) (5)	DOC margin of dumping, (average col. 3 − col. 4 if >0, else 0) (6)
January 5	100	95	95	0	5
January 24	100	96	96	0	4
February 7	100	97	97	0	3
February 27	100	98	98	0	2
March 15	100	99	99	0	1
March 29	100	100	100	0	0
April 11	100	100	100	0	0
May 3	100	101	101	0	0
May 20	100	102	102	0	0
June 1	100	103	103	0	0
June 14	100	104	104	0	0
June 30	100	105	105	0	0
Average	100	100	100	0	1.25

price and the U.S. price of same-day sales are identical, and the true margin of dumping is zero. In contrast, since the average foreign market price is also the average U.S. price, the DOC method yields "instances of dumping" for one-half of the sales and no instances of dumping (set equal to zero by the DOC method) for the other half. In this example, the margin of dumping calculated using the DOC method is 1.25 percent. Since this estimated average margin of dumping exceeds 0.5 percent, the DOC would render a positive dumping determination. If the ITC determined that the domestic industry is injured by these subject imports, *an antidumping duty order would be issued even though no dumping exists.*

If the true margin of dumping is quite high, say, 20 percent, this statistical bias will not be very large. Simulations indicate that the estimated margin of dumping will not exceed the true dumping margin by more than 10 percent in those cases where the true margin of dumping is large. Thus, if the true margin is 20 percent, the DOC methodology will *on average* yield an estimated margin of dumping of not more than 22 percent. However, if the estimated margin of dumping is small, the bias could be several times the magnitude of the true margin of dumping; in such cases it is more likely that no dumping exists.

A preliminary indication of the significance of this statistical bias is disturbing. In the first 200 cases decided under the 1979 legislation, the estimated margin of dumping was less than 5 percent in 20 percent of the preliminary determinations and 30 percent of the final determinations.[16] Although this does not necessarily mean that the DOC has a propensity to find dumping when none exists, its finding of dumping is likely to be in error in a significant number of cases because of the statistical bias in its methodology.

RECOMMENDATION. Clearly, the DOC should modify its statistical methodology to produce unbiased estimates of the margin of dumping. The bias inherent in the current DOC method could be significantly reduced by any of three straightforward modifications. First, the average foreign market value could be compared to the average U.S. price. Second, home market sales and U.S. sales could be matched as closely as possible by the timing of the transaction; this is the method used by the DOC in its compliance investigation to assess actual antidumping duties. Third, the DOC could subdivide the time period of its investigation into several subperiods and calculate a foreign market value for each. This revision would simply reduce the magnitude of the bias; the greater the number of subperiods, the smaller the bias.[17]

An alternative would be to raise substantially the de minimis threshold. The objective would be to set a threshold that offsets the bias inherent in the method of averaging. The appropriate threshold would depend on the statistical variation of the price date, which in turn would depend on the circumstances of each case. A methodology for setting the appropriate threshold could be developed by using classical statistical techniques, which would ensure that objectivity is maintained in determining the appropriate threshold.

Exclusion of Home Sales at Prices below the Cost of Production

The margin of dumping is the difference between the foreign market value and the U.S. price, adjusted to ex-factory prices and including the

---

16. This analysis includes only those cases in which the DOC estimated the margin to be greater than de minimis. Thus, negative determinations, terminated cases and suspended cases are not included. In some cases, more than one margin was estimated because more than one foreign firm was alleged to be dumping; the analysis treats each estimated margin as a separate DOC determination.

17. This technique has been used by the DOC for cases in which the exporting country is experiencing hyperinflation.

cost of packing for shipment to the United States. The higher the foreign market value, the higher the margin of dumping. And to the extent that the ITC uses the margin of dumping in its injury investigation, the higher the margin, the more likely the ITC will render a positive injury determination.

The antidumping duty law specifies that when the DOC determines that certain home market sales are made at prices below the cost of production, such sales will be disregarded in determining the foreign market value.[18] If the remaining sales (sales above the cost of production) are inadequate for purposes of establishing the foreign market value, the DOC is instructed to use the constructed value method.[19]

Clearly, any method that removes below-average observations from a sample will increase the resulting average. Thus, this aspect of the law, when used, will increase the average foreign market value and therefore increase the estimated margin of dumping. The petitioners understand the effect of this provision on the margin of dumping and consequently repeatedly allege that certain home market sales are below the costs of production. In many of these instances the DOC rejects a petitioner's allegation on the grounds that the petitioner does not submit sufficient evidence to substantiate the claim.

Nevertheless, in the vast majority of cases in which home market value is used, some home market sales are excluded. The published record, however, does not indicate how the DOC determines whether selected sales are below the cost of production. Presumably, the decision is based on evidence in the record.

This issue will not arise when there are inadequate home market sales or third-country sales, since in such cases the foreign market value is determined by using the constructed value method. This issue will arise only when sales between unrelated parties either in the home market or in third countries are adequate. The fact that the transactions are between unrelated parties means that the foreign producer (or exporter) has no surreptitious incentive to sell at prices below the costs of production.

RECOMMENDATION. The application of this provision should be removed from the law. If the DOC finds the sales to the home market and to third countries inadequate, because of low volumes or because the

---

18. The DOC is to disregard below-cost sales if such sales (a) have been made over an extended period of time and in substantial quantities, and (b) are made at prices that do not permit the recovery of all costs within a reasonable period of time. Commerce Regulations, sec. 353.7.

19. See 19 U.S.C. sec. 1677(b).

sales are between related parties, the constructed value method should be used. If the sales between unrelated parties are adequate, those prices should be treated as valid prices occurring in the normal course of business.

Cost versus Price Adjustments

The antidumping duty law is designed to remedy price discrimination whereby *identical merchandise is sold under identical circumstances, in identical quantities, and at the same level of commerce* in the U.S. market at a lower price than it is sold in the home market of the exporting country (or in a third market if home market sales are inadequate).[20] If sales of merchandise meeting all these conditions could be identified, the existence of dumping could easily be determined. If the U.S. price was lower than the home market price, dumping would exist; the margin of dumping would be equal to the difference between these two prices.

In the real world, however, the physical characteristics of the merchandise sold in different markets are seldom identical, the merchandise is rarely sold under identical circumstances, and prices are seldom observed at the identical level of commerce. Because of these differences, the DOC must adjust observed prices to obtain prices that are comparable.

The objective of the DOC adjustments is to obtain comparable ex-factory prices of sales in the home market and in the U.S. market.[21] The problem is to arrive at comparable market prices that do not include transactions between related parties. In some cases, for example, the U.S. importer is an affiliate of the foreign producer or exporter. Thus, the starting points for DOC price comparisons are (1) the first observed arm's-length transaction price for sales in the home market[22] and (2) the first observed arm's-length transaction price for sales to the United States. These observed transaction prices are then adjusted to obtain comparable ex-factory prices that include the cost of packing for shipment to the

20. Department of Commerce, "Study of Antidumping Adjustments Methodology and Recommendations for Statutory Change in Accordance with Section 624 of the Trade Act of 1984" (Washington, November 1985).

21. The antidumping duty law instructs the DOC to make price comparisons at the ex-factory level of commerce and to include the cost of packing for shipment to the United States. 19 U.S.C. sec. 1677(a) and (b).

22. If adequate home market sales do not exist, the DOC is instructed to first search for sales to third markets and, if such sales are inadequate, to use the constructed value method.

United States. The normal adjustments are for differences in the cost of packing, shipping costs, the quantities sold, the circumstances of sale, physical characteristics of the merchandise, and indirect taxes and duties.

As the DOC acknowledges, the statute is inconsistent in its instructions on how these adjustments should be made.[23] At times the adjustments are based on the actual costs incurred, and at others on the differences in the observed transaction prices; these two types of adjustments will be referred to as cost adjustments and price adjustments, respectively.

The distinction between cost and price adjustments is important. Cost-based dumping occurs when the difference between home market and U.S. prices cannot be explained by the differences in costs. If dumping occurs, per unit profits on home market sales would exceed per unit profits on sales in the United States—by the margin of dumping.

The purpose of price-based adjustments is to determine what the comparable foreign market price *would have been* had the merchandise been identical and sold under identical circumstances and in identical quantities, adjusted for any differences in packing costs for shipment to the United States not already included in the observed transactions prices. Any differences in costs that are not reflected in differences in price are ignored. Differences in cost that do result in price differences are included only to the extent that they alter price. The question is, to what extent are costs passed forward to prices?[24]

If the purpose of the antidumping statute is to prevent dumped imports from injuring domestic industry, all adjustments should be based on price. But if the objective is to discourage foreign producers or exporters from dumping and to coerce them into complying by means of excessive penalties, cost-based adjustments may be appropriate. The DOC has taken the latter approach, arguing that it is impractical, if not impossible, to base adjustments on anything but costs.

The DOC recognizes that price-based adjustments can be made only with the aid of an economic model of the facts surrounding the dumping experience. In most cases, important parameters of that model must be estimated. One is concerned no longer just with differences in cost, but

---

23. See Department of Commerce, "Study of Antidumping Adjustments Methodology and Recommendations for Statutory Change," Washington, November 1985.

24. In the jargon of economics, cost-based adjustments ask the question: by how much does the marginal cost curve shift? Price-based adjustments ask the question: by how much does the equilibrium price change because of a given (cost-based) shift in the marginal cost curve? The answer to the latter question also depends on the market structure and the slope of the demand curve facing the dumped merchandise.

with the impact that such differences, acting through the market forces of supply and demand, have on the market price.

To determine that impact, one would need extensive information about the foreign market as well as the U.S. market, and the analysis would, the DOC claims, take more time and resources than are available, given the statutory deadlines for reaching determinations. Moreover, the DOC is required to base its determination on verified information. Estimates of the price effect derived with an economic model would be impossible to verify. Consequently, the DOC uses cost-based adjustments.

RECOMMENDATION. The antidumping duty law authorizes a remedy against imports that are sold at prices below fair value. The remedy is an antidumping duty up to the amount of the price margin. Granted, it is difficult to estimate the price margin to be remedied, but that is precisely the task assigned to the DOC. The DOC has not been asked to estimate the costs associated with various adjustments in observable arm's-length prices that are needed to estimate the price margin.

The problem with making cost adjustments rather than price adjustments is that costs are seldom fully passed through to prices. Thus, the DOC's cost-based method includes an inherent upward bias in estimating the price margin. The bias may or may not be large. The solution, as the DOC recognizes, can be arrived at through economic theory and models. The economic modeling needed to translate cost adjustments into price effects is not difficult. The problem is that the modeling cannot be put into operation without estimates of the underlying economic parameters (but a solution is suggested in the next section). Nevertheless, if an economic model with estimated parameter values is needed to arrive at unbiased estimates of the price margin, the DOC should use such a model.

Verification versus Estimation

The objective of the antidumping law is to assure domestic firms that competing imports will be fairly priced. To arrive at an unbiased estimation of the dumping margin, one must introduce economic analysis into the process, remembering that the DOC should estimate a price effect rather than calculate cost adjustments on the basis of accounting data. The current law recognizes that certain verifiable costs might not be passed forward into prices. The DOC has argued, however, that price effects estimated from economic models cannot be verified. That is true. Nevertheless, the law instructs the DOC to estimate the price effect.

Thus, verifiability should be limited to the input data it uses in estimating the price effect.

Economic models and concepts have been used to administer other laws; in fact, the ITC is currently using an economic model to determine whether dumped imports cause material injury to the domestic industry. So long as the administering authority reveals the economic analysis being used and gives both petitioners and respondents the opportunity to comment on the applicability of the analysis in the particular case, the Court of International Trade supports the use of such tools in administering the antidumping law.

RECOMMENDATION. There is no justification for obtaining *strongly verifiable calculations* of the cost adjustments, because cost is not the objective of the legislated task assigned to the DOC. Instead, the DOC should verify, where appropriate, the data and other information needed to estimate the correct price adjustments. This can be done with the aid of standard, well-received economic theory, but certain parameter values will have to be estimated. The final result will be *weakly verifiable estimates* of the price effect of dumping, which is the relevant measurement.

That is to say, the end result would be an estimate rather than a fact. But this is not different from current practice. Claims of precision based on verifiable information are, in fact, false claims. Many examples can be cited in which the DOC has been forced to make one or more arbitrary decisions to reach a final calculation. And that says nothing about the cases in which the DOC must allocate verifiable cost elements across transactions, across products, across plants, and across time. Such allocations are estimates, not verifiable precise calculations.

To repeat, the DOC should develop methods of estimating the correct variables and should limit verification to the verifiable input data needed to put its method into operation. The objective should not be verification—but an unbiased estimate of the price effect. If possible, the DOC should also estimate confidence intervals or the range in which the correct number is most likely to fall.

Counterfactual Comparison

The price effect of the unfair practice of dumping gives rise to a counterfactual question: what would the U.S. price be if the foreign producer or exporter charged the same price for sales to the United States as for sales in the home market? In general the price effect of dumping is not equal to the margin of dumping as defined in the antidumping duty law.

Recall that the margin of dumping is simply the difference between the U.S. price and the foreign market price. However, if the foreign producer or exporter stopped dumping and instead set the same price in both markets, in all likelihood the U.S. price would be increased by a part of the difference between the prices, and the home market price would be decreased by the remainder of the difference. The price effect of dumping would be the amount by which the U.S. price would be increased.

Since the price effect of dumping is not directly observable, how would one quantify it? One method would be to construct an economic model of dumping that incorporates the underlying motive of the foreign producer or exporter. Alternatively, one could ask rather simple questions about the effect of the elimination of dumping on the profits of the foreign producer or exporter. Since to eliminate dumping the home price must be decreased, the U.S. price increased, or some combination of both, one can simply estimate the profit effects of each of these steps. If the foreign producer's sales were primarily destined for the home market, the reduction in home market price would have a large negative impact on revenues; in this case, the U.S. price would be increased by a large share of the difference between the prices. But if a large share of the sales was destined for the U.S. market, an increase in the U.S. price, and the resulting loss of market share in the United States, would be of greater concern; here, the main price adjustment would lower the price of sales in the home market. As a rule of thumb, one could estimate the extent to which the price would be decreased for sales in the home market and increased for sales to the United States by using the proportionate shares of foreign production that are sold in the respective markets.

The price effect of dumping is related to the magnitude of the injury to the domestic industry and, therefore, to the appropriate remedy. If the antidumping duty is designed to remedy injury to the domestic industry, an antidumping duty equal in magnitude to the margin of dumping is an excessive remedy. If, however, the motive of antidumping is to persuade the foreign producer or exporter to stop dumping, an excessive antidumping duty may be appropriate.

RECOMMENDATION. The antidumping duty law explicitly directs the DOC to estimate the margin of dumping. The resulting antidumping duty is greater than the difference between the U.S. price in the presence of dumping and the U.S. price in the absence of dumping. Thus, the margin of dumping exceeds the price effect of dumping, and it is greater than that required to remedy the injury caused by dumping. Although such a margin of dumping might be an appropriate penalty to discourage foreign firms from dumping in the U.S. market, it is not appropriate for determining whether dumping causes injury to the competing industry in the United States. This latter task, which is the responsibility of the ITC, requires information suitable for quantifying the price effect of the dumping practice. The DOC should either estimate the price effect of dumping, in addition to estimating the margin of dumping, or provide the ITC with the evidence needed to estimate the price effect of dumping. This issue may also be relevant to the GATT negotiations for revising the international rules governing antidumping practices and antidumping remedies.

Use of the Constructed Value Method

The constructed value method is one of the three methods the DOC uses to determine the foreign market value; it uses two methods to determine the U.S. price. The statutes provide strong guidelines for selecting a method to calculate the foreign market value. Whenever possible, the DOC is to use sales in the home market. If home market sales are inadequate, the DOC is to use sales to third countries. If such sales are inadequate or if third-country producers decline to cooperate, the DOC is to use the constructed value method. The base used to calculate the U.S. price depends on whether the first arm's-length sale takes place before or after the product leaves the country of exportation. If before, the purchase price is used; if after, the exporter's sales price is used. The critical question is whether the outcome is influenced by the method used to calculate the foreign market price and the U.S. price.

This question can be answered by counting the frequency of positive antidumping determinations made by the pricing methods (see table 2-3).[25] Positive outcomes of the two methods used to calculate the U.S. price occurred with similar frequency. However, the alternative methods used to calculate the foreign market value produced quite different results. The constructed value method was almost twice as likely to result in an affirmative dumping determination than were third-country sales. When home market sales were used, the results fell between these extremes but were closer to those for the constructed value.[26] These results indicate the importance of the method used to calculate the foreign market value.

25. The sample of cases includes those initiated under the Trade Agreements Act of 1979 and concluded before 1986, but excludes cases that were terminated or suspended.

26. An interesting explanation for this result was suggested at the Brookings conference: the petitioner cannot anticipate the outcome when third-country sales are used, because the selection of the third country is not known at the time the petition is filed.

Table 2-3. *Frequency of Positive Antidumping Determinations*

Means of calculating foreign market value	U.S. price					
	Purchase price		Exporter's sales price		Total	
	Number	Percent	Number	Percent	Number	Percent
Home market value	95	80	36	86	131	82
Third-country value	22	59	10	60	32	59
Constructed value	49	90	22	86	71	89
Total	166	80	68	82	234	81

When using the constructed value methodology, the DOC attempts to measure the full per unit cost of the item being sold in the U.S. market.[27] But the per unit cost is difficult to calculate because many factors need to be quantified: (1) the cost of inputs and variable factors of production (for example, labor and other elements of value added, which vary with the volume of output) that are directly attributable to the particular items in the shipment (that is, the transaction) being investigated; (2) the cost of other inputs and variable factors of production that must be allocated across various shipments of the product being investigated (so-called indirect operating costs); (3) the cost of still other inputs and variable factors of production across the various products put out by a multiproduct plant (this element may not be relevant in all DOC investigations); (4) the cost of selling and administration across various shipments, various products in a multiproduct plant, various plants in a multiproduct corporation, and possibly various divisions in a multidivision corporation; (5) the cost of fixed factors of production (such as plant and equipment) that must be allocated across various shipments and various products in a multiproduct plant and amortized over time; and (6) the cost of research and development across shipments, products, and time.

The DOC typically attempts to measure the direct operating costs per unit and then adds indirect operating costs; this latter involves some allocation of costs.[28] The result of these calculations would be what the economist calls average variable production costs. This calculation would

27. Economists normally divide costs into two components, variable costs and fixed costs; the distinction depends on whether the cost item varies with the volume of output. The full per unit cost would equal average fixed costs plus average variable costs.

28. The following sequencing of steps used to calculate per unit costs is an illustration rather than a factual description of how the DOC does its work.

include items 1 and 2 above, which can be clearly related to the product being investigated, plus that part of item 3 that is allocated to the product being investigated. Next, the direct and the allocated indirect selling costs (from item 4) are added to arrive at average variable costs.

Once the average variable cost has been calculated, the DOC must add the average fixed costs to arrive at the full per unit cost of the shipment or transaction. Fixed costs would include other elements of "general, selling, and administrative costs" (GS&A; from item 4 above), which cannot be clearly related to the volume of output or to sales, plant and equipment (item 5), and research and development expenses (item 6).[29] It takes substantial effort to allocate the average fixed costs across shipments, products, plants, and time, and this would vary greatly from case to case.

It is extremely difficult to construct per unit costs (that is, average variable costs plus average fixed costs). To begin with, variable costs have to be allocated across transactions and products and fixed costs across transactions, products, and time. To complicate matters, the DOC must also determine whether some cost elements are variable or fixed. In a multinational corporation, for example, top management costs (included in administrative costs) would increase as the size of the corporation increased; however, these costs would not be expected to change with the volume of output of a particular product from a particular plant. But plant management (also included in administrative costs) might expand if the volume of output increased over time, although plant management would not be expected to change for normal fluctuations in the volume of output.

Suffice it to say that average variable costs are extremely difficult to construct. Clearly, many arbitrary decisions must be made in identifying the elements of variable costs and determining how to allocate that cost item across shipments and products. Therefore, the final result will be an estimate and should be treated as such.[30]

Dealing with the fixed cost items is even more difficult. Not only must plant and equipment expenses be allocated across shipments and products, but they must be allocated across time. Instead of expensing such items, the DOC usually depreciates them using general accounting standards.

29. Items 5 and 6 are often included in GS&A; however, in what follows they are considered as separate costs.

30. Since the DOC does not distinguish between fixed and variable cost items, this point may be challenged as moot. The importance of the distinction, however, will become more obvious below.

Since accounting standards differ from country to country, the outcome of the constructed value exercise will depend on which country's standards are used. Where appropriate, the DOC uses the accounting standards of the country of the foreign producer. A second problem is that the accounting standards used in depreciation typically reflect a nation's tax codes, which seldom have anything to do with the economic value of fixed assets. Since profit-maximizing firms base their pricing policies on variable costs and not on fixed costs, depreciation, being a fixed cost, clearly has little to do with price—regardless of the particular accounting standards being used.

A similar, though more complex, problem exists in the treatment of research and development expenses. Although these clearly need to be included in per unit costs, the effect of these costs on price is another matter. Firms with heavy R&D expenses must, of course, set prices in a manner that will recover those expenses. But the expenses are recovered over time, often over a prolonged period of time. For example, the Boeing Aircraft Corporation will measure its R&D recovery period in decades rather than months or years. Such firms will design forward pricing policies to recover R&D expenses over time; forward pricing will have little connection with the costs constructed by using normal accounting standards. Given that R&D is a continuing process during which products are upgraded from time to time, it is highly likely that the expenses of many individual R&D projects are never recovered. This is also true for firms whose pricing practices are consistent with the norms for their industry, that is, for firms that price fairly.

Forward pricing is particularly important in the field of high technology, where products are often introduced at prices that are below average variable costs. The objective is to gain consumer acceptance so that production volumes can be increased and per unit costs lowered. Over time, both costs and prices will fall. But the costs will fall more rapidly, with the result that prices will eventually be above per unit costs, and producers will then be able to recover their full operating costs, capital costs, R&D costs, and a reasonable profit. As long as forward pricing is a normal pricing policy of an industry (practiced by U.S. firms as well as foreign firms), it should not be considered unfair simply because it departs from the normal method of constructing value.

There is also the problem that U.S. law specifies minimums for GS&A (at least 10 percent of operating expenses) and profit (at least 8 percent of operating expenses plus GS&A). These minimums yield upward-biased estimates of the margin of dumping whenever the actual GS&A or profit experience of the respondent firms is lower than the legislated minimums. In practice, these minimums are used quite often. Thus, whenever a foreign respondent participates in a competitive home market industry in which the profits are lower than the 8 percent minimum, that firm would be found guilty of dumping even if it charged equal prices on sales to the home market and the U.S. market.[31] A reasonable alternative for the DOC would be to use GS&A and profit rate minimums that are consistent with the norms of the industry in the exporting country. The established minimums, however, should not be the average GS&A or profit rate for the foreign industry; such a practice would de facto define better-than-average efficiency as an unfair trading practice.

RECOMMENDATION. The constructed value method is replete with difficulties. It is being used more and more, whereas it should be used only as a last resort. Because of the difficulty in allocating fixed costs (for example, the costs of capital and of R&D), the DOC should emphasize per unit variable costs. Where per unit variable costs are higher than the U.S. price, the suspicion that imports are being dumped is strong. Even in these cases, however, the resulting calculation might be unduly influenced by the allocation of variable GS&A costs. Allowance must also be made for industries in which forward pricing is the normal pricing behavior.

Exchange Rate Adjustments

Fluctuations in the exchange rate between the U.S. dollar and the currency of the exporting country present further difficulties for the DOC. At times, changes in the exchange rate can produce circumstances that lead to a finding of dumping. Suppose that a foreign firm contracts with its buyers on the first day of the year for shipments to be made over the ensuing year. Suppose further that the contract provides for the same prices throughout the year—local currency prices for home sales and U.S. dollar prices for sales to the United States.[32] As long as the exchange rate remains constant throughout the year, the foreign firm is not dumping. If the value of the foreign currency appreciated before the contract expires, however, the U.S. price (in U.S. dollars) would be lower than

31. Of course, if the volume of home market sales was adequate, an unbiased comparison of prices would yield an absence of dumping. However, home market sales are often considered inadequate, in which case the constructed value method would be used.

32. Assume that the U.S. dollar price is determined by converting the local currency price into dollars at the market exchange rate that prevails on the first day of the year.

the home market price (converted to U.S. dollars at the new appreciated exchange rate). In other words, the foreign firm would be dumping.

In this example, the foreign exchange risk has been borne by the foreign producer rather than by the U.S. importer, and the result is an incidence of dumping. If the foreign producer had contracted for all sales in local currency, the U.S. importer would have accepted the exchange risk (and lost), but the foreign producer would not have been dumping.

This broadens the definition of dumping to include the "unfair" assignment of exchange risk; fair trading requires the U.S. importer to accept the exchange risk! Over time, as contracts are renewed and trends in exchange rate movements become obvious, foreign firms should set prices for sales to all markets consistent with exchange rates. But this has little to do with the DOC methodology for coping with changes in the exchange rate.

In the DOC methodology for comparing the foreign market value and the U.S. price, foreign market value is usually converted into U.S. dollars by using the appropriate exchange rates. The DOC normally uses the quarterly exchange rate as determined by the Federal Reserve Board. If during any quarter the daily exchange rate departs from the quarterly rate by more than 5 percent, the appropriate daily rate will be used to compare the foreign market value and the U.S. price for the particular transaction.

Recall the bias caused by the method of averaging. DOC calculations can indicate dumping even when no dumping exists—except when the foreign producer charges constant local currency prices on sales to the home market and constant dollar prices on sales to the United States throughout the six months of the investigation. But even if exchange rates are relatively stable over the period of a DOC investigation, two (or maybe three) quarterly exchange rates will be used to convert foreign local currency prices into U.S. dollar prices. The use of at least two exchange rates will cause exactly the same type of bias caused by the method of averaging. And whenever the two exchange rates differ by at least 1 percent, the expected bias will yield a margin of dumping greater than the one-half of 1 percent de minimis level.

Under normal circumstances, the exchange rate problem will be much greater, especially when the U.S. exporter's sales price is used. The exchange rate used for ESP transactions is the one that is appropriate for the date of exportation. Since the U.S. price will be based on the first transaction between unrelated parties, the transaction will not take place until after the product has cleared customs in the United States and, possibly, undergone further shipping and distribution or even further processing. Clearly, the exchange rate date and the transaction date are not the same and may differ by a substantial period of time.

RECOMMENDATION. Incorporating exchange rate fluctuations into the DOC methodology to estimate the margin of dumping is a complex procedure, and a rule appropriate for one situation might be inappropriate for another. No specific recommendation will be made here. But as a general practice, the DOC should use the exchange rate that applies on the date the price was determined between the foreign seller and the first unrelated party. This suggestion seems consistent with the DOC practice in cases where the U.S. purchase price is used; ESP cases are much more complicated. In the final analysis, the most appropriate method to use will probably depend on the circumstances. In any event, the averaging bias caused by exchange rate changes must be recognized. Again, the threshold for positive dumping determinations should be raised to offset this bias.

Concluding Remarks

The job of administering the antidumping duty law is an extremely difficult one, but the methodology the DOC uses to this end yields biased estimates of the margin of dumping. Each administrative decision seems to favor domestic producers of the like product and go against foreign producers, exporters, U.S. importers, and U.S. purchasers. In many cases, the decision simply follows the dictates of U.S. law, which contains the bias.

Where do we go from here? First, the most important biases should be removed from the law and from DOC methodology, these being the ones that occur most often in practice and that impart the largest bias. Since this study has been completed without the cooperation of the DOC and without access to detailed information, I am not in a position to identify the most important biases. The DOC has the data base to conduct a detailed study of past cases and to identify the important biases. But given the possibility that an in-house study might justify past behavior, such a study would more appropriately be conducted by an independent agency or a private research group. To be effective, that agency or group would have to have access to confidential information collected during the course of DOC investigations.

Second, if Congress intends the antidumping duty law to comply with the spirit of GATT rules, the DOC should be attempting to estimate a dumping margin equivalent to the "price effect of the dumping practice." An unbiased estimation of the price effect cannot be achieved unless economic analysis is introduced into the process. It must be recognized that the DOC will be estimating a price effect rather than calculating cost adjustments on the basis of accounting data. Under the current law, certain verifiable costs might not be passed forward into prices. Thus, verifiability should be limited to the input data used by the DOC in estimating the price effect. Economic models and concepts have been used to administer other laws; in fact, they are currently being used by the ITC in its investigation into whether dumped imports cause material injury to the domestic industry. As long as the administering authority reveals the economic analysis being used and gives both petitioners and respondents an opportunity to comment on the applicability of the analysis in the particular case, the Court of International Trade supports the use of such tools in administering the antidumping law.

Finally, the DOC should certainly remove the obvious and easily correctable biases. For example, the bias imparted by the method of averaging could easily be removed by using matched transactions, as is done during compliance, or by subdividing the investigation period into several subperiods. As for the bias imparted by exchange rate variations, each transaction must be examined. If prices are determined on a contract date that differs from the shipment or import date, exchange rate changes during the intervening period could significantly influence the calculation of the margin of dumping. This bias can be removed by using the appropriate exchange rate.

Appendix: Stages of Antidumping Proceedings

Role of the DOC: To determine whether foreign merchandise is being sold in the United States at less than fair value (LTFV) and, if so, to estimate the margin of dumping.

Role of the ITC: To determine whether an industry in the United States is being materially injured or is threatened with material injury, or whether the establishment of an industry is being materially retarded by reason of LTFV imports.

Sales at less than fair value: Primary definition: when the price of imported merchandise sold in the United States (hereafter, U.S. price, or USP) is less than the price of similar merchandise sold in the exporter's home market, or if none, sold in other countries (hereafter, foreign market value, or FMV)—after adjustments for any differences in quantity, circumstances of sale, level of trade, physical characteristics, packing costs, and transportation costs. Secondary definition: when imported merchandise is sold in the United States at a price below the cost of production; in this case the foreign market value is the cost of production.

Margin of dumping: The margin of dumping is the amount by which the U.S. price is below fair value; it is calculated as FMV − USP and is usually expressed as a percentage of the USP.

Filing of petition: Investigations are initiated when an affected industry in the United States files a petition alleging that imports are being sold in the United States at prices below fair value, together with information reasonably available to the petitioner, including data to support the allegation; the petition must also include some evidence that an industry in the United States is being injured.

Summary investigation by the DOC: To determine whether the petition contains adequate information to support the allegation of sales at less than fair value and injury to an industry in the United States. A notice of "Dismissal of Antidumping Petition" or a notice of "Initiation of Antidumping Investigation" is then published in the *Federal Register*.

ITC preliminary investigation: Within forty-five days of the filing of the petition, the ITC is to determine, on the basis of "best available information," whether there is a "reasonable indication" of injury; if the ITC determines in the negative, the investigation is terminated.

The DOC investigation: The DOC gathers data from the manufacturer and exporter to establish the statutory values required for the price comparisons (see Commerce Regulations, sections 353.2 through 353.10).

The questionnaire: A questionnaire designed to gather transactional data, including all home market and export information necessary to make the price comparisons, is communicated to the manufacturer and exporter. The DOC representative explains the questionnaire and assists the respondent in determining the best method of selecting and presenting data to fit the circumstances of the case.

The sixty-day review: Within sixty days from the initiation of investigation, the DOC reviews all data gathered to decide if sufficient information is available to make a preliminary determination.

Waiver of verification: If the sixty-day review concludes with an affirmative decision, the petitioner and other parties are notified and given a disclosure of the results within an additional fifteen days. If the petitioner and other domestic parties furnish a waiver of verification of the information and indicate a willingness to have a preliminary determination made on the basis of the facts obtained during the first sixty days of the DOC investigation, a preliminary determination will be made within ninety days of the initiation of the DOC investigation. (Note: a waiver of verification applies only to information obtained during the first sixty days of the DOC investigation; it does not preclude verification of data received subsequently.)

If a waiver of verification is not forthcoming, the investigation will continue and a verification of the data will be conducted by the DOC. Failure of the manufacturer or exporter to allow verification will be noted and may affect the consideration of all information furnished.

The DOC preliminary determination: The DOC is to determine, on the basis of "best available information," whether there is a "reasonable likelihood" that imports are being sold at less than fair value.

Suspension of liquidation: If the DOC preliminary determination is that LTFV imports are likely to exist, liquidation of entry is suspended from the date of notice of the DOC preliminary determination. Imports of merchandise subject to the investigation may be cleared through customs, but final duties will not be quantified or assessed until the question of dumping is resolved. The importer is required to make a cash deposit or post a bond or other security to guarantee potential dumping liability. The amount of the security is based on the margin of dumping as estimated in the preliminary determination.

Suspension of liquidations may be made retroactive to a date ninety days prior to the date of notice of the DOC's preliminary determination if the DOC determines that *critical circumstances* exist. (Note: If the DOC preliminary determination is negative, the investigation continues without suspension of liquidation.)

Critical circumstances: If the petitioner alleges "critical circumstances" in the original petition or by amendment at least twenty days before the DOC's final determination, the DOC shall promptly determine on the basis of the best available information at that time whether there is adequate reason to believe or suspect (a) there is a history of dumping of the kind of merchandise in question in the United States or elsewhere, or the importer knew or should have known the merchandise was being sold at less than fair value, and (b) there have been massive imports over a relatively short period (see Commerce Regulations, section 353.40).

The DOC's final determination: The DOC makes its final determination whether imports are being sold in the United States at less than fair value on the basis of all facts gathered during the investigation, including facts obtained after the preliminary determination. If the DOC's final determination is negative, the investigation is terminated. If the DOC's final determination is positive, an estimate of the margin of dumping is also reported. Liquidation is suspended if the DOC's preliminary determination is negative; if it is positive, suspension of liquidation continues.

The ITC's final determination: The ITC is to determine whether an industry in the United States is injured by LTFV imports. If the ITC final determination is negative, the case is terminated. Any cash deposits made on imports subsequent to the suspension of liquidation are refunded in full; any bonds posted to guarantee the payment of antidumping duties are released. If the ITC's final determination is affirmative, an antidumping order will be issued. Importation will continue under suspension of liquidation subject to the assessment of antidumping duties on those particular imports found to be at less than fair value; under an antidumping order, importers are required to deposit estimated antidumping duties.

Termination or suspension of investigation: Antidumping investigations may be terminated at any time if the petitioner withdraws the petition. The investigation is also terminated upon (1) an ITC preliminary negative determination, (2) a final negative determination by the DOC, or (3) a final negative determination by the ITC.

An investigation may be suspended if the DOC and at least 85 percent of the exporters of the imports subject to the investigation agree that (1) LTFV imports will be eliminated, (2) shipments will cease within six months of the suspension, or (3) prices will be adjusted to eliminate the injurious effects of the LTFV imports. The DOC must consult with the petitioner regarding a suspension agreement and notify all interested parties and the ITC (see Commerce Regulations, section 353.43).

Collection of antidumping duties: The DOC shall make an *administrative review* at least once during each twelve-month period to determine the foreign market value and the U.S. price of each entry of merchandise subject to an antidumping order. Antidumping duties are collected for each entry in the amount by which the foreign market value exceeds the U.S. price; interest is paid (charged) on any overpayment (underpayment) of estimated antidumping duties as provided under the antidumping order.

In the case of imports that are subject to suspension of liquidation pursuant to a DOC preliminary determination but that enter before an antidumping order, antidumping duties will be assessed in the amount of the estimated antidumping duties or the antidumping duties determined during the administrative review, whichever is less.

Revision or revocation of antidumping duty: The initial antidumping duty is that estimated by the DOC and reported in its final determination. The antidumping duty will be revised to be the average antidumping duty assessed as the result of the most recent administrative review.

An application for revocation of an antidumping order may be submitted to the DOC together with information demonstrating that imports are no longer being sold at less than fair value. The DOC will normally consider such applications only if LTFV imports have not been made for a period of two years following the date of the antidumping duty order or suspension of the investigation. The DOC may revoke an antidumping order on its own initiative if it is determined that (1) there is no likelihood LTFV imports will be resumed, (2) sales at less than fair value have been terminated, or (3) other circumstances warrant the revocation of the antidumping order or termination of a suspended investigation.

Comment

Noel Hemmendinger

Most of Tracy Murray's points are well taken, but a number of his comments bear closer examination.

On the question of standing, amending the law would be helpful but is not essential. Instead, the International Trade Commission and the Department of Commerce could do something radical, such as coordinate their activities so that information from the preliminary ITC investigation is available for the DOC to act on in a timely fashion—if not as timely as might be desirable, at least at an early stage in the investigation, when it could be discontinued.

I question the desirability of making dumping and the margin of dumping two separate investigations, and the feasibility of looking at things that are economically relevant, such as predation and the profitability of the foreign enterprise. That would certainly not be manageable under the U.S. law or any foreseeable amendments. Raising the de minimis margin does not really require legislation. Again, it might be good, but most of us in Washington prefer to avoid like the plague the notion of having to go to Congress to improve something, at least in this field.

Best information available, especially in the preliminary investigation, should not be based simply on the petition. This is obvious and important. Also, the point on averaging is well taken and is now a familiar complaint that is even privately voiced at the Department of Commerce. However, what is called "spot dumping" does require some attention, although it may be just a figment of the imagination. Whatever the case, there are drafts in the Uruguay Round that work around that problem. The main point is that if the patterns of sales in the home and U.S. markets are much the same, a finding of dumping should be inconceivable.

Surprisingly, Murray's discussion of symmetrical comparisons has omitted one of the main complaints about the U.S. practice—that complaint can be framed either in terms of the level of trade or the circumstances of sale for selling expenses. There is an entirely unjustified discrimination between what are called "directly related" and "not directly related" expenses. The true test should be whether expenses are established by evidence under generally accepted accounting principles; the allocation of overhead expenses is perfectly normal and appropriate. And, ironically, this what the Department of Commerce does all the time in determining the exporter's sales price.

I entirely agree that below-cost sales should be taken out of the law. They should never have been put in. This was done with too little consideration of the consequences. However, the practice is deeply embedded now and has even been adopted by other leading nations that have dumping laws, so it would be a tough fight. No draft in the Uruguay Round tries to tackle it.

Where I part company with Murray is over cost- and price-based adjustments. The notion that in considering injury one should try to determine to what extent the foreign producer would adjust his home market price and to what extent he would adjust the U.S. price is an interesting one. It is the first time I have heard of it, but I just can't imagine that such an inquiry, in an already complicated case, could be made. It must be frustrating to economists that they have very sophisticated tools that they can't use because the data are no good; that is, the inputs are going to be guesswork.

I also have a difference of principle on this point. I think that the authorities should be trying to do something very simple in principle, which is to work back to ex-factory prices, as was explained long ago by the Treasury Department, and that the margin of dumping should depend on relative profitability. If one is looking at relative profitability of the markets, then one naturally uses cost. So cost is the only thing one can use, and it is the only thing one ought to use.

With respect to constructed value, Murray rightly states that the "emphasis" should be on unit variable costs, because a price that covers variable costs is likely to reflect normal business behavior that is not challengeable under U.S. law applicable to domestic transactions. But this is really a rejection of the international concept of dumping, not a serious proposal to amend the practice. I agree that minima of 10 percent for administrative expenses and 8 percent for profit are too rigid, and that forward pricing should be allowed. The head of the International Trade Administration, Assistant Secretary Eric I. Garfinkel, has understandably said he can't deal with forward pricing because it is speculative. It is an institutional problem for the Department of Commerce that people there feel they have to crunch numbers.

However, when businessmen are actually making cost and volume projections and basing their prices on them, it is unrealistic for the DOC to insist on actual accounting data. Historical data have little to do with pricing for a new product and cannot deal with economies of scale or economies from the learning curve. In a proper case, forward pricing can be established to the satisfaction of the courts and, I hope, even the Department of Commerce. But the burden is on respondents to produce the studies that would help managers decide on the price: these would be studies of the price that would yield a return over a reasonable time, and in all probability they would be based on respondents' experience with other products.

The Uruguay Round is in a critical moment, and the dumping issues are in a critical phase in that Round. If the impasse over agriculture can be surmounted, and the Round brought to a meaningful conclusion, there would be no excuse for not using the most recent paper produced by New Zealand as a basis for major revisions in the antidumping code. The question is very sensitive because if Assistant Secretary Garfinkel is going to deal with it successfully, he will have to do things that dozens of congressmen have asked him not to do and that he himself has said he would not do. It is essential to the success of the Uruguay Round—if there is a chance for success—that the United States make some major concessions involving many of the points we have been discussing.

If no major changes in the antidumping code are reached in the Uruguay Round, the issues discussed in this book will not go away. There is a growing sentiment in the United States and throughout the world that the application of antidumping laws by the four countries that have traditionally used them has been biased. As far as the United States is concerned, almost all the problems could be corrected by the Department of Commerce itself without new legislation. Let us hope it will begin to see the light.

At another level, we should face up to the possibility that the U.S. law is not administrable. The DOC cannot admit this. Every government agency has to claim that it "can do" and must therefore ask for more money and bodies. Some people believe there is a valid distinction between fair and unfair trade. Others would disagree but would nevertheless argue that antidumping serves as an essential safety valve. The trend over many years toward freer trade has always needed a safety valve. It was furnished for a time by the escape clause (GATT article 19, U.S. section 201), but when the administration became ideologically unwilling to impose restrictions on fair trade, the antidumping law became the safety valve. The trouble is that it imposes too heavy a burden on legitimate trade and is too expensive and too capricious in its results. So nobody is satisfied.

A system with more administrative discretion could no doubt be devised, but it is not realistic to turn the clock back. The constant tinkering with the law to deal with cases in which domestic industries have been dissatisfied with the results has a ratchet effect. There is no way to simplify. Perhaps the relevant analogy is deregulation. Once regulation has reached a certain point of complexity and bureaucratization, you have to abolish it and start over.

It may be that eliminating the biases in the antidumping law would reduce the number of cases to the point where the administration would become manageable. But that is doubtful. My pet solution has been to do without the antidumping and countervailing laws and to rely on section 201 ("safeguards" in international parlance) if imports are causing problems for a domestic industry that are regarded as justifying countermeasures. More and more practitioners agree, although many have said that section 201 puts undue political pressure on the president. But that is what he is there for, and he can be given authority to delegate all but the critical decisions. How much or little trade restriction ensues will depend, of course, on the times and the prevailing economic and political forces. Ideally, most of us would prefer to see no protection at all, but we do not live in an ideal world. Whatever we do should be done rationally, not blindly and mechanistically, and with an overt regard for the national interest. Although the trend is still in the other direction, I hope to live long enough to see it reversed.

Comment

Tom Emrich

Tracy Murray has focused on one of the basic problems with the dumping methodology—the inherent bias that comes from comparing individual U.S. sales with average home market sales. Like other contributors to this volume, he has approached the issue by comparing identical prices on the same day in both markets. The averaging methodology used by the Department of Commerce, he points out, may produce a dumping margin where none really exists.

I do not believe that a change in legislation is necessary to resolve this problem. It could be accomplished administratively in one of two ways. One approach would be to average U.S. prices along with prices in the home market. In most cases, this would be appropriate. The other approach would be to take into account negative margins, to offset positive dumping margins with negative dumping margins.

Nor does it require a change in the annual review process, a possibility the DOC is apparently considering behind the scenes. The idea would be to replace the department's traditional window-matching methodology with a single, weighted-average, home market price for the entire period of review. Such a change would merely compound the problems that already exist in using a six-month average price in the initial investigation.

A second important point Murray raises is that the de minimus standard is too low and needs to be raised. It is often impossible for a company operating under a dumping order to price in both markets in such a way that the result will be an average margin of less than 0.5 percent. Few companies have this degree of control over market prices.

One of the speakers at the conference suggested raising the de minimus level to 5 percent. I would support such a change. Perhaps the DOC could implement a two-tiered rate—a higher rate for the initial investigation and a lower rate for annual reviews. Once companies have participated in the original investigation and understand the department's dumping methodology, they can take greater affirmative actions in adjusting future pricing.

As Noel Hemmendinger has observed, the DOC needs to jettison the entire sales-below-cost test. It doesn't have any place in the process. Alternatively, the law as written could be administered in ways that would alleviate some of the basic problems inherent in the current approach to below-cost sales.

One problem is that the DOC cannot look into the future to evaluate claims that a company can cover its costs over an extended period of time. Unlike historical accounting data, projections into the future cannot be verified.

Since the DOC does not appear to be considering an expansion of its time frame for evaluating sales below cost, it could simply increase the current threshold in the cost test. Now the department uses a 10 percent threshold in determining whether to eliminate below-cost sales from the data base of home market sales. This is a standard established by the DOC itself and one that it can change on its own initiative, say, to 20 or 30 percent. Such a move would help the process considerably.

In Murray's view, the DOC should be introducing price-based adjustments, but it is unrealistic to think that the department could adopt such an approach. The DOC is simply not staffed to deal with the kinds of economic and theoretical issues that accompany price-based adjustments. Moreover, a respondent would have serious problems in an annual review process, where the transparency and the predictability of the process (to the extent that they now exist) are essential to understanding how pricing decisions in both markets will translate into future dumping margins.

At the same time, there are things the DOC might do from a practical standpoint to make the overall process work more smoothly. First, it should fight the tendency to track every adjustment to the fifth digit to the right of the decimal point. This overreliance on detail without regard to whether it makes any sense or is relevant to the dumping calculation is a serious problem for companies involved in a dumping investigation. The department should consider setting new standards for ignoring charges and circumstance of sale adjustments that are not significant to the case at hand.

Second, the department could make much better use of data from annual financial statements, which do not necessarily line up with the period of review or investigation. It could also continue the practice started in the antifriction bearings case—that is, it could establish a comment period before the annual review to allow all parties—petitioners and respondents—to comment on the basic methodological issues coming up in the review itself. Most of the people participating in the antifriction bearing review found this to be helpful.

Third, the DOC should put a halt to a growing trend toward requiring respondents themselves to prepare model matches, conduct the sales-below-cost test, and calculate weighted-average home market prices. This can only create additional work and serious problems for both respondent and the department. Few respondents have the capability to do these kinds of tasks. Perhaps more important, such an arrangement does not allow the department to make its own adjustments to data submitted by respondents but instead forces it to go back to respondents repeatedly for additional information, a process that is time-consuming, disruptive, and expensive.

CHAPTER THREE

The Antidumping Law: A Legal and Administrative Nontariff Barrier

N. David Palmeter

THE TRADE EXPANSION ACT of 1962, "the unifying intellectual principle of the New Frontier," paved the way for the Kennedy Round, the most significant of the post–World War II rounds of trade negotiations.[1] The entire law is set forth in just 32 pages of the United States Statutes at Large. Since then, there has been an unrelenting addition of legal requirement upon legal requirement that has greatly increased the complexity of already complex investigations.

The improvements in the antidumping and countervailing duty laws contained in the Omnibus Trade and Competitiveness Act of 1988 by themselves require no less than 28 pages. These are in addition to the 43 pages needed for the 1979 enactment of the current basic versions of these laws and the 20 pages of amendments added in 1984. Antidumping regulations of the Department of Commerce, which implement the law, today comprise 44 pages of the Code of Federal Regulations. Indeed, since each page is double-columned, the regulations may be said to be the equivalent of 88 "normal" pages.

This increased complexity is also reflected in the increasing length of the questionnaires the Department of Commerce presents to foreign exporters in antidumping investigations. A page count of the first questionnaire presented in each of the last four years suggests what is happening:

---

1. Joseph Kraft, as quoted in Arthur M. Schlesinger, Jr., *A Thousand Days* (Houghton, Mifflin, 1965), p. 847.

Year	Case	Pages
1987	Potassium chloride from Canada	52
1988	3.5-inch microdisks from Japan	73
1989	Small-business telephone systems from Japan	128
1990	Fresh and chilled Atlantic salmon from Norway	158

No doubt the page count has not been uninterruptedly upward since 1987. The length of a questionnaire depends in part on the nature of the product under investigation and on the structure of the trade.[2] But there can be no doubt that the trend has been upward—sharply and steadily. The complexity that is reflected in part by the increasing length of antidumping questionnaires adds further unfairness to an already unfair process. And the process, like any stacked deck that purports to be otherwise, truly is unfair.

This characterization of the law and its administration as unfair stands the usual antidumping rhetoric on its head. It is the act of dumping, we are told, that is unfair, even "pernicious."[3] Indeed, courts have described dumping as "predatory," as containing an element of "wrongdoing."[4]

2. Product complexity may explain in part why microdisks and telephones required longer questionnaires than did potassium chloride. It is doubtful whether this explains all, however, for both microdisks and telephones would seem to be "complex" products, and the disparity in their questionnaire sizes is greater than the disparity in questionnaire length between microdisks and potassium chloride. And what of salmon? In part the explanation for the length of the questionnaire in this investigation is explained by the fact that the total page count includes separate questionnaires presented to two separate groups in the Norwegian industry: exporters and fish farmers. But in fact, a total of 220 pages was issued initially to these two groups. The 158-page count nets out the pages to one group of farmers that subsequently were withdrawn, but not after the farmers had spent considerable resources in attempting to answer them. Moreover, there is undoubtedly an unmeasurable qualitative factor by which fewer pages to a small farmer are, to that respondent, more complex than more pages to a large manufacturer of microdisks or telephone systems. It should also be noted that, with the possible exception of the Canadian producers of potassium chloride (who might have been English-speaking) all these questionnaires are, to the respondent, in a foreign language and require responses in a foreign language—no small added burden. How would the average American farmer or manufacturer do in responding to a questionnaire in French, Japanese, or Norwegian?

3. *Trade Agreements Act of 1979*, S. Rept. 249, 96 Cong. 1 sess. (Government Printing Office, 1980), p. 37: "Subsidies and dumping are two of the most pernicious practices which distort international trade to the disadvantage of United States commerce." This is part of what Jagdish Bhagwati has called the "insidious growth of the 'fairness' issue." Jagdish Bhagwati, *Protectionism* (MIT Press, 1988), p. 123.

4. *Matsushita Electric Industrial Co. Ltd.* v. *United States*, 823 F.2d 505,509 (Fed. Cir. 1989); *Algoma Steel Corporation Ltd.* v. *United States*, 865 F.2d 240, 242 (Fed. Cir. 1989).

This is strong language for the simple practice of pricing differently in different markets—for, when all is said and done, dumping is nothing more than that. But this condemnatory rhetoric, with its connotation of moral deficiency, sets the tone and characterizes the nature of most discussions of dumping. The language is normative language, and in virtually every syllable it suggests that something unsavory is going on—that the dumpers, the foreigners, are up to no good.[5]

In this chapter, I assume, with the apologists for the antidumping law, that the foreigners—or, at least, many of them—are indeed up to no good. But even if that is true, the antidumping regime of the United States rarely answers accurately the basic question it asks: are prices to the United States from a particular exporter really below fair value?[6] The standards of the law, the procedures it uses, and the implementation of these standards and procedures by the Department of Commerce increasingly ensure that, at the end of the day, an exporter determined to have been selling in the United States below fair value has probably been doing no such thing in any meaningful sense of the word "fair." On the contrary, rather than being a price discriminator, a dumper is more likely the victim of an antidumping process that has become a legal and an administrative nontariff barrier.[7]

5. The terminology in common law terms is that of *malum in se*—an act that inherently and essentially is immoral, such as theft or murder. A person who commits such an act does not have to be aware of the details of the law to know that it is wrong. Differential pricing simply does not fall into this category. There is nothing inherently wrong with it. In common law terms, again, differential pricing that runs afoul of the antidumping laws is merely *malum prohibitum*—an act that is wrong only because it is prohibited by law, such as driving on the left side of most highways in the United States, or on the right side of most highways in the United Kingdom or Japan. This is similar to Jeremy Bentham's distinction between "original utility" and "expectation utility," which, "explains why certain laws must be the same in all societies, while others vary greatly from society to society. The former laws, resting in a substantial way on original utility, depend on largely invariant features of human nature, whereas the latter depend on expectations and these, in turn, on potentially widely variable beliefs, experience, prejudices, attitudes and practices." Quoted in Gerald J. Postema, *Bentham and the Common Law Tradition* (Oxford: Clarendon Press, 1989), p. 169.

6. "Fair value" is the statutory term. 19 U.S.C.A. sec. 1673. The use of this term leads directly to its opposite, "unfair," to characterize the practice of selling below fair value. The term used in the GATT Antidumping Code is the slightly more neutral "normal" value. "Agreement on Implementation of Article VI of the General Agreement on Tariffs and Trade, in General Agreement on Tariffs and Trade," *Basic Instruments and Selected Documents* (26th Supplement, Geneva, 1980), article 2:1.

7. It may seem illogical to term a law that may lead to increased duties a nontariff barrier, but the increased tariff is the result of a legal and administrative process. It is this process—which leads to the duties, and not the duties themselves—that I characterize as a nontariff barrier.

The Law and the Inquisition

The antidumping provisions of U.S. law are set out in title VII of the Tariff Act of 1930, as amended by the Trade Agreements Act of 1979. They provide for the imposition of a special duty to offset any margin of dumping of imported merchandise—the amount by which the price for export to the United States is less than fair value. The determination of whether imported goods are being sold at less than fair value is made by the International Trade Administration of the Department of Commerce.[8]

Antidumping investigations are characterized by massive amounts of data that must be generated by foreign respondents and presented in required form within an extremely short period of time.[9] In a normal antidumping investigation, Commerce must reach a preliminary determination within 160 days of the filing of a petition; a final determination must be made within 75 days of the preliminary. In extraordinarily complicated cases, the deadline for the preliminary determination may be extended by a maximum of 50 days and the final determination by a maximum of 60 days. In the face of these strict statutory time limits, Commerce, in turn, places severe time limits on respondents, who are normally given only 30 days in which to respond to questionnaires. Extensions are granted sparingly and rarely exceed two weeks.[10] Moreover, the time limits encompass calendar days, not business days. When,

8. Even if the Department of Commerce finds sales at less than fair value, an antidumping duty will not be imposed unless the International Trade Commission determines that an industry in the United States is materially injured or is threatened with material injury, or that the establishment of an industry in the United States is being materially retarded, by reason of the imports sold at less than fair value. 19 U.S.C.A. sec. 1673.

9. If the response contains business proprietary information (which is almost always the case), separate public versions of the response are required as well. Both the proprietary and the public versions must be submitted in multiple copies. So voluminous are these documents that more than a day can be consumed simply in the photocopying and binding operations—further encroaching on response preparation time. All sales data in the response must be submitted on computer tape in specified formats: the tape should be nine-track and can have a density of either 800, 1,600, or 6,250 BPI. Since the department cannot translate ASCII data, the coding requirements are quite specific and must be followed. The characters must be coded either EBCDIC or BCD alphanumeric. Cost of production information generally must be submitted on IBM-PC compatible 5.25" DS/DD floppy discs, using the LOTUS 123 financial spread-sheet program compatible with IBM-PC Disc Operating Software (DOS) versions 3.2 or lower. These are not necessarily computer capabilities every foreign producer will have.

10. The pressure on respondents is usually ameliorated somewhat because Commerce normally presents its questionnaires on a staggered timetable. The first portion, however, typically calls for a response in less than thirty days, often in as little as two weeks.

as often occurs, Commerce presents its questionnaire to counsel for the exporters on Friday afternoon, it is already day 3 of the 30-day response period by the time the exporter finds the questionnaire on its facsimile machine Monday morning.[11]

What strikes lawyers as particularly unusual about this entire process is its distance from the traditional American system of justice, the adversarial system in which two parties argue their case before an impartial arbiter and the complaining party has the burden of proof. Antidumping procedure at the Commerce Department, in contrast, is inquisitorial: a single office has the dual responsibility of investigating the allegations and deciding the issue.[12] This is the essence of the inquisitorial system: "conversion of the judge from an impartial referee into an active inquisitor who is free to seek evidence and to control the nature and objectives of the inquiry."[13]

Although this system obviously confers enormous power on Commerce, the department's position is less than enviable. Commerce is supposed to be at once the official, impartial judge and the thorough, relentless investigator on behalf of petitioners who are not always shy when it comes to taking their complaints to Congress. Indeed, complaints to Congress by petitioners are largely, if not totally, responsible for the extensive additions to the antidumping law in recent years. No matter what Commerce does in its investigative role, no matter what it accomplishes in the brief period of time available, the department always is subject to the allegation that it did not do enough. If one had set out to give a government agency a mission that is subject by its very nature to second guessing, it would be difficult to do better than this.

The impact on foreign respondents is predictable. Commerce seeks to leave no stone unturned, desiring to do as thorough an investigation as

11. I know of no data concerning the days and times when Commerce presents questionnaires. However, an informal survey of cases in my office puts Friday afternoon in first place. There may well be a simple, and innocent, explanation: like most of us, Commerce staffers probably like to clear their desks and in-boxes by the end of the week and thus not carry projects over the weekend. This is particularly likely to be true of time-sensitive projects. The questionnaire presentation date is an administratively important date in an antidumping investigation, and Commerce officials understandably want the record to show their efficiency. Better to have the weekend count against the exporter's response time than against the staffer's production time.

12. For a more detailed elaboration of this point, see N. David Palmeter, "Torquemada and the Tariff Act: The Inquisitor Rides Again," *International Lawyer*, vol. 20 (Spring 1986), pp. 641–57.

13. John H. Merryman, *The Civil Law Tradition: An Introduction to the Legal Systems of Western Europe and Latin America* (Stanford University Press, 1969), p. 135.

possible—to say nothing of responding to criticism and pressure generated by petitioners. But the burden of turning over those stones is placed on the respondents. That burden can range from the seriously harassing to the impossible. There is, at the administrative stage, no appeal to an independent arbiter of the reasonableness, the burdensomeness, the relevance of the requirements imposed unilaterally by Commerce. The department alone determines the nature and extent of these requirements, whether respondents have complied adequately, whether the answers of respondents are true, what sanctions will be imposed for the actual or perceived failure of the respondents to meet its demands. And, at the end of this process, Commerce puts on its black robe and reaches its quasi-judicial final determination. Respondents who balk at the demands of Commerce, or who simply cannot comply, risk being branded as uncooperative or unresponsive and risk paying the price of having Commerce reject their responses and base its determinations on the "best information available." From the perspective of the respondents, it would be more accurate to say "worst information available."

Best Information Available

The best-information-available requirement is the counterpart to the negative inferences rule that is a part of the everyday law of evidence. Its presence in the antidumping law is not, by itself, unusual or ominous. Triers of fact are entitled to assume that a party in possession of information, who refuses to produce it, is refusing because disclosure would not be in that party's interest. If there is a need for an antidumping law at all (a dubious proposition), there is a need for a best-information-available provision or something like it simply to ensure cooperation from respondents. The process requires it. To say this, however, is not to say that the best information rule as it seems to be evolving is justified.

The results of an antidumping investigation are based on the questionnaire responses of foreign exporters and producers and on the results of an on-site verification to determine the accuracy of those responses. A questionnaire-and-response procedure requires the cooperation of the respondents, and many, understandably, view cooperation with something less than total enthusiasm. Those who fear they are dumping may have an obvious reason for not wishing to cooperate, but even the others could do without the headache involved and would prefer to get by with as little effort as possible. Who, after all, enjoys answering any government questionnaire?

This is where the best-information-available provision comes into the law. It provides that in the absence of verified information supplied by the exporter, Commerce will use the best information available in its place.[14] Usually the only other information available—and, therefore, by default the best—is the information contained in the allegations of the complaining U.S. industry. Typically, these allegations, largely grounded in hyperbolic fantasy, yield extremely high dumping margins. The theory of the law is that the exporter, faced with such a penalty for default, will cooperate. Over the years, the provision has been successful. Most exporters did cooperate, and the best information available was rarely used.

That seems to be changing. There is evidence that the demands being placed on respondents are reaching intolerable levels. The administrative burden simply of furnishing the required information within the required time in the required form to the Department of Commerce has become so overwhelmingly difficult that more and more companies are failing to meet that burden, and, therefore, are being subject to determinations made on the basis of the best information available.

As a consequence of their being unable or unwilling to meet the administrative demands of Commerce, companies of the stature of Matsushita, SKF, and Toshiba have been subject to best-information-available determinations.[15] One major Japanese trading company—Mitsui & Co.—received a best-information-available determination because its routine program of disposing of records prevented it from providing Commerce with detailed information concerning transactions that had occurred as much as fifteen years earlier.[16] The fact that companies of this stature find compliance with the administrative requirements of the Commerce Department impossible says more about the nature of the requirements than it says about the companies.

---

14. 19 U.S.C.A. sec. 1677e(c).

15. *Antidumping; Antifriction Bearings from Various Countries; Notices*, 54 Fed. Reg. 18991, 19033 ff. (1989); *Preliminary Determination of Sales at Less than Fair Value: Certain Small Business Telephone Systems and Subassemblies Thereof From Japan*, 54 Fed. Reg. 31978 (1989); and *Final Determination of Sales at Less than Fair Value: Certain Small Business Telephone Systems and Subassemblies Thereof from Japan*, 54 Fed. Reg. 42541 (1989).

16. *Steel Wire Rope from Japan; Final Results of Antidumping Duty Administrative Review*, 54 Fed. Reg. 38541 (1989).

Calculation of Fair Value

Perhaps the characteristic of the U.S. antidumping process that best exemplifies the fact that a dumper is more likely to be a victim of that process than a price discriminator is the method by which fair value is calculated. Even if we assume, with the champions of the antidumping law, that international price discrimination is unfair, pernicious, predatory, and wrong, the methodology used by the Commerce Department to determine if price discrimination in fact exists is itself inaccurate, misleading, and unfair—if not pernicious, predatory, and wrong.

U.S. antidumping investigations typically encompass an exporter's sales to the United States and in its home market for the previous six months.[17] If no home market sales exist, sales to third countries are used. A weighted average of home market (or third-country) prices is calculated for the period, and the price of each sale to the United States is compared to this average.[18] Almost inevitably, a finding of dumping results because an average of different numbers necessarily will exceed some of its components. For example, if on the same day a foreign manufacturer sold identical quantities of merchandise to the United States and in its home market (or to a third country) for $100 a unit, and some days later sold identical quantities in both markets for $200 a unit, the average home market price, $150, would be termed fair value. Each sale to the United States then would be compared to this fair value, and the first, at $100, would be found to be "less than fair value," or "dumped." No allowance would be made for the fact that the $200 sale exceeds fair value by exactly the same amount.[19] Under U.S. antidumping practice, this exporter has a dumping margin of 50 percent on 50 percent of its sales.

17. 19 C.F.R. sec. 353.42(b) (1990).

18. This procedure is not readily apparent from the published text of most antidumping determinations. The issue is discussed, however, in the few cases (all involving agricultural products) in which a departure was made or urged. See, for example, *Certain Fresh Winter Vegetables from Mexico; Antidumping: Final Determination of Sales at Not Less than Fair Value*, 45 Fed. Reg. 20512 (1980) (average daily prices compared); *Final Determination of Sales at Less than Fair Value; Fall-Harvested Round White Potatoes from Canada*, 48 Fed. Reg. 51669 (1983) (each sale to the United States compared to weighted average foreign value for the day on which it occurred); and *Red Raspberries from Canada: Final Determination of Sales at Less than Fair Value*, 50 Fed. Reg. 19768 (1985) (each separate sale to the United States compared to twelve-month weighted average foreign value), *aff'd* as, *Washington Red Raspberry Comm'n v. U.S.*, 657 F. Supp. 537 (Ct. Int'l Trade 1987).

19. See *Antidumping and Countervailing Duties; De Minimis Dumping Margins and De Minimis Subsidies*, 52 Fed. Reg. 30660, 30662 (1987); and *Certain Iron Construction*

The system can produce even more perverse results. Suppose, in this example, that when the price in the exporter's home market rose from $100 to $200, the U.S. price increased only to $175. The seller, being an upstanding, law-abiding citizen anxious to comply with the antidumping law (to say nothing of wanting the higher price), refused to make the second sale to the United States and, instead, sold the merchandise for $200 in the home market. No dumping, right?

Wrong. In fact, the dumping is greater. The exporter now has three home market sales, one at $100 and two at $200, whose weighted average (assuming equal quantities) is $168. This means that the $100 U.S. sale now is being dumped by 68 percent. Yet, had the company sent the goods to the United States for $175, the fair value would have been $150 ($100 + $200 ÷ 2); the first sale, as before, would have been dumped by 50 percent, not 68; and the $175 sale, since it is above $150, would not have been dumped at all! So much for trying to obey the law.

One way to avoid the problem would be to compare individual sales to individual sales. There is an inherent difficulty in this method, however—the frequent absence of matches. On any given day, there may be no home market sale to compare to an export sale. In a fluctuating market, using either an earlier or later sale for comparison could lead to serious distortions.

A better way is to compare averages to averages. The missing match problem is overcome, and the comparison is "apples to apples." But no, some argue, comparing averages to averages does not deal with "targeted dumping"—an ill-defined concept that means, presumably, an isolated, rifle-shot export sale at a very low price. It is all very well, the argument seems to go, to compare averages to averages when prices in both markets fluctuate between, say, 95 and 105 with an average of 100. But what if one or two of those export sales are not at 95, but are at 75 or even 50?

Well, what if they are? Lower export prices simply will bring the export average down and thereby increase the likelihood of a dumping finding. If targeted dumping is the problem, average-to-average price comparison is the solution.

The present system of comparing individual export sales to foreign market averages is an inherently inaccurate, unfair, and distortive—if not ludicrous—method. It contributes greatly to the probability that a determination of dumping will be made when the economic data would seem to dictate otherwise. It is hardly a proper means by which to determine that pricing is unfair, pernicious, predatory, or wrong. Nevertheless, it is the measure by which Commerce, in the great majority of cases, chooses to make its determination of which foreign firms deserve those labels—chooses, because it is not required to do so. The law permits, but does not require, the use of averages in determining both U.S. price and foreign market value.[20] Commerce is in effect free to choose its method. Its use of weighted average prices to establish fair value is made worse by a bias in the law that provides for the exclusion of below-cost home market sales from the calculation of fair value.

Sales below the Cost of Production

The question whether a foreign respondent is selling below its cost of production is a central question in most antidumping proceedings. The question is addressed, however, in a way that tends to surprise both economists and antitrust lawyers. In antitrust law, the issue is raised when predatory pricing is alleged. The relevant question is whether sales have been made at prices below variable costs.[21] But despite its justifying rhetoric, antidumping law is not concerned as a legal matter with predatory pricing or predatory intent. Indeed, their demonstrated absence is no defense.

There are two crucial differences between the role of below-cost sales in antidumping investigations and the common assumption, growing out of broader knowledge of antitrust principles, of what the phrase "below-cost sales" means. First, it is not variable costs with which antidumping law is concerned, but *total* costs, a very different measure.[22] Although many might argue that sales below variable cost may be evidence of predatory pricing, few would make a comparable point about sales below total cost.[23]

Strange as reliance on total costs may seem, it is the second aspect of sales below cost in an antidumping investigation that truly is bizarre: the cost-of-production provision of the antidumping law does not even deal with sales to the United States; instead, it is directed to sales in the

20. 19 U.S.C.A. sec. 1677f-1.

21. Phillip Areeda and Donald F. Turner, *Antitrust Law: An Analysis of Antitrust Principles and Their Application* (Little, Brown, 1978), vol. 2, pp. 710–22.

22. 19 U.S.C.A. sec. 1677b(b).

23. No less a body than the U.S. Supreme Court has observed that "predatory pricing schemes are rarely tried and [are] even more rarely successful." *Matsushita Electrical Industrial Co. v. Zenith Radio Corporation*, 475 U.S. 574, 589 (1986).

exporter's home market.[24] How is it that a law, purportedly concerned with low-priced sales in the United States, suddenly is concerned with low-priced sales in a foreign country? Isn't this the opposite of the common notion of dumping, in which a foreign firm, predatory or not, safely sits in a high-priced home market and dumps its surplus on the world? Indeed it is. Then why does the antidumping law concern itself with low-priced sales in a foreign market? It is not logical.

"The life of the law," Oliver Wendell Holmes has told us, "has not been logic; it has been experience."[25] Although the antidumping law in many ways may serve as exhibit A in the case for the truth of Holmes's proposition, the cost-of-production provision, from the viewpoint of a protectionist, is not illogical at all since it increases the chances of protection. It is an example of the experience of once-unsuccessful antidumping petitioners and their skill in obtaining needed amendments to the law. The cost-of-production provision, which accompanied the upsurge of antidumping investigations that began in the 1970s, is an early example of the genre.

When home market sales fall below fully allocated costs, they may be disregarded in the calculation of fair value.[26] By requiring that the calculation of fair value be based only on sales above cost, which raises the weighted average, the law increases the likelihood that dumping will be found. It also may compel the use of constructed value, a statutory formula that is decidedly biased against exporters.

Constructed Value

Constructed value is used if there are no home market or third-country sales to provide the basis for a dumping comparison—either because there

---

24. 19 U.S.C.A. sec. 1677b(b). I use the term "home market" here as shorthand to include third-country sales that also may be the measure of fair value. 19 U.S.C.A. sec. 1677b(a)(1) (B). The cost of production provisions of the law apply to third-country as well as home market sales.

25. Oliver W. Holmes, *The Common Law* (Little, Brown, 1881), p. 1.

26. 19. U.S.C.A. sec. 1677b(b). The law provides that sales below total cost shall be disregarded in the calculation of fair value if they (a) have been made over an extended period of time and in substantial quantities, and (b) are not at prices that permit recovery of all costs within a reasonable period of time in the normal course of trade. Commerce interprets the extended-period-of-time requirement to mean its investigation period, usually the most recent six months; the substantial quantities requirement usually means 10 percent of the total sales, measured by volume; a 50 percent benchmark is sometimes used in cases involving fresh agricultural products. The second requirement is generally ignored.

are no such sales or because they have been disregarded for being below fully allocated costs. The exporter's variable costs—the materials and fabrication costs incurred in producing the merchandise exported to the United States—are the basis of constructed value. This part of the formula may be reasonable, but the rest of it is not, for it involves fully allocated costs and more. To materials and fabrication costs are added fully allocated fixed costs that by law must equal a minimum of 10 percent. An exporter with fixed overhead below 10 percent will be deprived of this efficiency when constructed value is calculated. Next, an allowance for profit is added that by law must equal a minimum of 8 percent of fully allocated costs. This total—constructed value—is then compared to the U.S. price to determine if there is dumping. At the very least, an exporter earning less than 8 percent on its U.S. sales will automatically be found to be dumping.[27]

The requirement of a minimum addition for general expenses and profit may appear to have some justification when the exporter concerned is a multiproduct organization theoretically capable of shifting general expenses away from a product subject to an antidumping investigation, or willing to take a lower than usual profit on a particular product in order to penetrate the export market. But, in fact, not even this questionable theory justifies these minimums. First, proper accounting procedures and adequate audits would make these manipulations difficult, if not impossible, to hide. More important, however, these minimums apply even to single-product companies that export all their merchandise to the United States. By definition, these are companies incapable of shifting expenses or obtaining higher, offsetting profits elsewhere. Finally, even in cases involving multiproduct companies, the actual amount of general expenses and profits must be calculated in any event in order to determine whether they are lower than the statutory 10 percent and 8 percent minimums.

Thus, these statutory amounts are not surrogates for data that are difficult to ascertain but are minimums to be used should the real amounts prove too low for the law's protectionist purposes. If general expenses in fact are greater than 10 percent, or if profit in fact is greater than 8 percent, those greater amounts will be used in lieu of the statutory minimums.[28]

27. See 19 U.S.C.A. sec. 1677b(e); and 19 U.S.C.A. sec. 1677b(a)(1).
28. See, for example, *Final Determination of Sales at Less than Fair Value: Antifriction Bearings (Other than Tapered Roller Bearings) and Parts Thereof from the Federal Republic of Germany*, 54 Fed. Reg. 18992, 19073 (1989): "In all cases, the actual general expenses

The Exporter's Sales Price Cap

One of the more notorious examples of the antidumping deck's being stacked against exporters is the so-called ESP cap. This concerns adjustments that are made to home market and export prices to ensure that they are compared at a proper level, that the comparison is one of apples to apples. For example, if a firm sells for cash in one market while extending credit in another, account will have to be taken of the cost of extending the credit in order to determine whether the net price to the credit customer is higher or lower than the price to the cash customer.[29]

The question of the ESP cap arises when the export sales are made through a wholly owned U.S. subsidiary, whose prices are termed the exporter's sales price, or ESP.[30] That subsidiary incurs overhead expenses that will usually differ from those incurred by the parent in its home market. To ensure an apples to apples comparison, an appropriate adjustment to the price of the goods should be made for the overhead charges attributable to each market. Fair enough, but that is not what occurs. Instead, all the overhead charges incurred in the United States are deducted when net U.S. price is calculated, but the deduction in the home market is capped by the amount of the U.S. deduction. In other words, if overhead is greater in the United States than in the home market, all overhead in each market will be deducted; but if the reverse is true, if home market overhead exceeds U.S. overhead, the home market deduction will be limited by the amount of expenses incurred in the United States.[31]

This comparison is "apples to oranges," not "apples to apples." The practice is not required by the antidumping law. It is a practice Commerce freely chooses, and it is a good example of administrative regulation in the service of protectionism.

Nonmarket Economies

Perhaps nowhere is the arbitrariness of the antidumping law as apparent as it is in its treatment of products from centrally planned or nonmarket

---

of the company exceeded the ten percent statutory minimum requirement so that no adjustment to general expenses was required."

29. 19 C.F.R. sec. 353.56 (1990).

30. 19 U.S.C.A. sec. 1677a(c). Because the exporter and importer are related, the transaction between them is disregarded.

31. 19 C.F.R. sec. 353.56(b)(2).

economies. Although many methods have been attempted or proposed, none has proved satisfactory because, as Jagdish Bhagwati has written, "there is no way in which 'true' or 'fair' costs and prices can be meaningfully determined for centrally planned economies in the first place."[32] This presents a policy problem: what should be done about nonmarket economies and the antidumping law?

Despite developments in Eastern Europe, the problem is not likely to disappear in the short term. First, it is not at all clear when a former nonmarket economy may be said to be a market economy for purposes of the antidumping law. And second, there are, of course, nonmarket economies in the world outside of Europe—most notably, China.

The alternatives are to exclude nonmarket economies from the strictures of the law, abolish the antidumping law entirely, or invent an artificial measure of fair value. The first choice is politically intolerable— the United States is not likely to exempt China, for example, from the antidumping law while continuing to apply that law to other countries. By the same token, domestic political realities do not seem likely to permit abolition of the antidumping law in the foreseeable future. Consequently, the third alternative—the invention of an artificial measure of fair value— has been adopted. Bhagwati is correct. This invention is indeed economically meaningless. But even more, it is arbitrary, and it is unfair.

The method that was invented to apply the antidumping law to nonmarket economies is the use of a "surrogate" country.[33] Economic data from a market economy country—the surrogate—are used to determine fair value for the nonmarket economy country. For example, in the investigation of paint brushes from China, Sri Lanka was selected as the surrogate and a dumping margin of more than 27 percent was found. This margin was based on a comparison of the prices charged by the exporter in China for sale to the United States to the prices charged by a Sri Lankan manufacturer for sale in Sri Lanka.[34] It is difficult to imagine a more irrelevant measure of what is or is not unfair or pernicious, predatory or wrong.

Of course, Sri Lanka was selected as the surrogate for China after the investigation began. There was no way the Chinese exporter could have predicted the choice of Sri Lanka. But even if there were some way by which the surrogate could be known in advance, the methodology is

32. Bhagwati, *Protectionism*, p. 51.
33. 19 U.S.C.A. sec. 1677b(c).
34. *Natural Bristle Paint Brushes and Brush Heads from the People's Republic of China; Final Determination of Sales at Less than Fair Value*, 50 Fed. Reg. 52812 (1985).

unfair because it is not possible for exporters in one country to obtain the necessary price information in advance from unrelated producers in another.

Indeed, it frequently has been impossible for the Department of Commerce itself to obtain prices in surrogate countries even after the fact. For this reason, although the law until 1988 gave preference to the surrogate country price methodology, two other methods of calculating fair value were sometimes used. These two methods, however, do not escape the basic flaw of the surrogate-country-price methodology. Both employ surrogates and, accordingly, under neither can the exporter know in advance the standard it must meet.

The first involves calculating fair value on the basis of the price of U.S. imports from other countries. As with the surrogate-country-price methodology, the exporter has no way of knowing in advance the country, or group of countries, whose export prices will be used to provide the measure of fair value. Recognizing this, as well as the problem with the surrogate-price methods, Congress in 1988 enshrined the other method—factors of production—as the preferred method.[35] Unfortunately, this, too, provides no escape from the problem.

Under the factors-of-production method, as the name implies, fair value is calculated by valuing the nonmarket economy factors of production for the merchandise exported to the United States. The factors include hours of labor expended, quantities of raw materials used, amounts of energy consumed, and capital costs. This approach, however, is nothing more than a variation on the surrogate-country-price methodology because surrogate data are used in the valuation of the production factors. All that is methodology is its elevation to preferred status. It has been used before.[36]

Administrative convenience is perhaps the only justification for the factors-of-production approach. Once the factors are obtained from the nonmarket economy exporter, their valuation usually will be easy because governments and international organizations publish great quantities of information concerning wage rates, energy costs, and material and com-

35. 19 U.S.C.A. sec. 1677b(c).

36. See, for example, Final Determination of Sales at Less than Fair Value; Shop Towels of Cotton from the People's Republic of China, 48 Fed. Reg. 37055 (1983); Final Determination of Sales at Less than Fair Value; Potassium Permanganate from the People's Republic of China, 48 Fed. Reg. 57347 (1983); Final Determination of Sales at Not Less than Fair Value; Barium Carbonate from the People's Republic of China, 49 Fed. Reg. 33913 (1984); and Final Determination of Sales at Less than Fair Value; Barium Chloride from the People's Republic of China, 49 Fed. Reg. 33916 (1984).

modity prices.[37] In general, this information is far easier to obtain than are internal prices for finished goods in third countries.

But if the factors-of-production methodology is administratively easier than are its alternatives, it is no more fair. It continues their lack of predictability. "The new methodology," one lawyer has written, "is simply the same bad wine in a new, and unattractive, vessel."[38]

Duty Deposits and Unlimited Contingent Liability

Any margin greater than one-half of 1 percent will satisfy Department of Commerce regulations for an affirmative dumping determination.[39] Such a small amount seems hardly onerous; after all, an additional tariff of one-half of 1 percent is not likely to remind many people of Smoot-Hawley. This reasonable conclusion is erroneous, however, because the scheme of the antidumping law puts any importer of goods subject even to apparently low margins at considerable risk of much higher duties—duties that in theory have no upper limit.

The key to this somewhat obscure point is that an announced dumping margin represents only an estimated duty, not a finally determined one. If Commerce finds sales at less than fair value, it does so, of course, only on the basis of the sales examined during its six-month investigation period. By the time this determination occurs, about five to eight months will have passed since the close of that investigation period. Consequently, an affirmative determination is simply a finding that sales below fair value occurred during the earlier investigation period; it has nothing necessarily to do with what may have occurred later, or with what may occur in the future. Subsequent changes in prices or adjustments may change considerably the margins on later transactions.[40] The payment of estimated

37. For example, in *Tapered Roller Bearings*, Chinese factors of production were valued on the basis of costs in India. Raw material prices were based on Indian prices published by the Steel Authority of India, adjusted for inflation by using the wholesale price index for India published by the International Monetary Fund. Values for labor were obtained from data published by the International Labor Organization. An addition for fringe benefits was based on data publicly available in India. *Tapered Roller Bearings from the People's Republic of China; Final Determination of Sales at Less than Fair Value*, 52 Fed. Reg. 19748 (1987).

38. Jeffrey S. Neeley, "Nonmarket Economy Import Regulation: From Bad to Worse," *Law and Policy in International Business*, vol. 20, no. 3 (1988), pp. 529–54.

39. 19 C.F.R. sec. 353.6 (1990).

40. The statute provides for annual administrative reviews of outstanding antidumping duty orders. 19 U.S.C.A. sec. 1675(a)(1). During these reviews, the actual dumping margins

dumping duties by the importer is much like the payment of estimated taxes by a taxpayer. Both are estimates only—the final assessment is made, and the final bill is rendered, only after the relevant period closes.

The uncertainties connected with this system can have a chilling effect on trade. Although the exporter would seem to have the opportunity to change its pricing practices to avoid future determinations of dumping, this is never easy, if it is ever possible, particularly because Commerce is permitted to change its methodology from one investigation or review to another, and does so.[41] Moreover, although it is the foreign seller's home market and export prices that determine whether dumping is occurring, it is the importer who pays the duty, and the importer essentially is powerless even to know—much less to affect—either the home market price of the exporter or the costs on which adjustments to that price will be based. Thus, any company that imports merchandise from an exporter subject to a dumping order is acquiring an open-ended contingent liability. Any company which assumes that a small estimated dumping duty deposit is the outer measure of its potential exposure under the law may be disastrously mistaken. Even a minuscule dumping margin can put an entire import trade at enormous risk. This is why petitioners fight so vigorously for affirmative determinations, no matter how small the margin.[42]

---

for the review period are determined, and the weighted average margin for this new period becomes the estimated antidumping duty deposit rate for the next period. Regulations governing this complex administrative procedure are set out in 19 C.F.R. sec. 353.22 (1990). Ordinarily, a firm may request revocation of an antidumping order only after three consecutive years of no sales at less than fair value. 19 C.F.R. sec. 353.25.

41. See, for example, *Barium Chloride from the People's Republic of China; Final Results of Antidumping Administrative Review*, 52 Fed. Reg. 313 (1987): "Neither the law nor the Commerce Regulations compel us to use precisely the same method of determining foreign market value as that used in the original investigation or a previous administrative review." The practice has been sustained on appeal, *Uddeholm Corporation v. United States*, 676 F. Supp. 1234 (Ct. Int'l Trade 1987).

42. As long ago as 1971, the Treasury Department, which at the time administered the antidumping law, almost seemed to crow about the uncertainty created by the process. Even if an exporter claims to an importer that steps have been taken to eliminate dumping, Treasury said: "So long as the dumping finding remains outstanding, the importer can never be sure that this is true. Even if the exporter is not stating a falsehood, he may have erred in his calculations. Moreover in a fast changing market, it is conceivable that an exporter may not be entirely certain that he has, in fact, eliminated his dumping margins in the case of all his sales. Given these circumstances, an American importer, if he has a choice, would prefer to deal with a supplier against whom no dumping finding is outstanding. Only then can he be absolutely sure that he will not have to pay dumping duties." Department of the Treasury, "Antidumping Duties," in *United States International Economic Policy in an Interdependent World*, Papers Submitted to the Commission on Inter-

Anticircumvention

"Circumvention" is another of those pejorative terms that seem to over-populate the antidumping law. The word smacks of craftiness and guile, of evasive schemes. No upright person would favor circumvention, and only a dumper—an unfair trader by definition—would engage in it. In the view of many, circumvention of antidumping orders is a major problem in international trade.

Yet, genuine circumvention probably occurred rarely in the many decades of the antidumping law's existence, and when it did occur, the law was able to take care of it quickly and cleanly. For example, when some exporters sought to evade an antidumping order on television sets by shipping disassembled sets in kits, Commerce found that the unassembled kits were still television sets and remained subject to the order. This was upheld on appeal.[43] If this case established any point, it was that minor tinkering with a product subject to an antidumping order need not be countenanced.

Despite this demonstrated lack of need, Congress in 1988 added an anticircumvention provision to the antidumping law.[44] At best this new provision is redundant. More likely, it will be used to reach transactions that are not, under any bona fide principle of law, genuine circumvention. And indeed that appears to be the case.

The issue of circumvention of antidumping orders has become intertwined with the complex issue of rules of origin. The real interest of the proponents of the anticircumvention provision seems to be in expanding the coverage of antidumping orders from goods originating in one country to goods originating in another without the necessity of proving dumping in the second country.

The trend began even before enactment of the 1988 amendment. Semiconductors assembled and tested in third countries using processed wafers or dice fabricated in Japan were included in a final antidumping determination covering semiconductors from Japan, despite the fact that the

---

national Trade and Investment Policy and Published in Conjunction with the Commission's Report to the President, vol. 1 (1971), pp. 395, 406.

43. See *Final Results of Changed Circumstances Review and Determination Not to Revoke Antidumping Duty Order; Color Television Receivers from Korea*, 52 Fed. Reg. 24500, 24501 (1987); aff'd as *Gold Star Co., Ltd. v. U.S.*, 692 F. Supp. 1382 (Ct. Int'l Trade 1988).

44. P.L. 100-418 1321, 102 Stat. 1192, adding 781 to the Tariff Act of 1930, as amended, 19 U.S.C.A. sec. 1677j.

U.S. Customs Service had previously ruled that the assembly and testing operations conferred origin on the country in which they occurred. Commerce held that in defining the scope of the product subject to an antidumping order, it is not bound by rulings of the Customs Service concerning origin. On a case after enactment of the 1988 amendment, involving microdisks from Japan, Commerce confirmed its authority to determine origin for antidumping purposes.[45]

The anticircumvention provision furthers a process that has been under way for nearly a decade, a process of using origin determinations for protectionist ends.[46] It does so by giving legislative sanction to the Commerce policy of ignoring Customs Service determinations that do not produce the desired result. In effect, the anticircumvention provision, like the Commerce policy it implements, stacks the antidumping deck further by giving origin issues in antidumping investigations a heads-we-win, tails-you-lose aspect.

Here's how it works: antidumping orders are issued against named articles from named countries—potassium chloride from Canada, for example, or 3.5-inch microdisks from Japan. To enforce an antidumping order, Customs must make an origin determination. Widgets from country A are subject to the order; widgets from country B are not. But what if a producer in country A sends semifinished widgets or components of widgets to country B, which exports the finished widget to the United States?[47]

As an initial matter, Customs will apply the rules of origin and ask whether the operations in country B substantially transform the material imported from country A, making it into a new and different article of commerce, one with a different name, character, or use. If not, if the country B operations are minor, cosmetic, and insubstantial, then the product will remain a widget from country A and will be subject to the antidumping order, notwithstanding the activities in country B.

The anticircumvention provision comes into play only when Customs decides that the transformation in country B of the materials from country

45. *Erasable Programmable Read Only Memories (EPROMs) from Japan; Final Determination of Sales at Less than Fair Value*, 51 Fed. Reg. 39680, 39692 (1986); and *Final Determination of Sales at Less than Fair Value: 3.5" Microdisks and Coated Media Thereof from Japan*, 54 Fed. Reg. 6433, 6435 (1989).

46. This process is detailed in N. David Palmeter, "Rules of Origin or Rules of Restriction? A Commentary on a New Form of Protectionism," *Fordham International Law Journal*, vol. 11 (1987), pp. 1–50.

47. The anticircumvention provisions also apply if the semifinished article or components are exported to the United States. The legal issues, however, are the same.

A is substantial. Notwithstanding a Customs Service ruling of "substantial" transformation, Commerce may determine that the value of the change is "small" and may apply the antidumping order to widgets that Customs determines originate in country B. Thus, if the exporter does not do enough in the third country to change origin, the widgets by definition are "from" country A and are subject to the order. Heads, we win. But if the change is substantial enough to confer origin on country B, Commerce may revisit the issue and find circumvention. Tails, you lose.

Recommendations

There is no dearth of recommendations that can be made for improving the antidumping law and its administration. There appears to be, unfortunately, an extreme dearth of political willingness to implement any liberalizing recommendations. Consider, for example, a recent letter from a bipartisan group of thirty-two members of the House of Representatives to the U.S. trade representative, urging that the United States "stand firm on its current antidumping negotiating position and reject" proposals to amend the Antidumping Code of the General Agreement on Tariffs and Trade (GATT) in ways that "would weaken U.S. trade law."[48] Among the more objectionable proposals being considered in GATT, in the view of the signatories to the letter, were those "that would change U.S. methodology in determining dumping margins by allowing a significant number of below-cost sales in the home market to be used as a basis for comparison with a foreign company's U.S. sales." Nonetheless, proposals for change should not be constrained, at least at the list-forming stage, by perceptions of political reality. Before political change can be made, the intellectual case must be made. The perceptions of policymakers must be changed.

When U.S. antidumping law was being amended in 1979 to implement the GATT Antidumping Code negotiated in the Tokyo Round, few voices were heard in dissent. In the larger world of trade policy, dumping was considered no more than a minor sideshow, of interest only to technicians incapable of appreciating the big picture. Events in the decade that has passed seem to have changed those views. More and more, the anti-

48. See, "House Letter to Hills on Antidumping," *Inside U.S. Trade*, October 5, 1990, p. 17.

dumping systems that the United States and many of its trading partners have erected are being seen for what they are: an attempt to provide a fig leaf of respectability for laws whose purpose and effect are purely protectionist.[49] This indeed is progress, but it is extremely doubtful that the case against antidumping laws is yet strong enough to prevail. The ball is rolling, however, and it well may have sufficient momentum, whenever the next round of negotiations occurs, to knock down the nontariff barriers that antidumping laws have established. When and if that day comes, the trade ministers of the world should consider the following actions:

1. Abolish antidumping laws altogether, while subjecting international price discrimination to the same laws that apply to domestic price discrimination. This would be particularly appropriate if creeping bilateralism continues and the world's trading entities move toward free trade blocks. Whatever else may be said for or against free trade areas, such as that existing between Canada and the United States or that proposed between Mexico and the United States, the existence of antidumping laws within them is anomalous. There is no artificial barrier or other market imperfection that would permit dumping to continue, or that otherwise would make normal competition law inapplicable.[50]

If Utopia does not result from the next round of negotiations, there remains considerable room for improvement in the existing antidumping law. Protectionists, such as the thirty-two members of the House of Representatives who wrote to the U.S. trade representative, would say that these proposals would weaken the law; a preferable description would be that they strengthen the law by bringing it more in line with the basic principles of both substantive and procedural fairness that we like to believe characterize the American legal system.

2. As a salutary step in that direction, change the procedure at the Department of Commerce from inquisitorial to adversarial by separating the decisionmakers in the department from the investigative staff. A more appropriate model for the process would be that of normal U.S. administrative law, which clearly separates the investigative from the decision-

49. One reason for this increased awareness may be the vulnerability of U.S. exporters to antidumping proceedings in other markets. See Eduardo Lachica, "Some Big U.S. Companies Favor Loosening Anti-Dumping Laws," *Wall Street Journal*, August 31, 1990, p. A2.

50. The use of competition or antitrust laws within free trade areas would require agreement of the countries on such issues as the reach of the judicial process of one country into the territory of another, standards for production of documentary and other evidence, and similar issues that have proved sensitive in the past.

making function within an agency.[51] This change may or may not require legislative consent.

Some improvements in the antidumping regime of the United States could be accomplished by Commerce on its own. These would include:

3. Exercise simple self-control and moderation in presenting questionnaires and in making other demands on respondents. At gatherings of trade lawyers these days, remarks are frequently made to the effect that the game at Commerce now is to make the demands so impossible that respondents will refuse or be unable to comply, thus requiring the use of best information available. This is the game, it is said, because best information available is easier for Commerce to handle than the accurate processing of volumes of complex data. No doubt there is enormous exaggeration in remarks of this kind, but exaggeration is not the same as pure invention—exaggeration merely enlarges, unjustifiably, a reality that is present to some degree.

4. Average prices in both markets or average prices in neither. The present methodology of comparing individual export prices to weighted average home market (or third-country) prices is unfairness in its rankest form. It is perhaps the most blatant kind of deck-stacking that goes on in an antidumping proceeding. There is no justification for it.

5. Use realistic criteria in determining whether home market (or third-country) sales below fully allocated cost should be excluded from any averages used. The statute calls for the elimination of these sales only if they (a) have been made over an extended period of time and in substantial quantities and (b) are not at prices that permit recovery of all costs within a reasonable period of time in the normal course of trade.

The approach of Commerce to these legal standards is totally wooden. The criterion of substantial quantities is, except for fresh agricultural products, deemed to be 10 percent regardless of the product involved. For fresh agricultural products, the standard is an automatic 50 percent. Commerce does not consider whether these self-imposed, inflexible benchmarks are realistic for a particular industry.

The two time periods referred to in the statute—the "extended period of time" over which sales in substantial quantities are made, and the "reasonable period of time" in which costs must be recovered in the ordinary course of trade—are both considered to be the six-month period of investigation. That an extended period of time for one industry might

51. I have set out specific recommendations in "Torquemada and the Tariff Act" (full cite in note 12).

be an extremely short period for another seems obvious, as does the fact that what is a reasonable period of time in the normal course of trade will be one period for one industry and something different for another. Commerce could improve the administration of the law by looking at these strict statutory criteria more intelligently.

6. Eliminate the ESP cap. There is no justification for capping deductions for indirect selling expenses in the home market by the amount incurred in the United States. The ESP cap rivals home market price averaging in the race for the "most arbitrary" title among the antidumping regulations. It should be eliminated from the race.

Other changes are likely to require legislation. These changes are called for, nonetheless, and their prospects would be enhanced by support from the Commerce Department. Congress should:

7. Eliminate the arbitrary and automatic minimums of 10 percent for overhead and 8 percent for profit in constructed value. Use of these minimums distorts reality. They serve only to find dumping margins for companies that otherwise, even within the remaining framework of the law and its administration, would not be dumping. They, too, are bereft of any justification beyond pure protectionism.

8. Eliminate the application of the antidumping law to nonmarket economies. The method of determining whether a nonmarket economy exporter is dumping truly is bizarre. Every alternative tried—surrogate prices, factors of production, average import values—is completely unsatisfactory. Each is the equivalent of blindfolding a person, spinning him around, and having him throw a dart at walls covered with numbers—with few, if any, of the numbers being zero.

A better approach is simply to look at injury. The standard objection to using injury alone is that the present injury, or market disruption, statute that applies to nonmarket economies, section 406 of the Trade Act of 1974, is ineffective because relief will not be granted, even if disruption is found, unless the president affirmatively acts to provide that relief.

This objection might be met by reversing the process, by providing that an affirmative finding will automatically lead to the relief recommended by a majority of the U.S. International Trade Commission unless, within a specified period, the president affirmatively acts to block the relief. The Trade Act of 1974 installed such a provision in section 337 of the Tariff Act, dealing with other forms of unfair competition (primarily patent infringement). Before that time, an ITC-recommended remedy under section 337 (an exclusion order) would not be implemented unless the president acted affirmatively to do so. Predictably, few exclusion orders went into effect. After 1974, when the president was required to step into the process to block an order, far more of them became effective.[52]

9. Raise the de minimis level of 0.5 percent to 5 percent. The current de minimis standard, 0.5 percent, pretends to a precision that is rarely achieved in antidumping investigations, and, if achieved, is reached only at enormous cost. A 5 percent standard has the virtue of being consistent with the exchange rate regulations of the department, which require conversion of all currencies involved in an antidumping investigation into U.S. dollars. The exchange rate used is the quarterly rate set in advance by the Federal Reserve Bank of New York. This rate is used throughout the quarter unless, on any particular day, the daily rate varies from it by more than 5 percent. When this happens, the daily rate is used for that day only.

This method can lead to some odd results. For example, if the preset quarterly rate is 100, it is applied to all transactions completed during a given quarter when the daily rate ranges from 96 to 104. But when the daily rate falls to 95 or below, or rises to 105 or above, the daily rate is used. Hence, a 104-106-104 rate pattern would be translated by Commerce as 100-106-100, whereas a 96-104-96 pattern would be 100-100-100. It is obvious that there is enough play in this exchange rate policy alone to make the 0.5 percent de minimis standard meaningless. Indeed, the 5 percent magnitude of flexibility in the exchange rate policy is ten times greater than the 0.5 percent de minimis level. There is no justification for this practice apart from pure protectionism.

10. Use rules of origin standards in anticircumvention determinations. The anticircumvention provision of the 1988 law is an example of codification by Congress of previous Commerce Department practice. Once Commerce determined that a circumvention problem existed, Congress could not resist. Nonetheless, the language of the circumvention provision is general enough for Commerce to appear to have the latitude to interpret its responsibility in conformity with standard-rules-of-origin determi-

---

52. A count of section 337 exclusion orders in 1984 revealed that from 1944 through 1969 no exclusion orders were issued. One was issued in 1969, and 2 in the early 1970s. By May 1, 1984, less than a decade after section 337 was changed from requiring presidential approval to requiring disapproval, 28 exclusion orders were in effect. N. David Palmeter, "The U.S. International Trade Commission at Common Law," *Journal of World Trade Law*, vol. 18 (1984), pp. 497–511. As of November 1, 1990, 51 exclusion orders were outstanding. U.S. International Trade Commission, *Calendar of Hearings and of Deadline Dates for Pending Investigations* (November 1, 1990), pp. 17–21.

nations of the Customs Service. This is not to say that the determinations of the Customs Service are always stellar examples of jurisprudence at its best. Far from it. But consistency in legal systems has a value of its own.

When Commerce insists that it can make its own origin determinations for antidumping purposes, serious inconsistencies can arise. Consider again the example of country A and country B, in which country A is subject to an antidumping order while B is not, and parts or materials are shipped from country A to country B for manufacture into the finished article that is subject to the order. If, in the view of Customs, the manufacturing operations in country B are substantial enough to confer origin, then importers would be required to mark the product with the name of country B (and could not use the name of country A even if it were more marketable); any quota applicable to the article would be the quota of country B; the duty rate that would apply would be the duty applicable to country B; the value of the product would count in the bilateral trade balance calculated for country B (a sum most economists say is irrelevant and many members of Congress seem to think is of vital concern). With all of this, to say that the product nevertheless is subject to an antidumping order from country A makes no sense.[53]

Conclusion: Worse than "Dog Law"

In his criticism of the English common law, Jeremy Bentham described the system as "dog law":

> When your dog does anything you want to break him of, you wait till he does it, and then beat him for it. This is the way you make laws for your dog: and this is the way the judges make laws for you and me. They won't tell a man beforehand what it is he *should not do* . . .

53. This practice, in fact, raises a serious question about the rights of country B under the GATT Antidumping Code, inasmuch as its exporters could be subject to antidumping orders without any specific findings having been made regarding them, and without their having had an opportunity to defend. The Antidumping Code provides, for example, in article 6, that "the foreign suppliers and all other interested parties shall be given ample opportunity to present in writing all evidence that they consider useful to the antidumping investigation in question." In the example given, this right would appear to be denied to exporters in country B. See, generally, N. David Palmeter, "The U.S. Rules of Origin Proposal to GATT: Monotheism or Polytheism?" *Journal of World Trade Law*, vol. 24 (1990), p. 25.

they lie by till he has done something which they say he should not *have done*, and then they hang him for it.[54]

Antidumping law is worse. Although it is true that the antidumping law and its regulations are published—voluminously, as noted at the outset of this chapter—the fact is that all these pages of law and all these regulations do not even permit a market economy exporter, let alone a nonmarket economy exporter, to know what price should be charged to the United States in order to sell at fair value. Just consider the variables attendant to the six-month weighted average used by Commerce to establish fair value: prices charged to the United States in November 1990 could be compared to a weighted average of home market prices running from November 1990 through April 1991. To know what the fair price in November 1990 should be would require a crystal ball.

In Bentham's dog law, the poor animal at least is eventually told the standard it must meet to avoid future beatings. It learns, albeit painfully, "Don't do that again." Not so the exporter. Not only are the standards of fair value unknowable, as in an initial matter, but they are unknowable even after the fact. A company found to be dumping cannot rely on the methodology used by Commerce to make that determination, for the department may change its methodology from one investigation or administrative review to another. Perhaps the only lesson to be learned is, "Don't export at all."

It shouldn't happen to a dog.

---

54. Quoted in Postema, *Bentham and the Common Law Tradition*, p. 277 (emphasis in original).

Comment

Patrick Macrory

A topic that hasn't received much attention in these chapters is verification, but it is a critical element in antidumping investigations.

The purpose of verification is to ensure that the information supplied to the Department of Commerce by the respondent is accurate and complete. The law requires that every item in the response be verified: the prices, all the charges and adjustments, and the relevant costs. Verification is performed by Department of Commerce analysts at the offices of the company in question by checking the information against the company's books and records. It is like a financial audit. Verification is an informal process. No transcript is kept. The analysts ask questions, make copies of documents that they think are relevant, and then write a report summarizing their findings. If a response cannot be verified by the department, it will use the best information available. This can lead to high dumping margins, as explained in chapter 7.

Verification is always conducted under the pressure of a deadline, and the company gets only one shot at proving its case. There isn't time to redo it. If a company submits a defective questionnaire response, the department normally issues a deficiency letter and gives the company a second chance. This is not so in the case of verification.

In the old days of clerks and quill pens, it was fairly difficult to fake entire accounting records. As long as a ledger had a sufficient number of coffee stains and ink blots, it was usually considered genuine. But now, any decent-sized company keeps its accounting records on computer. It used to be fairly easy to rig the data. Before the Department of Commerce was given the responsibility of administering the antidumping law, verifications were usually conducted by Customs Service officials attached to the local U.S. embassy who knew little about the case and even less about accounting procedures. There is a story of a verification in which a company produced a computer list, setting out all the home market sales that were listed in its response. The verifier asked to see a few invoices and records of payment of sales on the computer list. Naturally, everything matched up, and he pronounced himself satisfied. What he didn't know was that the response and the computer list both left out all the high-priced home market sales.

The Department of Commerce has developed sophisticated techniques to ensure that all sales have been reported. In particular, it uses the audited financial statements of the company as the touchstone, since the numbers in the statements have been checked and certified by outside accountants. The verifiers try to trace the numbers in the response through the accounting records, the monthly ledgers, and the trial balances, all the way into the financial statements. That is not an easy task, because a large multiproduct company will not show the sales of individual products in its profit-and-loss statement. It will simply record one figure for all sales to all markets. So the verifier has to trace sales for the individual product being investigated, which may represent a fraction of 1 percent of the company's total sales, all the way through the financial records. It is a laborious, difficult task that requires considerable knowledge of accounting techniques.

Imagine for a moment that you are a relatively new Department of Commerce analyst. You are sent out to verify a large response. By definition, you are in a foreign country, and you probably don't speak the language, so you can't understand any of the documents you are looking at. You are unable to communicate directly with any of the company representatives whom you are interviewing. You are totally dependent on an interpreter who is probably supplied by a local firm of interpreters; and you are not quite sure whose side he or she is on. You have one week, or possibly less, to master the accounting system of the company, including its standard cost system (if cost is an issue), and to verify a large number of individual data points. That is no small task.

But now imagine you are the company being verified. As the verification proceeds, you realize the analyst doesn't understand the difference between accrual-based accounting and cash-based accounting, or doesn't understand double-entry bookkeeping. Or the analyst spends four-and-a-half days checking a routine advertising adjustment and copies 1,000 documents in connection with that one adjustment. It hardly inspires confidence in the process. Yet these are all situations that have occurred in the last few years.

At the same time, these are exceptional cases. The majority of the Department of Commerce's analysts are conscientious and fair-minded. However, now and then one comes along who feels it is his or her job to find flaws in the response. Unless there is good reason to believe the company has not been forthcoming in its response, this attitude is inappropriate. The law intends the department to be a neutral arbiter of fact, not a prosecutor.

There are several problems with the system. First, because of the high turnover at the Department of Commerce, some of the analysts are relatively young, relatively inexperienced, and may have only rather elementary accounting training. The department seems to be trying to improve this situation with increased training, but that is asking a great deal of someone who does not have a thorough background in accounting to verify a complex response. Sometimes the verifier will spend far too much time focusing on tiny adjustments worth a fraction of 1 percent and simply fail to grasp the big picture.

A second problem is that the verifiers have almost unreviewable discretion. In many situations they have to decide on the spot what approach to take to verification or how far to go on a particular item and at what point to stop. In theory, presumably, that judgment could be overridden by a supervisor in Washington, but in all likelihood the person on the spot will be allowed to call the shots. Given the intensely factual nature of verification, it would be difficult to get the Court of International Trade to review a dispute arising out of verification. The only record would be some documents in a foreign language with a partial translation and the verifier's report, which is often cursory.

An even more serious problem relates to timing. The department used to conduct verification before the preliminary determination, so when the preliminary determination was issued, the department would have indicated clearly which items it considered to be verified and which it did not. The parties had an opportunity to run through verification issues before the department and produce documents proving that a given item was verified.

Now, in virtually every case, verification takes place after the preliminary determination. Some verifiers will tell you on the spot: "I think this is verified" or "I don't think it is verified." But many will just smile and say, "The record speaks for itself."

The verifier's report may not indicate whether the department regards a particular item as verified or not. Obviously, if it is simply a matter of verifying numbers, it is usually easy to tell whether the company has passed muster. But this is often not the case when more subjective judgments have to be made, such as whether transactions between related parties are affected by the relationship. A company may not know until the final determination comes out whether the decision is going to be based on best information available. Its counsel therefore has no opportunity to present arguments on the issue.

The process is also frustrating for the petitioner. The petitioner's counsel is not, of course, permitted to be present at the verification and until recently did not have access, even under protective order, to the documents taken by the department for the record. Because the verifier's reports are usually summaries, it may be hard to tell what took place.

But as already mentioned, verification is a critical part of the investigation process. The attorney on the case spends a good deal of time preparing for verification and participating in the verification itself. The company, too, puts time and effort into it. Yet it is subject to few if any of the safeguards that we have the right to expect in a system that is meant to be governed by some sort of rule of law. There are no magic solutions to these problems, but they are important, and the department should take a hard look at the issues and perhaps solicit ideas for improvement from the trade bar and from accounting firms.

But there would be little point in making verifications more like depositions, for example, by allowing the petitioner's counsel to be present and by keeping a stenographic record of the proceedings. This would add to the cost and probably inhibit the process.

The department should try, to have a trained accountant present at verifications. The department usually does that now in cost cases, but it should do so even when cost is not involved, because so much of the process consists of tracing items through the accounts of the company. A few years ago, the department retained a leading accounting firm to work on verifications, and most people who went through that experience felt that it worked well because the accountants understood exactly how companies kept their books. They knew the right questions to ask and could grasp the overall situation immediately. That practice has now lapsed, apparently for budgetary reasons.

The department should also do more to standardize its procedures. Some analysts prepare and send the company detailed outlines of what they wish to review at verification, and these help the company prepared for verification. But other analysts provide only the most general outlines.

It might be helpful if the department published general guidelines on what it expected to accomplish at verification and the types of procedures it planned to use.

Verifications are always performed under a tight schedule. There is no flexibility. The verifier usually has to go on to another company at the end of the week, and it often takes a day or more for the verifier to understand the company's basic accounting system. This may leave too little time for the verification of individual items. Recently, the department started sending out detailed pre-verification questionnaires, asking for details about the accounting system. That increases the pressure on the lawyers and the company for a response, but to the extent that it creates a less rushed atmosphere during the verification itself, it is probably a good practice. The department should also hold a pre-verification conference in Washington, where counsel (and company officials, if they choose to come to Washington) could discuss the company's accounting system so that the verifying officials could develop a better understanding of it ahead of time and explain what they plan to accomplish by verification.

Whenever the department believes a company has failed verification on one or more issues, it must notify the company in time for the company's counsel to present arguments on the issues. The department should also indicate what it plans to use as best information available, whether punitive or nonpunitive, so that each side will have an opportunity to present its views on this subject. After all, the purpose of issuing a preliminary less-than-fair-value determination is to allow both sides to present their views on the department's proposed decision. The respondents and the petitioners should, but currently do not, have exactly the same rights with respect to verification issues.

CHAPTER FOUR

Conceptual and Procedural Biases in the Administration of the Countervailing Duty Law

Joseph F. Francois, N. David Palmeter, and Jeffrey C. Anspacher

T HE EXPRESSED policy justification for applying the U.S. countervailing duty (CVD) law lies not in positive economics but in ethics and morality, the realm of normative economics. In the simple terms of maximizing national income and consumption, the imposition of countervailing duties to offset subsidies tends to harm the country imposing the duties. In this sense, if foreigners wish to subsidize our purchases of their goods, so much the better. As consumers, we should send a thank you note and ask for more.[1]

But such narrowly defined economic values are not our only values, and they are not cited in support of the countervailing duty law. The maximization of national income is not our government's only policy objective.

The Objectives of the Law

The countervailing duty law is justified by the need for fairness. The legislators who devised this law were not concerned with the potential

This chapter represents the personal opinions of the authors, and is not meant to reflect in any way the opinions or positions of the International Trade Commission, or the professional opinions or positions of any individual commissioners or of the ITC staff.

1. There has of course been a substantial growth in the formal trade literature on strategic trade policy, which can be cited as justification for the subsidization and protection of strategic trade sectors. However, none of the policy factors emphasized in that literature play an explicit role in the administrative process of the unfair trade laws. See the related discussion in chapter 7 of this volume. J. Bhagwati has compared the purchasing of "unfair" imports to accepting stolen goods at discount prices. See Jagdish N. Bhagwati, *Protectionism* (MIT Press, 1988).

gain to the nation resulting from access to subsidized imports; rather, they were concerned with the welfare of the firms and workers that compete with the producers of those imports. There is something unfair, the rationale goes, with having to confront competitors that are aided by national treasuries. A unanimous Supreme Court said countervailing duties are "intended to offset the *unfair* competitive advantage that foreign producers would otherwise enjoy from export subsidies paid by their government."[2] Note, too, that Congress put the amendments to the countervailing duty law in the Trade Act of 1974 under the portion of the statute dealing with "unfair trade practices."[3] And in its report on the Trade Agreements Act of 1979, the Senate Finance Committee termed the practice of granting subsidies "pernicious."[4]

The General Agreement on Tariffs and Trade (GATT)—with, to be sure, less colorful language—concurs. So unfair are subsidies, in the view of GATT, that its most basic provisions may be suspended to offset them: duty bindings may be broken so that countervailing duties may be imposed; most-favored-nation (MFN) treatment may be denied.

Clearly, conduct that earns such unfavorable terms—"unfair," "pernicious"—and that justifies the jettisoning of duty bindings as well as the suspension of MFN is not in the realm of the trivial. Presumably, such extreme consequence as the countervailing duty law should be reserved for extreme conduct—conduct beyond the pale, conduct that truly is unfair and pernicious.

Is it so reserved? In some instances. But in its actual implementation, the countervailing duty law, like the antidumping (AD) law, also routinely reaches conduct that by no stretch of the imagination can be labeled "unfair" or "pernicious." Behind the rhetoric of fighting unfairness, of attacking the pernicious, the countervailing duty law is also used as a tool to penalize imports for the age-old protectionist reason that they are imports, regardless of whether such imports are traded fairly. The law penalizes imports both through its explicit terms and in the way it is administered by the Department of Commerce (DOC).

This chapter explores the extent to which the countervailing duty law departs from its expressed justifications and exhibits a protectionist bias through its terms and procedures, even when its premises of unfair,

2. *Zenith Radio Corp.* v. *United States*, 437 U.S. 443, 455–56 (1978), emphasis added.
3. P.L. 93-618, 88 Stat. 1978, title 3—"Relief from Unfair Trade Practices," chap. 3.
4. *Trade Agreements Act of 1979*, S. Rept. 249, 96 Cong. 1 sess. (Government Printing Office, 1980), p. 37. "Dumping" shared the adjective "pernicious" with subsidies in the Senate report.

pernicious conduct are accepted. Before discussing the conceptual and procedural biases, however, we must explain the countervailing duty law and procedure.

The Legal Framework

The countervailing duty provisions of the Tariff Act of 1930 require the imposition of a special duty on imports to offset, or to "countervail," any subsidy if the imports receiving the subsidy cause material injury to an industry in the United States.[5] The Department of Commerce determines the existence and amount of any subsidy; the U.S. International Trade Commission (ITC) determines whether the requisite injury is occurring. This chapter focuses on the subsidy issues of concern to the DOC.

The threshold question is, what is a countervailable subsidy? The law, unfortunately, is not of great help. It defines the word "subsidy" in terms of a prior law that itself was far from clear and relies on examples rather than explicit definition.[6] A distinction is made between export and domestic subsidies. Export subsidies are defined with reference to the GATT Subsidies Code, which, in an annex, provides an illustrative list of a dozen schemes ranging from direct government subsidies contingent upon export and excessive remission of indirect taxes upon export to "any other charge on the public account constituting an export subsidy."[7]

Domestic subsidies, which present the far bigger problem, are described as the provision of capital, loans, or loan guarantees on terms

5. 19 U.S.C.A. sec. 1677b. Although the injury test applies to most countries, it does not apply to all. The injury provision of U.S. countervailing duty law was added in 1979 to implement the GATT Subsidies Code (see note 7) and applies only to signatories to the code or to countries that have assumed substantially equivalent obligations. For other countries, the prior countervailing duty law, section 303 of the Tariff Act of 1930, as amended, continues to apply. Under section 303, the injury test applies only to nondutiable merchandise. Dutiable merchandise continues to be countervailable, from countries subject to this provision, without an injury determination. The injury test of the countervailing duty law is phrased in terms of "material injury" and includes the threat of material injury or of the material retardation of the establishment of an industry. For the sake of brevity, the terms "injury" or "material injury" are used throughout this chapter to denote threat and material retardation, unless otherwise specified.

6. The full statutory text defining "subsidy" is set out in 19 U.S.C.A. sec. 1677(5).

7. "Agreement on Interpretation and Application of Articles VI, XVI, and XXIII of the General Agreement on Tariffs and Trade," in General Agreement on Tariffs and Trade, *Basic Instruments and Selected Documents* (26th Supplement, Geneva, 1980) (hereafter Subsidies Code).

inconsistent with commercial considerations; the provision of goods or services at preferential rates; the granting of funds or forgiveness of debt to cover operating losses sustained by a specific industry; or the assumption of any costs or expenses of manufacture, production, or distribution.[8]

These are considered subsidies if they are provided or if the government requires that they be provided to "a specific enterprise or industry, or group of enterprises or industries."[9] The department considers subsidy recipients to be enterprises or industries that are located within delineated geographic regions and that constitute a specific group under this definition. Thus, regional government programs, no matter how broad or generally available and no matter how motivated, are considered to be unfair and hence countervailable. This in effect covers all regional development programs, urban block grants, regional job training programs, income equalization programs, federally subsidized earthquake insurance, and the like. At the same time, "agriculture" is defined as a world unto itself—it is not a specific industry, but rather a generalized universe of industries, so that subsidies to "agriculture" are not "specific."[10] This reasoning explains why Canadian programs directed toward the poorest 5 percent of the population are considered unfair, whereas federal water subsidies to agriculture in California's Central Valley are not.[11]

This so-called specificity requirement has led to much confusion. At first, the DOC translated this requirement into a general availability test: if a subsidy was generally available, such as a subsidy to education or transportation, it was not considered to be industry-specific and was not countervailable.[12] But the Court of International Trade held that this general availability test is not good enough.[13] A subsidy may be generally available nominally, but in fact may be used by only a selected industry,

8. 19 U.S.C.A. sec. 1677(5)(ii). See, generally, Christoph Lehmann, "The Definition of 'Domestic Subsidy' under United States Countervailing Duty Law," *Texas International Law Journal*, vol. 22 (1987), pp. 53–86.

9. Lehmann, "Definition of 'Domestic Subsidy,' " p. 58.

10. *Final Negative Countervailing Duty Determination; Fresh Asparagus from Mexico*, 48 Fed. Reg. 21618 (1983); and *Certain Fresh Cut Flowers from Mexico*, 49 Fed. Reg. 15007 (1984). See also, *Roses, Inc. et al. v. United States*, 743 F. Supp. 870 (Ct. Int'l Trade 1990).

11. *Final Affirmative Countervailing Duty Determinations; Certain Fresh Atlantic Groundfish from Canada*, 51 Fed. Reg. 10041, 10045 (1986).

12. *Carlisle Tire & Rubber Co. v. United States*, 564 F. Supp. 834 (Ct. Int'l Trade 1983).

13. *Cabot Corp. v. United States*, 620 F. Supp. 722 (Ct. Int'l Trade 1985), *appeal dismissed*, 788 F.2d 1539 (Fed. Cir. 1986) (Cabot I); and *Cabot Corp. v. United States*, 694 F. Supp. 949 (Ct. Int'l Trade 1988) (Cabot II).

either because few industries are able to use the program or because of government policy. In response, the DOC has developed a "specificity" test of three factors:

(1) the extent to which a foreign government acts (as demonstrated in the language of the relevant enacting legislation and implementing regulations) to limit the availability of a program; (2) the number of enterprises, industries or groups thereof that actually use a program, which may include the examination of disproportionate or dominant users; and (3) the extent, and manner in which, the government exercises discretion in making the program available.[14]

This policy received explicit congressional approval in the Omnibus Trade and Competitiveness Act of 1988, section 1312 of which amended the Tariff Act to include a "special rule" on the subject of specificity. In determining whether a subsidy has been conferred "to a specific enterprise or industry, or group of enterprises or industries," Commerce is told: "Nominal general availability, under the terms of the law, regulation, programs, or rule establishing a bounty, grant, or subsidy, of the benefits thereunder is not a basis for determining that the bounty, grant, or subsidy is not, or has not been, in fact provided to a specific enterprise or industry, or group thereof."[15]

What this means in actual practice is an increase in the administrative burden faced by exporters. No longer will it be sufficient for a respondent to show that the law laying down a subsidy does not restrict its availability. De jure availability is not enough. De facto general use must follow, and it is up to the foreign respondent to prove it. Unlike all other areas of U.S. law, the unfair trade laws place no burden of proof on the complaining party—the burden, even the burden of proving the negative, is on the responding party. As a prominent British legal philosopher has noted, "Practical decisions often turn on the burden of proof."[16] Indeed they do.[17]

14. *Final Affirmative Countervailing Duty Determination and Countervailing Duty Order; Carbon Steel Wire Rod from Malaysia*, 53 Fed. Reg. 13303 (1988).

15. 19 U.S.C. sec. 1677(5)(B).

16. Tony Honoré, *Making Law Bind: Essays Legal and Philosophical* (Oxford, 1987), p. 118.

17. See N. David Palmeter, "Torquemada and the Tariff Act: The Inquisitor Rides Again," *International Lawyer*, vol. 20 (Spring 1986), pp. 641–58.

Domestic Subsidy Rates and Actual Competitive Benefits in Export Markets

The GATT Subsidies Code, like the U.S. law that ostensibly implements it, distinguishes between two broad classes of subsidies: domestic subsidies and export subsidies. The code permits countervailing duties against both domestic and export subsidies. Although the code makes it clear that export subsidies violate the intent of the GATT, no similar statement is made regarding domestic subsidies. On the contrary, "Signatories recognize that subsidies other than export subsidies are widely used as important instruments for the promotion of social and economic policy objectives and do not intend to restrict the right of signatories to use such subsidies to achieve these and other important policy objectives which they consider desirable."[18] Moreover, the code notes that "it is desirable [though not required] that the imposition [of countervailing duties] . . . be less than the total amount of the subsidy if such lesser duty would be adequate to remove the injury to the domestic industry."[19] As far as the U.S. countervailing duty law is concerned, these passages need never have been written. Indeed, although the code views export subsidies in a harsher light than domestic subsidies, U.S. practice ironically, if unintentionally, follows the precisely opposite approach. The United States treats domestic subsidies more harshly than export subsidies.

The duties that the Department of Commerce applies against domestic subsidies often far exceed those needed to counter the effects of domestic subsidies, in effect adding a punitive duty above that needed to counter the subsidy, while at the same time applying duties against export subsidies that come much closer simply to countering their effects. Does this mean that U.S. policymakers view domestic subsidies as even more "unfair" and "pernicious" than export subsidies? Hardly. More likely, this adverse treatment results simply from a failure to think through the implications of domestic subsidies. But, intentional or otherwise, the results are the same—U.S. countervailing duties tend to exaggerate the effects of domestic subsidies even more than the effects of export subsidies.[20] As a result, the DOC's practices regarding domestic subsidies do not

---

18. Subsidies Code, article 11:1.

19. Subsidies Code, article 4:1.

20. Under special circumstances, such as when the United States is the only export market or when all importing countries apply an identical countervailing duty, the rate set by the DOC does exactly counter the effects of export subsidies. Otherwise, even these effects are overcompensated for.

level the playing field; they tilt it. One distortion, introduced by domestic subsidies in foreign markets, is replaced with yet another that transfers income from downstream U.S. producers and consumers to the protected U.S. producers.

A Geometric Analysis

The distinction between export and domestic subsidies is important for the obvious reason that it determines the denominator over which the nominal subsidy amount is to be placed in calculating an ad valorem subsidy rate. Less obviously, perhaps, the distinction also is important for calculating the actual competitive benefit that subsidies provide and for determining the causal link between subsidization and material injury. The difference between identical ad valorem export and domestic subsidies can be seen in figure 4-1. We assume an initial foreign domestic market equilibrium characterized in the left panel by the supply and demand curves SS and DD. The supply curve measures the amount that the industry producing good Q in the subsidizing country will supply at a given price, and the demand curve maps out how much home market consumers will demand at a given price. Export supply (or import demand) is determined by the horizontal distance between these two curves. We map export supply in the right panel as the export supply curve X_sX_s. Export demand is represented by the export demand curve X_dX_d.

When a domestic subsidy is introduced, it causes the following events. There is an initial outward shift of the domestic industry's supply curve from SS to $S'S'$.[21] Along with this shift in supply, there is a corresponding shift of the export supply curve from X_sX_s to $X_s'X_s'$. The result is a fall in the domestic price level, an increase in domestic consumption from Q_0 to Q_1, and an increase in exports from X_0 to X_1. The actual relative increase in domestic and export sales consequent to a given domestic subsidy depends on the relative sensitivity of domestic and export demand to price changes (relative demand elasticities).

When a domestic subsidy is introduced, it shifts the domestic supply curve and thereby affects export markets indirectly, whereas an export subsidy acts directly on the export market. An export subsidy drives a wedge between the prices paid by consumers in the home market and

21. Applying a countervailing duty implicitly assumes that the subsidy is somehow tied to production. Otherwise, the subsidies are ineffective gifts, and there is no reason to expect producers to subsidize inefficient production themselves with the cash grant if they can pocket the money instead.

Figure 4-1. *Effects of a Domestic Subsidy*

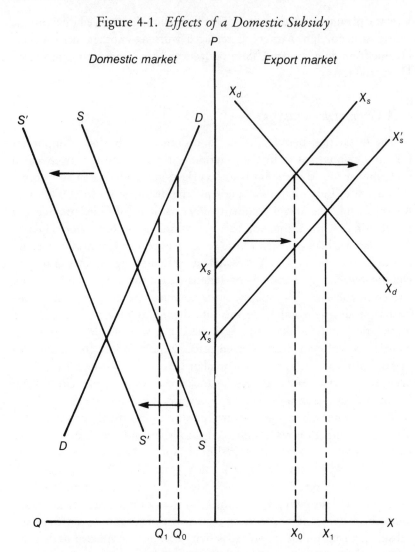

export markets. Now consider figure 4-2, where the introduction of an export subsidy for domestic producers shifts export supply from $X_s X_s$ to $X_s'' X_s''$. The result is an increase in exports from X_0 to X_1 and a fall in export prices from P_0 to P_1. At this new export quantity, domestic prices rise from P_0 to P_2. The wedge between export and domestic prices will be $(P_2 - P_1)$, which is determined by the export subsidy rate.

Because domestic subsidies act only indirectly on export markets, their effect is offset by an increase in domestic demand. Thus, an ad valorem

Figure 4-2. *Effects of an Export Subsidy*

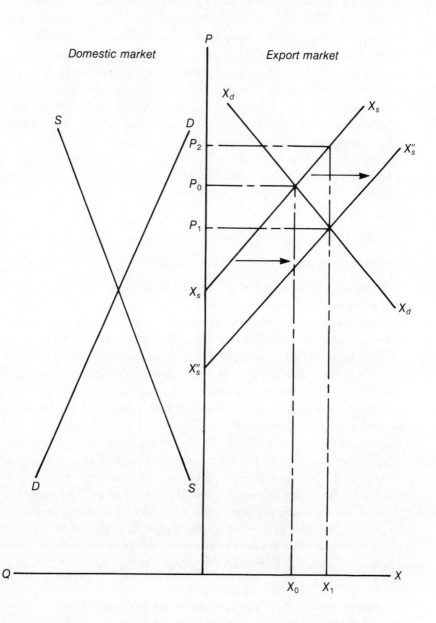

domestic subsidy will have less effect on export markets than an export subsidy at an identical ad valorem rate. To demonstrate this proposition, consider the equilibrium represented in figure 4-3, where we assume that the supply curve of the domestic industry is fixed (that is, it is perfectly inelastic). With the introduction of an export subsidy, domestic prices increase from P_0 to P_1 and exports from X_0 to X_1. As a result, domestic production is reallocated from domestic consumption to export sales. In contrast, because the total supply of the domestic industry is fixed, an ad valorem domestic subsidy will have absolutely no effect on the volume of exports. In more general cases where supply is not fixed, the effect of a domestic subsidy still will be less than that of an export subsidy at an identical rate, owing to the interaction of home market and export demand.

Quantifying the Implications of the Bias

When export subsidies are tied directly to the performance of exports to the United States, the duty calculated as that needed to countervail the competitive benefit of subsidization is identical to the duty calculated as the subsidy rate itself. In general, however, the two approaches can yield dramatically different results, both with domestic subsidies and with export subsidies that are also paid-for exports to other markets. The greatest divergence involves domestic subsidies.[22]

Table 4-1 presents countervailing duty rates based on the competitive benefits that foreign domestic subsidies have on export performance, assuming a 1 percent domestic subsidy. For a larger foreign domestic subsidy, we simply multiply the amount in the table by the domestic subsidy rate. The countervailing duty rate for competitive benefits is derived by calculating the export subsidy needed to give the exporting industry the same competitive benefit in export markets as a given domestic subsidy. This may overstate the competitive effect of the subsidy when there are other export markets as well. However, as long as we expect other countries to take similar action, this is an appropriate bench-

---

22. There has been some debate in the legal community about whether a cash-flow approach or a competitive-benefit or competitive-effects approach is most appropriate. See Richard Diamond, *A Search for Economic and Financial Principles in the Administration of United States Countervailing Duty Law* (Washington: Georgetown University Law Center, 1990).

Figure 4-3. *Effects of Subsidies with an Inelastic Domestic Supply*

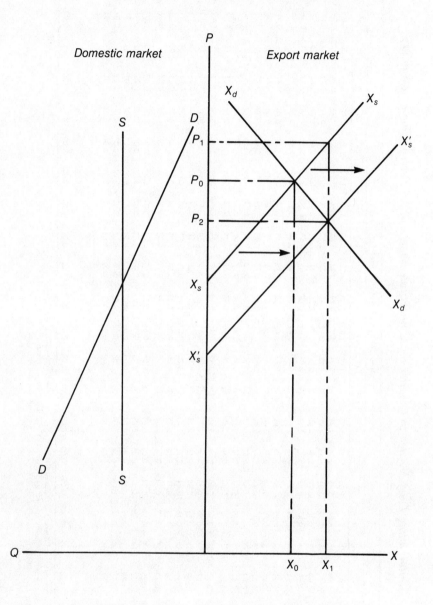

Table 4-1. Countervailing Duty Needed to Counter the Competitive Benefit of a 1 Percent Domestic Subsidy

Percent

Ratio (e_d/e_s)[a]	0[b]	Domestic consumption as a percentage of total production																			
		5	10	15	20	25	30	35	40	45	50	55	60	65	70	75	80	85	90	95	99.9
0.00[c]	1.00	1.00	1.00	1.00	1.00	1.00	1.00	1.00	1.00	1.00	1.00	1.00	1.00	1.00	1.00	1.00	1.00	1.00	1.00	1.00	1.00
0.25	1.00	0.99	0.98	0.96	0.95	0.94	0.93	0.92	0.91	0.90	0.89	0.88	0.87	0.86	0.85	0.84	0.83	0.83	0.82	0.81	0.80
0.50	1.00	0.98	0.95	0.93	0.91	0.89	0.87	0.85	0.83	0.82	0.80	0.78	0.77	0.76	0.74	0.73	0.71	0.70	0.69	0.68	0.67
0.75	1.00	0.96	0.93	0.90	0.87	0.84	0.82	0.79	0.77	0.75	0.73	0.71	0.69	0.67	0.66	0.64	0.63	0.61	0.60	0.58	0.57
1.00	1.00	0.95	0.91	0.87	0.83	0.80	0.77	0.74	0.71	0.69	0.67	0.65	0.63	0.61	0.59	0.57	0.56	0.54	0.53	0.51	0.50
1.25	1.00	0.94	0.89	0.84	0.80	0.76	0.73	0.70	0.67	0.64	0.62	0.59	0.57	0.55	0.53	0.52	0.50	0.49	0.47	0.46	0.45
1.50	1.00	0.93	0.87	0.83	0.77	0.73	0.69	0.66	0.63	0.60	0.57	0.55	0.53	0.51	0.49	0.47	0.46	0.44	0.43	0.41	0.40
1.75	1.00	0.92	0.85	0.79	0.74	0.70	0.66	0.62	0.59	0.56	0.53	0.51	0.49	0.47	0.45	0.43	0.42	0.40	0.39	0.38	0.36
2.00	1.00	0.91	0.83	0.77	0.71	0.67	0.63	0.59	0.56	0.53	0.50	0.48	0.46	0.44	0.42	0.40	0.39	0.37	0.36	0.35	0.33
2.50	1.00	0.89	0.80	0.73	0.67	0.62	0.57	0.53	0.50	0.47	0.44	0.42	0.40	0.38	0.36	0.35	0.33	0.32	0.31	0.30	0.29
3.00	1.00	0.87	0.77	0.69	0.63	0.57	0.53	0.49	0.46	0.43	0.40	0.38	0.36	0.34	0.32	0.31	0.29	0.28	0.27	0.26	0.25
4.00	1.00	0.83	0.71	0.63	0.56	0.50	0.46	0.42	0.39	0.36	0.33	0.31	0.29	0.28	0.26	0.25	0.24	0.23	0.22	0.21	0.20
5.00	1.00	0.80	0.67	0.57	0.50	0.44	0.40	0.36	0.33	0.31	0.29	0.27	0.25	0.24	0.22	0.21	0.20	0.19	0.18	0.17	0.17
10.00	1.00	0.67	0.50	0.40	0.33	0.29	0.25	0.22	0.20	0.18	0.17	0.15	0.14	0.13	0.13	0.12	0.11	0.11	0.10	0.10	0.09
20.00	1.00	0.50	0.33	0.25	0.20	0.17	0.14	0.13	0.11	0.10	0.09	0.08	0.08	0.07	0.07	0.06	0.06	0.06	0.05	0.05	0.05
30.00	1.00	0.40	0.25	0.18	0.14	0.12	0.10	0.09	0.08	0.07	0.06	0.06	0.05	0.05	0.05	0.04	0.04	0.04	0.04	0.04	0.03
40.00	1.00	0.33	0.20	0.14	0.11	0.09	0.08	0.07	0.06	0.05	0.05	0.04	0.04	0.04	0.04	0.03	0.03	0.03	0.03	0.03	0.02
50.00	1.00	0.29	0.17	0.12	0.09	0.07	0.06	0.05	0.05	0.04	0.04	0.04	0.04	0.03	0.03	0.03	0.02	0.02	0.02	0.02	0.02
60.00	1.00	0.25	0.14	0.10	0.08	0.06	0.05	0.05	0.04	0.04	0.03	0.03	0.03	0.03	0.02	0.02	0.02	0.02	0.02	0.02	0.02
70.00	1.00	0.22	0.13	0.09	0.07	0.05	0.05	0.04	0.04	0.03	0.03	0.03	0.02	0.02	0.02	0.02	0.02	0.02	0.02	0.02	0.02
80.00	1.00	0.20	0.11	0.08	0.06	0.05	0.04	0.03	0.03	0.03	0.02	0.02	0.02	0.02	0.02	0.02	0.02	0.01	0.01	0.01	0.01
90.00	1.00	0.18	0.10	0.07	0.05	0.04	0.04	0.03	0.03	0.02	0.02	0.02	0.02	0.02	0.02	0.02	0.01	0.01	0.01	0.01	0.01
100.00	1.00	0.17	0.09	0.06	0.05	0.04	0.03	0.03	0.02	0.02	0.02	0.02	0.01	0.02	0.02	0.01	0.01	0.01	0.01	0.01	0.01
x[d]	0.00	0.00	0.00	0.00	0.00	0.00	0.00	0.00	0.00	0.00	0.00	0.00	0.00	0.00	0.00	0.00	0.00	0.00	0.00	0.00	0.00

a. Ratio of the price elasticity of demand to the price elasticity of supply in the home market.
b. Corresponds to case of no domestic market, so that $(Q_d/Q_s) = 0$, and (e_d/e_s) is irrelevant.
c. Corresponds to case of fixed (inelastic) domestic demand, where export and domestic subsidies are then identical.
d. Note that with fixed (perfectly inelastic) supply, domestic subsidies have no effect on export performance.

mark. (The formal derivation of these results is discussed in the appendix to this chapter.)[23]

In table 4-1, the terms e_s and e_d represent the price elasticity of supply and demand in the home market. Thus, e_s measures the percentage increase in total production of the domestic industry that would result from a 1 percent increase in price, and the term e_d measures the percentage decrease in domestic demand that results from a 1 percent increase in price. When demand and supply are equally sensitive to price, the ratio (e_d/e_s) will equal one.

The estimates presented in table 4-1 highlight the fact that the greater the relative significance of home market sales, the greater the divergence between the duty applied by the DOC and the one actually needed to counter the competitive benefits of a domestic subsidy. For example, if demand is twice as sensitive to price changes as supply (that is, $[e_d/e_s]$ = 2) and domestic consumption accounts for 50 percent of total production, the duty rate, when based on the calculated per unit rate alone, will be twice as large as that actually needed to counter the effects of the domestic subsidy on producers in the import market. In other words, with a 10 percent domestic subsidy, the Department of Commerce will apply a 10 percent duty rate, even though only a 5 percent duty is needed to counter the actual effects of the subsidy on U.S. producers.

The different implications of these two approaches to countervailing the effects of subsidies should be apparent. When countervailing duties for domestic subsidies are based only on the actual subsidy received, they tend to exceed the amount needed to offset the injury caused by subsidized imports. The duty applied replaces the original distortion in U.S. markets, which favored foreign producers, with another distortion, which favors domestic producers. The result is a transfer of income from domestic consumers to domestic producers beyond the amount needed to provide a level playing field by offsetting the effect of the practice. Yet, for export subsidies, condemned by GATT and presumably far more unfair than domestic subsidies, duties are applied that come closer to merely countering the effects of subsidization. Countervailing duties for export subsidies are therefore closer to an effects-based model, whereas duties for domestic subsidies conform more to a punishment-based or "benefits" model.

23. If we do not expect other countries to take countervailing duty actions, the appropriate duty rate can then be found by redefining "domestic consumption," as in our analysis, to include all consumption other than consumption in the United States.

Whether the department continues to apply a duty rate based on the subsidy rate itself or bases it on the competitive benefits that result from subsidization, the results presented here are important for yet another reason. The International Trade Commission may use the subsidy rates calculated by Commerce in determining whether the subsidies have caused material injury. Because it is the competitive benefit of a subsidy, rather than the subsidy rate itself, that determines the link between subsidies and material injury, the relationship between subsidy rates and competitive benefits is an important one.

Procedural Biases, or "Real Measurement Issues"

To qualify for subsidies, the recipient often incurs costs that reduce, at least to some extent, the pecuniary advantages of receiving the subsidy. For regional subsidies, these costs may include the burden of relocating in a region, whereas for other programs it may mean increased tax liabilities (as when subsidies constitute or increase taxable income). These costs are referred to as offsets.

Offsets

Current U.S. law, as read by the Department of Commerce, is specific about what kinds of offsets are allowed in the calculation of the net benefits of a subsidy in such circumstances. It states that three categories of costs may offset a portion of the gross subsidy in the calculation of "net subsidy": (1) any application fee, deposit, or similar payment paid in order to qualify for, or to receive, the benefit of the subsidy; (2) any loss in the value of the subsidy resulting from its deferred receipt if the deferral is mandated by government order; and (3) export taxes, duties, or other charges levied on the export of merchandise to the United States specifically intended to offset the subsidy received.[24]

The fact that Commerce "may" offset these specified costs does not, of course, mean that it "may not" offset for others. However, the department has chosen to read the statute that way. In any event, these restrictions reflect the muddled nature either of the department's legislative mandate or of its administrative policy. Because of the restrictions

24. 19 U.S.C sec. 1677(6).

placed on offsets, current department practice measures neither the true cash-flow value of a subsidy nor the competitive benefit it implies.

REGIONAL SUBSIDIES. Regional subsidies are an area in which the department's policy regarding offsets departs explicitly from either a benefits or a competitive effects approach. Before 1979, the Treasury Department (which preceded the Department of Commerce in administering the law) calculated the net benefit of regional development programs as the cash value of gross benefits received directly or indirectly from the government, netted against the pecuniary disadvantages of locating in a region.[25]

As an example, suppose a company receives a production subsidy that is equal to 10 percent of its revenues to locate in an isolated, undeveloped region. Assume further that producing in this isolated region raises inland freight and shipping costs by an amount that equals 6 percent of revenues. Under the methodology used by the Treasury Department until 1979, the net benefit of the program would be 4 percent. In this calculation, the gross benefit is offset by the costs of relocating in the region. Conceptually, net benefits are measured by the share of revenues that can be attributed to program participation, assuming that otherwise firms would not have located in the subsidized region.

The DOC's interpretation of the law does not allow such offsets. As a result, the subsidy calculated in regional subsidy cases not only fails to measure the real competitive benefit that domestic subsidies give to exports but also generally exceeds the actual per unit subsidization of the exported product measured as a per unit share of total cash flow. Thus, for regional subsidies the distortions introduced to the market by the department's treatment of domestic subsidies is compounded by a biased calculation of the per unit value of the subsidy.

SECONDARY TAX EFFECTS. The Department of Commerce further interprets its legislative mandate so as to ignore secondary tax effects, which can have a significant impact on the calculation of the amount of a subsidy. This prohibition is consistent with the cash-flow model followed by the department, although it is at odds with subsidy measurements that focus on the link between subsidization and the actual production of the product under investigation.[26]

Historically, the department's interpretation of the term "secondary"

---

25. For example, see *ASG Industries, Inc.* v. *United States*, 610 F.2d 770 (Ct. Cust. & Pat. App. 1979); and *Michelin Tire Corp.* v. *United States*, 2 Ct. Int'l Trade 142 (1981).

26. As an example of the department's interpretation of the legislative mandate regarding secondary tax offsets, see *Preliminary Affirmative Countervailing Duty Determination; Fresh and Chilled Atlantic Salmon from Norway*, 55 Fed. Reg. 26727 (1990).

has been extremely narrow. Thus, the DOC classifies as secondary not only the tax effects of nontax benefits but also the tax implications of changes in a single tax program for related tax liabilities. Thus, if a tax-related benefit decreases some taxes paid by a company and simultaneously increases others, the department will focus only on those tax programs in which the amount paid has decreased.

To illustrate, consider a differential payroll tax that is paid in two tax regions, each of which has a different tax rate. The higher rate is applied in urban areas, and the lower is applied in the relatively undeveloped outlying counties. Payroll expenses, including payroll taxes, are deductible when calculating income for tax purposes, and a single income tax schedule (that is, not region-specific) is used to calculate the tax on profits. Therefore, companies that have relatively low payroll taxes because they employ people located in outlying counties will also have relatively higher income taxes.

The DOC finds these payroll tax arrangements to be countervailable. In calculating net benefits, however, it ignores the effects of reduced payroll taxes on profit taxes.[27] Such effects would be deemed "secondary," although both changes affect the level of total taxes paid.

To highlight the implications of treating these tax effects as secondary, suppose that two companies, both located in the outlying area, have revenues of $100,000 (before payroll taxes or payroll deductions), that the corporate tax rate is 50 percent, and that both have a payroll of $50,000. But suppose that their other expenses are quite different: one company operates at a profit, the other at a loss. Because of the differential payroll tax system, these companies, by virtue of being in the outlying county, pay $10,000 in payroll taxes, whereas they would have paid $20,000 if they were located in the capital. For tax purposes, the companies have accounts as presented in table 4-2.

What is the benefit to the producers in the outlying county? In a simple cash-flow analysis, the subsidy would be identical for both companies, equaling the simple reduction in payroll taxes, or $10,000, the reason being that cash flow (before income taxes but after expenses) has increased

27. See, for example, *Preliminary Affirmative Countervailing Duty Determination; Fresh and Chilled Atlantic Salmon from Norway.* In fact, following the department's reasoning, the U.S. Federal Tax Code also embodies unfair trade practices by allowing deductions for various state taxes, which vary by region. This is because the effective federal tax rate varies by state, being higher in states with low rates for federally deductible taxes. In addition, the department generally chooses the highest prevailing tax rate as a benchmark. Thus, under current U.S. practice, practically the entire U.S. economy could be countervailed because effective federal tax rates vary by locality.

Table 4-2. *Accounts of Two Hypothetical Companies in Outlying Areas*
Dollars

Category	Company A	Company B
Revenue	100,000	100,000
Minus: Payroll	50,000	50,000
Minus: Payroll taxes	10,000	10,000
Minus: Other expenses	10,000	60,000
Equals: Before-tax profit	30,000	(20,000)
Minus: Profit taxes	15,000	0
Equals: After-tax profit	15,000	(20,000)

by $10,000. From an accounting perspective, the effect on before-tax net income is thus identical for both companies.

Yet the benefits are far from identical. The profit taxes of the company operating at a profit increase $5,000 when the government reduces its payroll tax by $10,000. Net of income taxes, it thus keeps only $5,000. The company operating at a loss, however, has no such increase in profit taxes. It still pays none. As a result, its after-tax cash flow increases by the full $10,000.

The subsidies are different for another reason as well. Although the reduction in payroll taxes implies a reduction in the marginal cost of labor, the reduction is twice as large for one company as for the other. The subsidies will thus have different effects on input costs and hence on production for the two companies. Yet the department simply ignores such factors, deeming them irrelevant. Because the department focuses on an accounting rather than on an economic definition of subsidy, these different subsidies are treated identically.

DUTY DRAWBACK. Most governments, including that of the United States, refund to exporters the duties previously paid on imported material when a finished product made with that material is exported. These duty refunds, or drawbacks, are not considered to be a subsidy unless they exceed the duty paid on the materials used in the production of the exported article. This seemingly noncontroversial principle in fact leads to findings of subsidies where none exist because of the policies of the actual implementation of the procedure.

The case of *Stainless Steel Cooking Ware from Korea* is an example.[28] There, the government of the Republic of Korea refunded duties previously paid on imported raw materials that were physically incorporated into the exported article, stainless steel. It also refunded duties previously paid on imported materials that were consumed in the manufacturing

28. 51 Fed. Reg. 42867 (1986).

process, such as polishes. The DOC did not approve, however, of the practice of granting duty drawback on materials not physically incorporated in the product. Accordingly, the drawback granted by the government of Korea for duty paid on imported materials consumed in the manufacturing process was deemed excessive and was countervailed.

It may or may not be sound policy to grant a duty drawback on imported materials consumed in the production of a product as well as those physically incorporated in the product. By application of countervailing duties, however, the DOC has decided that it is unfair to do so, that it is in fact so pernicious a practice that it justifies overriding GATT's duty-binding and MFN obligations.[29]

There is more. In order to determine how much imported material is incorporated in an exported article, allowance must be made for waste. An agency of the government of Korea conducts biannual surveys of a wide variety of industries to determine average waste rates for their products. These provide the basis for the drawback amount. Thus, if the survey reveals an average waste rate of 25 percent, an exported finished product weighing 100 pounds will be presumed to have been manufactured with 125 pounds of a particular raw material. Individual manufacturers will vary from the mean, of course, and, given the fixed rate, all will have an incentive to become more productive and to attempt to beat the system.

The government of Korea asserted that its system was designed for administrative convenience, a justification the DOC frequently uses for its own practices. Rather than calculate actual wastage on a shipment-by-shipment basis, the government of Korea used standard rates, thereby expediting the administrative process. This position was not disputed; it was simply deemed irrelevant. To the extent that a drawback was granted to an exporter for wastage not actually incurred by the company because its wastage rate was below the mean, a subsidy was found—an unfair practice. The DOC added the benefits from the drawbacks granted on products not physically incorporated into the exported article to the benefits from an excessive wastage allowance and found a subsidy ranging from 0.15 to 0.20 percent.[30]

29. The U.S. law defining an export subsidy (19 U.S.C. sec. 1677(5) refers to annex A to the Subsidies Code, which sets out an illustrative list of export subsidies. That list includes, as an example of an export subsidy, excessive drawback (making normal allowance for waste) on imported goods physically incorporated into exported merchandise. This list is silent, however, about imported materials necessarily consumed in the manufacturing process and therefore not physically incorporated.

30. 51 Fed. Reg. 42867, 42871 (1986). The manner in which "excessive" wastage was found points up another problem area of countervailing duty law and practice: the damage

Accounting Measures and Use of Firm-Specific Information

In various applications of its regulations, such as the choice of short-term loan benchmarks and the allocation period for equity and grant benefits, the Department of Commerce ignores company-specific information, relying instead on sources of information that maximize administrative feasibility. Given often unrealistic statutory deadlines, a concern for administrability is understandable, although it would be more understandable were the department more willing to accord the same flexibility to other governments, which it was not willing to do, for example, with Korea's standardized wastage rates. Although administrative ease is a desirable feature of any administrative system, it does not justify replacing a correct analysis with an incorrect analysis. "A desire for consistency, administrability, and predictability is understandable, but it is not a substitute for evidence of record."[31] Yet Commerce does ignore evidence of record in countervailing duty investigations, evidence that it obtains as a matter of course in its verification of the records of individual firms. The department is in effect choosing to ignore firm-specific information to which it has access. In this section, we discuss some of the consequences of relying on arbitrary benchmarks rather than on firm-specific data.

SHORT-TERM FINANCING. The department evaluates short-term loans by comparing the lending terms of the investigated loan with "the average interest rate for an alternative source of short-term financing in the country in question."[32] In reality, the sample for this national average rate

---

to comity among nations. The waste rates calculated by the government of Korea were published in a loose-leaf binder, comparable to a published tariff schedule, containing several hundred pages of product descriptions and rates. This wasn't enough. The Korean agency concerned was asked, at verification of the government of Korea's official response to the government of the United States, to produce the backup documentation for the numbers. It was unable to do so because of normal records disposal practices. The Department of Commerce stated, "Because we were unable to check back to source documents we must consider the government calculation of the input ratios unverified." 51 Fed. Reg. 42867, 42870 (1986). See also Department of Commerce public file, Investigation C-580-602. It is interesting to speculate as to how the U.S. government would react—particularly how the legislative branch would enact—were another government to question its word in a comparable verification exercise, particularly when, as here, the calculated discrepancy is so trivial an amount.

31. *IPSCO, Inc.* v. *United States*, 701 F. Supp. 236 (Ct. Int'l Trade 1988).

32. International Trade Administration, *Countervailing Duties, Notice of Proposed Rule Making and Request for Public Comments*, 54 Fed. Reg. 23366, 23380 (1989) ("Proposed Regulations"). The Proposed Regulations, which have not yet become final, in the words

can range from curbside vendors to AAA-rated multinational corporations. As a result, any company able to obtain financing at less than the national average rate is assumed to be receiving a subsidy when the financing is obtained through government channels. There are, of course, cases in which a firm-specific rate is unavailable and some proxy is thus necessary. But Commerce prefers averages even when firm- or industry-specific rates are available. It justifies the use of an average rate by citing the need for administrative feasibility and by asserting that the terms of company-specific, short-term loans are unlikely to vary from national average terms.[33]

The practice of using national average interest rates as benchmarks for short-term loans ignores a fundamental reality of short-term credit markets—short-term lending rates can vary greatly according to risk. As a result, the department's methodology merely identifies those firms that borrowed at terms better than the national average. Thus, assuming that interest rates are distributed evenly around the mean, all companies have a 50 percent probability of failing this test.

The department's current method, although perhaps easier to administer, does not provide the information required. According to the statute, the department is supposed to be identifying loans that are provided "on terms inconsistent with commercial considerations," and only loans shown to be inconsistent with commercial considerations qualify as countervailable subsidies.[34] The department has not been mandated by Congress to countervail companies merely because their borrowing terms fall above or below national averages, regardless of the actual default risk of the company under investigation. Indeed, firms that are bad risks and that borrow at subsidized rates above the national average will not be countervailed under the current methodology.

The potential distortions introduced by the use of average-rate benchmarks are even more problematic outside the countries of the Organization for Economic Cooperation and Development, where many economies are characterized by much higher interest rates and by fragmented capital markets. In addition, money markets and financial institutions in these countries are often specialized in certain industrial sectors,

---

of the Department of Commerce, "codify much of the Department's existing practice with respect to the identification and measurement of subsidies." 54 Fed. Reg. 23366 (1989).

33. Proposed Regulations at 54 Fed. Reg. 23369 (1989) (citing Subsidies Appendix, 49 Fed. Reg. 18016, 18020).

34. 19 U.S.C. sec. 1677(5)(A)(ii)(I).

geographic regions, or even urban localities. Comparisons with an "average" or "prevailing" rate in these situations is a meaningless exercise.[35]

ACCOUNTING PRINCIPLES. The department's determination of whether a firm is creditworthy or equityworthy can be one of its most critical decisions in a particular case because this is what determines whether credit or equity infusions are consistent with commercial considerations.[36] Yet the department has never specified how these determinations are made, except to say that it will use, among other things, "the present and past financial health of a firm, as reflected in various financial indicators calculated from the firm's financial statements and accounts" to determine creditworthiness.[37] Similarly, in determining creditworthiness, the department simply states that it will examine, among other things, "current and past indicators of a firm's financial health calculated from that firm's statements and accounts, adjusted, if appropriate, to conform to generally accepted accounting principles."[38] But the department does not specify what it is seeking.

Under current regulations, foreign governments and firms have no way of knowing what financial standards guide the DOC. This uncertainty is compounded by the vague statement that a firm's accounts can be adjusted "if appropriate." Not only are potential respondents left in the dark about how their books will be evaluated, but they are not told whether their books or some "appropriately adjusted" version generated by the department will be used to determine equityworthiness.

In evaluating the financial health of companies, the department favors U.S. accounting practices. In fact, there seems to be an implicit bias against a national GAAP (generally accepted accounting principles) that does not correspond to U.S. practices.[39] In such circumstances, the department will often dismiss the financial statements of companies under

35. Similarly, the use of interest rates in comparable countries would be meaningless since the same problem would exist when identifying an average or prevailing rate. For more on the characteristics of capital markets in developing countries, see V. V. Batt and J. Merman, "Resource Mobilization in Developing Countries: Financial Institutions and Policies," *World Development*, vol. 6 (January 1978); Ronald I. McKinnon, *Money and Capital in Economic Development* (Brookings, 1973); U. Tun Wai, "Interest Rates Outside the Organized Money Markets of Underdeveloped Countries," International Monetary Fund, Staff Paper, Washington, November 1957, pp. 80–142; and Michael P. Todaro, *Economic Development in the Third World* (Longman, 1985).

36. 19 U.S.C.A. sec. 1677(5)(A)(ii)(I).

37. Proposed Regulation 355.44(b)(6)(i)(B), in 54 Fed. Reg. 23380 (1989).

38. Proposed Regulation 355.44(e)(2)(i), in 54 Fed. Reg. 23381 (1989).

39. See, for example, *Final Affirmative Countervailing Duty Determinations; Certain Steel Products from the Republic of Korea*, 47 Fed. Reg. 57535 (1982).

investigation and will instead recalculate the statements, after making adjustments to the accounting life of capital equipment and altering the treatment of currency transactions.[40] As a result, even though corporations are usually judged in national capital markets relative to other firms that follow the same accounting standards, the department, after the fact, introduces an alien (that is, U.S.) system of standards and then finds firms and governments guilty of unfair conduct for failing to meet the alien, after-the-fact, standard. It seems fair to say that this is a strained way of detecting unfair conduct.

It has also been the department's practice to allocate the benefits from certain nonrecurring subsidies—such as grants, long-term fixed-rate loans, and equity infusions—over a period of years. The rationale is that the cash-flow effect of these types of subsidies usually does not occur upon receipt of the benefit.[41] After determining the amount of the subsidy, the DOC chooses an allocation period over which it will spread the benefit (that is, a period during which it believes the cash-flow effect will occur) and, using a discount rate, constructs a stream of benefits for each year of the period.

The DOC currently relies on 1977 tables of the Internal Revenue Service (*no longer actually used by the IRS*) in determining the useful life of capital equipment. It has proposed to move to a fixed ten-year allocation period. The department explains its rationale for considering a fixed, ten-year allocation period in the following manner:

> The period selected must be substantively fair to the interests of both domestic and foreign parties. However, the Department must select a period which facilitates the administration of the statute in a timely manner, and which offers predictability for domestic and foreign parties. Thus far, the alternatives considered by the Department have suffered from one or more drawbacks. The use of firms' accounting

40. The final determination and the public file in *Korean Steel* (see note 39) provides an interesting example. Korean GAAP permitted, but did not require, amortization of foreign exchange gains and losses. The Korean respondent, POSCO, had adopted the practice of expensing these items if they were 5 percent or less and amortizing them if they exceeded 5 percent. The Department of Commerce determined that since this practice was not required, it was inconsistent with Korean GAAP (and hence that its accountants and auditors had been as well), and restated the company's books to expense all foreign exchange items. The change introduced by the DOC in reworking the books by this alternative accounting standard made the firm unequityworthy/uncreditworthy for the years in question. See also *Offshore Platform Jackets and Pipes from Korea*, 51 Fed. Reg. 11779 (1986).

41. Subsidies appendix, 49 Fed. Reg. 18016 (1989).

useful life as reflected in their records suffers from the fact that a firm may select a useful life for a variety of reasons, such as tax liability. Thus, to use firms' accounting useful life could result in drastically different benefit amounts even though firms might be receiving identical subsidies and might be otherwise identically situated. Likewise, the tax tables of other countries often are designed to promote certain governmental objectives, and do not necessarily reflect the useful life of assets. Moreover, to use the tax tables of the country under investigation would produce different benefit amounts between countries.[42]

This statement reflects the department's aversion in CVD cases to relying on data and benchmarks drawn directly from the financial data of foreign companies. Yet this preference is at odds with other practices of the department. The Court of International Trade pointed out in a recent decision that, although the department may reject a company's books even when in compliance with the home country's GAAP, in antidumping proceedings the International Trade Administration (ITA) generally does rely on the producer's accounting records for determining depreciation periods and for cost computations, provided that the company's records comply with the home country's GAAP and do not significantly distort the firm's financial position or actual costs.[43]

Upstream Subsidies

An upstream subsidy is one that is conferred upon a product in the production of an exported product. For example, a subsidy paid to a producer of wire could be an upstream subsidy in an investigation of coat hangers manufactured from wire. Even if a manufacturer of coat hangers receives no subsidies directly, it is possible that coat hanger exports are encouraged artificially by the subsidy paid on wire, an essential input. This would occur if the cost of the manufacturer's raw materials was reduced by reason of the subsidy paid to the input supplier.

In response to growing allegations that exporters of finished products benefit indirectly from subsidies conferred upstream on their inputs, Congress, in 1984, added a new provision to the Tariff Act, making countervailable any subsidy that

42. 54 Fed. Reg. 23376 (1989). Consider the department's stated need for a method that "facilitates the administration of the statute" with its refusal to extend the same privilege to the government of Korea (see notes 28–30 and accompanying text).

43. See *IPSCO, Inc.* v. *United States*, 701 F. Supp. at 238, n.3.

(1) is paid or bestowed by that government with respect to a product (hereafter referred to as an "input product") that is used in the manufacture or production in that country of merchandise which is the subject of a countervailing duty proceeding;

(2) in the judgment of the administering authority bestows a competitive benefit on the merchandise; and

(3) has a significant effect on the cost of manufacturing or producing the merchandise."[44]

COMPETITIVE BENEFIT. Technically, a competitive benefit exists if an upstream subsidy results in a reduced input price for downstream producers, such that production costs for downstream firms are lowered. It should be obvious that the existence of such benefits depends on the extent of passthrough from upstream producer to upstream consumer. Actual passthrough will depend on a number of factors, including the structure of demand for the input by all downstream industries for which it is used, the structure of supply for the input, and the competitive structure of the upstream market. Even in the simple case where an upstream industry is perfectly competitive and produces only one product, the effect of a subsidy on input prices nevertheless depends on supply and demand elasticities. With competitive markets, full passthrough occurs only as a special case where upstream supply is perfectly elastic or demand is perfectly inelastic.

With noncompetitive upstream markets, there is even less reason to expect even partial passthrough. For example, with an upstream monopolist, the extent to which an ad valorem subsidy translates into a reduction in prices depends on the sensitivity of upstream demand to price changes. If demand is highly elastic (that is, very sensitive to price changes), a firm with market power will pass through very little of the subsidy it receives.[45]

44. 19 U.S.C.A. sec. 1677-1, as added by sec. 613(a) of the Trade and Tariff Act of 1984, P.L. 98-573, Stat. 2948 (1984).

45. It is important to note that even when passthrough does occur, an upstream subsidy still will not yield a reduction in input prices equal to the full rate of the upstream subsidy, even when markets are perfectly competitive. As a result, the legal requirement that the department assume full passthrough in agricultural cases is not consistent with reality. For example, with upstream supply and demand elasticities e_{si} and e_{di}, the proportional reduction in input prices P_i consequent to the introduction of a subsidy on input i at rate s_i can be shown to be

$$dP_i/P_i = [e_{si}/(e_{di} - e_{si})]s_i.$$

Inspection of this equation reveals that unless the upstream industry has a perfectly elastic

The DOC avoids dealing with the issue of supply and demand factors in two ways. In most cases, it relies on direct input price comparisons. Even then, it runs afoul of important elements of market structure. For example, in *Steel Wheels from Brazil,* the DOC made a comparison between the Brazilian price for hot-rolled sheet and coil and the "world market" price.[46] The department relied on Korean sheet and coil prices to the United States because Korea is "one of the lowest-cost producers of steel." Because Korean c.i.f. (cost, insurance, and freight) prices to the United States were "on average over 50 percent higher than domestic Brazilian prices in 1987," the department found that a subsidy existed.

Notwithstanding the question of whether Korea was an appropriate benchmark country, the department ignored a more obvious and more fundamental problem with its price comparisons. Korean steel exports to the United States, like exports from most other suppliers, were controlled by voluntary restraint agreements (VRAs). In 1987, Korea was at 100.22 percent of its quota on plate and 99.16 percent of its quota on sheet and strip. Quota rents associated with the VRAs are captured by foreign producers and thus are often included in c.i.f. prices. In a market protected by quotas, the price in the United States obviously would be *above* world prices, reflecting these quota rents, because such quotas drive a wedge between the price of steel in exporting countries (such as Korea and Brazil) and importing countries (such as the United States). Because of the existence of quotas, an application of the department's methodology to steel prices in Korea would have found that domestic prices in Korea were also "significantly below" the U.S. export price, even though Korea was the benchmark country.[47] In such cases, using U.S. market prices as a benchmark is misleading at best and points out the myriad complications and pitfalls that can arise when relying solely on price comparisons for subsidy calculations. Clearly, a thorough anal-

---

industry supply curve, or unless demand is perfectly inelastic, an upstream subsidy will not translate fully into a downstream price reduction.

46. 54 Fed. Reg. 15527 (1989).

47. There is a scene in the movie *Monty Python and the Holy Grail* that provides a good metaphor for investigations that rely on consistent methods, regardless of what such methods actually measure. In the film, a woman is accused of being a witch. Concerned about the appearance of fairness and impartiality, the King then proposes to the accusers the following test: "What do we do with witches? We burn them. What else burns? Wood. What else does wood do? It floats. What else floats? A duck. Hence, if this woman weighs as much as a duck, she is a witch." The scale they then use to compare weights is itself biased. The woman weighs as much as a duck and hence is guilty of being a witch. But the system is at least consistent. Everyone knows what the investigation process involves. In such investigations, the accused stands a good chance of getting burned.

ysis of market conditions must be performed in order to make a fair decision.

SIGNIFICANT EFFECT. The department determines significant effect by multiplying the ad valorem subsidy rate on an input by its proportion of the total production costs of the article under investigation. If the input subsidy to the output product exceeds 5 percent, the DOC determines that a significant effect exists. If the subsidy is less than 1 percent, it finds no significant effect. Interestingly, if the subsidy rate is between 1 and 5 percent, the department then determines whether the input has a signif-icant effect on the competitiveness of the investigated product. This de-termination involves "case-by-case determinations of the degree to which demand for the merchandise is elastic."[48]

The department states that significant effect relates to the effect that upstream subsidies have on "the cost of manufacturing or producing the merchandise." Yet, in making the actual determination, the department ignores supply-side factors, relying instead on the elasticity of demand. This suggests either that the department does not understand the basic distinction between supply and demand, which is not likely, or that it is attempting to apply an economic effects test. Assuming that this is the case, the department's method illustrates its schizophrenic approach in interpreting its legislative mandate. Regarding both upstream subsidies and nonmarket economies, the DOC uses language consistent with an economic effects approach. Yet in other areas it deliberately avoids taking such an approach.

PROCESSED AGRICULTURAL PRODUCTS. There is no a priori reason to treat the analysis of upstream subsidies paid to agricultural producers any differently from subsidies paid to other upstream producers. Neverthe-less, the question of the application of upstream subsidy analysis in ag-ricultural cases has resulted in a double reversal of U.S. policy, with a possible triple reversal in the offing.

The issue arose in *Swine and Pork from Canada*, which involved the export of both live animals and meat.[49] Subsidies were paid to the farmers, but not to the meat packers. Hence, the issue was what, if anything, is the subsidy on exported meat? The DOC rejected an upstream subsidy analysis, under which it would not have been able to apply a counter-vailing duty on imports of meat absent a finding of a passthrough of

48. 54 Fed. Reg. 23374 (1989).

49. *Final Affirmative Countervailing Duty Determinations; Live Swine and Fresh, Chilled and Frozen Pork Products from Canada*, 50 Fed. Reg. 25097 (1985).

significant economic benefits to the meat packers. Rather, it determined that a live hog and pork meat are essentially the same product at different stages of production. If the upstream subsidy provision were applied to agricultural products, the agency argued, producers would be free to shift easily to the next stage of production to avoid the full impact of countervailing duties. According to Commerce, when the primary purpose of all segments of an industry is to produce a single end product (here pork meat) and when substantially all the raw agricultural product (live swine) is dedicated to the production of that end product, a true upstream situation is not presented.

Thus, live swine were not treated as a product upstream of pork meat, but rather the two were treated as the same product. This had the effect of increasing the calculated subsidy paid on the meat, and thus the countervailing duty. For example, if the subsidy on animals was valued at 1 cent per pound, the countervailing duty on a 200-pound animal would be $2.00. But if a 200-pound animal yielded only 100 pounds of meat, the same $2.00 subsidy would convert to 2 cents per pound. Thus, under the methodology adopted by the DOC in rejecting upstream analysis, the per pound benefit on the end product is higher than the per pound benefit on the input. Full passthrough is ensured, and the significant effect test is not applied.

The DOC's methodology was rejected by the Court of International Trade, which held that the "attempt by Commerce to carve out what would be an agricultural exception to the statutory method for determining upstream subsidies" was contrary to law.[50] Although the reasoning of the court was not undermined by the fact that the order was subsequently vacated on other grounds,[51] it was definitively undermined by Congress, which, in section 1326 of the Omnibus Trade and Competitiveness Act of 1988, overturned the court's holding and reinstated the DOC's reasoning.[52] A new pork investigation was launched, and the subsequent determination conformed to the 1988 amendment and the DOC's initial reasoning.[53] But in September 1990 a GATT panel ruled that the DOC's failure to, in effect, apply the upstream provision by determining how much of the subsidy to the hog growers was passed

50. *Canadian Meat Council* v. *United States*, 661 F.Supp. 622 at 628 (Ct. Int'l Trade 1987).
51. *Canadian Meat Council* v. *United States*, 680 F.Supp. 390 (Ct. Int'l Trade 1988).
52. P.L. 100-418, 102 Stat. 1203, 19 U.S.C.A. sec. 1677(4)(E).
53. *Final Affirmative Countervailing Duty Determination; Fresh, Chilled and Frozen Pork from Canada*, 54 Fed. Reg. 30774 (1989).

through to the meat packers violated the GATT Subsidies Code.[54] To what extent, if any, the United States will conform its law to the findings of the GATT panel, is, at this writing, unknown.

Domestic Consumption Subsidies

The absurd results that can follow from blind adherence to accounting-based rules of thumb may be best illustrated by domestic consumption subsidies. It should be obvious that a domestic consumption subsidy in foreign markets should help competing U.S. producers. After all, such a subsidy would normally divert sales from export markets to the home market. Yet under a simple accounting approach, such a program would be found to confer an unfair countervailable subsidy to export sales, one that is potentially harmful to U.S. producers, even though such programs actually have the opposite effect.

This is more than a hypothetical example. In fact, one of the more bizarre determinations of countervailability occurred in *Cheese from Norway*; in that country, in the 1970s, dairy products sold in the domestic market were subject to price controls.[55] No controls applied, however, to animal feed and other major costs incurred by the farmers who produced the milk. To compensate producers for the resulting squeeze, a consumer subsidy was paid for each unit of manufactured dairy product, such as cheese, sold to distributors for resale within the domestic market. However, the subsidy was *not* conferred on exported products. As a result, although the uncontrolled export price exceeded the controlled domestic price, the domestic price and subsidy together exceeded the export price.[56] The program diverted sales from export to domestic mar-

---

54. *International Trade Reporter* (BNA), vol. 7 (October 10, 1990), p. 1541.

55. *Cheese from Norway; Notice of Preliminary Countervailing Duty Determination*, 40 Fed. Reg. 54843 (1975); *Countervailing Duties—Cheese, Other than Jarlsberg, from Norway*, 41 Fed. Reg. 21766 (1976) (T.D. 76-152); and *Waiver of Countervailing Duties—Cheese, Other than Jarlsberg, from Norway*, 41 Fed. Reg. 21767 (1976) (T.D. 76-153). Because the announced determinations of the Treasury Department were not as complete as those currently published by the Department of Commerce, many of the details of cases from this era, including this one, can be gleaned only from the public files.

56. The fact that the export price was below the total return for domestic sales led the exporter to argue that an antidumping investigation rather than a countervailing duty proceeding was the appropriate remedy. The argument was rejected, however, presumably because at the time it was not necessary to show injury in order to impose a countervailing duty, while injury was then, as it is now, a requirement under the antidumping law. In its quest for quotas, the U.S. diary lobby studiously avoided any avenue that required an injury finding.

kets, which reduced the level of exports. The program was thus a positive *disincentive* to export. Elimination of the program would have led to reduced home market sales and increased exports to the United States.

Notwithstanding the fact that the program benefited U.S. producers, it was countervailed by the Treasury Department, which then administered the law.[57] Treasury reasoned that exports were being subsidized, since the entire subsidy was paid to Norway's single national dairy cooperative, and all of the co-op's farmer members shared in its proceeds, including those farmers whose milk was used to produce exported cheese. "Pooling" it was called. This "single-entity" notion does not, of course, change the fact that the program positively discouraged exports and that the cooperative received more funds to distribute to its farmer members from domestic sales than from exports. The reasoning simply was erroneous—if not perverse.

It should be noted that this decision was made by Treasury, not by Commerce, and that Commerce might well reach a different result were the issue to arise today. But it would be hazardous to be too sure: after all, responsibility for enforcement of the countervailing duty law was transferred from Treasury to Commerce largely because Treasury was perceived as being too lax in its enforcement of the law.

Nonmarket Economies and Economies in Transition

The need to introduce policy-level reviews before the imposition of countervailing duties is perhaps most apparent when viewed in the context of the current economic turmoil in Eastern Europe. Under the DOC's regulations, fair trade actions against nonmarket economies (NMEs) cannot be initiated under the CVD provisions of the law. Rather, such actions must be taken under the antidumping provisions of the laws. The department has determined, correctly, that "bounties or grants, within the meaning of section 303 of the Tariff Act of 1930 . . . cannot be found in nonmarket economies."[58] In particular, although subsidies cause mea-

---

57. The Department of Treasury's responsibilities for enforcement of both the antidumping and the countervailing duty laws were transferred to the Department of Commerce by Reorg. Plan No. 3 of 1979, 44 Fed. Reg. 69173 (1979) (codified as a note at 19 U.S.C.A. sec. 2171).

58. *Carbon Steel Wire Rod from Czechoslovakia; Final Negative Countervailing Duty Determination*, 49 Fed. Reg. 19370 (1984); and *Carbon Steel Wire Rod from Poland; Final Negative Countervailing Duty Determination*, 49 Fed. Reg. 19374 (1984).

surable distortions in market economies, in NMEs subsidies are part of the central planning process. Since market mechanisms are not the operational forces in an NME economy, the effect of subsidies are not measurable, and the concept of subsidy-related distortions is meaningless.

> In NMEs, resources are not allocated by a market. With varying degrees of control, allocation is achieved by central planning. Without a market, it is obviously meaningless to look for a misallocation of resources caused by subsidies. There is no market process to distort to subvert. Resources may appear to be misallocated in an NME when compared to the standard of a market economy, but the resource misallocation results from central planning, not subsidies.[59]

Although the DOC has been correct in its application of the CVD law to NMEs, the problem of transition from nonmarket to market economy is not addressed anywhere in the department's current regulations. This is not surprising, given the unexpected events of 1989. Even if transition rules were included, however, it is not readily apparent that a single government agency should be able to initiate, on its own, actions that severely restrict or cut off access to the U.S. market for NMEs in transition. A formal role is needed for other government agencies.

As if to illustrate this point, U.S. Customs, apparently on its own, decided in 1990 that "any existing dumping cases against companies in what is now known as East Germany will apply to the entire country," and vice versa for West German dumping cases. Thus, East German production not originally covered by AD bonding requirements will now be covered under the AD "all other" rate for West German cases. The same applies to West German producers with respect to East German AD duties. This decision was made even though, in some AD cases involving East Germany, West German producers had actually been chosen as the benchmark for price comparisons. In addition, quotas for East German goods were wiped out, with the West German quota levels being applied to the whole country. This set of decisions promises years of senseless and expensive litigation.[60] Coupled with the absence of any role for policy-related deliberations in the application of the CVD law, Commerce practice raises the specter of CVD bonding requirements being

59. 49 Fed. Reg. 19371 and 19375 (1984).

60. "Status of Goods from Territories formerly known as East Germany," memorandum from assistant commissioner, Commercial Operations, September 28, 1990.

applied against imports from Eastern European firms, such that the department, perhaps inadvertently, sabotages foreign policy efforts aimed at otherwise encouraging a peaceful and successful transition to market-based policies. A likely target is Polish or Czech government funds used to ease the transition pains associated with the plant closures and massive restructuring that accompany the transition process.[61] A sensible alternative would be for the Commerce Department to state explicitly that, during the transition from centrally planned to market driven economies, it will take many years for the resources of Eastern European countries to be allocated "properly." Economies classified as being "in transition" would then fall under the department's current CVD regulations regarding NMEs.[62]

If the Department of Commerce does initiate CVD actions against NMEs in transition, it will encounter numerous problems beyond the scope of its present regulations. In effect, it will be unable to measure the subsidy rates in existing markets because of distortions left by the central planning process and additional distortions introduced as part of the transition from a centrally planned to a market economy. The department will also have difficulty establishing a basis for comparison because there will be no historical basis to determine issues such as equity- and creditworthiness. The CVD law obviously should not be applied in such circumstances, since any comparisons will be meaningless. Yet, as its application of the AD law to NMEs makes clear, the department has not hesitated in the past to apply meaningless measurements in unfair trade cases against NMEs.[63]

Administrative Biases

Technically, the volume of information required in the investigative process and the burden of proof can be viewed as being a procedural rather

61. In its final negative determination on *Carbon Steel Wire Rod from Czechoslovakia*, the Commerce Department stated that "the economy of a country is an NME whenever it operates on *principles of non-market cost or pricing structures* so that sales or offers for sale of merchandise in that country or to countries other than the United States do not reflect the market value of the merchandise" (emphasis added). Thus, the department may well decide that Eastern European countries that have adopted the *principles* of market forces, although they have not yet undergone the transition from an economy based on centralized planning to an economy driven by market forces, are in fact subject to the countervailing duty laws.

62. This type of rationale was used in a DOC antidumping memorandum, "Use of Chinese Home Market Prices in the Chloropicrin Case" (August 1983).

63. See, for example, N. David Palmeter "The Impact of the U.S. Anti-Dumping Law on China-U.S. Trade," *Journal of World Trade*, vol. 23, no. 4 (1989), pp. 5–14.

than a measurement issue and thus perhaps beyond the scope of this paper. However, because the end result of the investigative process can be the use of punitive best information available (BIA), in reality it is also one of the most important measurement issues. Although technically this is true for both AD and CVD investigations, the actual application of BIA is much more common in dumping investigations.

Best Information Available

The significance of BIA for CVD investigations relates to the incentive it applies to foreign governments and producers to tolerate an incredibly intrusive administrative process. Imagine, for example, a judicial process in which, once accused, the defendant has an 85- or 160-day deadline in which to prove innocence. This is what foreign producers and governments face in CVD investigations.

BIA is justified by the department (and Congress) as an incentive to obtain the cooperation of investigated parties, and in the abstract, it is difficult to quarrel with the need for this incentive. Certainly, effective sanctions are needed for those who would refuse to cooperate. But the refusal to cooperate is not the only problem. An inability to meet the often unrealistic, overburdening demands of the department is also a common problem. Unfortunately, there are no effective administrative restraints placed on the department regarding the demands that may be made on respondents, and the failure to provide any subset of the information demanded by the department, whether such information can be provided realistically or whether it is relevant to the investigation, can result in use of punitive BIA. [64]

Another administrative bias related to BIA pertains to the volume of information requested by the department and the manner in which such information is requested and evaluated. In unfair trade investigations, small foreign producers often find themselves faced with fifty-page questionnaires and are asked to provide detailed financial data in English. Responses are usually due within thirty to forty-five days. These responses are then followed by an audit of financial records by officials of a foreign government (that is, the United States). This practice is forced

64. It is not unheard of for the DOC to demand ten- to fifteen-year-old financial data in administrative reviews. Given that such data are often not available in sufficient detail, the DOC must then resort to the use of BIA. Closely related to this matter is the timeliness of DOC reviews. See, for example, the discussion of *Steel Wire Rope from Japan* in chapter 5 of this volume.

upon the department by unrealistic statutory requirements. However, the department then compounds these legislatively imposed burdens by shifting the burden of proof to the respondents, requiring them to prove that the allegations made against them are not true. Unlike every other aspect of U.S. law, decisions of guilt and innocence in unfair trade investigations are then made by the same party that performs the investigator or prosecutor function.[65]

If information requests truly are unreasonable, there is of course the option of appeals to the courts. While under appeal, however, dumping and countervailing duty bond requirements are in effect and an appeal may take years. Even a subsequent victory on administrative grounds may thus be hollow. These deposits are real barriers from the outset.[66] In effect, regardless of subsequent court rulings, an initial affirmative determination by the department has the same effect on domestic producers, importers, consumers, and exporters whether or not the order is overturned years later.

To put current U.S. practice into perspective, imagine a decision by the Thai government to resolve its recent dispute over cigarette imports from the United States with a CVD investigation. Following U.S. practice exactly, competing producers in Thailand would be required to provide only evidence reasonably available to them that suggests that the U.S. government (or state, county, or municipal governments) pays subsidies to tobacco producers. Such evidence could be collected from the U.S. and Thai popular press. There would be an incentive for the Thai producers to stretch the bounds of credibility, perhaps alleging subsidy rates and dumping margins of 100 percent or more. They might begin by alleging regional subsidies on the basis of the impact of federal taxes on producers in different states.[67]

Suppose that the Thai government, presented with a petition, initiates a CVD investigation. It would then deliver a forty- to fifty-page single-spaced typewritten questionnaire in the Thai language to the U.S. Embassy in Bangkok, demanding that relevant portions be answered by government officials in the U.S. Department of Agriculture and probably in the Treasury and Commerce departments as well. Other portions of the Thai-language questionnaire would be directed to tobacco farmers, cigarette manufacturers, and state and county governments. The ques-

---

65. Palmeter, "Torquemada and the Tariff Act.
66. See our discussion below of uncertainty. Also see chapter 7.
67. See note 27 and accompanying text.

tionnaire would of course be delivered to the U.S. Embassy on a Friday afternoon, so that there would actually be only twenty-eight days to prepare a response.[68] Only short extensions would be granted.

The burden of proof throughout the investigation would be on the U.S. government and producers to prove that the accusations are not true. All responses would be required in the Thai language. Copies of all laws and regulations would have to be translated into Thai by U.S. respondents, few of whom are likely to be fluent in the language. To verify this information, Thai government officials would demand meetings with the officials who prepared the responses. They would also demand to go through the financial records of state and local agricultural agencies and through the financial records of individual tobacco farmers. If the United States failed to cooperate at any stage, or if the tobacco farmers failed to cooperate, or, more important perhaps, if they could not cooperate adequately, the Thais would then be forced to use BIA, with the resulting imposition of prohibitive duties.

With a procedure like that available—all perfectly GATT-legal—it is a wonder that any government needs to resort to illegal means to protect its industries.

Random Tariffs, or Protection through Uncertainty

There is a tremendous amount of uncertainty surrounding the duty rates actually charged on subsidized and dumped imports. This uncertainty adds to the protectionist aspect of the process. The deposits paid by importers of dumped or subsidized imports are *estimates* only, much like an estimated tax, the final amount of which will not be determined until the year is over. When a product under a CVD or AD order is imported, the importer deposits cash in the amount of the estimated duty, the actual value of which may not be known for years. Thus, the DOC does not determine the actual CVD or AD duty until long after the goods

68. See, for example, "Countervailing Duty Questionnaire, Oil Country Tubular Goods from the Republic of Korea," inv. no. C-580-402, July 13, 1984. This consists of forty-four single-spaced typewritten pages. The cover letter of the same date, to the Commercial Attaché, Embassy of Korea, states: "We are requesting that the government of Korea, the Korean producers which export the subject merchandise to the United States, and trading countries which export or import the subject merchandise to the United States, provide complete answers to all questions . . . we further request that (10) copies of each response be forwarded to this office by August 13, 1984." The date of presentation of the questionnaire, July 13, was Friday the thirteenth, unlucky for the respondents because the first two days of the thirty were the following Saturday and Sunday.

are imported—not until the DOC completes a long and behind-schedule process called an "administrative review." Importing thus becomes something of a crapshoot. This uncertainty is one of the primary reasons that a petitioner will go through the efforts of an AD or CVD case when the result may be estimated duty rates of only 0.5 percent. This point has largely been missed by the political economy literature, which tends to emphasize instead the harassment value of a countervailing duty or dumping case.[69]

The uncertainty surrounding AD and CVD orders comes from several sources. In the review process, the DOC can, and has, gone after programs not covered in the original CVD order. In addition, in particular reviews it has changed the procedures used to estimate subsidy rates, including benchmark countries. For dumping orders, uncertainty is a function of both the length of time that reviews take and the threat of best information available. For AD reviews, the department requires a record of each sale in the review period, including information on sales costs, shipping costs, and the like. Backup documentation (such as invoices) must also be made available for verification. Because such reviews are often completed four to ten years after the actual entry of imports, companies are required to supply information in detail that even the IRS would consider unreasonable in an audit. The result is BIA.

The uncertainty surrounding deposit rates means that importing from affected countries creates an open-ended contingent liability for importers that will probably not be settled for years. Given that liability is incurred by the *importer*, under the current implementation of CVD laws importers must know information on national, regional, and local industrial programs in excruciating detail so that they can asses the risks of increases over deposit rates associated with their suppliers (an impossible task), or else they must make general assessments of risk on the basis of their limited knowledge of the department's behavior in related reviews (a difficult if not impossible task). In AD cases, importers would need to know their suppliers' prices to other customers, including, perhaps, the importers' competitors, as well as their suppliers' costs. Possessing the information needed to make such an informed judgment would, at a minimum, pique the interest of antitrust authorities. The end result is often that any dumping or countervailing duty, no matter how small, is prohibitive.

---

69. But see Bhagwati, *Protectionism*, p. 52; and N. David Palmeter, "The Capture of the Antidumping Law," *Yale Journal of International Law*, vol. 14 (1989), p. 182.

Summary, Conclusions, and Recommendations

Trade subsidies distort the outcome of international trade and hence may hinder the efficient global allocation of resources, reducing global income while providing an unfair competitive edge to subsidized producers. Even in the context of strategic policy, competitive subsidization schemes conjure up images of beggar-thy-neighbor trade policies. For these reasons, the basic provisions of the GATT can be suspended when a country believes its producers are injured by another country's subsidies to exporters. Yet not all subsidies reduce national income, and not all government action has a significant effect on producers in other countries.

If one believes the rhetoric justifying the CVD laws, the laws are meant to target pernicious and unfair practices that are serious enough to merit the suspension of the basic tenets of the GATT. As currently administered, however, the laws are routinely applied in cases that simply do not fit this description. The result is that the CVD laws, in their administration, have become a tool for protecting producers from all imports, fair and unfair alike. But the need for reform goes beyond the Commerce Department's administration of the laws, in some instances to the laws themselves. The following are the more obvious reforms that are needed.

1. *Change the law and the department's procedures so that they are limited in application to unfair trade practices.* The department routinely applies the CVD laws against practices that are also followed by the U.S. government. Since the U.S. government hardly considers itself to be unfair and pernicious, at the minimum the practices in which the United States engages (either at the federal, state, or municipal level) should not be countervailable. Beyond the obvious point of hypocrisy, such a reform is justified because it is in the long-term self-interest of the United States. It is only a matter of time before the administrative procedures used by the department are used by U.S. trading partners. Following its current path, the United States will have little ground for opposing such actions when the time comes. For example, under the department's current reasoning on regional subsidies, the U.S. Federal Tax Code alone justifies countervailing practically the whole U.S. economy.

2. *Change the department's procedures regarding domestic subsidies so that countervailing duties target the actual competitive benefits that unfair practices provide to exports.* By definition, all government action involves intervention into the market, whether to provide infrastructure and public education, implement social policies, equalize the distribution of income, collect revenues, or promote macroeconomic stability, economic devel-

opment, and growth. These are the basic functions of government. Certainly, they are not normally classified as unfair or pernicious. Yet the department routinely includes such actions in CVD investigations. In effect, almost any government action is fair game. The department then applies duties that can greatly exaggerate the actual trade implications of domestic government policies.

The purpose of having CVD laws (presumably) is to protect U.S. producers from the consequences of unfair trade practices, not to punish foreign producers because their governments pursue legitimate domestic policy goals with the same tools used by the U.S. government. The department should thus be concerned with the trade implications of government actions, rather than with the actions themselves. To this end, the department should implement a methodology for domestic subsidies that quantifies the trade implications of domestic subsidies. This approach is feasible. The fundamental principles are presented in this chapter and in chapter 5.

3. *Modify the general availability requirements for the specificity test.* De jure general availability should be enough, absent an affirmative showing of bad faith, to prove general availability. Therefore, section 1312 of the 1988 Act (19 USCA section 1677(5)(B)) should be repealed, and Cabot cases and their progeny should be rejected.

4. *Raise the de minimis standards, and apply them on a program-by-program basis.* Currently, the department perpetuates the myth of accounting precision by applying a ridiculous de minimis standard of 0.5 percent. This standard is applied after all the net benefits attributed to various programs have been summed. Yet the department's procedures are subject to errors of assumption and measurement that apply on a program-by-program basis. In *Canadian Pork*, for example, the department found a total net benefit of Can$ 0.079657 per kilogram.[70] This was rounded up to Can$ 0.080000, a difference of "only" Can$ 0.000343. Yet this rounding error was greater than the benefits from ten of the eighteen individual programs that the department countervailed. These programs were by and large domestic programs that had no discernible effect on trade performance. For some programs, the department found net benefits ranging from one ten-thousandth of a Canadian cent to sixty-six ten-thousandths of a Canadian cent per kilogram. All were included in the final duty rate.

Introducing a program-level de minimis standard would reduce the

70. 54 Fed. Reg. 30774 (1989).

administrative costs associated with future administrative reviews; reduce the future costs faced by the department, petitioners, and respondents; and cause little or no discernible change in effective duty rates.

5. *Apply a 5 percent de minimis standard for domestic subsidies.* Domestic subsidy programs do not have the same effect on export performance as export subsidies at identical rates. In addition, domestic subsidy programs can be used as legitimate policy tools and are recognized explicitly as such in the GATT Subsidies Code. Even if the department continues with its current cash-flow approach to the determination of subsidy rates, a higher de minimis standard for domestic subsidies would be a simple way to recognize the distinction between export and domestic subsidies that is drawn in the GATT Subsidies Code.

6. *Eliminate the uncertainty surrounding AD and CVD bonds, perhaps by applying the results of administrative reviews to future entries, not past entries.* The risks created by the current bonding and review process compound the duties collected by the Department of Commerce. These uncertainties are not trivial, and in themselves may mean that a 1 percent CVD bond rate represents a prohibitive import barrier. Yet such uncertainty is not needed to counter the effects of unfair trade practices, although it certainly provides additional protection from imports. It could be eliminated, either (a) by fixing the duty rate at that determined in the final determination made by the department, as the European Community does, with the results of future reviews then being applied against future entries, or (b) by setting fair value target prices, as Canada does.

7. *Change department practice regarding offsets.* The department should offset the costs of locating in disadvantaged areas when dealing with regional subsidies. It should also consider secondary tax effects. Drawbacks for materials consumed in the production of goods for export and reasonable standardized rates, established for bona fide administrative reasons, should be accepted.

8. *Introduce a policy-level review before the application of unfair trade duties.* Nowhere in the investigative process at the department and the subsequent injury determination at the International Trade Commission are the implications of unfair trade actions for downstream producers and consumers considered. Nor is any weight given to the antitrust implications of unfair trade actions. The foreign policy costs of such actions are ignored as well. Under current U.S. law, if future AD or CVD actions run counter to broader U.S. interests (such as actions against NMEs in transition), the duties are applied anyway.

In theory, the AD and CVD laws target unfair trade practices and hence are focused on the consequences of such unfair practices for competing U.S. producers. Competition with fair imports is supposed to be covered under section 201, which gives weight to the broader consequences of protection. Yet in many ways the AD and CVD laws have replaced section 201, providing an administrative mechanism for protection from the effects of fair as well as unfair competition. Thus, the process needs a formal mechanism for weighing affected U.S. interests beyond those represented by petitioners.[71]

Appendix

This appendix presents a formal analysis of the distinction between export and domestic subsidies. This framework is then used to compare CVD rates calculated as simple ad valorem rates with those that are actually needed to counter the competitive benefit that domestic subsidies provide for export performance. We specify the domestic market with constant elasticity supply and demand curves:

(4-1) $$Q_s = (k_s P_d^{e_s})(1 + s_d)^{e_s}$$

(4-2) $$Q_d = k_d P_d^{e_d}.$$

In equations 4-1 and 4-2, Q_s and Q_d refer to the supply of the domestic industry and to domestic demand, P_d is the domestic market price, s_d is a domestic ad valorem subsidy, expressed as a production subsidy, and e_s and e_d are the domestic supply and demand elasticities.[72]

We represent the export market by the equations

71. Note that President Bush's recent initiative to give GSP status to Andean products was effectively defeated before it began because of a combination of VRAs, MFA restrictions, and AD duties on all the products that really mattered to the Andean countries (apart from coca). As an example, despite the broader interest the United States has in encouraging legitimate, alternative exports from cocaine-producing countries, the department and the ITC did not weigh such factors in the application of dumping duties against flowers from Colombia.

72. Note that upstream (input) subsidies can be incorporated by calculating the ad valorem production subsidy equivalent of the upstream subsidy.

(4-3)
$$X_s = Q_s - Q_d$$

$$= k_s P_d^{e_s} (1 + s_d)^{e_s} - k_d P_d^{e_d}$$

(4-4)
$$X_d = (k_{xd} P_d^{e_{xd}}) (1 + s_x)^{-e_{xd}},$$

where X_s represents export supply (which is identical to excess supply in the domestic market) and X_d is export demand. Since export markets clear when domestic markets clear, we focus our analysis on the export market. Note that, as specified, we solve for equilibrium in export markets by solving for the domestic price (because we have specified the effect of an export subsidy as a perceived shift in export demand). To solve for the actual shift in export prices, we introduce the additional equation

(4-5)
$$P_x = P_d/(1 + s_x).$$

Equation 4-5 measures the wedge driven between domestic and export prices by an export subsidy. In the case of domestic subsidies, this wedge collapses, and $P_d = P_x$.

Consider the effect of a domestic subsidy. We assume that $s_x = 0$. Thus, setting 4-3 = 4-4 and taking derivatives, we have

$$e_s k_s P_d^{e_s - 1} (1 + s_d)^{e_s} dP_d + e_s k_s P_d^{e_s} (1 + s_d)^{e_s - 1} ds_d$$

$$- e_d k_d P_d^{e_d - 1} dP_d = e_{xd}(k_{xd} P_d^{e_{xd} - 1}) dP_d.$$

Rearranging, and substituting dP_x for dP_d and P_x for P_d per equation 4-5, we have

$$\partial P_x/\partial s_d = -[e_s k_s P_x^{e_s} (1 + s_d)^{e_s - 1}]$$

$$/[e_s k_s P_x^{e_s - 1} (1 + s_d)^{e_s} - e_d k_d P_x^{e_d - 1} - e_{xd}(k_{xd} P_x^{e_{xd} - 1}) dP_x].$$

From an initial free-market equilibrium (that is, $s_d = 0$), we thus have

(4-6) $$\partial P_x/\partial s_d|_{s_d, s_x = 0} = e_s Q_s/[(dX_d/dP_x) - (dX_s/dP_x)].$$

Next consider an export subsidy. We first use equation 4-5 to replace P_d in equation 4-3 with

(4-7)
$$P_d = (1 + s_x)P_x.$$

Next we assume $s_d = 0$. Setting 4-3 = 4-4 and taking derivatives, we now have

$$e_s k_s P_x^{e_s-1} (1 + s_x)^{e_s} dP_x - e_d k_d P_x^{e_d-1} (1 + s_x)^{e_d} dP_x$$

$$+ e_s(k_s P_x^{e_s})(1 + s_x)^{e_s-1} ds_x - e_d(k_d P_x^{e_d})(1 + s_x)^{e_d-1} ds_x$$

$$= e_{xd}(k_{xd} P_x^{e_{xd}-1}) dP_x.$$

Rearranging, we have

$$\partial P_x / \partial s_x = [e_d(k_d P_x^{e_d}) (1+s_x)^{e_d-1} - e_s(k_s P_x^{e_s}) (1 + s_x)^{e_d-1}]$$

$$/ [e_s k_s P_x^{e_s-1} (1 + s_x)^{e_s} - e_d k_d P_x^{e_d-1} (1 + s_x)^{e_d} - e_{xd}(k_{xd} P_x^{e_{xd}-1})].$$

From an initial free-market equilibrium (that is, $s_x = 0$), we thus have

(4-8) $\partial P_x / \partial s_x|_{s_d, s_x=0} = [e_s Q_s - e_d Q_d]/[(dX_d/dP_x) - (dX_s/dP_x)],$

where $P_x = P_d$ in a free-market equilibrium.

We examine the effects of export and domestic subsidies with reference to a free-market (that is, no subsidies) equilibrium. When starting from an initial free trade equilibrium, export and domestic prices are identical. The denominators of equations 4-7 and 4-8 are thus identical. This means we can calculate a linear approximation of the relative change in prices in the export market consequent to introducing an export or domestic subsidy as

(4-9) $$\phi = \frac{(e_s Q_s - e_d Q_d)}{e_s Q_s} \frac{s_x}{s_d}.$$

Thus, for an export subsidy to have an equivalent marginal effect on prices in the export market as a domestic subsidy, it must be true that $\phi = 1$, or identically that

$$[(e_s Q_s - e_d Q_d)/e_s Q_s] (s_x/s_d) - 1 = 0.$$

With further manipulation, it can be shown that this condition holds only if

(4-10) $$s_x^* = [1/(1 + \Theta)s_d],$$

where

$$\Theta = \frac{|(e_d)\,(Q_d)|}{(e_s)\,(Q_s)}.$$

In equation 4-10, the term s_x^* denotes the export equivalent of a domestic subsidy.

Comment

Gary Horlick

The substantive difference between antidumping and countervailing duties is an important point that is sometimes missed. Countervailing duty laws are based, at least in part, on a grain of truth, which is the distortion caused by subsidies. Antidumping laws, as has accurately been pointed out, are about 90 percent pure protection. Presumably, there are some cases of dumping that represent predation or other economic behavior not normally permitted. But the antidumping law requires no showing of a closed market, of predation or recoupment, of cross-subsidization.

Much of the rhetoric about countervailing duties follows the same lines as antidumping, and mistakenly. To impose a countervailing duty in the United States, you have to show that there was some foreign government action not directed at the entire economy. Obviously, that leaves room for dispute, but even so there is a legitimate basis for a countervailing duty law, and one that is not far off current U.S. practice.

As for the question of countervailing domestic subsidies, every government has a sovereign right to subsidize anything it wants to, but it doesn't have a sovereign right to sell that product in another country. This is a fairly clear example of what is called the effects test for extra-territorial jurisdiction, which is accepted international law. It is also really not an issue of morality. Obviously, whenever we get into political debates in the United States, we clothe everything in terms of morality because that is the way we do things. It drives other countries crazy. But the basic issue is whether some sort of countervailable distortion is going on that would not have occurred but for the government action. Again, a grain of truth exists there that is often missed.

The real question posed by Francois, Palmeter, and Anspacher, however, is, what are the *trade effects* of domestic subsidies? The trade effects of export subsidies can be traced out fairly well, and one reason that it was so easy to agree to get rid of the subsidies was that even ministers could not ignore—in fact, ministers could understand—their trade effects.

The trade effects of domestic subsidies are the missing link in U.S. countervailing practice. No one looks at the trade effects of domestic subsidies. The Department of Commerce does not, and its view—I think a correct one—is that it should not. The statute does not tell it to do so. Whether the ITC should be doing it is a question for the experts.

Whoever tackles the job will find it difficult because what you really want to do is to measure the shift of comparative advantage within the exporting country and within the importing country. Although there is enough economic talent around to come up with good proxies, it is too much to expect a consensus on one proxy or formula. Administrators, however, need something that is widely accepted, not one of ten competing theories. So, the search for the measurement of the trade effect of domestic subsidies should go on.

I also want to take issue with the claim that the Department of Commerce did not look at de facto *specificity* until the Cabot case. This is a canard, of course, and everyone repeats it. Commerce looked at de facto specificity from at least June of 1982 and, indeed, in the famous Carbon Black case that is exactly what it did in the administrative review.

The basic problem in the specificity test is Commerce's addition, somewhere in the mid-1980s, of a discretion test. That is to say, there could be a program that is de facto not specific—meaning it is widely used throughout the territory—yet Commerce finds the government intended it to be specific. In essence, Commerce has substituted government intent for a de facto test, and as long as it only uses this to *find* subsidies, rather than *not* to find them, this will doubtless meet with approbation in Congress. But Commerce has completely undercut its rationale for the de facto specificity test. The statute—passed in 1988—does not include a discretion test.

Also note that all judges and legislators, when confronted with the specificity test the first time, automatically reject it on the grounds that "you mean, if I give it to one company it is a subsidy, but if I then give it to everyone else, it is no longer a subsidy?" The economics profession obviously has a lot of educating to do.

Francois and his colleagues are correct on the question of *offsets*. The policy on offsets is wrong. It is also statutory. There is nothing Commerce can do about it. One could hardly have clearer statutory language or legislative history. Obviously, it makes no sense. Offsets should work both ways.

One problem, by way of background, is that the Department of Treasury, in its alleged desire to pander to foreigners, did claim that it should adjust for offsets that would be favorable to the exporter but not adjust for offsets that would not be. This one-sided approach did not endear it to the Finance Committee in 1979.

On regional subsidies, Commerce also does it wrong, and the problem here is not statutory. It turns out that the issue—the holding, if you will—in the legislation is about offsets. There is nothing saying that if one bit of a country is left out, the entire country becomes a region. This is of more than passing interest to any U.S. company that fears it might someday be subject to a countervailing duty case overseas. Although I doubt that Commerce would actually countervail the income tax situation that David Palmeter laid out in chapter 3, Commerce has stated, as its rule for determining whether something is regional "whether one region gets more money than another even with neutral criteria." Using that rule, virtually everything the U.S. government does leads some regions to get more money than others. Thus, irrigation water in California might be countervailable because they get it on different terms in the Central Valley than they do elsewhere.

A few other points should also be mentioned. First, secondary-tax effects are an intriguing idea but administratively difficult (note that the European Community is ignoring secondary-tax effects in administering their internal-subsidy rules, article 92). Second, the search for firm-specific information is like the search for perfect justice. Commerce, as Francois and his colleagues point out, uses national rather than firm-specific information for administrative convenience; and unless you want to be condemned to do all those investigations, you would do the same. Third, the failure to use foreign-accounting principles and foreign information in general is a little more serious. As a matter of principle—and, I would suspect, law—Commerce should not be using U.S. information to measure foreign subsidization, except as best information. This has usually come up in the question of over what period of time you should spread out subsidies.

One of the mysteries here is that Commerce keeps insisting that it is using U.S. information. The original choice of fifteen years for steel was not based on IRS information; it was the closest you could come to an acceptable median based on the practice in several other countries. (Brazil and Britain were using fifteen years.) But also note the equity problem. Suppose there are cases against five companies in five different countries, each of which got the identical amount of money from its government on the same conditions, and those five countries used depreciation periods of one year, three years, seven years, ten years, and fifteen years, respectively. You would get completely different countervailing duty rates in the same circumstances. That is not going to fly, and that is why Commerce's drive for something that would yield neutral results is understandable. But Commerce should not use U.S. data.

Fourth, Commerce has not dealt with upstream subsidies adequately. It uses the wrong data consistently. There is legislative history to show that what Commerce does is illegal. Commerce chooses to ignore it, and someday it will get to court or the GATT.

Finally, the authors raise the intriguing question, what if someone did this to the United States? Well, the fact is that no one does. Canada had the only countervailing duty case against the United States and didn't take it very seriously. Since Canada could find 65 percent subsidies from three price-support programs, it didn't have to look at all the little programs at which the United States would look.

The United States has been pushing hard for subsidy discipline, but it has been looking at domestic subsidies, not countervailing duties. These are prohibitions, limits to be backed up by multilateral decisionmaking. Canada, for example, presumably does not consider it rational to impose high countervailing duties on products going into Canada, which Canadians want to buy. That does not strike Canadians as sensible. Canada might feel much less constrained about going to a multilateral body to ask it to require the United States to raise the price of irrigation water in the Central Valley or the entire Tennessee Valley Authority. The United States, needless to say, might well do the same to Canada. This is what most economists would call a first-best solution, and most lawyers would also, since it promises to keep us quite busy.

Comment

Richard Diamond

There is much to applaud in the efforts of Francois, Palmeter, and Anspacher to formalize the relationship between market conditions and the effect of subsidies on U.S. producers. Some of the methods now widely in use for calculating countervailing duties were formulated without the benefit of modern economic analysis and were designed to cover only a narrow subset of the subsidies covered by today's laws.[1] Rigorous analysis, such as that performed by the authors, provides the tools necessary for improvement.

But is it appropriate to mix this kind of analysis with such terms as "unfair," "pernicious," and the "level playing field"? The use of these pejoratives suggests that the authors have failed to analyze the Department of Commerce's actions with the same rigor they apply in their own work and, specifically, that they have neglected to start with first principles in evaluating current countervailing duty rules. An understanding of this methodological difficulty is vital if we are to achieve meaningful reform of the U.S. countervailing duty system.

Francois and his colleagues refer to two conflicting systems for determining whether countervailing duties should be assessed. One is referred to as an "effects-based-model" or as a "competitive benefit approach" to countervailing duty law; the other, as a "benefits model" or a "cash-

---

1. For a review of this subject, see Richard Diamond, "A Search for Economic and Financial Principles in the Administration of United States Countervailing Duty Law," *Law and Policy in International Business*, vol. 21 (1990), pp. 507–607.

flow approach."[2] The discussion implies that two alternative models of countervailing duty law exist, that answers can be derived from each model, and that the question is which model to choose. On close inspection, however, one finds that the authors' egalitarian approach to these models is flawed and that the message conveyed is somewhat misleading.

To understand why, it is necessary to ask what an economic model is. In this context, such a model must have two parts. First, the model must have an object—that is, it must be possible to identify the object or relationship that is being modeled. Second, the model itself must consist of a set of logical statements that simulate or represent the object being modeled. The success of the model is judged in terms of the ability of the model's logical constructs to represent the object accurately.

In the light of this definition, let us examine the two models the authors refer to. The competitive effects or entitlement model identifies its object: protection of the competitive position that U.S. producers would have occupied had the foreign subsidy not existed.[3] Economic theory is then

---

2. The names given to various systems for assessing countervailing duties have not been standardized and thus can be confusing. The authors' term "effects-based model" refers to a system that determines countervailability on the basis of the competitive effect of the subsidy on U.S. producers. This model has also been referred to as an "entitlement model" since, as formally developed, it conceptualizes the purpose of countervailing duty law as an entitlement of U.S. producers to be free from the effects of foreign subsidies. See Charles J. Goetz, Lloyd Granet, and Warren F. Schwartz, "The Meaning of 'Subsidy' and 'Injury' in the Countervailing Duty Law," *International Review of Law and Economics*, vol. 6 (June 1986), pp. 17–32; and Richard Diamond, "Economic Foundations of Countervailing Duty Law," *Virginia Journal of International Law*, vol. 29 (Summer 1989), pp. 767–812. The authors also use the term "competitive benefit approach," or "competitive effects approach," when speaking of this system.

The rules employed by Commerce do not evaluate the competitive benefit that the subsidy provides to foreign producers or the subsidy's competitive effect on U.S. producers. Rather, in general, Commerce attempts to neutralize the additional cash flow that a subsidy provides to a foreign producer. For this reason, Commerce's approach is sometimes referred to as a "cash-flow approach." In its terminology, Commerce sometimes uses the phrase "countervailable benefit." See *Countervailing Duties, Notice of Proposed Rulemaking and Request for Public Comments*, 54 Fed. Reg. secs. 355.42, 355.44, 355.48 (1989) (hereafter *Rulemaking*). The meaning of the term "benefit" is never defined by Commerce and sometimes, but not always, refers to an increase in cash flow resulting from the subsidy. It is in this sense, as distinguished from the term "competitive benefit approach," that the authors refer to Commerce as having a "benefits model."

3. This objective is consistent with the Supreme Court's analysis of the purpose of U.S. countervailing duty law, as noted in *Zenith Radio Corp.* v. *United States*, 437 U.S. 443, 455–56 (1978). For a more detailed discussion of the entitlement of U.S. producers that may be protected by countervailing duties, see Diamond, "Economic Foundations," pp. 778–82.

used to model the relationship between U.S. and foreign producers and the effect that subsidies have on that relationship. From this model, applicable rules may be derived for determining when countervailing duties should or should not be assessed to achieve the objective of the model. For example, economic theory indicates that a countervailing duty is never required unless a subsidy lowers the marginal cost of a foreign firm, since unless the recipient's marginal cost is lowered, it will not change its behavior in a manner that will endanger the entitlement of U.S. producers. If marginal cost is lowered by the subsidy, the amount of duty, if any, that is needed to protect the entitlement of U.S. producers will depend on certain characteristics of the firm's marginal cost function and the various market conditions that the firm faces.[4]

In contrast, Commerce's benefits or cash flow approach does not satisfy the definition of a model. Although the DOC has issued proposed rules and numerous rulings, it has never coherently defined the object of its model or what countervailing duty law is intended to achieve. Indeed, the DOC's proposed rules, issued in 1989, indicate only that the department defines a subsidy as "a distortion of the market process for allocating an economy's resources."[5] This definition suggests that the purpose of countervailing duty law is to preserve economic efficiency. However, such a belief cannot be squared with the rules DOC proposes. Its methodology ignores information that is needed to determine whether a subsidy is efficient. Moreover, some countries may provide efficient subsidies that are detrimental to U.S. producers. There is no indication that Congress intended such subsidies to be exempt from U.S. countervailing duties. In summary, the choice is not between two models, as the authors would suggest, but between a model with derived coordinated rules, designed to achieve a stated objective, and an incoherent assemblage of directives without a stated purpose.

It is important to understand how Commerce's failure to state a purpose for countervailing duty law affects the nature of the legal and academic debate over specific countervailing duty rules. Here, a metaphor is helpful. Think of a small forest with numerous trails. The trails branch right and left, and the traveler must decide which branch to take. All groups enter from the south. Into this forest comes one group, representing those who espouse the entitlement model of countervailing duty law. Just as they have specified the goal they wish countervailing duty

---

4. Diamond, "Economic Foundations," pp. 786–806.
5. "Rulemaking," p. 23367.

law to achieve, so here they know the destination they wish to reach. Let us say that they wish to get to the western edge of the forest. Since they have identified their destination, this group can formulate rules governing which trail branches to take. One rule to get to the west is to take whichever branch goes toward the sunset. A second rule is to take branches going away from the sunrise. Judges and academicians observing this group can evaluate its rules in terms of the group's goal. Moreover, since the rules are all designed to achieve the same goal or purpose, they can be reviewed for internal consistency. Thus, the conditions necessary to evaluate the rules and to ensure that administrative actions are not the product of individual predilection are present.

Suppose that the DOC enters the same forest. It comes to a fork in the trail. It needs to formulate rules about which branch to take. What does it do? It does not identify a desired destination. Rather, it notes that a senator in the appropriate committee had spoken favorably of rain.[6] Therefore, a rule is promulgated to take whichever fork of the trail goes toward rain.

Consider now the task facing those who are attempting to analyze the DOC's action. Can they determine whether the "rain rule" is good or bad? The answer is that they cannot. In our metaphor, Commerce has never specified the destination it wishes to reach, and without knowing the destination, there is no basis for evaluating the rule. Similarly, in the case of countervailing duty law, without a purpose, without a defined objective, there can be no basis for evaluating substantive or procedural rules.

The debate surrounding countervailing duty law has always had an ethereal quality. Intricate arguments are made in regard to many factual and theoretical details; however, the arguments seem to stand on their own, without any relationship to basic propositions. The story of Commerce's "rain rule" explains this phenomenon. Given such a rule, the largest Washington law firms would assign associates to write detailed memoranda on crucial weather questions. Debate would rage over how the DOC should determine the difference between rain and drizzle, or

6. See, for example, the following discussions of Commerce's attempt to establish how countervailing duties should vary with time and of the agency's reliance on Senator Heinz's comments: Alan F. Holmer, Susan A. Haggerty, and William D. Hunter, "Identifying and Measuring Subsidies under the Countervailing Duty Law: An Attempt at Synthesis," in *The Commerce Department Speaks on Import Administration and Export Administration, 1984*, Corporate Law and Practice Course Handbook Series 455 (Practicising Law Institute, 1984), vol. 1, pp. 301–460; and Diamond, "Search for Economic and Financial Principles," pp. 579–86.

when it could assume rain solely from the kind of cloud cover. A heated international dialogue would ensue over whether Commerce could choose to ignore the weather reports of foreign governments (we all know they are biased) and accept only reports taken according to U.S. government procedures. Finally, after years of litigation, Commerce would argue to the Court of International Trade that courts have no expertise in weather and should defer to the agency on all questions regarding the "rain rule."

Excuse the metaphor, but it makes the point. It is all too easy to get caught up in the minutiae of individual countervailing duty rules and miss the most important fact. To reform the U.S. countervailing duty system, policymakers must first formulate a coherent purpose that the system will serve and then derive rules stating when duties must and must not be charged to achieve that purpose. No amount of detailed argumentation can provide a basis for evaluation if the basic purpose of the system is not specified.

Francois, Palmeter, and Anspacher have a coherent view of the purpose of countervailing duty law. Though they never explicitly state it, they seem to adopt the foundations of the entitlement model. In analyzing Commerce's actions, however, they do not always begin with the tenets of this model. In at least one area—their claim that, although Commerce correctly counters the effects of export subsidies, it is "biased" against domestic subsidies and reacts with too great a duty—this failure has led them to an erroneous conclusion.

As noted above, the basic premise of the entitlement model is that countervailing duty law is intended to protect U.S. producers from the effects of foreign subsidies. It follows that it is necessary to impose a countervailing duty only when a subsidy lowers the marginal cost of the foreign recipient and leads the recipient to increase production. Moreover, it is only necessary to charge a duty in the amount required to ensure that the foreign recipient's sales in the United States will not exceed what they would have been had the subsidy not been provided.[7] Given this foundation, the relationship between subsidy and duty that the authors explore may be analyzed as a composite of two effects that particular types of subsidies have on marginal cost. First, there is one case in which a duty will totally neutralize the effect of a subsidy on the foreign producer.[8] When the duty charged exactly equals a per unit or ad valorem

7. See Diamond, "Economic Foundations," pp. 791–98. Under certain market conditions, it may not be necessary to charge a duty to protect the entitlement even when the recipient's marginal cost curve is lowered.

8. Diamond, "Economic Foundations," pp. 798–99.

subsidy and the subsidy is provided only on goods exported to the United States, the effect of the duty will be to remove all of the subsidy that the foreign firm has received. The firm will therefore perceive no change in its marginal cost, and the status quo ante will be preserved.

The second effect is illustrated in the authors' description of the Norwegian dairy cases. Under most market conditions, if a good is subsidized when sold in some markets but is not subsidized when sold in other markets, the result will be an increase in the subsidy recipient's marginal cost of production (that is, in the marginal cost, not counting the effect of the subsidy) and an increase in the price of the good in all markets in which its sale is not subsidized. For this reason, when a foreign government subsidizes sales made either in the foreign country's domestic market or in non-U.S. export markets, but does not subsidize sales made in the United States, the subsidy will work to the detriment of U.S. consumers and in favor of U.S. producers.

It follows that if a foreign subsidy applies *both* to goods shipped to the United States *and* to goods sold elsewhere—either in the foreign firm's home market or in export markets other than the United States—a U.S. duty equal to the amount of the subsidy will be higher than is needed to neutralize its effect on U.S. producers. Such a duty will reflect the drop in marginal cost that arises from the subsidization of goods shipped to the United States (the effect that hurts U.S. producers), but it will not reflect the increase in marginal cost that results when subsidized goods are shipped elsewhere (the effect that helps U.S. producers).

According to the authors, U.S. duties closely counter the effects of export subsidies, whereas duties in regard to domestic subsidies are too high. They continue: "Countervailing duties for export subsidies are . . . closer to an effects-based model, whereas duties for domestic subsidies conform more to a punishment-based or 'benefits' model." In light of the above analysis, these conclusions must be amended. First, the authors are correct in saying that Commerce will charge duties that exactly neutralize the competitive effect of the subsidy in some cases and duties that are higher than required to countervail such effects in others. However, the dividing line is not between export subsidies and domestic subsidies, as they propose. Rather, Commerce's duty will be correct merely on a small subset of export subsidies, those that are provided only on goods shipped to the United States. In regard to all other subsidies, including domestic subsidies and export subsidies applying to markets other than the United States, Commerce's duty will be unnecessarily high.[9]

Of greater importance, the authors suggest that Commerce's approach to export subsidies differs from its approach to domestic subsidies and that these two approaches correspond to the competitive effects model and the cash-flow model. First, as explained above, Commerce's approach cannot be termed a model at all. Second, Commerce's calculations of the countervailing duties that must be assessed on export and domestic subsidies proceed from the same premise. Subject to the specificity test, the market standard, and apportionment, the duty should neutralize the increase in cash flow arising from the government's action.[10] Finally, although the duties that Commerce assesses in regard to ad valorem export subsidies limited to U.S. sales will coincide with those required to protect the entitlement of U.S. producers, Commerce's actions are not based on, nor intended to correspond to, a competitive-effects model. Suggestions that some underlying rationale is responsible for the resemblance between Commerce's duties and the correct duties in this small subset of cases merely diverts attention from the fact that the basic methodology Commerce currently uses to evaluate *all* subsidies is severely flawed.

The authors also criticize many individual Commerce Department rules, and, in most cases, it is easy to agree. However, the analysis may be clarified by differentiating between three types of problems that may call for very different types of solutions.

The first type of problem, as already discussed, arises from the fact that administrators have failed to define the purpose of countervailing duty law and to formulate an economic model which achieves that purpose. Questions regarding the formula by which duties should be calculated for export and domestic subsidies fall into this category.

A second type of problem involves portions of the U.S. countervailing duty statute that are inconsistent with the purpose Congress has specified. The offset rules contained in the definition of net subsidy present an example.[11] The authors quote section 1677(6), which limits offsets to

---

9. In a small subset of cases involving foreign firms with market power producing at a point at which marginal cost is declining, Commerce's duties will be too low to counteract the competitive benefit arising from the subsidy. See Diamond, "Economic Foundations," p. 796.

10. See Holmer, Haggerty, and Hunter, "Identifying and Measuring Subsidies," pp. 314–16, 322–25, 328–67.

11. 19 U.S.C. sec. 1677(6)(1982 & Supp. 1989).

three specific types. However, they do not read the statute as precluding Commerce from taking other offsets into account and, consequently, attribute Commerce's failure to do so to the way it "has chosen to read the statute."

It is difficult to square the authors' interpretation of the statutory provision and consequent criticism of Commerce with the applicable legislative history. The Senate report accompanying the 1979 Trade Act stated that the three offsets were "narrowly drawn and . . . all inclusive."[12] The House report stated: "For purposes of determining the net subsidy amount, the Authority may subtract from the gross subsidy only items described in subparagraphs (A), (B), and (C) of subsection (6)."[13] In this case, it appears that Commerce has not reasoned incorrectly. Rather, it has correctly read an explicit legislative directive that is inconsistent with the general purpose of the statute.

The question then becomes how the administrators of the statute can accommodate a section that is inconsistent with the theory and purpose that seemed to guide Congress in passing the statute. Two approaches suggest themselves. First, the administrators can treat the statute as attempting to achieve two inconsistent but equal objectives. While this may have been the intention of the statute's drafters or the result of their inability to agree among themselves, it creates great difficulties.[14] Any attempt to model the purpose of the statute and derive specific rules of application will be defeated by the inherent conflicts. Unless criteria can be found to indicate when each of the two objectives should take precedence, administrators will have no basis for deciding how to act nor will judges be able to assess their actions. As a result, duties will be applied when, and to the extent that, the administrators feel they are needed.

Alternatively, the inconsistent statutory provision may be treated as an exception to an otherwise coherent statutory scheme. For example, research may show that the inconsistent provision was a reaction to a specific peripheral concern. Although the language of the provision and comments in the applicable legislative history may not support the broad purpose of the statute, administrators may conclude that the theories

12. *Trade Agreements Act of 1979*, S. Rept. 249, 96 Cong. 1 sess. (GPO, 1979).
13. *Trade Agreements Act of 1979*, H. Rept. 317, 96 Cong. 1 sess. (GPO, 1979).
14. For an interesting discussion of the origins and consequences of inconsistent legislation, see Ronald A. Cass, "Trade Subsidy Law: Can a Foolish Inconsistency Be Good Enough for Government Work?" *Law and Policy in International Business*, vol. 21 (1990), p. 609.

supporting the provision were not intended as a general reformulation of the purpose underlying all other sections of the statute. In such a case, a coherent model of the statutory purpose may be created and rules derived. However, specific exceptions to this consistent structure will be required to accommodate the inconsistent provision.

The offset rules of section 1677(6) may well fit such a category. They were developed at a time when the administrator, the Treasury Department, was accused of failing to enforce the countervailing duty law. Specifically, Treasury seemed intent on accommodating foreign claims that the benefit of subsidies should be offset by disabilities that the recipient firms assumed. In one often-cited decision, criticized by the U.S. Court of Customs and Patent Appeals in *ASG Industries, Inc.* v. *United States*,[15] Treasury accepted as evidence the unverified oral statement of an official of the German government. Given this background, the offset rules contained in the 1979 Trade Act may be seen as an attempt to deal with specific problems regarding control of the agency rather than as an indication that Congress wished to redesign the purpose of the entire countervailing duty system.

A third category of problems raised by the authors pertains to the use of surrogates or other imperfect sources of information, often justified by claims of "administrative convenience." By way of example, the authors discuss the relative merits of using IRS depreciation tables or firm-specific U.S. or foreign accounting information. Given staffing problems and the time limits that must apply for countervailing duty cases to be effective, it is difficult to quarrel with the use of such imperfect sources. The question raised is, what limits must be placed on agency decisions to accept or reject particular surrogates in individual cases or in formulating rules?

One minimal standard governing the use of surrogates is suggested by the Subsidies Code of the GATT and section 1671(a).[16] The former refers to duties that are "calculated"; the latter, to duties "equal to the amount of the net subsidy." Both statements imply that the level of the duties imposed must be the result of a rational calculation, grounded in fact,

15. 610 F.2d 770, 778(Ct. Cust. & Pat. App. 1979). The court characterized as "totally inadequate" the agency's statement: "The German Government has advised the Treasury Department that these benefits [that is, the benefits of the alleged subsidy] have the effect of offsetting disadvantages which would discourage industry from moving to and expanding in less prosperous regions."

16. Subsidies Code of the GATT, article 4:2 (in note 15, the code also states: "An understanding among signatories should be developed setting out the criteria for the calculation of the amount of the subsidy."); and 19 U.S.C. sec. 1671(a)(1982 & Supp. 1989).

and must not be set as an arbitrary fine. At a minimum, this would require that the Commerce Department demonstrate the rational relationship between the surrogate employed and the data for which it is substituting.

The authors seem to suggest that questions concerning surrogates are technical, involving mainly the relative veracity of the information. On the contrary, it is impossible to analyze surrogates without addressing fundamental questions about U.S. countervailing duty law. In the example above, the authors question whether, in "allocating the benefits" from grants, Commerce should use the depreciable life of machinery reflected in the 1977 IRS table, that reflected under the recipient firm's generally accepted accounting principles, that which would have been reflected under U.S. GAAP, or an arbitrary ten-year period.[17] The depreciation periods provided under the standards above may correspond to the physical life of the machine or they may reflect social policies, such as a wish to promote capital investment. The proposed ten-year period evidences Commerce's conclusion that, although it is dealing with the economic effect of subsidies on competing producers, "no economic or financial rules . . . mandate the choice of an allocation period."[18] To decide between these alternatives, it is necessary to determine what information is needed. To determine what information is needed, it is first necessary to state the purpose of countervailing duty law, how duties must be calculated to achieve that purpose, and what information is needed to make those calculations.

Commerce's grant methodology, of which the allocation question is a part, allows duties to be assessed even when the program has no effect whatsoever on U.S. producers and cannot be reconciled with any acceptable purpose of countervailing duty law. Given this system, none of the choices mentioned is rationally related to a proper statutory purpose. Under the entitlement model, it is necessary under most market conditions to charge a countervailing duty for the period during which, as a

17. Note here the application of the "rain rule." The authors argue that the IRS tables are no longer used in the United States, that Commerce's decision reflects an aversion to relying on data drawn directly from the financial records of foreign companies, and that the International Trade Administration does rely on foreign accounting records in antidumping proceedings as long as application of home market accounting principles does not significantly distort the firm's financial position. As discussed below, crucial questions concerning the relationship between the information sought and the purpose of countervailing duty law are lost.

18. *Rulemaking*, p. 23376. Commerce goes on to justify the arbitrary period it has chosen on the grounds of fairness and administrative convenience.

result of the subsidized purchase of a new machine, the marginal cost of the recipient firm is lowered. This formulation suggests that Commerce should examine the IRS tables and U.S. and foreign accounting methodologies to determine which most accurately reflects the effect of the new machine on the foreign firm's marginal cost. Of course, other sources of information may also be available. Questions of access to information and verifiability must also be considered.

In the end, my disagreement with Francois and his colleagues relates more to how they have stated and justified their conclusions than to the conclusions themselves. Their criticism of the Department of Commerce's procedures is certainly warranted. And their rigorous treatment of the relationship between market conditions and duties certainly carries us one step closer to rationality.

CHAPTER FIVE

The Economic Implications of the Administration of the U.S. Unfair Trade Laws

Richard Boltuck, Joseph F. Francois, and Seth Kaplan

THE UNITED STATES has entrusted two agencies with administering its trade laws pertaining to dumping and countervailable subsidies. The International Trade Administration (ITA) at the Department of Commerce is charged with determining the existence and level of the unfair practice, and the U.S. International Trade Commission (ITC) determines whether a domestic industry producing a "like product" is injured by the subject imports. If determinations at both agencies are in the affirmative, duties are imposed on the imports under investigation.

Economists tend to view the administration of these laws as a "technical" process and to forget that it is strongly influenced by political forces in Congress and the executive branch (both directly through the president and indirectly through the Office of the U.S. Trade Representative).[1] Recent research suggests that unfair trade administration is subject to politicization on two distinct fronts. First, determinations at the ITC are often in the affirmative when the complaining industry is located in the state of a senator belonging to the Senate Finance Committee.[2] The Finance Committee oversees the ITC budget and, more important, plays a major role in the confirmation of political appointments in agencies and departments with trade-related portfolios.

Second, biases enter through the statutory interpretations of the ad-

---

1. J. M. Finger, H. Keith Hall, and Douglas R. Nelson, "The Political Economy of Administered Protection," *American Economic Review*, vol. 72 (June 1982), pp. 452–66.

2. Michael O. Moore, "Rules or Politics? An Empirical Analysis of ITC Antidumping Decisions," working paper, George Washington University, Washington, January 1990.

ministrative agencies.[3] It is well known that the reviewing courts generally defer to trade administrators on issues of interpretation. This discretion allows for radically different approaches to the same statutory imperative and thus for systematic and pervasive biases. That has been the case in determinations of both the ITC and the ITA.

The biases present in the Commerce Department's method of measuring dumping margins and countervailable subsidy rates are the subject of this chapter. We examine the economic framework of the procedures used by the ITA in constructing dumping margins, the method of calculating countervailing duty rates, and the costs of increased uncertainty created by the review procedures for dumping and subsidy rates

Statistical Biases in Dumping Margin Calculations

The institution of duties following a dumping investigation is meant to offset the harm suffered by a domestic industry as a result of an unfair act. Foreign firms are found to be "price" dumping when they lower the price of an import below its ex-factory price in the home market. Dumping is also found when insufficient home sales are above cost and the price of the import is below the price of the product in a third market. If more than 90 percent of these sales are also below cost and an adequate third market cannot be identified to serve as the price reference market, the department then looks for "cost" dumping. Cost dumping occurs when sales have been below an estimate of the average total of production, called "constructed value."[4] The dumping law thus targets two practices: international price discrimination and export sales below the average total

3. Richard Boltuck, "Creative Statistics: Biases in the Commerce Department's Calculation of Dumping Margins," paper prepared for the Western Economics Association Conference, Vancouver, July 10, 1987; and Seth Kaplan, "Injury and Causation in USITC Antidumping Determinations: Five Recent Approaches," in P. K. M. Tharakan, ed., *Policy Implications of Antidumping Measures* (North Holland, 1991), pp. 143–73.

4. Note that the other major set of laws concerned with price discrimination, the antitrust laws, focuses on sales below average *variable* cost, rather than average total cost. The implication of the department's approach is that if U.S. trading partners followed the same set of criteria as Commerce, U.S. firms would have to recover R&D, product development, and fixed overhead costs as they are incurred or else be subjected to AD duties. There would be no allowance for forward pricing or pricing over the business cycle. This practice would make it difficult for the United States to export products that require a number of years to recover product development costs (such as pharmaceuticals). In fact, current U.S. practice in applying these laws is being studied as possible models by such countries as Mexico and Turkey.

cost of production. Under both these definitions, dumping lowers the price of the import in the U.S. market below the price that would have prevailed in the absence of dumping. The fall in the price of the import causes a decrease in demand for the U.S.-produced "like" product, which is a consumer substitute for the dumped import. The decline in demand, in turn, injures the domestic industry by reducing profitability, sales, employment, and other indicators relative to a market equilibrium with no dumping.[5]

Once the fair value of the good in the exporters home market is determined, the Department of Commerce must identify individual sales to the United States to compare prices.[6] However, the product produced for home consumption often differs from the product produced for export. Comparison becomes difficult when sets of product options that are available in the home market are not available in the export market. The difficulty is compounded when the differences are nonphysical. Unfortunately, the usual procedure for identifying similar merchandise is to compare physical characteristics. Hedonic comparisons using physical and nonphysical characteristics (such as delivery time and service) are seldom attempted. Adjustments are usually based on the cost of production and not on the market valuations of the product differences.

For several well-known reasons, the ITA's calculation of dumping margins are statistically biased measures of the true extent to which exportable products destined for sale in the United States sell for less than the same product destined for sale in the exporter's home market. These biases extend beyond those associated with the comparability of product types. The most important of these is the department's continued practice of comparing average prices in one market to individual prices in another. This practice is not required by law; rather, it represents a deliberate decision by the department to continue using a method that is known to be biased, as discussed in chapter 4. A stylized model of the ITA's statistical methodology for calculating dumping margins can be then used to demonstrate the magnitude of the biases implied by a variety of export

5. See Richard Boltuck, "Assessing the Effects on the Domestic Industry of Price Dumping," in P. K. M. Tharakan, ed., *Policy Implications of Antidumping Measures* (North-Holland, 1991), pp. 99–141.

6. Commerce has, on rare occasions, acceded to the blandishments of respondents who urged an alternative methodology, namely a comparison of each particular export sale to a temporally coincident home market sale. In the great majority of cases, Commerce rejects this proposal because the data do not provide consistently comparable coincident sales in the two markets. Commerce ordinarily requires sales to occur on the same day before they will be considered coincident.

industry production and global demand conditions. Statutory and other nonstatistical sources of bias are not included in the following analysis.

General Procedures

In principle, the dumping margin is the proportional difference between fair value (based on either home market prices, third country prices, or constructed value) and the U.S. sale price of the same merchandise. All prices are evaluated at the factory gate. After the product leaves the factory for various national markets, it incurs differential costs of marketing, transportation, insurance, taxes, and duties such that subsequent price comparisons would be invalid.

The basic definition of a dumping margin may be written algebraically as

$$(5\text{-}1) \qquad DM = (FV - P_{exp})/P_{exp},$$

where DM is the dumping margin, FV is fair value, and P_{exp} is the U.S. sale price of the exportable. Since both home market prices and U.S. export prices typically vary within the ITA's six-month investigation period, DM is a statistic of the price sets.

On the surface, this definition suggests little cause for alarm. If the fair value is the average home market price and the U.S. export price is the average of ex-factory prices for U.S. export, the expected margin would appear to be zero whenever the two sets of prices were identically distributed. This notion of the absence of dumping is adopted here.

The ITA, however, is guided by different lights. Even when both sets of prices are selected from identical distributions, the margin calculated by the ITA's method will not be zero. Commerce does not compare population means. Rather, it calculates fair value first and then generates a vector of dumping margins based on the price of each U.S. export transaction. Negative margins are set to zero, and the elements of the vector are averaged. Naturally, it introduces a bias by counting only positive margins. Moreover, as explained below, fair value is an upwardly biased measure of home market prices whenever it is based on home market prices, and thus the true margin is overstated even further. When fair value is based on true production costs, it would be slightly downward biased if we removed the biases associated with assumptions such as profit margins and the exporter's sales price (ESP) cap. However, the assumptions Commerce makes in calculating constructed value tend to bias its estimate above the true production cost.

Price Comparison Margins

The ITA ordinarily regards home market prices that fall short of production cost as not being "in the ordinary course of trade." (It attempts to calculate the minimum total average cost of production; no distinction is made between fixed and variable costs.) Under GATT rules, such prices may be disregarded in finding price-based fair value. When the ITA determines that sufficient home market transactions have occurred at prices above the production cost, it averages these prices and sets fair value.

Clearly, the ITA engages a tortured concept of market pathology when it contends that undistorted, competitive markets will clear only at or above the total average production cost. Any market subject to demand uncertainty will be characterized by prices that are sometimes less than the minimum average cost and sometimes above it. Indeed, competitive market equilibrium in an industry comprising risk-neutral firms requires the *expected economic profits* to be zero, but flow profits at any particular moment may be either positive or negative. By excluding prices below cost, the ITA biases fair value upward and consequently the dumping margin on which it depends.

Cost Comparison Margins

If the ITA finds an insufficient proportion of home prices above production cost and cannot identify a suitable third-country reference market, it will set the fair value equal to the constructed value. If the department believes that third-country sales are below cost as well, it will again rely on constructed value. If calculated correctly, this measure would slightly understate the true fair market value. However, this effect on the measure of fair market value does not offset the bias associated with zeroing out negative margins.

The constructed value itself introduces biases, above those associated with zeroing-out negative margins. The additional biases introduced by cost dumping are twofold: first, the use of constructed value rather than price comparisons inflates dumping margins; second, the conventions used in constructing cost are often biased upward. The use of constructed value applies a veneer of legitimacy to dumping calculations by relying on verifiable accounting data either directly from the foreign firms under investigation or from suitably chosen proxies. Closer examination, however, reveals that the conventions and proxies used in the calculations do not reflect the economic costs associated with production.

These additional biases include arbitrary assumptions about profit margins, overhead, and the ESP cap. With constructed value, the department assumes a minimum of 10 percent of production costs for overhead and 8 percent for profit. Under the ESP cap, overhead deductions charged to home market prices are capped by overhead charges for U.S. subsidiaries. In cases in which the home market overhead is higher than in the United States, this practice generates artificial margins.[7] For trading companies and others with low overhead, the 10 percent minimum also biases cost estimates.

Bias Assessment Model

To assess the determinants of the magnitude of overstatement inherent in the ITA's methodology of applying individual U.S. sales to an average measure of fair market value, while zeroing out negative margins, consider an export industry in competitive equilibrium that is subject to stochastic global demand for its product. We assume that at each instant during the ITA's investigation it charges the same price in all markets and hence does not dump.[8] Realized prices over the period are triangularly distributed with respect to time, as illustrated in figure 5-1.[9] Also superimposed on the figure is the industry's profit function, which exhibits the usual convexity conditions.[10] Because firms expect high or low prices to regress

---

7. See N. David Palmeter, "The Capture of the Antidumping Law," *Yale Journal of International Law*, vol. 14 (1989), pp. 182–89.

8. For a somewhat different treatment of stochastically distributed pricing and dumping, see M. P. Leidy and B. M. Hoeckman, "Production Effects of Price- and Cost-Based Antidumping Laws under Flexible Exchange Rates," *Canadian Journal of Economics*, vol. 23 (November 1990), pp. 873–95.

9. Note that the standard deviation of the temporal price distribution, σ, equals $B/\sqrt{6}$. Approximately 97 percent of the frequency is within $\pm 2\sigma$.

10. Specifically, the profit function is exponential, taking the form, $\pi = \exp(\epsilon_s P) - A$, where P is the product price, and $1 - A$ is the vertical intercept. Note that minimum average cost (MAC), where $\pi = 0$, occurs when $P = \ln(A)/\epsilon_s$. Note also that MAC exceeds the temporal average price. By using Hotelling's theorem, it may be verified that ϵ_s is the short-run (no entry or exit) supply elasticity (or equivalently, the elasticity of marginal cost), assuming fixed factor costs, evaluated at the normalized average price of 1.

Figure 5-1. *Profits and the Distribution of Price*

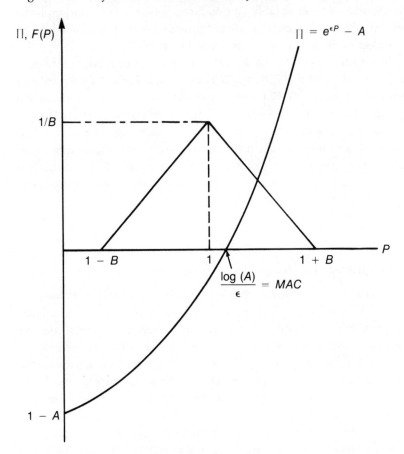

to the normalized mean of one, each firm earns an expected profit of zero, and there are no incentives for entry or exit.

When the ITA bases fair value on home market prices, it discards prices below the minimum average cost. Furthermore, it weights observed prices by the quantity transacted, and since output—and presumably sales in each market—increase at higher prices, the higher the price, the greater the quantity weight. Price-based fair value, therefore, may be found by calculating

(5-2) $$FV_P = E(V|P > MAC) / E(Q|P > MAC),$$

where the numerator is the average value of transactions occurring at prices greater than the minimum average cost (*MAC*), and the denomi-

Table 5-1. *Statistical Biases in the International Trade Administration's Reported Dumping Margin*
Percent

Standard deviation	Supply elasticity	0.1	0.6	1.0	5.0	10.0
0.01	DM_P	0.9	0.9	0.9	0.9	0.9
	DM_C	0.4	0.4	0.4	0.4	0.4
0.05	DM_P	4.8	4.8	4.8	4.8	4.6
	DM_C	2.1	2.1	2.1	2.2	2.2
0.10	DM_P	9.8	9.7	9.7	9.3	8.1
	DM_C	4.5	4.5	4.5	4.6	4.5
0.25	DM_P	25.9	25.4	24.7	17.2	9.8
	DM_C	12.8	12.8	12.7	10.9	7.9

nator is the average quantity of such transactions. (We are assuming that the Department of Commerce accurately calculated the average cost of production.) The ratio is the average quantity-weighted price.

The average *positive* dumping margin is based on U.S. export prices (distributed identically as home market prices, by assumption) that fall below fair value. Consequently,

$$(5\text{-}3) \quad DM(+)_P = [FV_P - E(V|P < FV_P)/E(Q|P < FV_P)] /$$
$$[E(V|P < FV_P)/E(Q|P < FV_P)].$$

The actual dumping margin, calculated as a percentage of total sales, includes a similar calculation for sales made *above* fair value (that is, negative margins). The average dumping margin reported by Commerce, however, counts such negative margins, whenever they occur, as if they were zero. Formally, this margin is calculated as

$$(5\text{-}4) \quad DM_P = Pr(P < FV_P) \times DM(+)_P + Pr(P > FV_P) \times 0,$$

where Pr (.) connotes a probability. Cost-based margins follow a similar procedure, only in this event $FV_C = MAC$. Equations 5-3 and 5-4 apply with the appropriate substitution.

Table 5-1 presents dumping margins based on equation 5-4 and the various combinations of underlying temporal price dispersion (σ) and short-run supply elasticity (ϵ_s).[11] The values presented in table 5-1 represent the margins that the department would calculate when a company was charging the same price in both markets. Since by construction no true dumping is occurring, the reported margins are thus a direct measure of bias in the ITA's methodology. A firm that charges the same price in all its markets will be found to be dumping at a margin roughly equal to the normalized standard deviation of price in the price-dumping cases, and roughly equal to half the standard deviation in cost-dumping cases. Even when firms charge the same price in both markets, the department will still find dumping. In layman's terms, if a company charges the same price in U.S. and other markets and its prices normally vary within 10 percent of the average price charged, the department will calculate a dumping margin of 10 percent.

In effect, the department punishes firms for failing to price-discriminate. The only way to avoid dumping duties under the department's usual procedures is to charge substantially more in the United States than in other markets. If firms charge the same price in the United States as in other markets, they are at risk of being subject to dumping duties.

Countervailing Duties

The statutory intent of a countervailing duty differs from that of a dumping bond. Rather than being calculated to offset the *injury to the domestic industry* owing to the unfair act, the countervailing duty is calculated to offset the *benefit to the foreign firm*.[12] This is a significant distinction because the department does not calculate countervailing duties on the basis of the competitive benefit that subsidies give to exports; rather, it relies on a strict accounting definition of benefit. With the exception of a per unit export subsidy, a duty calculated to offset the benefit to the

11. Since the temporally average price has been normalized to 1, σ is the coefficient of variation.

12. For an explanation of the legal foundations of this distinction, see Ronald A. Cass, "Trade Subsidy Law: Can a Foolish Inconsistency Be Good Enough for Government Work?" *Law and Policy in International Business*, vol. 21 (Fall 1990), pp. 609–61. In the case of export subsidies, the accounting measure of benefit and the economic measure of competitive benefit coincide. Significant differences emerge with domestic subsidies, such as regional development programs and upstream subsidies. Thus, the department's current calculation of the benefit of a subsidy cannot be said to generally approximate the competitive edge that subsidies give to producers in their export markets. Rather, in the case of domestic subsidies, the department sets a CVD rate that usually exceeds this competitive benefit.

foreign firm thus differs significantly from a duty calculated to offset injury to the domestic industry. Given the wide variety of subsidy schemes—input, output, regional development, relocation, research and development, and so on—the divergence between the injury or competitive benefit approach and the accounting-based approach to defining benefits has strong real-world implications. Although the dumping bond is calculated to return the domestic economy to a pre-dumping state, the countervailing duty often creates further distortions in the domestic market.

The General Agreement on Tariffs and Trade (GATT) is (perhaps deliberately) vague in its strictures on countervailing duty (CVD) rates. A broad range of duties is allowed, extending from zero to the per unit value of a subsidy. The rate actually needed to offset the injury caused by subsidies falls somewhere within this range. For export bounties, the maximum rate allowed (the per unit rate) is the same as that needed to offset injury. For domestic production and upstream subsidies, however, this rate will be less than the allowed maximum and in some cases will be closer to the lower end of this duty spectrum. Although the GATT urges countries to choose the duty from this range that is needed to counter the effects of foreign subsidies on producers in exporting countries, the department in its implementation of U.S. law follows the easy road, always setting the CVD rate at the allowed maximum. As a result, the department's subsidies are in effect duties that distort U.S. markets in that they protect import-competing U.S. industries from fair competition as well as unfair competition and add yet another tilt to the playing field of international competition.

The department has failed to recognize some of the distinctions between export bounties and domestic subsidy programs in part because of historical inertia. The precursor to the current set of CVD laws, the Tariff Act of 1897, was targeted specifically at export bounties and related export incentives.[13] Under the 1897 laws, the secretary of the treasury was directed to impose on dutiable imports an additional duty equal to the amount of the export bounty. In this context, the application of a strict accounting approach makes complete sense and coincides with the duty needed to offset the competitive benefit of export subsidies. Problems do

13. See Jacob Viner, *Dumping: A Problem in International Trade* (A. M. Kelley, 1966; University of Chicago Press, 1923). Viner noted that "it will be possible for any Secretary of the Treasury with protectionist leanings to make of the countervailing provision an instrument for the establishment of a substantial measure of additional protection applying to a wide range of commodities coming from many countries" (p. 177).

not emerge until we attempt to apply the same set of rules to domestic subsidy programs.

The types of subsidies currently countervailed by the Commerce Department can be grouped into three main classes: export subsidies, domestic production subsidies, and domestic upstream subsidies. Export subsidies are contingent on export performance; domestic production subsidies go directly to a firm but are not contingent on export performance; and upstream subsidies are not subsidies in the sense of money or other benefits conferred directly on a producer but represent the secondary effects of a government program that is actually directed at upstream producers.[14]

The primary reason the department draws a distinction between domestic and export subsidies has nothing to do with the completely different mechanisms by which these two classes of subsidies affect export performance. Rather, the reasoning is grounded in the accounting approach taken by the department. The determination of the export or domestic subsidy simply establishes the denominator over which the nominal value of a subsidy is to be placed. That is because the department's objective is simply to determine the ad valorem equivalent of a nominal subsidy amount, where this amount measures only the nominal value of total cash flow, in an accounting sense, that can be labeled as a subsidy. For domestic subsidies, the value of the subsidy is allocated across the value of total sales, whereas an export subsidy is spread out only across export sales.

The accounting measure of the nominal benefit does not take into account the effects of subsidization on actual production levels, nor does it recognize that a given per unit subsidy might have a different effect on export performance, depending on whether it is an export or domestic subsidy. This method also ignores most economic distinctions between types of subsidies. Thus, although a subsidy that directly affects labor costs (such as a payroll tax rebate) has a different effect on production than an outright cash gift, both are treated identically. In the case of domestic subsidies, no consideration is given to the role of domestic market demand and supply conditions, or to the relationship between these factors and material injury. Yet it is this accounting measure of

14. Such subsidies can involve actual government expenses (see *Steel Wheels from Brazil*, 54 Fed. Reg. 15527 [1989]), or government trade policies such as export bans or export taxes on raw materials used by downstream industries (see *Leather from Argentina*, 55 Fed. Reg. 40212 [1990]).

subsidy rates, calculated without regard for any of these effects, that is supplied to the ITC for use in determining injury.

Notwithstanding the department's decision to adopt an accounting rather than an economic definition of subsidy, its methodologies have procedural problems that still introduce biases, even from a naive accounting perspective. For example, it uses average short-term interest rates that ignore company-specific risk premiums or discounts (such that all low-risk companies are potentially countervailable), follows arbitrary rules about duty drawbacks and offsets, and makes arbitrary determinations about the useful life of capital equipment. Because the department relies on average data rather than firm-specific data, justified by references to administrability and feasibility, subsidy findings are based simply on the fact that firm characteristics (such as risk discount factors) vary from national and industry averages (see chapter 4).

Although many biases are conceptual or methodological, some of the most significant ones are administrative. They arise in part from uncertainties generated by the department surrounding actual duty rates. Simply placing imports under bond, even at 0.5 percent, can cut off access to the U.S. market. In addition, the lack of administrative restraint mechanisms, combined with the fact that the burden of proof is placed on the accused (that is, the exporters), means that legal, accounting, and economic fees can be tremendous, even for frivolous cases.[15] These costs themselves are a significant trade barrier.

The Implications of Accounting-Based Measurement

The Department of Commerce shows a distinct preference for accounting approaches to subsidy rate calculation, as illustrated in the case of dumping margins. Accounting methods promise greater replicability and are arguably less subject to the suspicion of subjective or judgmental, case-by-case, administrative bias than are economic methods. Accounting generally values paper trails and rules of thumb at the expense of customized judgment and detailed, impartial scientific inquiry. Thus, accounting methods are used for tax assessment and financial disclosure statements where self-interest would otherwise hopelessly contaminate the exercise of impartial scientific judgment.

15. Note that the current policy debate about allowing successful petitioners to recover legal fees is completely asymmetric. No one has publicly suggested that successful respondents should be able to recover such fees as well, although they tend to be several times higher than those faced by petitioners.

Clearly, the image of objectivity and consistency conferred by accounting techniques in the application of mechanical methodology has many desirable and appealing properties. This has helped shield Commerce from its critics. After all, how can the department be biased if it is consistent and predictable in its methods? To those critics who allege that Commerce is controlled by protectionist domestic interests, the department simply argues that it lets the chips fall where they may and lacks discretion to do otherwise.[16] Thus, it cannot nudge outcomes in politically desirable directions. Nonetheless, accounting methods that are arcane and ad hoc may indeed be responsible for biased results, as has been shown in the case of dumping. The methods themselves—not the application—contain the seeds of bias.

In countervailing duty investigations, accounting procedures inevitably rely on rules of thumb that embody economic assumptions. Although these assumptions will not precisely reflect the economic reality of individual cases, they can nonetheless prove to be a useful and powerful compromise between administrability and formal, case-by-case economic analysis. However, such rules of thumb must then be based on assumptions that are realistic and explicitly recognized. When such assumptions are unrealistic, unreasonable, or simply not made explicit, the techniques may be consistently applied to cases where they are inappropriate at best or biased and unfair at worst.

The department introduces biases by restricting the selection of methodologies to accounting procedures that ignore supply and demand factors and then extending every benefit of the doubt to domestic petitions in selecting its methods. Thus, the department allocates subsidies to the less-than-fair-value (LTFV) product rather than to other products manufactured by the same firm. The department calculates a countervailing duty rate for domestic subsidies as if all subsidized sales were exported. For processed agricultural products, the department is required by law to simply assume full passthrough of upstream subsidies. In the case of offsets, the department excludes almost all adjustments to subsidies that would reduce the estimate of net benefit. In short, biased accounting methods may create the appearance of fairness and a rules-based procedure and yet be answering the wrong questions.

Regardless of whether the department continues to rely on a strict

---

16. In fact, the Department of Commerce does have discretion over the amount of information it demands and over its flexibility with administrative deadlines. Such factors are critical in determinations that end in BIA.

accounting approach to measuring subsidies, it could still benefit from giving more weight to the economic context of the facts in an investigation, such as domestic demand elasticities, domestic consumption, industry cost structure, and the competitive nature of upstream markets. Such an application of economic methods, perhaps through additional rules of thumb and a checklist approach to the applicability of the assumptions they embody, would help the department focus its efforts more efficiently on activities that are truly unfair and injurious.[17]

An Alternative Approach to Setting Countervailing Duties

In this subsection we develop rules of thumb that formally incorporate measures of supply and demand conditions. These rules are applicable in a broad set of circumstances. Their limitations, which apply both to the methods presented here and those currently followed by the department, are discussed under the heading of market structure. The methods presented here explicitly recognize the distinctions between upstream, production, and export subsidies. As such, they serve as a useful point of reference for examining the distortions under the department's current methods. Because Commerce focuses on strict accounting procedures that are frequently inappropriate, the duties it applies tend to be protectionist, transferring income from U.S. downstream producers and consumers to the protected industries in amounts in excess of that needed to offset injury.

An obvious criticism of the methods presented here is that they rely on parameter estimates that cannot be measured with certainty. Yet one could argue that the department already makes implicit assumptions about these parameters every time it follows its present approach. At the least, by giving no consideration to these factors, the ITA introduces additional distortions into the U.S. market that were not included in the department's legislative mandate. In contrast, the ITC regularly relies on informed subjective analysis of similar parameters in a variety of circumstances, ranging from injury determinations to trade policy analysis. Such esti-

---

17. Although not as precise as accounting data, economic data and analysis in legal contexts need not be egregiously unobjective. In fact, economic modeling has already infiltrated other areas of administrative law, overcoming initial resistance and settling more or less comfortably among the various tools of analysis. Objectivity in the use of economics at Commerce would be enhanced by open proceedings and the sharp exposure of data and reasoning to peer examination, disinfectants that kill the pestilence of political bias. Consider the Justice Department's *Merger Guidelines* or the CADIC model at the ITA's sister agency, the International Trade Commission.

mates are routinely obtained through structured questionnaires and checklists that allow government industry experts that may have little or no background in formal economic theory to organize and present information in a manner that allows informed judgment of likely parameter ranges.

Consider a foreign market characterized by competitive upstream and downstream markets. Downstream producers are assumed to produce both for domestic consumption and for export. If we introduce a subsidy, its effect on export performance (and hence its translation into material injury in export markets) will depend on the type of subsidy introduced. For example, a per unit subsidy on the production of an upstream product will not necessarily translate into an identical reduction in input prices for the downstream producers. Thus, it will not usually be identical to an identical per unit subsidy provided directly for the downstream producer. Similarly, a production subsidy paid directly to the downstream industry will not have the same effect on exports as an identical per unit export subsidy. That is because a domestic subsidy will increase domestic consumption in a way that absorbs a share of any increase in production. In contrast, an export subsidy shifts downstream sales directly from domestic to export markets.

Suppose that a per unit subsidy at rate s is introduced either as an upstream or input subsidy, a production subsidy, or an export subsidy.[18] We define the export equivalent of such a subsidy as the export subsidy needed to have the same effect on export prices (and hence on producers in export markets) as a given upstream or domestic production subsidy. By definition, competing U.S. producers and consumers would be indifferent between a foreign domestic subsidy at rate s and an export subsidy set at the export-equivalent rate. Hence, the export equivalent of an export subsidy is, by definition, equal to the actual subsidy rate. This export-equivalent subsidy measures the duty needed to countervail the effects of a given per unit subsidy in export markets. If we assume a per unit subsidy rate of s, then the export-equivalent SX of this rate will be as follows:

$$\textit{Export subsidy:}$$

(5-5)
$$SX = s$$

---

18. An upstream or input subsidy and a production subsidy can be treated identically by specifying a production subsidy as an input subsidy provided at an identical rate to all inputs.

Domestic production subsidy:

(5-6) $$SX = s\{1/[1 + (|e_d Q_d|/e_s Q_s)]\}$$

Domestic upstream subsidy:

(5-7) $$SX = s\{1/[1 + (|e_d Q_d|/e_s Q_s)]\} \{\alpha\beta[e_{su}/(e_{su} - e_{du})]\}.$$

These equations are derived formally in the appendix to this chapter, and are based in part on the results of the appendix to chapter 4. They are based on a model that includes home market and export sales to the United States. When a product is exported to third-country markets as well, equation 5-5 needs to be replaced by a modified version of 5-6. The parameters e_d and e_s denote the home market demand elasticity and the downstream supply industry, respectively; e_{du} and e_{su} are upstream supply and demand elasticities; Q_d and Q_s are downstream home market demand and total downstream production; α is the cost share of the upstream input in total downstream production costs; and β is the downstream output elasticity of the subsidized upstream product.

The additional information required to apply these equations can be obtained directly or estimated in a manner similar to that followed by the ITC (that is, with the aid of worksheets and checklists). The department currently estimates only s, which is the strict accounting measure of the subsidy rate.

The Department of Commerce tries to measure the change in input prices $\hat{w}$ consequent to an upstream subsidy directly by comparing observed input prices with a constructed benchmark price. This approach, although more difficult to implement than the comparative statics simulation of the subsidy in the upstream market that underlies equation 5-7, is conceptually legitimate. The benchmark method appears to require less information because it does not depend on knowledge of the upstream demand and supply elasticities. In fact, this approach is more information-intensive because, if it is to be implemented properly, the department has to account for the contribution of all nonsubsidy factors to the difference between the observed input price and the benchmark price. If the department could properly control for all factors other than the subsidy, it could then use the following modified version of equation 5-7:

(5-8) $$SX = \{1/[1 + (|e_d Q_d|/e_s Q_s)]\}\beta\alpha\hat{w}.$$

The alternative methods embodied in equations 5-6, 5-7, and 5-8 can realistically be implemented if adequate evidence is collected in the investigation. Any effort to evaluate the export-subsidy equivalent would no doubt generate controversy about the value of market-behavior parameters embedded in these equations, the appropriate adjustment period (which would determine the use of short-run or long-run parameter estimates), and the sensitivity analysis used to reflect the degree of uncertainty attached to each parameter. Experience at the ITC with the CADIC model suggests the exercise is feasible with commitment, organization, persistence, effort, and qualified staff.

The parameters in equations 5-6 and 5-7, and 5-8 indicate what factors need to be considered in applying a countervailing duty that seeks to target the competitive benefits of unfair trade practices without introducing protection against fair trade practices as well. These factors include the relative importance of home market consumption and the price sensitivity of supply and demand in upstream and downstream markets. The output elasticity β highlights the relationship of input subsidies to production technologies (a factor not explicitly recognized by the department at present) and emphasizes the fact that subsidies may target traditional technologies or inferior inputs. For example, subsidies for the use of hand looms would have a different effect on production than a subsidy on the use of modern weaving machines.

The Role of Market Structure

Market structure (that is, the competitive nature of markets, the effect of trade restrictions on competitive behavior, and the like) is an important determinant of the competitive effects of foreign subsidies on competing U.S. producers. Market structure is also at the heart of the motivation for dumping and the economic implications of dumping for importing countries.[19] Nevertheless, the department generally ignores the role of market structure when evaluating the competitive benefit conferred by subsidies and thus merely exacerbates the problems inherent in its accounting approach to measuring benefits.[20]

There is a vast literature on trade and market structure, and it would

19. Recognition of the importance of market structure in accounting for dumping dates back at least to Gottfried Haberler, *The Theory of International Trade with Its Application to Commercial Policy* (London: William Dodge, 1936).

20. As an example, see the discussion of the treatment of upstream subsidies by the department in chapter 3. We recognize that under a noncompetitive market structure the methods discussed in the previous section on CVD determination would have to be modified.

be impossible to address all the implications of various market structures for the application of the unfair trade laws. We therefore focus on a single issue, the passthrough of upstream subsidies to downstream producers. This example is particularly relevant, since the department's positive subsidy determination for Canadian Pork was recently rejected by a GATT panel because the department failed to address this very issue.[21] This example demonstrates how important it is for the department to evaluate subsidies in an economic context.

The Department of Commerce relies on a combination of price comparisons and ad hoc assumptions about passthrough when measuring the benefits of upstream subsidies (see chapter 4). In agricultural cases, for example, the department is now required to assume full passthrough of upstream subsidies to downstream consumers.[22] Thus, although the effect of an upstream subsidy on the price paid for an input by downstream producers depends on several factors, including the market power of the upstream producer, Commerce generally does not consider such factors. As a result, CVD rates will reflect actual benefits only on rare occasions, and otherwise will be biased upward.

Suppose that an upstream producer who prices as a monopolist receives a production subsidy. Consider the difference between calculated benefits that are based on actual passthrough and benefits that are based on the department's common assumption of full passthrough. When an upstream monopolist competes in a relatively large global industry, upstream subsidies generally have no effect on input prices for downstream producers, because competing suppliers limit the ability of the domestic producer to influence prices. As a result, upstream subsidies tend to yield either a shift from imported to domestic input supplies (when inputs are imported) or an increase in exports of the upstream product (when the upstream industry exports). In either case, there will be no significant effect on input prices for the downstream industry. To assume full passthrough is misguided at best in such circumstances.[23]

---

21. *Canadian Pork*, 54 Fed. Reg. 30774 (1989). At the time this chapter was written, the United States had successfully blocked the panel report. The final outcome may become clear after the Uruguay Round concludes.

22. 54 Fed. Reg. 23383 (1989), sec. 355.45(g). The department was explicitly required by Congress to assume full passthrough on agricultural cases. See *Omnibus Trade and Competitiveness Act of 1988*, House Conference Report, 100 Cong. 2 sess. (GPO, 1988), sec. 1313.

23. In general, the factors that would affect the ability of upstream producers to influence prices include the substitutability of the domestic and rest-of-world inputs, the price elasticity of demand for the input, and the relative size of the domestic and global industries.

Figure 5-2. *The Effect of Upstream Subsidies on Input Price with Perfectly Elastic Input Demand*

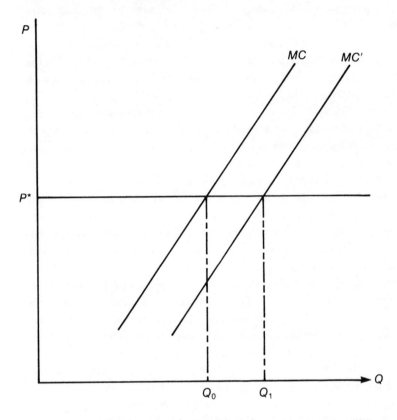

This proposition is demonstrated geometrically in figure 5-2, where world supply fixes prices at P^*, which represents both the demand curve and the marginal revenue curve for the upstream producer. The curve MC represents the industry marginal cost curve. Both an industry monopolist and a competitive market equilibrium will yield equilibrium supply at point Q_0. When we introduce an upstream subsidy, the MC curve shifts to MC', with an increase in upstream output from Q_0 to Q_1. If there is no change in input prices, however, the only effect on downstream markets is a shift from imported to domestic inputs, without any change in input prices.

Because passthrough depends on global market conditions, the effect of upstream subsidies on downstream producers depends both on the tradability of the input and on the ability of the subsidized upstream

Table 5-2. *The Input Subsidy Equivalent of a 1 Percent Upstream Subsidy under Upstream Monopoly*[a]

e_{du}	e_{su}							
	0.00	0.25	0.50	0.75	1.00	2.00	5.00	∞
0.25	0.00	0.50	0.67	0.75	0.80	0.89	0.95	1.00
0.50	0.00	0.33	0.50	0.60	0.67	0.80	0.91	1.00
0.75	0.00	0.25	0.40	0.50	0.57	0.73	0.87	1.00
1.00	0.00	0.20	0.33	0.43	0.50	0.67	0.83	1.00
2.00	0.00	0.11	0.20	0.27	0.33	0.50	0.71	1.00
5.00	0.00	0.05	0.09	0.13	0.17	0.29	0.50	1.00
∞	0.00	0.00	0.00	0.00	0.00	0.00	0.00	. . .

a. e_{su} equals $(1/(\epsilon_i - 1))$, where ϵ_i is the output elasticity of total cost. If the upstream industry were competitive, this would be the supply elasticity. e_{du} represents the total price elasticity of demand for inputs by downstream producers, or the sum of the elasticities of individual consumers weighted by quantity.

producer to influence prices. With tradability, even if prices did fall in upstream markets, such a fall would benefit both domestic *and* foreign downstream producers. Thus, for an upstream subsidy to provide a *competitive* benefit to home market downstream producers, such that the home market producer is incrementally better off than producers in export markets, the domestic input market must somehow be isolated, either by significant transport costs or by trade taxes.

Even when the upstream industry is isolated from global markets, if demand for the upstream product is highly elastic, there will be little or no passthrough to downstream consumers by a monopolist. (This is analogous to the case in which upstream prices are fixed in global markets.) In contrast, relatively inelastic demand for the upstream product will tend to result in higher passthrough. Between these two extremes, the passthrough of an upstream subsidy depends on the relative importance of the subsidized input in the total cost of downstream production for the various downstream users. This measure of cost share, as well as the relative importance of demand by the various downstream industries using the input, determines the price elasticity of demand for the subsidized upstream product (see the appendix for details).

Table 5-2 presents estimates of the input subsidy equivalent of a domestic upstream subsidy with an upstream monopolist. The table is based on an upstream subsidy that, in the case of full passthrough, would yield an input subsidy equivalent of 1.0 percent. Thus, in assuming full passthrough, the department would also calculate a subsidy of 1.0 percent. Actual input subsidy equivalents are presented as a function of the upstream elasticity of demand and the elasticity of the industry marginal cost curve.

Table 5-2 shows that with an upstream monopolist, full passthrough occurs only when the marginal costs curve is perfectly horizontal (that is, infinitely elastic) or when upstream demand is highly inelastic. In most circumstances, however, the actual passthrough is not complete and can be significantly less than full. For example, in the case of equally elastic demand and marginal cost curves, an assumption of full passthrough, such as is made in agricultural cases, yields an input subsidy equivalent that is twice as large as the "correct" amount. It should be obvious from table 5-2 that such biases can be quite significant and can lead to the application of duties when there is no discernible competitive benefit or injury to U.S. producers.

The Role of Uncertainty in Both CVD and Dumping Compliance

Under U.S. law, any dumping margin greater than one-half of 1 percent justifies an affirmative determination. Domestic firms consider such findings to be a victory, even though one might expect a duty rate of 0.5 percent to have an insignificant competitive effect. It has been argued that such findings demonstrate that the harassment value of dumping and countervailing duty investigations often justifies the effort and expense required of domestic petitioners, even if the outcome is barely above de minimis.[24] Such observations miss a crucial point. The very existence of antidumping (AD) and countervailing duties, no matter how small, carries tremendous significance simply because of the uncertainties they introduce. These effects go well beyond the value of present and future administrative harassments.

Importing under an AD or CVD order increases the chance of incurring much higher duties than those originally paid. These duties, in theory, have no upper bound. That is because the bonds initially posted on import are only estimates of the final duty, in effect a "deposit" on a final amount to be determined later. At the end of each year, the Department of Commerce offers interested parties the opportunity to request an annual administrative review of outstanding AD and CVD orders. If no interest is expressed in such a review, the department declares that the estimated deposit rate equals the final duty rate and "liquidates" the imports. In such cases, no additional liability is placed on the importer. If a review

24. Jagdish N. Bhagwati, *Protectionism* (MIT Press, 1988).

is requested, however, the department usually takes three to four years to determine the final duty rate. Because of the biases inherent in its methods and because the department does not feel constrained to follow a consistent approach in subsequent reviews, the outcome of the administrative review process is a random shot, and the final duty rates charged by the department will vary considerably.

Because of the uncertainty surrounding deposit rates, importing from countries and firms under AD and CVD orders amounts to an open-ended contingent liability. If a review is requested, this liability may not be settled for years.[25] Once it is settled, the Department of Commerce charges interest (at a rather high rate) on underpayment. Given that liability is incurred by the *importer*, the net effect is that importers of goods subject to countervailing duties are required to have detailed information on national, regional, and local industrial programs in the exporting country before they can assess the risks of increases over deposit rates associated with their suppliers. Given the biases in the calculation of dumping duties, they must also assess the uncertainties surrounding final dumping duties.

Since a dumping duty equals the difference between actual home and export prices, it seems designed to create an incentive for the exporter to cease dumping. In essence, an exporter who continued to dump would be deciding to share revenue with the U.S. Treasury that it could have captured itself by raising the export price to the U.S. price. That the liability falls on the importer and not the exporter, however, introduces moral hazard and may thus create less incentive for the exporter to stop dumping. The importer bears the risk, whereas the exporter is responsible for the pricing behavior. To the extent the exporter cares more about current profits from price discrimination than long-term profits from a sustained business relationship with the importer, the importer will have less opportunity to transmit proper incentives to the exporter to stop dumping.

Theoretical Considerations

Random tariffs have a number of implications for import demand. Some measurements of the actual variability of AD and CVD duties are

---

25. This creates an interesting problem for accounting firms auditing such importers, which must assign some value to the contingent liabilities incurred by importing affected imports.

discussed in the next subsection. Consider import demand for commodity X_m. This product is assumed to be an imperfect substitute for the domestic product X_d. We represent the markets for these two products in figure 5-3. When an export subsidy is placed on the imported product, export supply shifts to S'_m from S_m. In the new equilibrium, the domestic industry is injured because of the reduction in shipments and price consequent to the introduction of the subsidy on the imported product. In the figure, the demand for the domestic product falls from X_d to X'_d. If we place a countervailing duty on the imported product that is known with certainty and equals the export subsidy rate, the market returns to its original equilibrium, and the distorting effects of the subsidy are exactly countered.

As an extension of this analysis, assume that representative consumers and importers of the imported good are risk averse. We formalize this assumption by defining the random shock variable δ. The variable δ measures proportional deviations in the import price from its expected value. The actual price is not known until after the decision to import has been made. We assume that δ is normally distributed with mean zero and variance σ^2. The mean and variance parameters are known—although in all likelihood importers have a poor understanding of the parameters and uncertainties involved. The consumer is assumed to expose himself to this random shock each time he imports a unit of the commodity X_m under a random AD or CVD order. (By assumption, the expected value of the duty on imports is not affected by the introduction of this uncertainty parameter, which has a mean of zero). For any random duty with mean t_r, we thus know that there exists some fixed duty rate t^* that will have the same effect on import demand as t_r, where

$$(5\text{-}9) \qquad t^* = f[t_r, E(\delta), \sigma^2], f_1, f_2, f_3 > 0,$$

and where $t^* > t_r$.[26] In figure 5-3, the introduction of uncertainty means that, when we introduce a tariff subject to a shock parameter δ with expected value $E(\delta)$ and variance σ^2, the fixed tariff equivalent is some rate t^* greater than the actual rate of the subsidy.[27] The greater the variance

---

26. See Jack Meyer, "Two-Moment Decision Models and Expected Utility Maximization," *American Economic Review*, vol. 77 (June 1987), pp. 421–30.

27. This means that the United States is imposing random antidumping and countervail duties that (including the implicit insurance premiums) always exceed the actual estimated dumping margins and subsidy rates.

Figure 5-3. *The Effects of Random Import Duties*

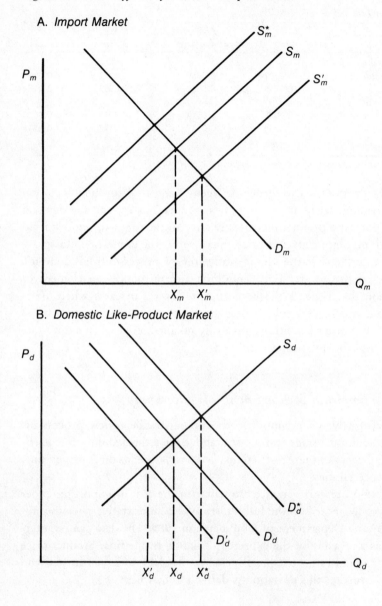

A. *Import Market*

B. *Domestic Like-Product Market*

Table 5-3. *Variance Estimates for Import Prices under Countervailing Duty Orders*

Item	Steel	Textiles and apparel	Other	Total
Conditional				
Mean value of δ	-0.0411	0.0089	-0.0070	-0.0067
σ	0.0748	0.0639	0.0363	0.0451
Unconditional				
Mean value of δ	-0.0078	0.0044	-0.0019	-0.0020
σ	0.0254	0.0337	0.0172	0.0248
Average years[a]	3.5	3.5	2.5	3.0

a. From beginning of review period to publication of final rate.

on t_r, the greater the divergence between t^* and t_r. With the imposition of this random tariff, import supply is reduced to S_m^*, and the demand for the domestic product increases relative to the original, nondistorted equilibrium. Shipments and prices increase for the domestic industry.

The uncertainty in the administrative review process distorts domestic markets relative to free-trade equilibria and introduces an element of protection that benefits the domestic producers. In cases where σ^2 is significant and plays a role in determining $t^* - t_r$, the initiation of an AD or CVD case by petitioners is easily justified, even when a duty rate of only 0.5 percent is expected.

Some Empirical Measurements of Uncertainty

Conceptually, uncertainties in the administrative review process introduce additional trade restrictions, above the estimated duty rate itself. The significance of these restrictions, however, depends on the magnitude of the uncertainties.

Table 5-3 presents variance estimates for the cost of importing under a CVD order, based on the full set of CVD administrative reviews published by the Department of Commerce in 1989. The data can be interpreted as a measure of the expected deviation of the final product price from the initial estimated price inclusive of CVD duties, estimated and actual. Formally, this deviation is defined as δ, where

$$(5\text{-}10) \qquad \delta = (t_1 - t_0)/(1 + t_0),$$

and where t_1 and t_0 represent the final duty rate and the original deposit

Table 5-4. *Conditional Variance of Import Prices under Antidumping Orders*

Item	Steel	Other manufactures	Agriculture and fisheries	Total
Conditional				
Mean value of δ	−0.0093	−0.0443	−0.0809	−0.0384
σ	0.1279	0.1990	0.0811	0.1280
Unconditional				
Mean value of δ	−0.0027	−0.0049	−0.0359	−0.0059
σ	0.0584	0.0496	0.0623	0.0516
Average years[a]	7.75	4.0	2.5	5.5

a. From beginning of review period to publication of final rate.

rate under which the goods were imported. This deviation is thus measured as a proportion of the initial duty-inclusive price.

Two estimates are provided: (1) the conditional variability of price, given that a review will occur with probability 1, and (2) the unconditional variability of price, without prior knowledge of whether a review will occur (the sampling techniques and probability estimates are discussed more fully in the appendix). Thus, for a product imported under a CVD order, the unconditional standard deviation of the variation between the final price and the initial price, as a percentage of the initial price, is 2.54 percent for steel products, 3.37 percent for textiles and apparel, and 1.72 percent for other products. In other words, without prior knowledge of whether a review will occur, there is approximately a 95 percent probability that an importer of steel products under a CVD order will pay a price within two standard deviations or ±5.08 percent of the original price. An importer is only 68 percent certain that his final price will vary no more than 2.54 percent, or one standard deviation from the original price. For products that will be reviewed with certainty 1, the confidence interval is much broader. A steel importer is 95 percent certain his final price will fall within ±14.96 percent of the expected price. In fact, he can only be 68 percent certain that his price will not vary by more than 7.48 from the expected price.

Table 5-4 presents data for AD duties from a sample covering over 85 percent of the AD administrative reviews completed from January to June 1989. In this sample, goods imported under AD orders are subject to much higher variability than CVD orders. An importer of steel products expecting an administrative review is only 68 percent certain that his price will vary by no more than ±12.79 percent from his initial price. He is 95 percent certain that his final price will not vary by more than 25.58 percent from the original price.

The Suspension of Dumping Orders

In cases where dumping has actually occurred, dumping duties remove the incentive for price discrimination.[28] Thus, if AD duties actually reflected the degree of past price discrimination and if ending price discrimination meant that such duties would be lifted, we would expect reviews to lead to suspension of duties on a regular basis. In fact, bonding rates on average decline following reviews. However, the average reduction is quite small compared with actual bonding rates, so that almost all AD orders tend to remain in place.

The department lifts AD bonding requirements only after three years of a proven absence of dumping. Given the biases cited earlier, the only way to get a duty lifted is to (1) stop exporting to the United States or charge substantially higher prices in the United States than in all other markets and then to (2) request three subsequent annual reviews. Other reviews are likely to be requested by petitioners while the relevant reviews are being completed. In cases where firms are not dumping but continue to sell in the United States, the department's practice of comparing individual sales in one market with average prices in another practically guarantees continued findings of dumping. Because administrative reviews take an average of 5.5 years to complete, the termination of a dumping order thus involves a decision not to export or to export low volumes at high prices to the United States for a total, on average, of 8.5 years. These facts are reflected in the actual data on reviews. Although the average bonding rate in our sample is 13.7 percent, the expected (unconditional) reduction in this bonding rate is only 0.8 percent. Dumping bonds are forever.

Conclusions and Policy Implications

The purpose of the antidumping and countervailing duty laws is to ensure that international competition conforms to a concept of commercial fairness that views some commercial practices as unfair or beyond the pale of proper competitive behavior. If these laws are properly applied, the

28. Richard D. Boltuck, "An Economic Analysis of Dumping," *Journal of World Trade Law*, vol. 21 (October 1987), pp. 45–54.

rationale goes, the distribution of national product and income will approximate that which would have prevailed in the absence of such unfair and pernicious acts by foreign producers and governments. The gains and losses of domestic producers then presumably would depend on their own performance in a competitive market, as they should, rather than on their ability or inability to compete with unfair practices.

Although this may be the ideal outcome of the unfair trade laws, the actual outcome is quite different. In effect, the unfair trade laws have replaced section 201 and are applied as a modified escape clause that provides potential relief from all imports. This is especially true of the dumping law. In the way the department calculates dumping margins, almost any company accused of dumping will be found to be doing so. This finding of dumping will have no relationship to the actual definition of dumping. Rather, the margins calculated by Commerce depend on the variability of prices over time and on the ability of a company to overcome the administrative biases that favor the use of "best information available" (BIA).[29] Only if a company is actually charging substantially more in the United States than in foreign markets, such that the price premiums overcome the significant biases inherent in the department's methodologies, will a company avoid positive margins. The decision whether to apply duties against imports thus hinges on the injury test at the ITC. In this way, the application of the unfair trade laws has become an escape clause for domestic producers.

Although the administration of the unfair trade laws has turned them into trade relief laws, there is a considerable difference between their application and that of the legitimate escape clauses of U.S. law and the GATT. In particular, the ITC is limited to considering only those producers injured by imports. No consideration is given in the ITC's injury deliberations to the effect of imposing Commerce's duty rates on downstream consumers and producers. In view of the department's methodology, we do not know whether such imports actually are unfair. Although the actual escape clause mechanism considered by the GATT and embodied in U.S. law considers the broad effect of trade relief on the U.S. economy, the focus is much narrower under the unfair trade laws. Producers that are in poor health, and that thus can pass an injury test at the ITC, can more easily petition for and receive protection from imports

29. In fact, exchange rate movements have also been linked to findings of dumping. See Robert M. Feinberg, "Exchange Rates and 'Unfair Trade,'" *Review of Economics and Statistics*, vol. 71 (November 1989), pp. 704–07.

under the unfair trade laws, whether or not their health is related to the effects of unfair competition.

The specific exclusion of the interests of downstream producers and consumers from injury determinations magnifies the distortions introduced by Commerce's application of these laws. For example, Commerce and the ITC recently applied tariffs ranging above 200 percent on imported bearings, with absolutely no consideration of the effect that such a price increase would have on U.S. production and exports of heavy machinery, copier machines, and a number of other products that use bearings. In fact, practically the whole world was found to be dumping bearings in the United States, largely on the basis of the use of BIA. None of the testimony of downstream producers was deemed relevant.

Because of the biases inherent in the administration of the unfair trade laws, their application implies a transfer of income from downstream producers and consumers to producers through the administered protection of import-competing producers from fairly traded imports. Even when unfair trade practices do exist, the unfair trade laws do not merely correct the distortions introduced by these practices. Rather, they twist the distortion in the other direction, transferring income in the process. These costs and distributional effects are compounded by the uncertainties inherent in the application of duties, which impose additional nontariff barriers on imports. The net effect is that the unfair trade laws punish not only fair and unfair imports alike but also domestic consumers and downstream industries.

The losses to consumers and downstream producers will, of course, be captured in part (but only in part) by an increase in tariff revenues. However, because foreign governments can and do collect countervailing duties instead of the U.S. government, even this part of the loss to consumers may be deadweight loss. In the case of dumping, exporters can capture the duties by raising export price. Even more important, however, is the fact that one of the primary costs imposed unintentionally by the administration of these laws is unrelated to the actual magnitude of dumping or subsidization and to the resulting import duties. This is the nontariff barrier inherent in the costs of uncertainty. Given that the actual duties collected are random and likely to vary greatly, their imposition implies implicit self-insurance costs that are never collected as actual duties. The losses to consumers and downstream producers represented by these implicit premiums are thus a true deadweight loss. In many cases, this last barrier has the same welfare costs as the imposition of prohibitive trade barriers.[30]

The current application of U.S. dumping and countervailing duty laws is sometimes defended as a strategic trade policy. A number of theoretical arguments in the recent literature on trade under imperfect competition explain why certain industries might be defined as strategic.[31] However, none of these arguments are considered by the Department of Commerce or the ITC. Although one would expect strategic industries to be dynamic, high-technology industries that generate external benefits in the form of technical spinoffs, falling production costs for related industries, or similar external economies, protection under the current laws is just as likely to go to labor-intensive, agricultural, or primary industries such as textiles, raspberries, baseball uniforms, low-end electronics, and fish.

Appendix

In the text we suggested that accounting methods should not ignore the economic context of subsidies if they are to be applied to questions that are fundamentally economic in nature. The model developed here illustrates the important elements of an economic approach to measuring subsidy rates. Although we strive for generality and simplicity, we cannot claim that the model is universally applicable. With creative effort, however, assumptions may be relaxed or new assumptions imposed and the model thus modified to fit particular cases. The selection of the proper model is itself an exercise in economic judgment. The essential point is that the tools are available to the Department of Commerce for evaluating such factors.

30. There is also strong evidence to suggest that the imposition of dumping duties on upstream industries is correlated with the filing of downstream dumping cases. This suggests that upstream demand for administered protection generates a derived demand downstream for more administered protection. See Robert M. Feinberg and Barry T. Hirsch, "Industry Rent Seeking and the Filing of 'Unfair Trade' Complaints," *International Journal of Industrial Organization*, vol. 7 (September 1989); Feinberg, "Exchange Rates and Unfair Trade"; and Robert M. Feinberg and Seth Kaplan, "Fishing Downstream," working paper, U.S. International Trade Commission.

31. See Elhanan Helpman and Paul R. Krugman, *Trade Policy and Market Structure*, (MIT Press, 1989); Kelvin Lancaster, "Protection and Product Differentiation," in Henry K. Kierzkowski, ed., *Monopolistic Competition and International Trade* (Oxford: Clarendon Press, 1984), pp. 137–56; and Daniel Gros, "A Note on the Optimal Tariff, Retaliation and the Welfare from Tariff Wars in a Framework with Intra-Industry Trade," *Journal of International Economics*, vol. 23 (November 1987), pp. 357–67.

Subsidy-Rate Model

Consider competitive upstream and downstream industries. We focus on the export subsidy equivalent of domestic production and upstream subsidies. Output subsidies are then a special case of upstream subsidies where all inputs are effectively subsidized, whereas export subsidies, which may be measured directly, are analytically trivial. When the upstream producer is subsidized, the marginal costs of each downstream firm shift when the price of an input changes as a result of the subsidy. We assume that in the short run (which usually corresponds to the period covered by unfair trade investigations) downstream firms adjust production to be on their marginal costs curves, whereas in the long run firms enter the industry to dissipate extraordinary returns generated by the subsidy. In the case of fixed input prices, this would imply a horizontal long-run industry supply curve. We assume further that each downstream firm is small (that is, a price taker) in the market for the upstream product. Any of these assumptions may of course be modified on a case-by-case basis.

In the model, we distinguish between the short and long run. It is important for Commerce to have in mind the likely nature of adjustment over the period of time permitted in its analysis. In industries where entry and exit take place over a period of years (such as steel, autos, or semi-conductors), or in industries large enough to be characterized by discernibly upward-sloping supply curves even in the long run, the relevant model will correspond to the short-run case presented here; in industries where entry and exit are rapid (such as apparel), the long-run case is appropriate.

With a horizontal long-run supply curve, and under the other assumptions detailed above, a downstream industry is in long-run competitive equilibrium when marginal cost equals average cost for each representative firm and total demand equals total supply. These conditions may be represented by

$$(5\text{-}11) \qquad M(\mathbf{w}, y) = A(\mathbf{w}, y)$$

$$(5\text{-}12) \qquad P(ny) = M(\mathbf{w}, y),$$

where marginal cost, M, and average cost, A, are based on the cost function of a representative firm, $\mathbf{w}$ is a vector of factor prices, y is a representative firm's production volume, $P(.)$ is an inverse market demand function, and n is the number of firms in the industry.

Alternatively, in the short run, or in the long run with less than perfectly elastic industry supply, condition 5-12 must hold in equilibrium.[32] Logarithmically differentiating 5-12 with respect to the factor price for factor 1, w_1, holding n unchanged, yields

$$(5\text{-}13) \qquad (1/e_d)\,(\hat{y}/\hat{w}_1) = \hat{M}/\hat{w}_1 + (\hat{M}/\hat{y})\,(\hat{y}/\hat{w}_1).$$

Note that $\hat{M}/\hat{y}$ is just $1/e_s$, where e_s is the representative firm's marginal cost curve elasticity (and hence also the short-run supply elasticity). The term $\hat{M}/\hat{w}_1$ may be evaluated by Young's theorem and Shephard's lemma, and shown to equal $\alpha\beta$.[33] By making the appropriate substitutions, we may solve for $\hat{y}/\hat{w}_1$ and obtain equation 5-14 below, where the percentage change in the LTFV product price, $\hat{P}$, caused by a $\hat{w}_1$. percentage change in the input price, w_1, is thus

$$(5\text{-}14) \qquad \hat{P} = [(\beta\alpha e_s)/(e_s - e_d^*)]\hat{w}_1.$$

In equation 5-14, β is the output elasticity of the input, α is the cost share of the input, e_s is the elasticity of supply (and hence measures the elasticity of the industry marginal cost curve), and e_d^* is the elasticity of total demand for the downstream product (including both domestic and foreign demand).[34] Note that the department currently attempts to measure $\hat{w}_1$ directly with upstream subsidies.

Equation 5-14 emphasizes that the change in price depends on supply

32. With constant returns in terms of both technology and input prices, short-run equilibrium is characterized by enough time for firms to alter production so as to remain on their marginal cost curves, but too little time to permit entry or exit.

33. For a typical derivation of a closely related result, see, for example, Eugene Silberberg, *The Structure of Economics: A Mathematical Analysis* (McGraw-Hill, 1978), pp. 208–11.

34. An output elasticity is the percentage increase in the use of an input associated with a 1 percent increase in production, holding all input prices unchanged. If all output elasticities are equal, the expansion path must be a 45-degree line from the origin. Constant returns to scale correspond to a cost-share weighted average output elasticity of one; increasing returns to scale correspond to an average output elasticity of less than one. Output elasticities are negative in the case of inferior factors. An inferior factor is used less as an industry expands because efficient technologies differ according to scale. For instance, artisans may be used for small-scale manufacture but be replaced by assembly lines at bigger scales. All demand elasticities are negative.

and demand in the product market and on the production technology, captured by the parameter β.[35] Not surprisingly, it also depends on the one factor the Commerce Department currently takes into account, namely, the cost share, α. In general, the greater the output elasticity, the bigger the production response to a change in input price, and hence the bigger the change in price. In its current approach to upstream subsidies to agricultural products, the department implicitly assumes that (1) $\beta = 1$ (that is, input coefficients are fixed) and either (2a) $e_s = \infty$ or (2b) $e_d^* = 0$ (that is, there is full passthrough to downstream consumers).

In equilibria involving horizontal industry supply curves, the same general approach is used, but condition 5-11 (ensuring zero profits) as well as condition 5-12 must hold. Furthermore, in competitive equilibrium, firms produce at minimum average cost, so $\hat{A}/\hat{y} = 0$. By taking the total logarithmic derivative of 5-11 and solving for $\hat{y}/\hat{w}_1$, we find that

$$(5\text{-}15) \qquad \hat{y}/\hat{w}_1 = (\hat{A}/\hat{w}_1 - \hat{M}/\hat{w}_1)/(\hat{M}/\hat{y} - \hat{A}/\hat{y}).$$

Once again, Young's theorem and Shephard's lemma may be applied to show that $\hat{A}/\hat{w}_1$ equals α. Given also than $\hat{A}/\hat{y} = 0$, and $\hat{M}/\hat{y} = 1/e_s$, we find that

$$(5\text{-}16) \qquad \hat{y}/\hat{w}_1 = \alpha e_s (1 - \beta).$$

Now, when condition 5-12 is totally differentiated logarithmically, n must be allowed to vary to reflect entry or exit. Thus,

$$(5\text{-}17) \qquad (1/e_d)[(\hat{n}/\hat{w}_1) + (\hat{y}/\hat{w}_1)] = \hat{M}/\hat{w}_1 + (\hat{M}/\hat{y})(\hat{y}/\hat{w}_1).$$

By substituting 5-16 and 5-17 and by recognizing that $\hat{M}/\hat{w}_1 = \alpha\beta$ and $\hat{M}/\hat{y} = 1/e_d$, we may solve for $\hat{n}/\hat{w}_1$,

$$(5\text{-}18) \qquad \hat{n}/\hat{w}_1 = \alpha(e_d - e_s + \beta e_s).$$

We know that the total change in price with respect to a change in input price, $\hat{P}/\hat{w}_1$, is given by the expression

---

35. The role of the demand elasticity is recognized in Commerce Department regulations under certain conditions. See chapter 4.

$$\hat{P}/\hat{w}_1(1/e_d) = [(\hat{n}/\hat{w}_1) + (\hat{y}/\hat{w}_1)].$$

This expression may be simplified by substituting 5-16 and 5-18 for the appropriate terms, yielding,

(5-19) $$\hat{P}/\hat{w}_1 = \alpha.$$

In the long-run case as defined herein, we have assumed a horizontal long-run marginal cost curve, such that free entry keeps the long-run supply curve horizontal. Equation 5-19 reflects the role of entry in re-establishing production at the minimum average cost of the representative firm.[36] In other words we are assuming, in the long run, that the industry is characterized by constant returns to scale, not just in technology but also in input prices.[37]

The relationship between equations 5-14 and 5-19 is apparent: in the long run, the entry and exit of firms imply that the supply elasticity, e_s, approaches infinity and the output elasticity, β, approaches one. It should be noted that all the market-behavior elasticities, although not subscripted S or L, are also generally greater in the long run than in the short run, and these differences with respect to time should be taken into account.

Next, consider the relationship between the change in the price of the input, $\hat{w}$, and the ad valorem upstream subsidy, s_u, summarized in

(5-20) $$\hat{w} = [e_{su}/(e_{du} - e_{su})]s_u,$$

where e_{su} is the upstream industry's supply elasticity in the relevant adjustment period, and e_{du} is the elasticity of demand for the upstream product. This demand elasticity depends on conditions in the downstream market under consideration and on conditions in other industries that used the upstream product as an input.

In cases where the downstream industry is the only one that uses the input, e_{du} can be expressed as

(5-21) $$e_{du} = \alpha(e_d^* - \sigma),$$

36. Note that the assumption of a horizontal long-run supply curve is not realistic for sectors large enough to experience long-run increases in input prices as production increases. In such cases, equation 5-14 should be applied, with long-run elasticities substituted for short-term elasticities.

37. Increasing or decreasing returns to scale at the industry level require additional modifications to the model presented here.

where σ is the cost-share weighted-average Allen elasticity of technical substitution between the upstream input and each other input (cost shares are normalized to sum to one). Clearly, the Commerce Department's accounting assumption of full passthrough in agricultural cases is true only under special conditions (that is, when demand is completely inelastic or supply is perfectly elastic), even in the long run. Proper analysis requires an examination of supply conditions in the upstream industry as well as any substitutability among production factors for the upstream input, as measured by σ. In cases where we have fixed input coefficients, $e_{du} = \alpha e_d^*.$[38]

To establish the production subsidy equivalent of the upstream subsidy we must find the production subsidy that would cause the same price effect as the upstream subsidy. Such a production subsidy, s_p, would induce the price effect given by

$$(5\text{-}22) \qquad \hat{P} = e_s/(e_d^* - e_s)s_p.$$

By substituting equation 5-20 into equation 5-14 (for the short run) or equation 5-19 (for the long run), and then setting equations 5-14 or 5-19 equal to equation 5-22, the value of s_p may be found. These rates, s_{pL} and s_{pS} are given by equations 5-23 and 5-24, respectively,[39]

$$(5\text{-}23) \qquad s_{pL} = [(e_s - e_d^*)/e_s][\alpha e_{su}/(e_{su} - e_{du})]s_u$$

$$(5\text{-}24) \qquad s_{pS} = (\beta\alpha e_{su})/(e_{su} - e_{du}^*)s_u.$$

The assumed upstream subsidy is absolutely equivalent to the calcu-

38. Hence, in cases of upstream monopoly, the greater the share of an input in downstream costs, the greater the upstream elasticity of demand and the less the passthrough of upstream subsidies.

39. It is useful to note that the price change calculated by substituting equations 5-23 and 5-24 into equation 5-25 would be appropriate for the International Trade Commission to incorporate as the first step in its injury analysis. The ITC must then determine by how much the demand for the U.S. like product declined when the price of the import decreased. This step would require an inquiry into the composite U.S. demand elasticity for the product, the degree of substitutability (the Armington elasticity of substitution) between the LTFV import and the like product, the market shares of each product, and the supply elasticity and degree of substitutability with any nonsubject imports. Next, the ITC would decompose the reduction in demand for the like product into a price and volume effect by considering the elasticity of supply of the like product.

lated production subsidy rate from the perspective of U.S. consumers
and U.S. import-competing industries; U.S. residents should be absolutely indifferent between an upstream subsidy of s_u and a production
subsidy of s_{pS} or s_{pL}, as the case may be. Both upstream and overall
production subsidies affect all production, not just exports. For that
reason, the equivalence of the two is a reasonable basis for converting
one into the other. It thus seems reasonable to attribute the same benefits
at the margin to the exporting industry in the two cases.

Given the domestic production subsidy or production subsidy equivalent of an upstream subsidy, our next step is to find the export subsidy
rate that would have the same effect on export performance as a given
domestic subsidy. This export-subsidy equivalent SX is the rate of duty
that would just offset the effects of the upstream subsidy on U.S. producers of the like product. From the appendix of chapter 4, we know
that the export subsidy equivalent of a domestic subsidy is

(5-25) $$SX = e_s\{1/[1 + (|e_dQ_d|/e_sQ_s)]\}s_d,$$

where SX is the export subsidy equivalent rate. In equation 5-24, Q_d and
Q_s represent downstream home market demand and total downstream
production. Equation 5-25 is presented in the text as equation 5-7. It
may be substituted into equations 5-23 or 5-24 to yield the long- and
short-run equivalences, respectively, of upstream subsidies.

(5-26) $$SX_L = \{1/[1 + (|e_dQ_d|/e_sQ_s)]\} \{\alpha[e_{su}/(e_{su} - e_{du})][(e_s - e_d^*)/e_s]\}s_u$$

(5-27) $$SX_S = \{1/[1 + (|e_dQ_d|/e_sQ_s)]\} \{\alpha\beta[e_{su}/(e_{su} - e_{du})]\}s_u.$$

We emphasize that for industries where entry or exit is not rapid or for
industries facing rising long-run costs, such as steel or autos, equation
5-27 should be applied, with the use of long-run elasticities as appropriate.
Equation 5-27 is reported in the text as equation 5-7.

Upstream Subsidies

Assume the downstream market is characterized by the industry cost
curve

$$(5\text{-}28) \qquad\qquad C = f(\mathbf{w})Q^\epsilon,$$

where $\epsilon > 1$, $f(\mathbf{w})$ represents composite input prices, and ϵ is the output elasticity of total industry cost. The marginal cost curve for the downstream industry will then be

$$(5\text{-}29) \qquad\qquad MC = dC/dQ = \epsilon f(\mathbf{w})Q^{\epsilon-1}.$$

We make the further assumption that demand in the downstream market is characterized by the equation

$$(5\text{-}30) \qquad\qquad Q_d = k_d P_d^{e_d},$$

where e_d is the elasticity of demand. Finally, we assume downstream markets are competitive. We are thus able to solve for demand in upstream markets as follows. By manipulating the downstream marginal cost equation, downstream supply can be shown to equal

$$(5\text{-}31) \qquad\qquad Q_s = k_s P_d^{e_s} f(\mathbf{w})^{-e_s},$$

where $e_s = (1/(\epsilon-1))$, and k_s is a constant. Setting supply equal to demand, equilibrium output in downstream markets will be

$$(5\text{-}32) \qquad\qquad Q = k[f(\mathbf{w})]^{e_s e_d/(e_s - e_d)},$$

where k is again constant. Consider the case of fixed-input technologies, where inputs are combined in relatively fixed proportions.[40] To formalize this assumption, we specify

$$(5\text{-}33) \qquad\qquad f(\mathbf{w}) = \Sigma \, \alpha_i q_i,$$

where α_i represents the price of input i, and q_i represents the unit input coefficients. From our cost equation 5-28, and from equation 5-32, the demand for composite inputs F will thus be

40. The Department of Commerce implicitly makes the same assumption when it weights an ad valorem upstream subsidy (measured as a reduction in input cost) by the relative importance of a given input in downstream cost. Upstream subsidies often do affect products that are used in relatively fixed proportions, such as raw materials. However, a more generalized approach would recognize the availability of input substitutes.

(5-34)
$$F = a_d f(\mathbf{w})^{e_{du}},$$

where $e_{du} = \epsilon e_d e_s/(e_s - e_d)$, and a_d is a constant. The demand for any particular input i will thus be

(5-35)
$$F_i = a_{di} f(\mathbf{w})^{e_{du}},$$

where $a_{di} = a_d q_i$. This represents demand for the upstream input, as a function of all input prices.

To represent supply for the upstream input, we first assume that the upstream industry is characterized by the industry cost curve

(5-36)
$$C_i = k_i F_i^{\epsilon_i},$$

where $\epsilon_i > 1$. The marginal cost curve will thus be

(5-37)
$$MC_i = k_i \epsilon_i F_i^{\epsilon_i - 1}.$$

Generally, a profit-maximizing monopolist in the upstream market would set marginal revenue equal to marginal cost. Consider a case in which the upstream producer receives a subsidy of s_i. The monopolist's pricing decision then means that

(5-38)
$$k_i \epsilon_i F_i^{\epsilon_i - 1} = (1 + s_i)[1 + (1/e_{du})]\alpha_i.$$

By making a substitution from equation 5-35 and differentiating, we can derive the term

(5-39) $\quad d\alpha_i/ds_i = \alpha_i/\{[1 + s_i][q_i\alpha_i/f(\mathbf{w})]e_{du}(\epsilon_i - 1) - (1 + s_i)\}.$

Consider an initial free-trade equilibrium (that is, $s_i = 0$). In this case, a linear approximation of the proportional change in input prices α_i consequent to the introduction of a subsidy at rate s_i can be derived from equation 5-39, yielding

(5-40) $\quad \partial\alpha_i/\alpha_i|_{s_i = 0} = -[1/(1 + |e_{dui}/e_{su}|)]s_i,$

where $e_{dui} = [q_i\alpha_i/f(\mathbf{w})]e_{du}$, or the aggregate input elasticity of demand for inputs, weighted by the relative importance of input i in total production costs. The term $e_{su} = (1/(\epsilon_i - 1))$. Equation 5-40 is used to derive the input subsidy equivalents presented in the text.

In more general terms, when several industries utilize the input in downstream production, the term e_{dui} can be replaced by e_{du}, where e_{du} is then the aggregate elasticity of upstream demand for the input, which equals the average elasticity of demand for individual users/industries, weighted by quantity.

Uncertainty Measurement Methodology

A brief comment should be made about the sampling methodology used to derive the mean and variance estimates for the effects of administrative reviews presented in the text. The final liquidation rates published in *Federal Register* notices of final determinations of administrative reviews were compared with the actual bonding rates in effect for the period of the review. This required tracing the history of previous reviews for the same AD or CVD order, since each of these reviews resulted in a change in the bonding rate. In many cases, the bonding rate changed several times during the review period. In addition, different companies often received different rates under the same order, either as a bonding rate for the entry of imports or when the final rate was set for the liquidation of imports. Each unique pairing of an initial bonding rate for the entry of imports with a final rate for liquidation was treated as a separate observation. Thus, each observation represents an observation of (1) the initial rate at which imports could enter the United States and (2) the final duty rate set by the Department of Commerce on those imports.

The conditional estimates of mean deviations and variances for both AD and CVD orders were based on these observations of rate pairings. Using the full set of AD and CVD orders in effect during the sample period and the full set of actual administrative reviews published, we estimated the probability that a given AD or CVD order would be subject to an administrative review. This also determines the probability that a review will not occur. From the full set of actual rate pairings observed in the reviews, we were thus able to estimate the size of the set of rate pairings that remained unchanged because, lacking a request for review, imports were liquidated at a final duty rate set equal to the original bonding rate. This full sample of (1) rate pairings based on administrative reviews and (2) estimated identical rate pairings based on the set of AD and CVD orders that were not reviewed was used to estimate the unconditional mean deviations and variances.

The sample for countervailing duty administrative reviews included all reviews published in calendar year 1989. The CVD data set included nineteen final determinations that involved forty-four different rate pairings. The rate pairing data set for antidumping duty administrative reviews included all reviews published between January and June of 1989 except for two.[41]

The AD data included twelve final determinations that involved thirty-two different rate pairings. The data set did not include suspension of bonding requirements because of changed circumstances, such as changes in treaty obligations or suspension agreements. The sample thus covers those rate pairings that resulted from the application of AD and CVD methodologies covered in this chapter. The estimates of the average age of an administrative review are based on the age of actual reviews (not rate pairings), and have been calculated from the *full* twelve-month set of CVD reviews and the *full* six-month set of AD reviews, including those published for *Steel Wire Rope from Japan* and *Television Receivers from Japan*.

41. The two orders not included in the AD sample would probably have resulted in a higher estimated variance. One was *Steel Wire Rope from Japan*, 54 Fed. Reg. 6373 (1989), which actually consisted of several reviews covering the period from 1974 to 1984. Many of the determinations made in this review were based on BIA. The other order not included was *Television Receivers, Monochrome and Color, from Japan*, 54 Fed. Reg. 13917 (1989), which covered the period from 1981 through 1988. Although the department routinely publishes reviews that are eight to ten years late, foreign companies are regularly victims of BIA for failing to meet the department's own thirty- and forty-five-day deadlines.

Comment

Brian Hindley

Several contributors have commented that the United States may in the future face problems as a consequence of other nations copying U.S. attitudes and practices regarding dumping and subsidization. There is thus some interest in seeing what the European Community (EC) has done with the U.S. example and in examining the technology it has developed to exploit the protectionist potential of unfair trade laws, which may in some ways be superior to the equivalent U.S. technology.

The European Community has few countervailing duty cases compared with the United States. In large part, that is because the EC Commission thinks that many EC practices might be countervailed by the United States and does not want to provide EC precedents that the United States might use against it in arguments over such cases. Hence, what would be subsidy cases in the United States are often dealt with by the European Community as antidumping cases. For that reason, I focus my remarks on antidumping action.

In the calculation of dumping margins, there are clear similarities between the United States and the EC. Both introduce biases into the calculation of dumping margins by rejecting below-average-cost sales in the home market of the alleged dumper and counting sales in the export market that were in fact made at a price greater than the reference price as if they had been made at the reference price.

The European Community does not apply the ESP cap, it does not use a rigid 8 percent rule for profit, and it does not assume that overheads are 10 percent of production costs. But its procedures for constructing prices and moving backward and forward between ex-factory and the first arm's-length sale contain their own biases.[1] This may be the principal source of bias in the EC's calculation of dumping margins.

A major difference, however, is that antidumping action in the European Community is under the control of the EC Commission and the Council. Private parties complain to the Commission, and initiate action in that sense, but the Commission makes the decision to proceed with a case, and the Commission and the Council decide how to proceed with it. So a political element is always potentially present. That is true in quite another sense in the United States. Antidumping legislation in the United States is clearly designed in part for protectionist purposes, and private parties can and do exploit that element. But specific antidumping cases are not under political control, as they are in the European Community.

Another difference, which increases the importance of the political factor, is that EC antidumping cases are more frequently settled by undertakings than by the imposition of antidumping duties. Leaving aside cases involving nonmarket economies, if the European Community imposes antidumping duties, there is a good chance that the product involved comes from East Asia. There are good protectionist reasons for this targeting.

Another difference concerns the determination of injury. No separate body, such as the U.S. International Trade Commission, makes injury determinations in the European Community. Within the EC Commission's antidumping unit, dumping margins and injury are determined by different people, but they are all in the same unit, and one side is under the same administrative control as the other.

Moreover, what is to be determined regarding injury differs in the European Community and the United States. In the United States, the ITC is asked whether there has been injury and, if so, whether the injury has been caused by the dumped imports. If the answer to those questions is yes, an antidumping duty equal to the dumping margin calculated by Commerce is applied. In the EC, the fact of injury and its causation by imports is of course determined, as under GATT law it must be (although the political element in some of these determinations is rather plain). But when these questions have been answered in the affirmative, the Commission will go a step further and calculate an "injury margin"—that is, the antidumping duty needed to remove the injury to EC producers. The duty applied will be the injury margin if that is smaller than the dumping margin.

1. Brian Hindley, "Dumping and the Far East Trade of the European Community," *World Economy*, vol. 11 (December 1988), pp. 445–64.

That may sound reasonable, in comparison with U.S. practice, but now we come to the matter of refunds of duty. Boltuck and his colleagues have explained the uncertainty to which an importer is subject in the United States as a result of having been found to sell dumped goods, and the differences between final and initial determinations. That seems to be important in assessing the economic costs of U.S. antidumping action.

In the European Community, however, there is little or no uncertainty. In the first place, the assessment of definitive duties rapidly follows the assessment of provisional duties. Perhaps more important, if you market in the European Community through an associated sales company (which is to say, by and large, if you are Japanese), you won't get back the duties you have paid. To a first approximation, there is no uncertainty because you know that the European Community will keep them.

At first glance, the EC regulations seem to say that, if you cease to dump, you will get back the duties you have paid. But the regulations also say that in constructing the ex-factory export price, antidumping duties must be deducted from the price of the first arm's-length sale. Thus, suppose a product is found to have a dumping margin of 50 percent, that an antidumping duty of 20 percent is imposed, and that the exporter raises his EC prices by the amount of the duty. In EC law, the product still has a dumping margin of 50 percent—the dumping margin was originally calculated in the absence of an antidumping duty, but now there is one and it has to be deducted from the export price, which, hypothetically, was raised by the amount of the duty. So the ex-factory export price—as the EC Commission will calculate it—is unchanged. To stand a chance of getting back the duties he has paid, the importer must raise his prices in the European Community by the injury margin *plus* the dumping margin. The legal process for reclaiming duties is reported to be arduous—and that, together with the effect on their business of raising prices by the required amount, is likely to deter many importers from attempting to do so.

Antidumping duties paid in the European Community are therefore a real cost to the importer, and it is likely that importers will pay quite a lot to avoid them—"pay" by charging higher prices in the European Community than they otherwise would. That way, they are more likely to avoid complaints from their EC competitors, and, if there is a complaint, will stand some chance of being found not to dump, even with the biases in the Commission's calculations.

This is why the greatest economic cost to EC residents of EC activity in this area is likely to come, not from the effects of antidumping action on those products that are actually hit by the action, but from the impact of the threat of antidumping action on the prices of products that have not been hit by such action. This effect of antidumping action creates the worst economic consequences of a voluntary export restraint, seen from the point of view of the importing country. It restricts imports and is likely to create rents for foreign firms—a clear loss of welfare for the importing country.

The Canadian law is at the opposite extreme and therefore serves to drive the point home. Once a reference price has been established, no duty is charged on imports that enter Canada at a price equal to, or above, that reference price. In effect, the penalty for being found to dump in Canada is that the exporter raises his price to the reference price—and, unlike the position in the European Community, can keep the additional profit per unit so generated. An exporter who thinks that the Canadian authorities will find a 50 percent dumping margin on his product will probably not pay very much, in the form of higher prices, to avoid it. If he expects such a finding in the European Community, however, he will be prepared to raise his prices by something like 50 percent. Therefore, antidumping action seems likely to cast a much longer shadow in the European Community than in Canada, and the economic costs of antidumping action, in terms of the effects on the prices of products that have not been hit be antidumping duties but may be, are likely to be much greater for the European Community than for Canada.

Where does the United States fit into this picture? Boltuck and his colleagues seem unclear on the answer to that question. David Palmeter has said that a lawyer dealing with these matters in the United States could no longer advise a client on the action he might take to avoid being hit by U.S. antidumping duties. I take it, however, that the higher the price charged by an exporter, the lower the dumping margin that will be claimed by Commerce and the lower the probability that he will be found to dump at all. Therefore, there is probably an incentive for exporters who think they might be hit by antidumping action in the United States to raise their prices.

If it is in the interest of exporters to raise the price to the United States of products that have not yet been hit by antidumping duties, but may in the future be, then, for the United States as for the European Community, that effect will represent a major cost of antidumping action. An analysis of that question should therefore be central to an assessment of the economic costs of antidumping action to the United States.

Comment

Robert M. Feinberg

As others have mentioned in this volume, there is a need for empirical work in determining in actual cases what has been the effect of the various biases in Commerce Department calculations, and whether or not it is much ado about nothing. It would be particularly important to see a systematic discussion of any offsetting biases that favor respondents, along with some discussion of what the net effects are. I think that would be a useful complement to the essays in this volume.

Boltuck, Francois, and Kaplan note that the exclusion of home market sales below average cost imparts an upward bias to fair value in price-comparison dumping cases and that the minimum 18 percent overhead plus profit margins tend to have the same impact in cost-comparison cases. What they do not mention is that pricing below average cost is especially likely when demand declines in industries with high fixed costs. My research with Barry Hirsch has shown that these are the industries most likely to file antidumping and countervailing duty petitions in the United States. To the extent that demand conditions, by industry, are correlated across countries, then those most likely to file petitions, when demand falls, are also those most likely to have dumping margins significantly biased upward. It does seem to be the case—just as a casual observation—that when the steel industry in one country is doing poorly, it tends to be doing poorly in other countries as well.

The authors ignore one bias related to the market definition used. By typically focusing on narrow product definitions in dumping cases, there is more likelihood that export and home market varieties will be sufficiently different to prompt the use of third-country or constructed cost measures. It also makes cost allocations in the home market more important; if too much overhead is allocated to a particular product line under review, there will then be a bias toward eliminating too many below-cost sales and an upward bias in fair value and, therefore, in the dumping margin.

Similarly, too narrow a market definition in the United States may lead to an overemphasis on small numbers of relatively low prices that happen to be at the low end of a price distribution on related imports by a particular country. It may be preferable to employ more of an antitrust notion of market definition in terms of a range of products closely substitutable in demand and supply. This issue is probably even more important in the injury analysis by the International Trade Commission than in the determinations by the Department of Commerce.

Another problem that needs attention is not a bias in Commerce's calculations at all but an inherent conflict between the six-month period used in calculating dumping margins at Commerce and the much longer time period considered in ITC injury investigations, generally three years or longer. Under the trend analysis favored by many ITC commissioners, negative trends over the past three years in measures of such items as profit, sales, and employment are often taken as evidence of the injury a domestic industry has suffered from dumping or countervailable subsidies. Without getting into the issue of the validity of trend analysis, the point remains that, in a dumping case, most (or even all) of the decline observed occurs during a period in which there is no evidence of dumping and, in fact, no finding of dumping—before the six-month period.

Similarly, little effort has been made in countervailing duty cases to tie trends suggesting injury to the timing of subsidies. Again, this is not a criticism of Commerce, but it does seem to represent an inherent conflict between the analysis done at Commerce and that done at the ITC.

One general point needs to be made about cross-case or cross-industry empirical analysis. Depending on what is to be explained, it may be important to redefine the unit of observation as independent groups of cases, rather than the cases themselves, as defined by Commerce or the ITC. Defining the unit of observation by the case numbers used at the government agencies tends to explain largely steel and chemical cases; whereas, if cases are grouped by some notion of an independent case, it may be possible to explain more generally independent incentives to file cases or the effects of cases. That distinction is not always made.

An empirical investigation that would be particularly useful would be to examine the extent to which market definitions, employed in Commerce and ITC proceedings, correspond to antitrust notions of the market and how this relates to outcomes. Another question to ask here is whether there is more likelihood—or less—of getting a positive determination when the market definition takes more account of demand and supply substitutes.

In addressing the risk-premium question raised by Boltuck, Francois, and Kaplan, it would be interesting to examine whether imports from a particular country under a dumping order tend to cease completely or to fall by a greater amount than predicted by the imposition of the initial dumping duty. These effects might suggest that importers are taking into account the increased liability inherent in the uncertainty mentioned.

The importance of best information available as an upward bias in initial duty rates could be examined by comparing the movement from initial duty rates to adjusted duties after a first review in two situations: one when the initial duty is based on BIA but the review is not—instead it is based on actual data—and one when both are based on actual respondent-company records. Baldwin and Moore in chapter 7 discuss the effect of BIA, but in a different way: if you found dramatic reductions in duty rates when the initial duty rate was generated by BIA, you would have some reason to think that the initial duty rate was biased upward.

The moral hazard issue is another important subject for empirical analysis. It arises when duties are imposed on importers but it is the foreign exporter who determines the pricing strategy and the price discrimination. It would be interesting to examine contractual relations between exporters and importers to see if there is any explicit mechanism to deal with this question. There may be ways in which this liability is shared by exporter and importer. If not, there may be implicit, standard mechanisms for dividing this liability to try to offset the moral hazard problem.

In view of the numerous upward biases pointed out for both dumping and CVD, one is led to wonder why 20 percent or so of the determinations of Commerce are negative. Eighty percent affirmative is a high number, but 20 percent is not trivial. The general impression seems to be that anyone who files a case can always—or almost always—get an affirmative determination at Commerce. Then why do 20 percent of them fail? It would be interesting to find out what causes a negative determination in those cases. Why are they filed? Are they clearly frivolous actions?

Finally, in evaluating the importance of these biases, one also would want to know the distribution of margins that actually occur. A number of people have talked about the possibility of raising the de minimus threshold from 0.5 percent to some higher value. How many margins that are calculated are in, say, the 0.5 to 10 percent range? If only fairly small numbers are in that range and if most are in the 30 to 40 percent range, then it is not clear that these biases—although we may not want to ignore them—are often pushing Commerce from negative determinations to affirmative findings. Again, that is an empirical exercise that would aid in evaluating the importance of these biases.

CHAPTER SIX

Antidumping and Countervailing Duty Law: The United States and the GATT

Ronald A. Cass and Stephen J. Narkin

T HE GENERAL Agreement on Tariffs and Trade (GATT) relies on two overarching principles to promote liberalization of the various national rules governing international trade. First, overt constraints on trade, such as tariffs, are subjected to a one-way ratchet: trade barriers are supposed to come down and not go up, and the most visible barriers are subjected to the most intense pressure. Tariffs are usually bound at a given level and cannot be increased without risking costly retaliation. The second principle is the commitment to generic rather than specific treatment of trade issues: all countries that can secure most-favored-nation (MFN) status are entitled to have their goods treated similarly by the host country. MFN treatment prevents trade from being diverted as a result of the selective lowering of high trade barriers and reinforces the lowering of trade barriers by preventing selective increases in trade barriers. Together these principles have supported the progressive, broad decline of tariff barriers for the past forty years.

Recent concern about the current health of the GATT and its future prospects center on the deteriorating force of these two principles. The sources of erosion include the rise of nontariff barriers, the use of selective gray-area measures such as voluntary export restraints (VERs, also known as voluntary restraint agreements, or VRAs), the expansion of bilateral or regional free-trade agreements, and, perhaps most threatening to the underlying GATT regime, the growth of antidumping and countervailing duty (AD and CVD) actions. In all cases, the erosion of GATT rules follows a predictable course: if the GATT makes a politically attractive action (country-specific increases in trade barriers to protect influential constituencies from particular threats to their livelihood) much more difficult in one form than another, governments will channel their actions into the second form. And if the second form of trade protection is less visible (is a less obvious trade barrier), domestic political opposition to it will be reduced.[1]

The form of trade protection that has proved most flexible and least costly in political terms—both domestically and internationally—is the imposition of antidumping or countervailing duties. The GATT explicitly provides for exceptions in regard to both base principles when domestic industries are injured materially from dumping (generally, goods sold abroad at prices below those charged in the exporters' home market) and certain types of government subsidies (broadly, those that promote exports).[2] Although economists today are skeptical of the national welfare claims for protection against these practices, both international price discrimination and government-subsidized export promotion were seen by those who fashioned the GATT as unfair, beggar-thy-neighbor policies that merited specific countermeasures, in each case the imposition of duties that offset the unfair practice.[3]

At the same time, each unfair practice differs only marginally from practices commonly accepted as fair. The GATT does not, and could not practicably, make *any* government subsidy an occasion for firm-specific or country-specific duty increases. So, too, if the GATT tried to counteract the practice of pricing goods to sell at different competitive prices in markets with different supply and demand conditions, it would be

1. Arguments to this effect have been made persuasively in numerous contexts. See, for example, Elmer E. Schattschneider, *Politics, Pressures, and the Tariff: A Study of Free Private Enterprise in Pressure Politics as Shown in the 1929–30 Revision of the Tariff* (Prentice-Hall, 1935); and I. M. Destler, *American Trade Politics: System under Stress* (Washington: Institute for International Economics, 1986). See also Ronald Cass, "Damage Suits against Public Officers," *University of Pennsylvania Law Review*, vol. 129 (1981), pp. 1110–88; and Kenneth A. Shepsle, "The Strategy of Ambiguity: Uncertainty and Electoral Competition," *American Political Science Review*, vol. 66 (1972), pp. 555–68. Close examination, however, raises questions about the strength of the effects of reduced visibility on political action. See Ronald A. Cass and Warren F. Schwartz, "Causality, Coherence, and Transparency in the Implementation of International Trade Laws," in Michael J. Trebilcock and Robert C. York, eds., *Fair Exchange: Reforming Trade Remedy Laws* (Toronto: C. D. Howe, 1990), pp. 24–90.

2. General Agreement on Tariffs and Trade, article 6 (1947). See Kenneth W. Dam, *The GATT: Law and International Economic Organization* (University of Chicago Press, 1970).

3. An influential theoretical work by a noted economist condemning dumping, well known to GATT's drafters, is Jacob Viner, *Dumping: A Problem in International Trade* (University of Chicago Press, 1923). Early argument to the contrary is presented by Gottfried Haberler, *The Theory of International Trade with Its Applications to Commercial Policy* (London: William Dodge, 1936), pp. 296–333. For more recent critiques, see, for example, Jagdish Bhagwati, *Protectionism* (MIT Press, 1989).

engaged in a massive supervention of market prices; except for a few commodities traded at world prices, all goods moving in international commerce would be potentially subject to special duties.

Thus, the problem is separating bad pricing and subsidy practices from good, GATT-consistent practices or, viewed from the other end, that of separating legitimate AD duties and CVDs from illegitimate, GATT-violative trade restraints. Theoretical tools could draw these lines with some precision (although, given the data at hand, usually not to too great a degree), but political consensus has not coalesced around any such theory of AD or CVD practice. Indeed, politicians and political interests have long been uneasy over any alternative mechanism for clarifying the contours of these remedies, each theoretically coherent approach seeming to threaten either infinite expansion or infinite contraction of the remedies. GATT is, hence, understandably ambiguous in striking particular compromises between disparate approaches.

Nations implementing the GATT have taken different views of its commands with respect to identifying and measuring dumping and countervailable subsidies. In this chapter, we examine several aspects of AD and CVD administration in the United States.

Three sorts of questions can be raised about the administration of international trade laws. One kind of question asks whether the administration comports with accounting principles: do the rules employed reflect neutral treatment of the data through the consistent application of accepted accounting practices? A second kind of question asks how the administration conforms to economic principles: do the rules ask the right questions, given some assumed goal for the administration of the law, and go about answering them the right way? Yet another kind of question asks whether the administration violates a legal constraint.

This last question is the one we address here, asking how well U.S. administration of these regimes fits the GATT and in some cases also whether administration exceeds the strictures of national law. This inquiry to some degree recapitulates the other inquiries in this volume insofar as the law arguably requires either fidelity to standard accounting measures or reference to particular economic rationales. Here, however, we conclude that many decisions that may fail to implement either good accounting principles or economic rationality nonetheless may be found consistent with governing legal rules. After all, legal rules at times are sufficiently spongy to be forgiving of many different approaches; and at times, legal rules mandate actions that would make professors of accounting or economics blush. Still, many AD and CVD practices that raise potential questions under the GATT are also those that seem problematic from accounting or economic perspectives.

Issues Relating to Antidumping Law

Although the GATT, both in article 6 and in the Antidumping Code, prescribes a unified test for the imposition of AD duties (they may be imposed only after a finding that dumped imports are, through the effects of dumping, causing material injury to a domestic industry), the United States has bifurcated responsibility over the relevant decisions. The Department of Commerce determines whether the imports at issue have been dumped and, if so, at what discount from the foreign market (or surrogate) price (the "dumping margin"). The U.S. International Trade Commission (ITC) decides whether the dumped imports have materially injured a domestic industry.

In this section, and in the chapter in general, we address only the set of issues committed to the Department of Commerce. Indeed, although some of the points raised relate to general issues of Commerce's administration of the AD laws, our discussion focuses particularly on areas in which there is arguable tension between that administration and the governing national or international legal regime. The discussion does not purport to be a general treatment of the administration of these laws.[4]

The Framework of U.S. Law and the GATT

The principal question for judging Commerce's administration of the antidumping laws is its consistency with the basic requirement of the GATT rule for dumping calculations—the requirement that there be a fair comparison between prices of the investigated goods sold domestically and those sold overseas. Article 2:6 of the GATT Antidumping Code sets forth that requirement:

> In order to effect a fair comparison between the export price and the domestic price in the exporting country (or the country of origin) . . .

---

4. For an excellent and readable summary of how the Commerce Department calculates dumping margins in practice, see Michael Coursey and David L. Binder, "Hypothetical Calculations under the United States Antidumping Duty Law: Foreign Market Value, United States Price and Weighted-Average Dumping Margins," *American University Journal of International Law and Policy*, vol. 4 (1989), pp. 537–53.

two prices shall be compared at the same level of trade, normally at the ex-factory level, and in respect of sales made at as nearly as possible the same time. Due allowance shall be made in each case, on its merits, for the differences in conditions and terms of sale, for the differences in taxation, and for the other differences affecting price comparability.[5]

Other code provisions specify various additional requirements and other parts of article 2 outline the basic methodology of dumping calculations, but the crux of the code's substantive limitation is the fair comparison language of 2:6.

In broad terms, the text of title VII of the Tariff Act of 1930, the U.S. statute that, in its present form, is specifically intended to implement and be consistent with the GATT, is in accordance with at least the basic structure outlined in this provision.[6] Moreover, Commerce's effectuation of that statute generally meets the GATT injunction to make meaningful and fair, apples-to-apples price comparisons. The department essays to take out of its price comparison various influences on ultimate price that are outside the producer-exporter's control. Commerce also attempts to ensure that the price comparisons are based on thick enough markets to be relatively reliable, excluding information that might represent idiosyncratic considerations in a particular sale. Where no meaningful market exists, Commerce also endeavors to allocate various costs in a way that reflects economic reality. The complex nature of most of the calculations that generate Commerce's findings and the general insulation of the civil servants making those calculations from effective political influence further increase the expected coincidence of Commerce's dumping assessments with the GATT's instruction.

Commerce Department Practices: Price Comparisons

The real question, however, is whether there are particular aspects of U.S. law, as set forth in the statute or as administered by Commerce, that are not consistent with the overriding requirement that the relevant

5. See "Agreement on Implementation of Article VI of the General Agreement on Tariffs and Trade," in GATT, *Basic Instruments and Selected Documents* (26th Supplement, Geneva, March 1980). Hereafter GATT Antidumping Code.

6. *Trade Agreements Act of 1979*, S. Rept. 249, 96 Cong. 1 sess. (Government Printing Office, 1979), pp. 57, 87; H. Rept. 317, 96 Cong. 1 sess. (GPO, 1979), p. 49; *Trade Agreements Act of 1979: Statements of Administrative Action*, H. Doc. 153, 96 Cong. 1 sess. (GPO, 1979), pt. 2, pp. 388, 389–93; and *Algoma Steel Corporation, Ltd.* v. *United States* 688 F. Supp. 639 n. 6 (Ct. Int'l Trade 1988), *aff'd*, 865 F.2d 240 (Fed. Cir. 1989).

price comparisons be fair. Several aspects of the administration or structure of U.S. law arguably conflict with this requirement.

TREATMENT OF SALES ABOVE FAIR VALUE. The second most striking manner in which the Commerce Department's calculations in antidumping proceedings depart from the fair comparison required under the GATT (the most striking manner will be addressed below) involves the department's treatment of sales made at prices above fair value. In essence, such sales are disregarded in the dumping calculation.

In determining the existence and magnitude of dumping, the department normally compares individual sales made by the subject foreign producers in the United States with a weighted-average foreign market value (FMV) of merchandise sold by those producers overseas.[7] For cases in which the individual U.S. sales price (USP) is determined to have been made at prices below this weighted-average FMV, a unit margin is calculated, which is included in an aggregate figure used to calculate a weighted-average dumping margin. However, when the USP for a particular transaction is above the weighted-average FMV, a unit margin of zero is used to calculate the weighted-average dumping margin.[8] Above-FMV sales thus cannot be used to offset the margins reflected in sales below FMV.

The bias in such a procedure is evident. As long as Commerce determines that any sales were made in the United States at prices below the weighted-average FMV, Commerce will find that dumping of some magnitude occurred. This will be true even if the vast majority of sales made by the subject foreign producers in the United States were at prices higher than the weighted-average FMV. It will also be true when price volatility is the sole explanation for the purported dumping.

A simple example should illustrate the bias in this one-way averaging process. A Japanese manufacturer of television sets sells 100 television sets in the United States and an equal number in Japan each month for a period of six months, say, from June 1 through December 31. The sets are sold in pairs, one set in Japan and one set in the United States, at exactly the same instant and exactly the same price. Plainly, any fair comparison would find no dumping, since all sales are at identical prices at any given time. Now, without modifying the assumptions in this example, introduce price variation over time: say that prices in both

---

7. Coursey and Binder, "Hypothetical Calculations," pp. 539–52. See also 19 C.F.R. sec. 353.20.

8. This practice is explained and critiqued in Richard Boltuck, "Creative Statistics: Biases in the Commerce Department's Calculation of Dumping Margins," paper prepared for the Western Economics Association Conference, Vancouver, July 10, 1987.

markets rise as Christmas approaches and drop sharply immediately after the holiday. Under Commerce's methodology, dumping will be found— even though at no time were prices in Japan higher than those in the United States for the TV sets, the *average* Japanese price over the six-month period will be above the price of *some* of the U.S. sales. The dumping margin calculated by Commerce in this setting will depend on the magnitude and distribution of the price variation over this period. If, in comparison with the July 1 price, prices are 30 percent higher on October 1, 40 percent higher on November 1, 50 percent higher on December 1, and 10 percent lower on December 26, with ten sets sold at the reduced price the last week in December and all other sets sold each month at the first-of-the month price, Commerce would find a margin of nearly 20 percent on the dumped imports and of nearly 10 percent on the entire 600 sets sold in the United States.

There is nothing in U.S. law that requires the department to stack the deck this way. Indeed, Commerce has itself not uniformly adhered to this practice. In a number of agricultural cases, beginning with *Winter Vegetables from Mexico* in 1980, Commerce has calculated and compared weighted averages for both the FMV and the USP.[9] This practice avoids the unfair treatment of sales made above the FMV, as described above; the foreign producer is found to have dumped or not to have dumped, depending on the actual similarity in average prices over the period examined.

Commerce has thus recognized the argument for comparing FMV and USP averages in cases involving perishable goods, which may be sold at higher prices early on and at much lower prices later on in their short life cycle. In those circumstances, Commerce recognizes that its standard practice for other cases would almost inevitably generate huge margins that in no way reflect dumping. Commerce has not, however, recognized that its standard approach can have similar effects in nonagricultural cases.

Congress arguably has appreciated the fact that Commerce's standard practice, as described above, may not be appropriate in many cases. In 1984 Commerce amended title VII to give Commerce explicit authority to use averaging techniques in determining the USP as well as the FMV. The operative language reads as follows: "For the purpose of determining [United States price] or foreign market value under this section . . . [Commerce] may—(1) use averaging or generally recognized sampling tech-

---

9. 45 Fed. Reg. 20512 (1980).

niques whenever a significant volume of sales is involved or a significant number of adjustments to prices is required."[10]

Although Commerce routinely uses this authority to justify its reliance on average prices for the FMV portion of the comparison, it has rarely chosen to use this authority in computing USP. That general reluctance is particularly striking in investigations, such as *Antifriction Bearings*, involving tens of thousands of individual items and even larger numbers of sales. Such cases clearly are the sort for which Congress contemplated that the averaging and sampling authority would be used.[11]

No convincing defense has been offered in support of Commerce's standard approach. For example, some have claimed that the magnitude of the dumping margin originally calculated by Commerce is of no consequence because it merely establishes the "cash-deposit rate" that will be in effect only until the subsequent administrative review that may be performed by Commerce under 19 U.S.C. sec. 1673f. Such a review is typically carried out on a transaction-by-transaction basis and does not involve the use of comparisons to a weighted-average FMV of the kind calculated by Commerce in the initial antidumping proceeding.

This argument, although plausible on its face, is not in fact a defense of Commerce's initial methodology. It hardly justifies one analytical approach to assert that a more appropriate and accurate approach will be used later. The argument is more confession and avoidance than explanation.

Furthermore, the dumping margin originally set by Commerce does matter, for at least two reasons. First, the dumping margins calculated by Commerce affect the probability that duties will be imposed. Commerce's inconsistent use of average prices at times can find dumping where none exists, and it also can alter the ITC's injury finding, which is the other legal requisite for AD duties. Commerce's margins have been relied on routinely by at least some members of the ITC in determining whether less-than-fair-value (LTFV) pricing has caused injury to a domestic industry.

Second, actual or prospective exporters or importers of a product that

---

10. 19 U.S.C. sec. 1677b(f).

11. *Final Determination of Sales at Less Than Fair Value: Antifriction Bearings (Other Than Tapered Roller Bearings) and Parts Thereof from the Federal Republic of Germany,* 54 Fed. Reg. 18992 (1989). These rare exceptions include *Certain Fresh Winter Vegetables from Mexico,* 45 Fed. Reg. 20512 (1980), *aff'd, Southwest Florida Winter Vegetable Growers Association* v. *United States,* 584 F. Supp. 10 (1984); *Rock Salt from Canada,* 50 Fed. Reg. 49741 (1985); and *Fresh Cut Flowers from Canada, Chile, Colombia, Costa Rica, Ecuador, Kenya and Mexico,* 52 Fed. Reg. 2126 et seq. (1987).

is subject to an antidumping order regard the dumping margin originally set by Commerce as an important factor in estimating the probable costs of the order. A high initial margin suggests the probability of higher costs—attorneys' fees and other transactional costs—in any subsequent administrative review aimed at persuading Commerce either that dumping did not occur or that it occurred to a lesser extent than reflected in Commerce's final dumping determination. More important, in all likelihood the review will not take place for several years. The cash-deposit rate set by the dumping margin directly determines the cost of duties during the period between the initial order and review. Given the time value of money, even firms that are certain at some point to recover the lion's share of this deposit may conclude that the interim out-of-pocket costs are too high to continue the pattern of importation that would be consistent with the product's expected final price (including the duty ultimately assessed). Furthermore, the delayed review produces uncertainty over the ultimate duty; this uncertainty is itself costly and also increases the costs associated with a too-high dumping margin. Since the foreign and domestic markets are subject to numerous, often disconnected forces that affect sales prices, there is virtually no way to predict what the ultimate Commerce margin will be. The problem of prediction, serious in any case, is greatly exacerbated by the prospect that Commerce, on review, may use a *less* accurate measure of relative prices, such as constructed value or best information available. In the meantime, only the current duty rate is certain, and it sets the likeliest final rate (in a Bayesian world, certainly, no rate is more likely). Commerce's unequal use of averages in computing dumping margins thus has substantial effects.

Surprisingly, the department's standard practice of using a weighted-average FMV and treating sales above fair value as irrelevant has not been subject to meaningful scrutiny in the courts or before the GATT. There are, however, some straws in the judicial wind. In a 1989 case, for example, Judge Tsoucalas of the Court of International Trade commented: "The Court questions whether the impact of Commerce's current averaging policy relieves administrative burden to the extent that it leads to 'loss of reasonable fairness in the results.' "[12]

DISREGARDING SALES BELOW THE COST OF PRODUCTION. The Commerce Department's dumping calculations also are often skewed by its practice of disregarding sales in the foreign market it finds to be below

---

12. *N.A.R., S.p.A.* v. *United States,* 707 F. Supp. 553, 559, quoting from H. Rept. 725, 98 Cong. 2 sess. (GPO, 1984).

the foreign manufacturer's cost of production. This practice stems originally from a statutory provision, contained in the Antidumping Act of
1921 and used only in rare cases, that was designed primarily to prevent
importers from misstating import prices for purposes of customs valuations.[13] The scope of this provision was greatly enlarged in the Trade Act
of 1974, when the law was changed, with little, if any, discussion, to
authorize the administering authority (then the Treasury Department) to
disregard such sales in determining FMV when it: "determines that sales
at less than cost of production (1) have been made over an extended
period of time and in substantial quantities, and (2) are not at prices which
permit recovery of all costs within a reasonable period of time in the
normal course of trade."[14]

This provision has become extremely important in U.S. antidumping
law. According to one commentator, about 60 percent of all antidumping
cases decided in the United States since 1980 have been based in part on
allegations of sales below cost. Consequently, this provision has "become
the centerpiece of U.S. antidumping law and policy—without any serious
consideration being given to the phenomenon."[15]

Two aspects of the Commerce Department's rules for implementing
this statutory provision are questionable. One rule, known as the 10-90
rule, applies to nonagricultural cases. In essence, this rule provides that
if less than 10 percent of all sales made by the foreign producer in its
home market are made below its cost of production, none of its sales
will be disregarded in determining FMV.[16] If, on the other hand, 90
percent or more of home market sales are made below the cost of production, as calculated by Commerce, all home market sales at any price
will be disregarded. In such cases, the long-standing practice of Commerce is to resort to constructed value as the measure of FMV. In cases
where sales below the estimated cost of production amount to between
10 and 90 percent of home market sales, just those sales made below the
cost of production are to be disregarded.

The rule seems directly opposite to what common sense would suggest.
Plainly, fictitious sales at prices too low to be credible should not be
permitted to obscure real instances of dumping. But the 10-90 rule does

13. See Gary N. Horlick, "The United States Antidumping System," in John H. Jackson and Edwin A. Vermulst, eds., *Antidumping Law and Practice: A Comparative Study*
(University of Michigan Press, 1989), pp. 99–166.
14. 19 U.S.C. sec. 1677b(b).
15. Horlick, "U.S. Antidumping System," p. 136. The quotation is from p. 133.
16. See *Timken Co.* v. *United States*, 673 F. Supp. 495, 513–514 (Ct. Int'l Trade 1987).

not identify such cases. Instead, it excludes exactly those sales that are *most* likely to have been real sales at market prices. If 90 percent or more of the sales in a foreign market are below what is calculated to be the cost of production, one might be *more* suspicious of that cost calculation than if less than 10 percent of sales were below that figure. Unless the business is one that, as in the old joke, loses money on every sale but makes it up on volume, continued sales at a consistently low price are unlikely to be below cost. Of course, "below the cost of production" is a term of art; just as automobile dealers can sell profitably "at cost" because the dealers buy below "cost," foreign producers can profitably sell below the officially determined cost of production for years.

Again, in agricultural cases the rules are different. Because Commerce recognizes that sales below cost are a common occurrence in such cases, Commerce will not disregard sales made at prices below the cost of production unless they amount to at least 50 percent of the sales under investigation. Still, the concept animating Commerce's rule, if taken at face value, is that the greater the volume of sales, the more likely the sales will be below the seller's own cost.

In fairness, this concept cannot be attributed wholly to Commerce. The law requires that exclusion be based, among other things, on a finding that sales below cost were made for "an extended period of time." As discussed below, however, the extended-time concept may have a different implication when seen in conjunction with the substantive rules for calculating when sales *are* below costs.

The courts have sustained the department's 10 percent threshold for disregarding below-cost sales, but they have also suggested that some applications of this rule will face tough sledding on review. In *Timken Co. v. United States*, the Court of International Trade upheld as a reasonable statutory interpretation Commerce's use of the 10 percent rule "as a benchmark only, to be applied absent indication on the facts before [Commerce] that use of the percentage will not implement legislative intent." The court went on to note, however, that the 10 percent threshold did not take into account the specific statutory requirement that to be excluded from FMV calculations, below-cost sales had to be made at prices that would not "permit recovery of all costs within a reasonable period of time."[17] The court also observed that Commerce's inquiry did not clearly establish that the excluded sale took place over a sufficiently extended period.

17. 673 F. Supp. at 516, 515.

In a subsequent case, *Toho Titanium Co.* v. *United States*, the Court of International Trade sustained the particular Commerce ruling at issue but reemphasized these cautionary notes. The court held that Commerce had established that the respondents' pricing practices would not recover costs within a reasonable period of time. The opinion warned, however, that "in the absence of formal rulemaking proceedings . . . Commerce should not assume as matter of Department practice . . . that company cannot recoup its costs in reasonable period even where 100% of home market sales over the investigatory period are made below cost."[18]

The *Toho Titanium* dictum recognizes the relation between the percentage of sales deemed to be below cost and the way in which Commerce determines whether sales are indeed below cost. The chief criticism of Commerce on this latter score is its arbitrary decision that almost all costs associated with the foreign-made product must be recovered within a six-month period. Plainly, the shorter the recovery period used by Commerce, the higher will be the cost-based FMV found by Commerce and the greater will be the number of sales found to have been made in foreign markets below the manufacturers' cost of production.

In *Daewoo Electronics Co.* v. *United States*, the Court of International Trade questioned even more strongly whether Commerce is taking seriously the statutory command that sales below cost not be disregarded when they are made at prices that permit recovery over a reasonable period of time in the normal course of trade. In that case, respondent Daewoo had argued that Commerce should treat certain management, marketing, and advertisement expenses related to a previous acquisition by Daewoo as "start-up costs" that can be amortized over time. This treatment would bring unit costs in current periods down to a level below the price at which they were being sold in the home market, and hence preclude the treatment of sales below cost. Commerce rejected this argument, concluding that start-up costs are limited to investments in long-term capital assets, such as manufacturing facilities and machinery, or to expenses directly associated with the development of a new product.

The *Daewoo* court disagreed with Commerce. The court noted that the statute did not specify the type and length of sales below cost that might be permissible, and it rejected Commerce's practice of automatically using a six-month period for determining whether the foreign producer's pricing practices permit recovery of all costs. The court stated that, in making such determinations, "the statute requires Commerce to

18. 693 F. Supp. 1191, 1194 (Ct. Int'l Trade 1988).

determine a prospective period of time, which reasonably corresponds to the long-term nature of the business expense in question, over which period the expense should be amortized in order to determine whether all costs would be recovered at the observed sales prices."[19]

The court correctly found that the department's rules on below-cost sales as currently implemented conflict with the statute by failing to distinguish between sales that are below cost by any conventional accounting or economic measure and sales that are below cost only by virtue of an administrative reallocation of costs in a manner inconsistent with accepted business practices. The U.S. statute is sensitive to this distinction at least insofar as it requires Commerce to disregard sales below cost only when they are in fact outside the normal course of trade.

Although the statute is less problematic than Commerce practice under the GATT fair-comparison principle, it still is open to question whether the statute itself that Commerce has been attempting to administer comports with the requirements of the GATT. The GATT permits data on actual sales transactions to be disregarded only when such sales are not in the "ordinary course of trade . . . or when, because of the particular market situation, such sales do not permit a proper comparison."[20] This language is admittedly ambiguous. However, there is nothing in the relevant GATT provision that requires or even authorizes a contracting party to the GATT to disregard price data on actual sales transactions simply because the sales price was below the cost of production estimated by that contracting party. Moreover, it is noteworthy that in the United States sales of domestically made goods at prices below fully allocated production costs are not automatically regarded as suspect under U.S. antitrust law. In this sense, it could be said that the United States treats imported merchandise less favorably than domestically produced goods, which raises the question whether U.S. law, as codified and administered, violates not only the fair comparison required of dumping calculations but also the national treatment requirements established by article 3 of the GATT.

Other Statutory and Administrative Issues: Constructing Value

Under U.S. law, in making the comparisons necessary to determine whether dumping has occurred, the Commerce Department is directed

19. 712 F. Supp. 931, 942 (Ct. Int'l Trade 1989).
20. GATT Antidumping Code, article 2:4.

to rely ordinarily on the foreign market value of the imported merchandise, as reflected by the prices at which such merchandise is sold for consumption in the exporting country (the "home market"). However, when the merchandise in question is not sold in sufficient quantities in the home market, Commerce is directed to establish FMV by looking at the prices at which such merchandise is being sold in third-country markets by the exporting country, or by calculating the constructed value of the merchandise.[21]

Commerce's practice is to view the home market as inadequate for purposes of price comparisons if sales in the home market are less than 5 percent of sales to third countries.[22] In the ordinary case, when the home market is too small (or nonexistent), Commerce is expected to use data on sales to third countries as the measure of FMV if such data are available; constructed value as the measure of FMV is, in theory at least, a last resort.[23] In reality, however, constructed value is used as the measure of FMV in a significant number of cases, and a closer look at this alternative shows why it is so appealing to U.S. petitioners.

MINIMUM GENERAL EXPENSES AND PROFITS. When calculating constructed value, Commerce is directed by statute to include in its cost calculations certain minimum amounts for general expenses and profit, irrespective of what the foreign producer's actual experience may have been. For general expenses, the law provides that the minimum cost allocated to the foreign producer shall be no less than 10 percent of the direct costs of production. The law further provides that the amount allocated for profit shall be no less than 8 percent of the combined general expenses and cost of production.[24]

On their face, these statutory provisions appear incompatible with the GATT. Article 2:4 of the Antidumping Code, states that in cases where constructed-value measures of FMV are used, a contracting party may include as part of the cost calculation "a reasonable amount for administrative, selling, and any other costs and for profits." Article 2:4 adds, "As a general rule, the addition for profit shall not exceed the profit normally realized on sales of products of the same general category in the domestic market of the country of origin." In short, the GATT clearly

21. 19 U.S.C. sec. 1677b(b)(1).

22. 19 C.F.R. sec. 353.41.

23. Formerly, this was made explicit in the statute. Now, Congress's intent on this issue is evident only from a reading of the legislative history. See *Trade Agreements Act of 1979*, S. Rept. 249, pp. 95–96.

24. 19 U.S.C. sec. 1677b(e)(1)(B).

appears to contemplate that each contracting party will determine general expenses and profit attributable to the foreign merchandise by considering the actual experience of firms in the industry at issue. It does not authorize a contracting party to simply set arbitrary, minimum amounts to be applied across the board for each category of cost.

There is no persuasive defense for the approach the United States has taken. One explanation that has been offered is that the qualifying language in the code—which states that, "as a general rule," profit is to be determined on an industry-specific basis—provides sufficient latitude to sustain the long-standing 10 percent general expense and 8 percent profit minimums. This language does imply that exceptions to industry-specific determinations are permitted. That acknowledgment, however, provides at best a weak reed for the U.S. approach. Far from stating the exceptional circumstances that would support a departure from industry-specific assessment, U.S. law transparently establishes a general rule that is entirely at odds with the sort of industry-specific analysis contemplated by the GATT.

SELECTING SURROGATES FOR NME COUNTRIES. At the outset of our discussion of potentially problematic U.S. practices in the administration of the antidumping law, we noted that Commerce's averaging rule was only the second most striking way in which U.S. implementation of the law might depart from the fair comparison required under the GATT. The practice that might be most difficult to sustain under the GATT, and that certainly has been the source of most merriment among commentators, involves the selection of surrogate countries for constructing the value of imports from countries with nonmarket economies (NMEs).

Both the primary definition of dumping, as international price discrimination, and the secondary definition, as sales below the cost of production, require a foreign market as a reference point. Information about the foreign market will establish either the price at which the imported goods trade in the exporter's home market or the cost of production (through the prices of factors used in the production of exports). In nonmarket economies, where prices are set by the state on bases quite different from those that control prices in market-based economies, this information is not useful for establishing a benchmark against which to test the fairness of the price of exports when sold into the United States.

To address this difficulty, Commerce has compared the USP of goods imported from NME countries with the cost of producing the same goods with the same inputs in another country that is similar to the NME but that has a functioning market economy. In theory, this is a sensible approach, but the action here is all in the theory's application. Two aspects of the application, in particular, present considerable difficulties under the GATT fair-comparison standard.

First, the surrogate country need not in fact produce the product at issue, so that the exercise in construction of costs may require extrapolation not only across countries but also across factors. The process began under the Treasury Department with the famous case of *Electric Golf Carts from Poland*.[25] In this dumping case, there was no direct comparison possible between the USP of the golf carts imported from Poland and the price for which the carts sold in Poland; not only was Poland at the time an NME country, but it also had no golf courses and, hence, no need for golf carts. Treasury thus asked what prices were charged for golf carts manufactured in a similar country, using Canada (!) as a country similar to Poland. However, no golf carts were made in Canada, so Treasury had to work from the prices charged for other carts made in Canada that were arguably similar to electric golf carts.

In extending this methodology since then, the Department of Commerce has compared the USP of actual imports to the constructed cost of production based on factors of production from countries that did not make even generally similar products.[26] Furthermore, Commerce now frequently takes the third-country price of the relevant factors of production, weighting them according to the proportions used in the country at issue; in effect it asks, if the golf carts made in Poland had been made in Canada using the same combination of ingredients used in Poland, what would the cost have been? This game can be played in an earnest and straightforward manner, and quite reasonable surrogates for the factors not actually traded in the surrogate country can usually be found.[27] But there is also the opportunity for straying far from what actual costs are when playing this double hypothetical game.

The second and more serious problem is that the selection of the surrogate country provides boundless opportunity for biasing the outcome, and there is more than a little evidence that Commerce has availed itself of this opportunity on occasion. The key consideration in selecting a surrogate should be to find a country that has a generally similar economic structure to that of the NME country and is at a similar stage of

---

25. 40 Fed. Reg. 25497 (1975).

26. See, for example, *Tapered Roller Bearings from Hungary*, 52 Fed. Reg. 17428 (1987).

27. For a defense of this "simulated constructed cost" approach, see Peter D. Ehrenhaft, "The Application of Antidumping Duties to Imports from 'Non-market' Economies," in Jackson and Vermulst, pp. 302–10.

development. With those criteria, however, it would be hard to find (as Commerce has found) that a combination of the Federal Republic of Germany, Japan, France, Canada, Switzerland, and the Netherlands represents a good surrogate for the People's Republic of China or that the United Kingdom or the Federal Republic of Germany are suitable surrogates for the Soviet Union.[28] It is certain that prices of many factors, especially labor, in each of these surrogate countries are much higher than those that would obtain in China or the USSR, if it had sufficiently well-functioning markets to yield reliable cost-of-production data.

Indeed, the higher cost of labor (not adjusted for productivity) is one reason that goods made in advanced economies tend to rely on higher ratios of capital to labor than goods made in less developed economies. A comparison of the USP of Chinese-made or Soviet-made goods with the cost of producing those goods in Western Europe or Japan with Chinese or Soviet factor proportions and Western factor prices will necessarily yield dramatically inflated dumping margins. Commerce's practice in this regard is difficult to square with the comparison mandated by the GATT.[29]

TREATMENT OF SELLING EXPENSES AND THE ESP CAP. Another curious feature of U.S. antidumping law is its treatment of the expenses incurred in selling the foreign merchandise under investigation. To understand this aspect of U.S. law, it is necessary to distinguish two ways of establishing the U.S. price with which the foreign sales price or FMV will be compared. The alternatives are (1) to use the price paid by the U.S. purchaser (compare purchase price, PP) or (2) to use the net received by the exporter from the U.S. sale (compare exporter's sales price, ESP). These two bases for comparing the USP with the FMV do not treat selling expenses in the same way. When the foreign merchandise is sold through an importer unrelated to the foreign producer, the purchase price of the goods sold at their first level of trade in the United States (what the first U.S. buyer pays) is used as the USP to be compared to the FMV (a PP comparison). These PP comparison cases, do not adjust for selling expenses—even major expenses that virtually any firm would regard as directly related

28. These cases are discussed, and Commerce appropriately twitted, in Charlene Barshefsky, "Unfair Trade Laws and Non-Market Economies," *Boston University International Law Journal*, vol. 8 (forthcoming).

29. The Commerce Department's reliance on the price of third-country factors has, however, been supported by the passage of the Omnibus Trade and Competitiveness Act of 1988, which makes the simulated constructed value approach the preferred method for establishing the FMV when information is insufficient to determine product prices in the exporting NME country. See 19 U.S.C. Sec. 773 (c).

to sales of the goods in question are treated as indirect expenses, which are not to be subtracted from the USP or the FMV for the purpose of a price comparison.[30] These expenses may vary from country to country for reasons unrelated to pricing decisions of the manufacturer-exporter, and thus their inclusion in both USP and FMV may distort the comparison. At the same time, there is a reasonable basis for arguing that the exclusion of these expenses would be more distorting. What is most important is that PP comparisons generally involve equivalent (reciprocal) treatment of these selling expenses in both the United States and foreign markets.

This reciprocal treatment is lost, however, when Commerce compares foreign prices and exporter's sale prices in the United States. When the foreign exporter makes its sales through a related party, the Commerce Department will compute an exporter's sales price and compare that to the FMV. In such cases, the governing statutory language has presented the department with special difficulties that it has recognized and struggled with but has resolved to the satisfaction of virtually no one.

In a nutshell, the problem is as follows. Title VII of the Tariff Act of 1930 provides that in ESP transactions, unlike PP transactions, the USP is to be reduced by the deduction of commissions and other selling-related expenses, but the statute does not contain any provision directing Commerce to adjust the FMV by deducting similar expenses incurred in the home market. Standing alone, this is patently unfair to foreign firms, since it will systematically inflate the foreign price relative to the USP. Like the averaging rule, this can lead to a finding of dumping when foreign and U.S. prices are identical or can inflate dumping margins when prices do indeed diverge.

Unlike the situation with averaging, however, officials at Commerce have recognized the distortions this treatment of selling expenses produces. Accordingly, Commerce has had a long-standing practice that, subject to a cap, most selling-related expenses can be deducted from the FMV to offset the deductions from the USP allowed for such expenses.

Commerce's experience with this ESP offset practice may explain its reluctance to address other distortions. Indeed, the ESP offset story is perhaps best summarized by the aphorism, "no good deed goes unpunished." Commerce's practice has raised objections from both domestic and foreign interests, the former arguing that no statutory authority for

---

30. See generally 19 U.S.C. sec. 1677a-b. See also 19 C.F.R. secs. 353.41, 353.56.

such an adjustment exists, the latter disputing the propriety of capping these expenses in only one market.

In marked contrast to parties to Commerce's investigations, U.S. courts have been supportive of Commerce's efforts to make sense out of the conflicting statutory provisions on selling expenses. In *Smith-Corona Group, SCM Corp. v. United States (SCM I)*, the U.S. Court of Appeals for the Federal Circuit sustained the department's practice of deducting selling expenses from the FMV to offset the ESP deduction. In so doing, the court was forced to go through a number of contortions. The court observed that no provision for an ESP offset was in fact provided for in the statute. The court also noted that the ESP offset might be characterized as being at odds with the overall objective of the statute. According to the court, "Congress sought to afford the domestic manufacturer strong protection against dumping, seeming to indicate that the Secretary should err in favor of protectionism."[31] The court even questioned whether the ESP offset did, in fact, represent Commerce's long-standing practice and, if so, whether Congress had acquiesced in that practice as respondents claimed.

Notwithstanding these doubts, the court sustained the ESP offset because one of the goals of the statute is to guarantee "the fair value comparison on a fair basis—comparing apples with apples."[32] The court noted that any other result would lead to unfairly inflated dumping margins, which the court believed were not intended by Congress.

Invocation of this common fruit metaphor could take litigants only so far. The necessity for making a fair, apples-to-apples comparison was of little consequence in a related case decided by the same court two years later, *SCM Corp. v. Silver Reed America, Inc. (SCM II)*.[33] In that case, respondents challenged the cap that Commerce had imposed on the amount of the ESP offset to be permitted. This ESP cap provides that the foreign respondent shall not receive an ESP offset in excess of the amount by which the ESP was reduced by deduction of U.S. selling expenses. The first court to address this cap in *SCM II*, the Court of International Trade, held that the cap was invalid under the rationale of *SCM I*, that is, on the grounds that it did not "comport with the underlying statutory objective of an efficient and fair comparison of prices in two markets."[34] If the necessary implication of a congressionally required deduction of

31. 713 F.2d 1568, 1576 (Fed. Cir. 1983).
32. 713 F.2d at 1578.
33. 753 F.2d 1033 (Fed. Cir. 1985).
34. 581 F. Supp. 1290, 1295 (Ct. Int'l Trade 1984).

selling expenses in one market was the deduction of selling expenses in the other market, it followed that the *amount* as well as the *existence* of the deduction should be treated reciprocally. If the deduction from the USP was not limited in relation to the expenses incurred abroad, then foreign expenses should not be limited when they exceed domestic selling expenses.

The appellate court in *SCM II* did not so much reject this argument as ignore it. The federal circuit ruled that the ESP cap was a reasonable exercise of Commerce's "discretion." The court quoted at length from a portion of its earlier opinion in *SCM I*, a passage seemingly at odds with the basic logic underlying that earlier decision:

> The Tariff Act of 1930, as amended by the Trade Agreements Act of 1979, establishes an intricate framework for the imposition of anti dumping duties in appropriate circumstances. The number of factors involved, complicated by the difficulty in quantification of these factors and the foreign policy repercussions of a dumping determination, makes the enforcement of the antidumping law a difficult and supremely delicate endeavor.[35]

Reaching for reasons going beyond a simple statement that the department could do essentially whatever it wanted to do, the court went on to observe, without elaboration, that the ESP offset might distort the price comparison in favor of foreign manufacturers in some unspecified way, and that the cap "does aid in efficient administration and assists the agency in meeting the exigencies of time and staff limitations."

Arguments such as these might be sufficient to sustain the ESP cap under U.S. law. Whether they would also be sufficient to fend off a challenge based on a claim that the cap is at odds with the fair comparison required by the GATT is highly questionable.

Issues Relating to Countervailing Duty Investigations

For all its difficulty, Commerce's calculation of dumping is subject to challenge only on the mechanics of its measurement rather than on the most basic principles that underlie its administration of the law. The reverse is true with subsidy law. The two principal issues faced in subsidy

35. 753 F.2d at 1039.

calculations—what is a subsidy, and how do you measure it—have both proved problematic. As explained below, the difficulties with these issues are related.

What Is a Subsidy?

The Commerce Department's difficulty in determining what a countervailable subsidy is, chronicled recently with great clarity, should not be surprising.[36] After all, the governing statute contains no meaningful definition of the term "subsidy." In the main countervailing duty statute, title VII of the Tariff Act of 1930 (which applies to cases involving GATT signatories), the term "subsidy" has "the same general meaning as the term 'bounty or grant' " has in section 303 of the Tariff Act (the former version of the countervailing duty statute, which still applies to cases involving imports from countries not party to the GATT). However, section 303 does not define the terms "bounty" or "grant."[37] The only other guidance respecting the meaning of the term "subsidy" provided by the statute is the elaboration of examples of subsidies; the law states that subsidies include

(A)Any export subsidy described in Annex A to the [GATT Subsidies Code]. . . .

(B)The following domestic subsidies, if provided or required by government action to a specific enterprise or industry, or group of enterprises or industries, whether publicly or privately owned, and whether paid or bestowed directly or indirectly on the manufacture, production, or export of any class or kind of merchandise:

(i)The provision of capital, loans, or loan guarantees on terms inconsistent with commercial considerations.

(ii)The provision of goods or services at preferential rates.

(iii)The grant of funds or forgiveness of debt to cover operating losses sustained by a specific industry.

(iv)The assumption of any costs or expenses of manufacture, production or distribution.[38]

36. See Richard Diamond, "A Search for Economic and Financial Principles in the Administration of United States Countervailing Duty Law," *Law and Policy in International Business*, vol. 21 (1990), pp. 507–617.

37. 19 U.S.C. sec. 1677(5); and 19 U.S.C. sec. 1303.

38. 19 U.S.C. sec. 1677(5).

BASIC DIVISIONS: EXPORT-DOMESTIC AND GENERAL-SPECIFIC. The problem with the statutory instruction is its substantial ambiguity, an ambiguity rooted in the GATT Subsidies Code, which the U.S. law generally tracks. The code distinguishes between export and domestic subsidies, clearly making the former persona non grata; although limited allowance is given to the grant of export subsidies for primary products (raw materials), export subsidies on nonprimary products are completely prohibited under the GATT.[39] Because the entire basis for an export subsidy is to increase competition by goods from the subsidizing country in other markets, the effect of such a subsidy is felt directly by other countries. Indeed, these subsidies replicate the effect that is of concern in dumping cases—the erosion of market share and profitability in the importing country through the sale of imports at prices that have been lowered for reasons other than comparative advantage.

The code explicitly recognizes, however, that domestic subsidies (not tied directly to the export of the subsidized good or factor) may be socially or economically desirable for reasons that have nothing to do with improving the competitive position of a given industry in selling to other countries. Governments, even in the most market-oriented economies, underwrite much economic activity and regulate much other activity, changing the position of various constituent groups each time. Money is spent on public works projects; the production or transportation of natural resources (coal or oil or uranium, for instance) is subsidized to generate increased energy use or is taxed to encourage conservation; highways and rail lines are built and maintained at government expense; tax incentives are given to locate in particular regions; grants are given to promote research in certain technologies. The notion, now being formalized in academic writings on "rent seeking," that governments function principally as vehicles for transferring wealth from one group to another within the society underscores the point that domestic political purposes not directly related to GATT concerns can underlie government subsidies.

The problem is that the intent and the effect of these various government actions are terribly difficult to segregate into purely export-oriented and purely domestic categories. Export subsidies are not provided strictly for their external effects, without regard for the redistribution of wealth

---

39. "Agreement on Interpretation and Application of Articles VI, XVI and XXIII of the General Agreement on Tariffs and Trade" (GATT Subsidies Code), *Basic Instruments and Selected Documents*, article 9.

such subsidies effect domestically, and domestic subsidies need not be undertaken without regard for their potential external effects. The GATT recognizes that domestic subsidies no less than export subsidies can affect competitors in other countries. If a domestic subsidy falls within the ambit of subsidies deemed sufficiently likely to have such effects, the GATT Code (article 11:1) allows any country in which the subsidy causes material injury to a competing domestic industry to impose duties to countervail the subsidy.

Having distinguished export subsidies from domestic subsidies, the GATT Code does not provide, any more than U.S. law, any determinate principle for circumscribing the array of government actions that constitute countervailable subsidies. This leaves open the possibility of classifying as countervailable the provision of all kinds of basic government goods and services—the building of roads and infrastructure, the creation of educational systems, and the maintenance of a national defense, just to name a few—that could be said to constitute domestic subsidies because they benefit domestic industries. Commerce has long recognized that it is not the intent of Congress or of the GATT to make such government action the basis for the imposition of countervailing duties.

Until fairly recently, the Commerce Department sought to "screen out" these desirable or unoffensive subsidies by the application of its "general availability" criterion, which posited that a domestic subsidy is countervailable only if provided to a specific enterprise or industry, or group of enterprises or industry, but not if the subsidy is "generally available" to all industries in the domestic economy.[40] Although this test could effectively distinguish between subsidies that functioned mainly to promote a single industry's exports and general investment in education or infrastructure, it had two serious drawbacks. First, it in no way differentiated between different subsidies on the basis of their likely effects in export markets. Second, the distinction on which it did focus—between truly general investment and narrowly targeted subsidies—could not readily be made in many cases on the evidence before the department. The choice faced by Commerce was between a formal test (was the subsidy open to more than one industry?) and a functional one (did the subsidy in fact disproportionately benefit one industry?).

As a result of the second difficulty, in particular, the general availability

---

40. See *Final Affirmative Countervailing Duty Determinations and Countervailing Duty Orders: Certain Steel Products from South Africa*, 47 Fed. Reg. 39379 (1982); and *Certain Softwood Products from Canada*, 48 Fed. Reg. 24159 (1983).

test became politically controversial. The controversy was sparked when Commerce used the test in reaching a negative determination in various cases involving Mexico where the domestic petitioner alleged that Mexican firms were being unfairly subsidized by low energy prices in Mexico.[41] At the same time, the courts began to question Commerce's application of the general availability principle. In *Cabot Corp.* v. *United States*, for example, the court overturned Commerce's ruling that the provision of carbon black feedstock by the Mexican government at subsidized prices was not a countervailable subsidy because such feedstock was theoretically available at the same price to industries other than the carbon black industry under investigation.[42] According to the court, Commerce had not appreciated the distinction between general benefits and generally available benefits that in fact accrue to specific recipient industries; the court indicated that the latter category of benefits, unlike the former category, may be countervailed. In other words, the court decided that Commerce had erroneously used a formal instead of a functional test for general availability.

In the Omnibus Trade and Competitiveness Act of 1988, Congress confirmed the position taken by the *Cabot* court, declaring:

> The administering authority, in each investigation, shall determine whether the bounty, grant, or subsidy in law or in fact is provided to a specific enterprise or industry, or group of enterprises or industries. Nominal general availability, under the terms of the law, regulation, program, or rule establishing a bounty, grant, or subsidy, of the benefits thereunder is not a basis for determining that the bounty, grant, or subsidy is not, or has not been, in fact provided to a specific enterprise or industry, or group thereof.[43]

After this revision of U.S. law (referred to in the legislative history as a "special rule"), the formal generality of a foreign domestic subsidy program is not conclusive on the issue of countervailability.

EFFECTS TESTS. The movement to a functional, rather than a formal, general availability test increases the probability that a domestic subsidy will be deemed countervailable. This makes understanding the substantive

41. See *Anhydrous and Aqua Ammonia from Mexico*, 48 Fed. Reg. 28522 (1983); and *Carbon Black from Mexico*, 48 Fed. Reg. 29564 (1983).
42. 620 F. Supp. 722 (Ct. Int'l Trade), *appeal dismissed*, 788 F.2d 1539 (Fed. Cir. 1985).
43. 19 U.S.C. sec. 1677(5)(B).

principle dividing licit from illicit (or at least countervailable) subsidies critical.

Unfortunately, the GATT contains no clear principle for making this distinction. The GATT does not make all government benefits countervailable, nor could it. Not only would that allow countervailability to be based on almost any governmental activity in the exporting country; it also would present insuperable problems of allocation at the measurement stage in attempting to assess the aliquot share of benefits of education, stable currency, and so on, represented in the exported goods. This stretches the concept of a countervailable subsidy beyond the imagination of even the most trade-restrictive participant in drafting the code.

Shy of this bloated subsidy concept, one might have limited countervailability to export subsidies. That, as noted above, was not done. Many participants in drafting the GATT code tried to confine the ambit of countervailability as close to the export subsidy line as possible. Having passed that line, however, there is no ready foothold in the GATT or in U.S. law to stop at.

How Much Is a Subsidy?

In the absence of a principle for readily constraining the scope of subsidies, the important issue becomes how one measures them. Here again, the search for a reasonably determinate principle becomes both critical and difficult. This point has been made by several recent writings focused on the difference between two different conceptions of what trade subsidy law endeavors to do.[44] One conception, labeled the deterrence model, is that the law is designed to deter foreign governments from granting subsidies that may harm competing domestic producers. The alternative conception, termed the entitlement model, is that the law is

44. See Diamond, "Search for Principles"; Diamond, "Economic Foundations of Countervailing Duty Law," *Virginia Journal of International Law*, vol. 29 (1989), p. 767; and Charles J. Goetz, Lloyd Granet, and Warren F. Schwartz, "The Meaning of 'Subsidy' and 'Injury' in the Countervailing Duty Law," *International Review of Law and Economics*, vol. 6 (1986), pp. 17–36. Before paring the conflicting concepts down to two, Goetz, Granet, and Schwartz, and Diamond reject a third alternative: that trade subsidy law is designed to promote allocative efficiency. Their conclusion that the contours of subsidy law conflict with allocative efficiency in numerous respects is compelling. Goetz, Granet, and Schwartz, ibid., pp. 17–18; and Diamond, "Search for Principles," pp. 22–26, 31–35. See also Ronald A. Cass, "Trade Subsidy Law: Can a Foolish Inconsistency Be Good Enough for Government Work?" *Law and Policy in International Business*, vol. 21 (1990), pp. 609–61.

designed to protect competing domestic producers against the effects of subsidized imports that, as a result of the subsidies, enter the domestic (importing) market at a lower price. Thus, the purpose of the design under the entitlement model is not to prevent subsidies but to offset their effects in the importing country.

The measure of certain subsidies and the rate set to countervail them will vary appreciably in most cases, depending on which view of the law one takes. A deterrence-based subsidy law would focus on the benefit a subsidy confers on a firm exporting to the United States and set duty rates sufficiently high to offset that benefit.[45] An entitlement-based approach, on the other hand, would focus on the effect of a subsidy on the cost of the recipient firm's exports and set duty rates at the level that offsets any reduction in the marginal costs of exports to the United States, since that reduction represents the only aspect of a subsidy that can adversely affect U.S. producers through conduct in the United States.[46]

The entitlement model, focusing on export effects rather than on the receipt of a benefit, falls closer to the basic concerns of the GATT than the deterrence model. The entitlement model also admits of some greater promise of consistent application, for it expressly incorporates economic principles respecting the distribution of costs that must in some form be part of any effort to measure subsidies for CVD purposes.[47] Unfortunately, the entitlement approach runs into two problems: although probably more consistent and less unruly than any alternative, the entitlement approach entails complex calculations to segregate the effects of subsidies within the cost functions of firms; more important, the entitlement approach conflicts with several aspects of U.S. law and to a lesser extent with the apparent understanding underlying the GATT Code. This latter tension is revealed in the code's instruction (in article 4) that countries should impose duties no greater than the subsidy and preferably less if some lower amount will offset injury in the importing country; the implicit assertion is that the principles underlying subsidy measurement are not the same as those underlying assessment of their effects.[48]

A deterrence approach (focusing on benefit), however, is subject to at least as serious difficulties in practice. Anyone using this approach will

---

45. Diamond, "Search for Principles," pp. 27–31; and Goetz, Granet, and Schwartz, "Meaning of 'Subsidy' and 'Injury,' " pp. 19–25.

46. Diamond, "Search for Principles," pp. 51–52; and Goetz, Granet, and Schwartz, "Meaning of 'Subsidy' and 'Injury,' " p. 20.

47. See Diamond, "Search for Principles."

48. See Cass, "Trade Subsidy Law," pp. 639–56.

constantly encounter the problem of establishing the baseline against which benefit is measured. For example, an input subsidy, such as a government payment for labor of certain types, may significantly reduce that component of a firm's costs but may not affect the firm's costs overall, simply causing the firm to substitute one source of labor for another or to substitute labor for capital. The effects-oriented analysis asks what the net reduction in the firm's costs consequent to the subsidy. What question would a benefit-oriented analysis ask?

The explanation most commonly given is that the Commerce Department looks at benefit in terms of the capacity of a subsidy to alter a firm's cash-flow with respect to the subsidized factor rather than in terms of net effects on firm costs. This cash-flow approach, however, could produce absurd results in some cases. Richard Diamond uses the following example to describe the limitations of the cash-flow approach: a foreign government makes a $50 million grant to a firm to build a factory; when political conditions change, the government requires the firm to tear the factory down and makes a second, $5 million grant to tear it down. If any payment or program that affects a firm's cash flow constitutes a countervailable subsidy, the hypothetical firm has received a $55 million subsidy against which Commerce would assess a duty.[49] Commerce then would have to determine the period of time over which the subsidy would be thought to operate so as to allocate the total subsidy across the articles produced by the firm and then apportioned among the exports to the United States, presumably deciding that the relevant period of benefit was the period for which the factory was in operation.

Commentators who have examined Commerce's administration of trade subsidy law do not accuse Commerce of similarly outrageous decisions. Rather, the consensus, perhaps most sharply stated by Diamond, is that Commerce has avoided manifestly silly results by declining consistently to apply any given set of subsidy measurement principles.[50] Instead, Commerce modifies its cash-flow analysis to incorporate some elements of an effects-oriented approach.

The result has been some increased difficulty in persuading U.S. courts that Commerce has appropriately applied the governing law. Courts at

49. Diamond, "Economic Foundations," pp. 765–66. The example is telling in part because it is extreme. Plainly, the hypothetical firm does not contemplate the need for a finding by the International Trade Commission that the subsidy injured American producers. It also relies on a version of the cash-flow principle that accepts even a transitory alteration of foreign firms' cash flow as the basis for duty imposition.

50. Diamond, "Economic Foundations," pp. 21–41, 96–157.

times have vacated Commerce subsidy determinations after finding a lack of coherent principle behind many specific determinations.[51] In other cases, the courts have concluded that Commerce relied on a benefit-focused approach when it should have been looking at effects or that the department's calculation simply failed to produce a result sufficiently consonant with fair measurement to satisfy U.S. or GATT law. In *Armco Inc.* v. *United States*, for example, the Court of International Trade suggested that Commerce's focus should now be on the general concept of "unfairness" and on whether the benefits at issue "peculiarly benefited" the industry. Among other things, the court stated that "even ignoring the problems of focusing on availability, if a particular benefit did constitute an unfair, countervailable subsidy when granted to a certain company or companies, the fact that other companies may also be eligible for the benefit, or even that other companies also utilized the benefit, would not . . . change the fact that the benefit was unfair, and thus countervailable, when granted to the first company."[52]

More recently, however, that court appeared to direct the department to undertake a different mode of analysis, dependent in large part on an assessment of the competitive effects of the alleged subsidy at issue. In *Roses, Inc.* v. *United States*, the court repeatedly declared that it is the effect of the subsidy, not the intention behind it, that must be considered.[53] The court also noted that the legislative history behind the special rule respecting the definition of subsidies introduced in 1988 to obviate the general availability test stressed that, when benefits are broadly available, the department should assess "whether there is a sufficient degree of competitive advantage in international commerce being bestowed upon a discrete class of beneficiaries that would not exist but for government action."[54] This confirmed for the court the understanding that an effects-oriented, export-price-focused analysis was required to measure the degree to which a government program was countervailable. Export effects, however, are only a necessary, not a sufficient, condition. Thus, the court went on to say that general availability is still "one of several relevant factors to be considered in determining whether or not a benefit or com-

51. See, for example, *IPSCO, Inc.* v. *United States*, 687 F. Supp. 614 (Ct. Int'l Trade 1988); and *Michelin Tire Corp.* v. *United States*, 4 CIT 252 (Ct. Int'l Trade 1982). See also Diamond, "Search for Principles," (discussing a series of disagreements between the Court of International Trade and Commerce over subsidy calculations).

52. 733 F. Supp. 1514 (Ct. Int'l Trade 1990).

53. 743 F. Supp. 870 (Ct. Int'l Trade 1990).

54. 743 F. Supp. at 877.

petitive advantage has been conferred upon a 'specific enterprise or industry, or group of enterprises or industries.' "[55]

Although the recent instructions of the Court of International Trade suggest the degree of confusion over the test for the existence of countervailable subsidies and the means for measuring them, they should not be taken as establishing a judicial commitment to a principle strongly contrary to Commerce's approach. Even *Roses* does not provide evidence of an intention to deploy a thoroughgoing export-price-effects approach to subsidy measurement. There is no indication that when, for instance, Commerce encounters a foreign input subsidy it must take the steps necessary to effectuate such an approach: analyze the output elasticities of the subsidized factor and other factors, assess the effects of the subsidy on substitution among factors and on firm output, and trace the output effects through to export ("excess supply") effects. Rather, the court seems simply to be stating the view Commerce already has been acting on: that the alteration of some component of a firm's cash flow cannot, of itself, suffice to constitute a countervailable subsidy and that the magnitude of that cash-flow alteration cannot be the principal means for measuring the subsidy.

That said, if Commerce's basic approach to subsidy determination and calculation remains an acceptable interpretation of U.S. and GATT law, the courts have not provided any sure basis for determining whether a given application of that approach will be affirmed or reversed. Outside of agriculture, many government programs for supporting industry have been abandoned as the world moves increasingly toward competitive, market economies and away from centralized controls (or in some cases as the insolvency of governments becomes manifest and their ability to commit funds declines). These changes have eased the pressure on CVD regimes. But at the same time, Western governments increasingly speak fondly of policies that reflect a "government-business partnership" or that build "critical, technology-driving sectors" of the economy, adumbrating greater need to identify with clarity just what subsidy law is designed to do and how administering authorities, like Commerce, are expected to do it. Unlike some of the issues pertinent to the administration of U.S. antidumping laws, this problem, most visible in the United States because of our near monopoly among GATT contracting parties on CVD investigations, is properly addressed to the GATT.

55. Slip op. 90-44, quoting from H. Rept. 40(I).

Initiating and Processing Antidumping and Countervailing Duty Investigations

As anyone who has been involved in a title VII investigation knows well, such an investigation imposes tremendous burdens—in terms of time and money—on the parties to the case and on the government officials charged with carrying out the investigation. Furthermore, for many of the same reasons given earlier for believing that Commerce's initial dumping calculation has significance, the market disruption occasioned by these proceedings can be substantial, regardless of their outcome. Accordingly, one might expect that the law would permit such an investigation to be triggered only by a party that truly represents the industry in whose name the case is brought. This has not been the practice under U.S. law.

Standing

The standards that the government uses in determining who is entitled to initiate and prosecute an antidumping or countervailing duty investigation—the standing rules—raise two issues. One is substantive, the other procedural.

The procedural issue is which of the two agencies that share responsibility for title VII cases—the Commerce Department or the U.S. International Trade Commission—has the authority to decide standing issues. This is a difficult practical issue, given the opportunity for conflict between the agencies, the peculiar division of authority (including initiation authority) between them, and the sequence of decisions by the two agencies (Commerce/sufficiency, ITC/preliminary, Commerce/preliminary, Commerce/final, ITC/final). We return to this issue below.

In practice, the ITC has deferred to Commerce on this issue, and the Commerce Department in turn has employed a substantive approach that essentially abandons any efforts to assess standing.[56] In only one case has the department ever ruled that a petitioner did not have the standing required to bring a title VII case.

The basic GATT rules on standing in AD proceedings set the frame-

---

56. The commission has not shied from direct statement of that fact; see, for example, *Sweaters Wholly or in Chief Weight of Manmade Fibers from Hong Kong, the Republic of Korea, and Taiwan,* USITC Pub. 2234, inv. nos. 731-TA-448-450 (Preliminary) (November 1989), p. 14, n. 35: "The Commission has consistently declined to decide issues of standing." Uneasy argument for ITC deference to Commerce can be found on pp. 33–38 ("Additional Views of Vice-Chairman Ronald A. Cass").

work for discussion. Article 5 of the Antidumping Code states that "an investigation to determine the existence, degree and effect of any alleged dumping shall normally be initiated upon a written request by or on behalf of the affected industry." The term "industry" for this purpose, in turn, is defined in article 4 of the code: "In determining injury, the term 'domestic industry' shall be interpreted as referring to the domestic producers as a whole of the like products or to those of them whose collective output of the products constitutes a major proportion of the total domestic production of the products." These provisions are themselves ambiguous. It is, for example, possible to interpret the term "major," in the phrase "major proportion of the domestic production," as meaning either a majority or as meaning simply great in rank or importance. The difference between these interpretations could be substantial.

The standing provision in U.S. law, which is parallel to the GATT, is that investigations not initiated by the government on its own motion (a power at present assigned only to Commerce) must be initiated by petition "on behalf of the affected industry." In *Gilmore Steel Corp.* v. *United States*, on appeal of Commerce's only no-standing determination, the Court of International Trade restated the standing requirement: to file a valid petition, a petitioner must not only "be a member of the affected industry, i.e., be an 'interested party,' it must also show that a majority of that industry backs its petition."[57] This formulation suggests a reading of U.S. law as mandating that more than half the industry (presumably, firms accounting for more than half the industry's output) must support an AD or CVD position. After finding that Commerce was authorized to implement this test, the court concluded that Commerce had correctly found that the *Gilmore Steel* petitioners lacked standing.

Since *Gilmore Steel*, however, Commerce has made no serious effort to evaluate the position of most of the industry. Commerce assumes that the requisite standing exists unless the opposition to a petition can show that it constitutes a majority of the relevant industry.[58] In other words, Commerce has turned on its head the burden of proof described by the court in *Gilmore*. Whatever the GATT's standing rule means, Commerce's post-*Gilmore* standing decisions almost certainly violate both GATT and U.S. laws.

Court decisions since *Gilmore*, however, have been inconsistent. In at least two cases, the Court of International Trade, in an apparent retreat

57. 585 F. Supp. 670, 676 (Ct. Int'l Trade 1984).
58. Horlick, "U.S. Antidumping System."

from *Gilmore*, has stated that Commerce "has discretion to dismiss, but is not required to dismiss, petitions that are not shown to be actively supported by a majority of the domestic industry."[59] Quite recently, that court went in the opposite direction, rebuking both Commerce and the ITC for their positions on standing. Judge Musgrave, writing in *Suramerica de Aleaciones Laminadas, C.A.* v. *United States*, held that the absence of proof that a majority of the industry affirmatively supported a petition rendered both agencies' decisions on the petition invalid.[60]

At the same time as Judge Musgrave decided *Suramerica*, a GATT panel ruled that the U.S. approach to standing violated the GATT. Sweden had complained about the "presumptive standing" rule (along with a failure to distinguish American producers of the narrowly defined product closely similar to the imports under investigation) under which the United States found jurisdiction to proceed with an antidumping complaint against a Swedish specialty steel company. The panel report, which has not been publicly released, finds in favor of Sweden on this issue.[61]

Suramerica reached another issue. In addition to passing on the substantive standard for determining standing to petition for the institution of AD and CVD investigations, Judge Musgrave addressed the more difficult procedural question of the division of authority over standing between Commerce and the ITC. In the ordinary case, quasi-adjudicative administrative agencies have clear authority to pass on jurisdictional issues such as standing. That, indeed, was a predicate for the *Gilmore* decision. As far as Commerce is concerned, the ordinary rule appears fully applicable. The Commerce Department, when it passes on the sufficiency of AD and CVD petitions, clearly has authority to find that a petition does not meet the requisites for the institution of investigations because it is not supported by a majority of the industry.

In the bifurcated world of U.S. AD and CVD proceedings, however, things are not so simple. Although Commerce could reject any petition that does not carry evidence of such support, Commerce seldom has information adequate for a precise definition of the industry or for determining with any degree of certainty the inclinations of entities not formally parties to the petition. The ITC, in its preliminary investigation,

---

59. *Comeau Seafoods Ltd.* v. *United States*, 724 F. Supp. 1407, 1411 (Ct. Int'l Trade 1989), citing *Citrosuco Paulista S.A.* v. *United States*, 704 F. Supp. 1075, 1085 (Ct. Int'l Trade 1988).

60. 746 F. Supp. 139 (Ct. Int'l Trade 1990).

61. "GATT Panel Rules against U.S. in Case Involving Duties Levied on Swedish Steel," *BNA International Trade Reporter*, vol. 7 (August 29, 1990), p. 1335.

develops information that is better suited to that end. The ITC, however, does not have the authority to initiate its own motion, and hence might be thought less properly the locus of the determination concerning whether to go forward with an investigation on grounds apart from the evidence of injury from the unfair trade practice. Moreover, at the time of the preliminary determination, the ITC frequently lacks the basis for a conclusive industry definition. And its ultimate definition of the domestic industry must be based in part on a consideration of the decision made by Commerce in defining the relevant class of imports, since the industry definition is derivative of the like product definition, which in turn is informed by the nature of the imports that the domestic products must be like.

The opportunity for interagency conflict if both agencies can make standing determinations in the same AD or CVD proceeding had suggested to ITC commissioners, including one who had disagreed strongly with the substantive test used by Commerce, that only one agency should make a standing determination.[62] Judge Musgrave sharply disagreed, although it is unclear whether that disagreement rests on a view that both the ITC and Commerce have authority independently to determine standing in the same proceeding, even if the determinations conflict, or instead rests on a belief that if Commerce fails to employ the correct substantive test for standing, it is incumbent on the ITC to do so.[63] In all events, it is plain that Judge Musgrave's decision on the substantive point in *Suramerica*, if followed generally, will bring U.S. law into compliance with the GATT on the standing issue.

Procedural Fairness

Many observers have criticized as inherently unfair various aspects of the title VII process. One commentator has gone as far as to equate the Commerce Department's role in this process with that of Torquemada in the Inquisition.[64]

Critics' objections focus on four principal issues. First, title VII proceedings, as a matter of statutory law, must be completed within tightly

62. *Certain Electrical Conductor Aluminum Redraw Rod from Venezuela*, USITC Pub. 2103, inv. nos. 701-TA-287 and 731-TA-378 (August 1988).

63. See *SurAmericana de Alaeciones Laminadas, CA, v. United States*, 746 F. Supp. 139, 146-53.

64. N. David Palmeter, "Torquemada and the Tariff Act: The Inquisitor Rides Again," *International Lawyer*, vol. 20 (Spring 1986), pp. 641-58.

compressed time frames.[65] Few other legal proceedings in the United States are subject to such constraints. Second, it is frequently alleged that the Commerce Department routinely makes excessive or unnecessary requests for information. Clearly this is a feeling deeply held by many foreign respondents; respondents frequently have elected to accept a default judgment by the department rather than comply with its demands that they evidently regarded as too onerous to meet.[66] Third, the department has been attacked as a less-than-impartial decisionmaker in title VII proceedings because the department assertedly serves as judge, jury, and prosecutor.[67] Fourth, the department has been charged with unfairly and frequently using as best available information data submitted by the petitioner, simply because respondents have failed in some minor respect to satisfy all of Commerce's demands for information.

The objections to Commerce's procedures almost certainly would fail if brought as claims under U.S. law. All could be classed as constitutional fairness (due process) claims, but none of them seems likely to succeed on those grounds. Putting aside the question of the rights at issue (the trigger for due process scrutiny of procedures), the processes exceed constitutional minima. Respondents may indeed be handicapped in these proceedings, but the proceedings are not so manifestly unfair on their face as to be unconstitutional.

The Commerce Department certainly is sufficiently impartial to pass due process muster. The claim is not that particular individuals at the department have direct financial interest in the outcome of these cases but that a more subtle bias is at issue. The "judge-jury-prosecutor" analogy is inapposite, since Commerce formally is not so much charged with pressing for an outcome as with investigating facts. That falls well shy of any constitutionally impermissible combination of functions.[68] The real claim is not that bias stems from Commerce performing multiple functions in AD and CVD investigations but that Commerce is politically

---

65. 19 U.S.C. secs. 1671b, 1671d, 1673b, 1673d.

66. For example, Palmeter, "Torquemada and the Tariff Act," pp. 646–47. Perhaps the most striking example of this occurred in the recent cases, *Final Determination of Sales at Less Than Fair Value: Certain Small Business Telephone Systems and Subassemblies Thereof from Taiwan*, where two Japanese respondents, Matsushita and Toshiba, dropped out of the investigation knowing full well that this would likely result in the imposition of antidumping duties in excess of 100 percent. 54 Fed. Reg. 42543 (1989).

67. Palmeter, "Torquemada and the Tariff Act," pp. 641, 657.

68. Constitutional and statutory "combined functions" issues raised in respect of a broad array of administrative decisions are addressed in Ronald A. Cass and Colin S. Diver, *Administrative Law: Cases and Materials* (Little, Brown, 1987), pp. 654–75.

influenced to favor domestic over foreign interests, a claim that could be made even if all initial investigative tasks were devolved on another agency. Again, this claim is far from enough to make out a case, as it argues for removing "policy" influences from this process rather than for removing specific individuals with clearly stated predispositions on particular cases.[69]

The complaint about summary process would fail in the ordinary case unless there was a *very* strong showing of the impossibility of any reasoned presentation within the time allowed, a doubtful matter. This complaint should be viewed in tandem with complaints about excessively burdensome requests for information. The time frames involved in the response to specific requests of particular parties in any given investigation may indeed be too short to allow a meaningful response, especially when a translation is required, and some of these might provide a basis for a judicial determination that Commerce behaved improperly (abused its discretion) in requesting specific data within a compressed period in a particular proceeding. But the *overall* time constraint is not so tight as to preclude a reasoned response in many cases.

The issue of burdensome requests also can be viewed separately: are the requests made of respondents by Commerce so costly as to be unreasonable under constitutional or general administrative law doctrines? Again, assuming that there is a substantial basis for complaint, the more likely avenue for relief is a finding under administrative law doctrines that particular requests from Commerce constitute an abuse of discretion, and this would be an unusual occurrence. Certainly, any such challenge would be an uphill climb if for no other reason than that many of the major trading partners of the United States employ antidumping procedures that are similar to those used in the United States (few countries ever invoke CVD measures). This is a factor that would almost certainly be considered, implicitly if not explicitly, by any U.S. court or GATT panel asked to determine whether the U.S. procedures are legally flawed.

Those who criticize U.S. procedures for being GATT-inconsistent are not without arguments. The GATT contains several unambiguous provisions stating that respondents in antidumping and countervailing duty proceedings must be given a full opportunity to defend against the charges leveled against them. For example, article 6:1 of the GATT Antidumping Code states: "The foreign suppliers and all other interested parties shall

69. See, for example, *Withrow* v. *Larkin*, 421 U.S. 35 (1975); *Friedman* v. *Rogers*, 440 U.S. 1, *reh'g denied*, 441 U.S. 917 (1979); *Association of National Advertisers, Inc.* v. *Federal Trade Commission*, 627 F.2d 1151 (D.C. Cir. 1979), *cert. denied*, 447 U.S. 921 (1980).

be given opportunity to present in writing all evidence that they consider useful in respect of the antidumping investigation." Article 6:7 goes on to provide: "Throughout the antidumping investigation, all parties shall have a full opportunity for the defense of their interests."

These provisions do not go far in spelling out the contours of a GATT-consistent hearing, and it probably cannot be said as a general rule that Commerce's procedures fail to measure up to these standards. However, there clearly have been cases in which a plausible argument could be made that Commerce's treatment of foreign respondents has not comported with the requirements of the GATT. In a recent investigation, for example the department assertedly demanded that English-language translations of thousands of pages of foreign-language documents be provided in several days or less. In such cases, it seems at best doubtful that Commerce could persuasively argue that it has given respondents an ample or full opportunity to present their defense.

Realistically, it is much less likely that a U.S. court could be persuaded that the department's procedures fail to comply with U.S. law. The legislative history of title VII makes it crystal clear that Congress intended that foreign respondents be given only a limited time (and therefore, almost by definition, a limited opportunity) to present their defense. Accordingly, a broadly based challenge to Commerce's procedures—such as one arguing that those procedures usually fail to meet the basic requirements of due process—would not be likely to succeed. Again, however, in particularly egregious situations, this might not necessarily be the case, even given the deference that the courts have traditionally given to administrative agencies.[70]

The appellate court that reviews determinations by Commerce under title VII, the U.S. Court of Appeals for the Federal Circuit, recently gave what may be a sign that it intends to scrutinize more carefully one of the department's practices deemed most objectionable by respondents—that is, the use of data (including the alleged dumping margin) presented by the petitioner as the best available information simply because Commerce has decided, in its own discretion, that a respondent has not complied satisfactorily with all of Commerce's commands. In *Olympic Adhesives v. United States*, the court warned, among other things, that the International Trade Administration (ITA) "has not been given power [in the

---

70. See, for example, authorities noted in Cass and Diver, *Administrative Law*, pp. 131–41; and Ronald A. Cass and Colin S. Diver, *Administrative Law—1990 Supplement* (Little, Brown, 1990), pp. 53–56.

form of the best available information rule] that can be 'wielded' arbitrarily as an informal club."[71] The court later went on to say that the ITA may not properly conclude that resort to the best information rule is justified in circumstances in which a questionnaire is sent and completely answered, just because the ITA concludes that the answers presented do not definitely resolve the overall issue presented. Although the ITA may properly request additional supplemental information, if needed, to resolve the issue, section 1677(e) clearly requires noncompliance with an information request before resort to the best information rule is justified, whether owing to mere refusal or mere inability. Whether this case signals that the court is becoming generally wary of Commerce's frequent resort to the best-information-available rule remains to be seen, however.

Conclusion

It does not seem fitting to end so cursory an exploration of so unclear an area of law with any firm conclusion. Surely, the ambiguity of the apposite GATT codes in many critical respects precludes strong assertions about the consistency or inconsistency of the U.S. administration of AD and CVD laws with the GATT. Surely, too, several important elements in Commerce's administration of those laws raise questions respecting their legality vis-à-vis the GATT that cannot be lightly dismissed.

More important than the narrow legal points discussed above, the administration of AD and CVD laws raises a question of attitude. Lawyers sometimes represent clients who from the outset of a business relationship see that relationship as adversarial. There are a few clients (these tend to be quite regular sources of legal business) who see virtually all relationships as adversarial. Some greater number see only an occasional relationship in that light. Other clients see all relationships as essentially cooperative. They use lawyers to help structure joint relations in ways that avoid pitfalls and occasionally also use lawyers to salvage as much as possible after a relationship turns out to have been less cooperative than the client had expected. No one who has even a modicum of life experience believes that any of these attitudes is ideal all the time or that a savvy operator can always figure out which is right in a given circumstance. But even a small amount of experience will persuade us that, over the broad run of cases, attitude influences outcomes.

71. 899 F.2d 1565, 1572, 1574 (Fed. Cir. 1990).

Although any simple characterization of a large set of decisions, on complex issues, by various officials, and at different times, risks caricature, it seems fair to describe the dominant attitude revealed in the Commerce Department's handling of AD and CVD cases as falling closer to the confrontational than to the cooperative end of the spectrum. Commerce certainly has *not* operated without rules, constantly favoring one set of parties—the ESP offset story is ample refutation of that. But Commerce has deployed a set of practices that both preserves a large degree of administrative discretion and that by and large makes it more likely that higher levels of dumping and subsidization will be found than would be the case under rules that could be more readily defended on professional grounds (accounting, economic, legal). There is at least a coloration in Commerce's practice of an effort to protect the home team against the opposition, to tilt the field slightly in our favor, no doubt with the honest suspicion that fields elsewhere—defined by other countries' trade practices—are more tilted against us.

We do not mean to suggest conscious distortion, even at the margin. There are enough ambiguities in the governing law and subtle pressures on administrative officials to explain more than the degree of bias observed. The industries frequently petitioning for AD and CVD relief are well organized and often have legitimate complaints about biases elsewhere. Their representatives can convincingly argue to Commerce that a given AD or CVD measurement practice was intended by Congress, does not unduly prejudice outcomes, is administratively easier, and is necessary to offset other biases. Only moderate accession to these arguments is required to produce a system such as that now in place.

The problem is that tilting the system is neither costless nor corrective. Even in the short term, our adversarial posture is questionable, since we inevitably find ourselves on both sides of each AD or CVD case. These cases do formally pit American businesses against foreign businesses; but those foreign businesses may import products with as much or more U.S. value (total U.S.-source inputs) as the domestic products, and in all events some American producers and consumers are hurt by increased AD and CVD duties. This makes our lax substantive rule for standing particularly ill advised.

Although even in the short term American interests are not unambiguously helped by an "us-versus-them" approach to trade adjudication, in the longer run our unwillingness to live with truly neutral administrative rules is considerably more problematic. It is likely to encourage less fidelity to GATT rules among our trading partners and to undermine efforts to put more bite in GATT constraints against protectionism. Who would want to enter negotiations when we assert our commitments to free trade and the rule of law while defending Commerce's averaging rule for AD determinations or its choice of surrogate countries for NME cases? As other countries increasingly see AD and CVD as cheap vehicles for protection, our less-than-even handed application of those laws is apt to set the pattern for a distortion of trade. For the United States, the world's largest exporting nation, that is hardly good news. Ultimately, the important question may not be whether our AD and CVD administration has been consistent with the GATT, but whether it has been consistent with our own best instincts and our own best interests.

Comment

Michael Coursey

For the most part, the contributors to this volume focus on five or six practices at the Department of Commerce that they find to be theoretically bankrupt and unfair. On close inspection most of this criticism seems to be much ado about nothing. Had the proposals discussed here been implemented ten years ago, there would be few different meaningful outcomes in the subsequent initial investigations under the dumping and countervailing duty laws than there have been today without those changes.

Since many of the authors represent respondents, one would expect them to provide specific examples of trade law injustice—cases in which specific foreign exporter was wrongfully convicted of dumping because, for example, weighted-average foreign prices were used or a respondent was found guilty of dumping because Commerce employed the notorious ESP cap. But no such examples of injustice are brought forth. The information needed to substantiate such examples, if they exist, is available to counsel who have represented respondents in past investigations. It could be presented at seminars such as this conference or at congressional hearings convened to consider changes to the antidumping and counter-vailing duties laws. Examples would be far more effective in achieving changes than the purely theoretical attacks on Commerce practice that have been the staple of this kind of criticism.

Treatment

One of the criticisms that has been voiced concerns the treatment of U.S. sales above fair value. The complaint is basically that a foreign company is not given any credit for nondumped U.S. sales. Presumably, if one U.S. sale is 10 percent above and one is 10 percent below foreign market value, the sales should cancel themselves out. There should be no finding of dumping. Instead, according to the arguments presented here, the nondumped U.S. sale is ignored, and the exporter is found to be dumping on the basis of the single dumped sale.

Technically, no one seems to have considered how nondumped U.S. sales are actually treated under long-established Commerce methodology. Nondumped sales are not simply disregarded, but are actually given some credit. That is, the value of the nondumped sale is included in the value of the dumped sales (the denominator) that will be divided into the combined unit margins of the dumped sales to determine the dumping margin. This inclusion of value has the effect of diluting the dumping margin, making the margin lower than it would otherwise be if, as implied by the discussants, these sales were totally disregarded and were not given any credit at all in the analysis.

Suppose, for example, that the foreign market value (FMV) is $10.00 and one U.S. sale is $9.00 and the other is $11.00. The dumping margin will be divided by $20.00, that is, the $1.00 that the one dumped sale was below the FMV divided by the total value of *both* U.S. prices ($20.00). This results in about a 5 percent dumping margin. If the nondumped sale was disregarded, the margin would be $1.00 divided by $9.00, or about 11 percent—more than twice as high as the margin that is actually calculated.

The critics of Commerce methodology will not be appeased by this technical explanation, of course, for their position would be that nondumped U.S. sales should be allowed to totally offset dumped sales. Yet the actual treatment of nondumped U.S. sales has much less impact on the dumping margin than they might think. Perhaps that is why no specific cases have been presented of an exporter being found to have dumped despite the fact that many or most of its U.S. sales were not dumped.

Some also say that there is no justification for Commerce's practice in this regard. At the same time, they seem to be struggling to understand exactly what Commerce might have in mind in not offsetting dumped U.S. sales with nondumped sales in initial investigations. The explanation is simple: this methodology is designed to combat a practice known as spot dumping or rifle shooting, in which a foreign competitor gains U.S. customers not by dumping all at once, but by dumping to customers one or a few at a time.

Suppose once again that the FMV value is $10.00 and one U.S. sale to customer A is $9.00 and the other sale to customer B is $11.00 (the same example as earlier). Since the exporter has decided to win the two U.S. customers one at a time, were the positive unit value of $1.00 from the nondumped sale to be included in the numerator, that dollar would wipe out the negative unit volume of $1.00 from the dumped sale, resulting in a dumping margin of zero; and no initial finding of dumping would be made. But Commerce methodology allows an initial finding of dumping to be made so that subsequent activity can be monitored.

One commentator argued that this type of practice just wouldn't occur frequently, if ever. However, the experience at Commerce in dealing with U.S. companies that believe they are being hurt by dumping indicates that U.S. companies are frequently exposed to spot dumping.

To demonstrate that the concept of spot dumping is widely recognized, one has only to look at New Zealand I, the early November 1990 draft of the GATT Antidumping Code. New Zealand I was sponsored by those countries interested in weakening the code and was summarily rejected by the European Community, the United States, and others. That draft, in proposing that all U.S. sales be averaged in the usual investigation, makes an exception for cases in which spot dumping or rifle shooting is demonstrated. Thus, even critics of the dumping law recognize that there can be circumstances in which Commerce's methodology is justified and is not simply an irrational practice.

Disregarding Home Market Sales below the Cost of Production

Consider, now, Commerce's practice of disregarding prices below the cost of production in home market sales in developing FMV. The main complaint here is that Commerce's method of calculating costs must be rigged against foreigners because no business would rationally sell large volumes over an extended period of time at prices that do not allow for an adequate recovery of costs. How can a foreign manufacturer continue to sell products at below cost and stay in business? The answer: cross-product leveraging, or government subsidization.

Take, for example, a diversified company that produces many products profitably, say, a company in consumer electronics or a vehicle-related industry. This company decides to sell a new product where there is tough competition in both the home and targeted markets, such as the United States. This company enjoys reasonable profits on its established, mature products, which it can use to support below-cost sales of the new product in both the home and export markets.

What happens is this: the U.S. industry exposed to cross-product leveraging knows it is facing low-priced competition in the United States. It also knows that the foreign competition is not leveraging its low-priced U.S. sales with high prices of the same product in the home market (that is, is not engaging in price discrimination) because, for example, the U.S. industry is losing market share in that country owing to the low foreign industry prices there. (This is precisely what happened in the Japan semi-conductor cases.)

The law quite logically provides that below-cost prices in the home market should not be used as a benchmark for determining whether sales in the U.S. market are at or above fair value, since below-cost prices are by their nature not fair. But only the below-cost home market prices are excluded from the development of the FMV benchmark unless over 90 percent of home market sales are below cost. In such a case, the law provides that all home market prices are to be discarded, and U.S. prices are to be compared with the products' constructed value—its cost of production plus an amount for profit.

Commerce's methodologies should be subject to constant reality checks to ensure that they are not out of line with commercial reality. In cases where Commerce has excluded home market sales prices as being below cost, one such reality check might be a comparison between the actual financial performance of the home market product under investigation as recorded on the company's records and Commerce's finding that the performance has not been profitable. To my knowledge, no foreign producer has ever gone public with such a comparison. In the absence of such examples, one must assume that Commerce's below-cost methodology largely reflects commercial reality.

Cass and Narkin point out that the general antidumping requirement that prices be at or above fully allocated production costs differs from the judicial interpretation of our antitrust law, which usually requires that a good be sold at less than the variable costs of production before antitrust liability will be found. The authors suggest that this is why foreign exporters to the United States are treated "less favorably" than domestic producers. First, under the antitrust laws, the locus of a product's manufacture is irrelevant; the U.S. sale of products made in Japan must comply with the antitrust laws to the same extent as domestically made and sold products. Foreign-made products thus do receive national treatment under the U.S. antitrust laws. U.S.-made products, of course, are not subject to the U.S. antidumping law; only foreign-made goods are. One could no doubt construct a respectable argument that our municipal price discrimination law, the Robinson-Patman Act, denies national treatment to foreign exporters to the United States, since the antidumping law is more restrictive than the Robinson-Patman Act.

Constructed Value Calculations

As Cass and Narkin also point out, the U.S. antidumping law requires that minimum amounts be included in the constructed value (CV) calculation for general, selling, and administrative expenses (GS&A) and for profit.

IMPUTATION OF A MINIMUM AMOUNT FOR GS&A. It has been incorrectly stated that the reputed 10 and 8 percent amounts are included in the analogous cost-of-production (COP) analysis. This mistake is understandable, for those new to the field often confuse the COP and CV concepts, which differ in several material respects. When Commerce is looking at whether a foreign company is selling in its home or third-country markets at below cost, it looks at the company's actual costs. The 10 percent amount of the cost of manufacturing for GS&A must be included in CV calculations. A 10 percent GS&A is not imputed in a below-cost calculation unless the company does not present Commerce with its actual GS&A cost. If the GS&A happens to be 4 percent, that amount—not 10 percent—is used.

There is no question that the 8 percent profit amount required by statute for CV calculations is not included in COP calculations, because only the manufacturer's costs are at issue there. Profit is irrelevant for COP purposes.

GS&A MINIMUM. Cass and Narkin legitimately criticize the antidumping requirement that the amount of GS&A in a CV calculation must be equal to at least 10 percent of the company's costs of manufacturing. The 10 percent minimum seems to be a holdover from old procedures used by the U.S. Customs Service in valuing imports in situations in which actual GS&A figures were not available.

As just mentioned, antidumping investigations use actual GS&A figures to develop the COP. Whenever Commerce rejects home market prices as being below cost and bases FMV on CV, it most likely has (and thus could use) the actual GS&A amounts in calculating the CV. Furthermore, actual GS&A figures are often submitted to and used by Commerce in price-to-price cases.

In other words, Commerce has often asked for, receives, and verifies actual GS&A information. Although at one time there may have been a concern that foreign exporters could hide their actual GS&A amounts in their books, that simply is no longer a concern, given the sophistication of Commerce's current verification techniques. Thus, there appears to be no reason that the minimum requirement for GS&A should not be dropped from the statute.

This is another area in which it would be useful to have some examples of injustice caused by the 10 percent GS&A minimum. While I was at Commerce, we never had, to my recollection, an exporter claim that its CV amounts were artificially higher than they would have been if its actual GS&A amount were used. There is some suspicion that the 10 percent GS&A minimum actually cuts in favor of exporters, since GS&A amounts are often, if not typically, greater than 10 percent. An exporter under current Commerce practice can choose not to report actual GS&A expenses if they are greater than 10 percent of the cost of manufacture and can have the 10 percent minimum amount imputed instead.

PROFIT MINIMUM. As for the 8 percent (of the cost of manufacture plus GS&A) profit minimum imputed by the statute in CV calculations, remember that profit is relevant only to the calculation of constructed value. Constructed value is relevant only on those occasions when the home or third-country market prices on which FMV typically is based are not available. This happens only on two occasions. One is when there is no viable home market or third-country market on which to base the FMV. In such situations, in which the foreign producer is not selling in the home market in sufficient quantities to allow those sales to be used as a basis for comparison with U.S. sales, what sense does it make to use whatever positive or negative profit figures the foreign company has from those few sales? In essence, the market has been disregarded for purposes of comparison.

Constructed value is also used as foreign-market value whenever prices have been eliminated, because almost all the sales in the home or the third-country market—that is, more than 90 percent of such sales—have been at levels that don't fully recover allocated production costs. Again, some wrong assumptions have been made about what Commerce does with constructed value. Commerce will not base FMV on constructed value until 90 percent of the sales are eliminated. Up to that point, it just throws out the below-cost prices and uses only the prices that are above cost.

Let's say a foreign producer has been making 90 or 95 percent of his sales in the home market at below-cost prices. How could one credibly claim that a profit figure from the few above-cost sales should be used as a reliable figure for profit in a constructed value calculation? One has a difficult time making that argument.

Another surrogate for profit in cases where a company has been making virtually all home market sales at below-cost prices could be the profit from the competitors of that company in the same market. However, it is likely that the profit margins of such competitors will have been squeezed paper-thin by the below-cost selling of the company in question, so it doesn't seem legitimate or appropriate to use the profit margin of those competitors.

When you go through all the options for profit in CV calculation, you are left with having to use some assumption, such as the 8 percent amount currently provide in the law. It is difficult to get around that fact. Whether or not 8 percent is generally reasonable is open to question. But if the antidumping law was amended so that actual profit figures had to be used in CV calculations, the cases would become impossibly complex.

Selecting Surrogates for Nonmarket Economy Cases

The criticism of the nonmarket economy cases is merited, although their unsatisfying outcome is largely the result of the fact that there have been no appropriate market economy countries to use as "surrogates" for nonmarket. The reason Commerce has ended up with Great Britain or Germany as a surrogate for China is that all the more appropriate market surrogates either are being or have been investigated for dumping the same product. They have been accused of dumping. It is not appropriate to focus on the same merchandise at that point.

In the last decade Hungary was what some would call a country with a nonmarket economy, and for that period Commerce treated it as a market economy. Indeed, Commerce goes to great lengths—perhaps too far—to treat nonmarket countries as market-economy countries. Two years ago it came within a hair's breadth of treating China as a market economy in its dumping investigation of headwear. Thus, given the profound changes taking place in the world—in Eastern Europe, in particular—before too long Commerce will probably be treating all such countries as market economies. Then those countries will find that they are exposed to the U.S. countervailing duty law, from which they now have some immunity. One wonders if status as a market-economy country is a briar patch into which the former Warsaw Pact countries really want to be thrown.

The Treatment of Indirect Selling Expenses and the ESP Cap

A few additional points can also be made about the apparent unfairness in Commerce's ESP (exporter's sale price) cap methodology. The GATT Antidumping Code requires that when the export price (or the U.S. price, under the antidumping law) is to be based on the ESP methodology (that is, the price offered to the first unrelated buyer in the export market), certain cost deductions "*including* duties and taxes, incurred between importation and resale, *and profits accruing*," should be made (article 2:6, emphasis added). This language is preserved in the most recent draft of the code (New Zealand I) in proposed article 2:4.

This instruction to deduct profits attributable to value added in the export (that is, U.S.) market seems perfectly logical. The U.S. price should not be inflated by the inclusion of value added in the United States. However, it has long been Commerce's practice, to the strenuous objection of U.S. industries, *not* to follow the code's command to deduct the amount of profit that can be attributed to the *value added* in the United States by the foreign producer's U.S. subsidiary through services such as selling.

At the same time, the code in article 2 does not appear to compel Commerce to allow foreign producers to offset these ESP deductions to U.S. price under Commerce's ESP cap methodology. U.S. industries complain (to Commerce *and* Congress) that the United States should not both violate the code (by *not* deducting from U.S. price the profits attributable to U.S. subsidiaries) and give the foreign producer the benefit of an ESP cap deduction on the FMV side of the equation, since this deduction is not authorized by the code.

The logical solution would be to amend U.S. law to require the deduction of U.S.-related profits from U.S. price (as now required by the code) and to amend the code to provide that the amounts related to the export market are also deducted from the export price on the normal value side without reference to a cap.

Regarding the contention that there is no justification for the ESP cap, since indirect expenses should be greater the further from home a producer is operating, indirect selling expenses in the home market should rarely be greater than selling expenses in the export market.

Procedure Fairness

Another criticism leveled at Commerce is that it makes excessive or unreasonable requests for information on foreign companies. In fact, Commerce's requests for information are minuscule compared with the information foreign respondents would be required to present were the investigations conducted, as others have suggested, before an administrative law judge under rules analogous to the Federal Rules of Civil Procedure.

Furthermore, Commerce's information requests apply equally to petitioners and respondents. You can ask any petitioner who has tried to present a case lately what his costs are. It is a sword that cuts both ways. As for the respondents, they may be a little guilty of wanting to have it both ways, that is, wanting to be able to submit whatever information is deemed relevant to show that foreign producers are not engaging in dumping, yet protesting every time Commerce requests information that the respondents do not deem to be relevant.

The fact that Commerce questionnaires are longer does not necessarily indicate that Commerce is requesting more information. In many cases, this represents a request for more specific information, which means that less information is actually being submitted. In chapter 3, David Palmeter commented on the great number of pages in Commerce's questionnaires in the ongoing antidumping investigation of salmon from Norway. It should be noted that the initial questionnaire response of the seven salmon farms under investigation averaged only eighteen pages—eight for text, ten for attachments (including full-page covers).

In chapter 8, Terence Stewart touches on the point about foreigners who decide not to respond to questionnaires for strategic reasons—because they have determined that they will make out better with the dumping margins alleged in the petition. Note, too, that Commerce does not blindly accept petition allegations in BIA (best-information-available) situations. In one investigation it went back and recomputed and then substantially lowered the rates alleged in the petition because they seemed unreasonably high.

A BIA decision at the Commerce Department is taken seriously. There is no analyst, program manager, division director, or office director who has the power to make a BIA call. It is a decision that requires considerable review, analysis, and the concurrence of virtually all those involved in the investigation.

Exchange Rates

To return to the point that a great deal of what has been said is much ado about nothing, consider the flurry of complaints over the exchange rate issue. Everyone knows that as foreign currency appreciates over the dollar, foreign exporters to the United States will receive less in their home market currency in exchange for the dollars they earn in U.S. sales. This means that exporters will have to either cut costs or raise U.S. prices to keep meeting their production costs. Raising prices in the United States typically means relinquishing market share, which many foreign companies are loath to do in any market.

The point is that those exporters who adjust their prices within a reasonable period in the face of pronounced appreciation of their home market currency over the dollar will have a lagged exchange rate applied to their sales to offset the downward pressure on their U.S. prices caused by the appreciation. Yet no foreign respondent has ever taken advantage of this access to lagged exchange rates. The reasonable inference is that foreign companies exposed to such currency trends wait an unreasonably long period to adjust their U.S. prices upward, and thus are allowing their U.S. prices to fall below fair value.

Comment

Robert Herzstein

I have attempted to assess whether the various issues that Cass and Narkin discuss could be dealt with under the current GATT, as an adjudicated matter, or whether they would need to be dealt with in a future GATT— as a legislative matter if we wished to correct the problem they identify.

Antidumping Issues

First, the practice of disregarding foreign sales below cost of production is clearly one—at least, in the right situation—that could be considered in an adjudication to be inconsistent with the GATT.

Second, the inclusion in constructed value—in all cases—of an arbitrary 10 percent for general expenses and 8 percent for profit is the sort of practice that probably could be successfully challenged in the GATT, again depending on the circumstances. This is one of those legal issues in which, if your facts aren't right on appeal, you are liable to lose, and the precedent is liable to carry into many other cases. But in a specific case if those arbitrary allowances are clearly inconsistent with how business is done in the industry, one might have a winning argument, even under a vague standard such as that contained in the "fair-comparison test" in the GATT.

Third, the refusal to allow deductions for certain selling expenses incurred in the home market when making comparisons under the exporter's selling price is in the same category. In the right situation, one would have a strong case under the current GATT.

Fourth, the choice of inappropriate surrogate countries for comparisons dealing with a product from a nonmarket economy is a bit less clear. Many have grappled with the question of how to apply the antidumping laws to trade from nonmarket countries, but no one has yet come up with anything better than the surrogate-country technique. Everyone usually agrees that it is the least-worst approach to that problem. How closely can we govern the discretion of the U.S. antidumping investigators in choosing an appropriate country to serve as surrogate? Except for a few comparisons—say, between China and the Federal Republic of Germany—the choice of the country to serve as surrogate will be hard to challenge.

Fifth, the most significant antidumping issue that Cass and Narkin discuss is the Department of Commerce's practice of disregarding U.S. sales made above market value and comparing the remaining U.S. sales individually with a price that is the average of sale prices in the foreign market. It is somewhat surprising that this practice hasn't yet been challenged in the GATT. After all, in the case of perishable agricultural products, the U.S. government has acknowledged that a comparison of U.S. average selling prices with an average of foreign selling prices is permissible. That case begins to lay a basis for arguing that, in principle, there is a rational basis for comparing average prices for nonperishable products. (Of course, the practical argument for comparing averages is more compelling in the case of perishable products.)

Sixth, another issue relating to antidumping that needs some attention is the shifting of arbitrary accounting judgments by Commerce Department officers as they do their analyses. This is an important question but probably can't be dealt with under the current GATT. It is hard to argue that one accounting practice is fairer than another. What one needs, simply, is consistency, as the accountants and business people keep telling us. Consistency in accounting can be dealt with through amendments to the GATT code or through some kind of regulation-making process to estabish accounting conventions that could be adopted by the GATT Antidumping Code Committee and then used by all the countries. In that way, we could achieve a degree of consistency over a period of time.

To say that some of the antidumping issues mentioned could be reviewed in the GATT assumes that you can get them to a GATT panel. One of the problems with antidumping under the GATT is that the respondent in an antidumping case is a private company or group of companies and not a government. It is hard for a company to interest its government in an antidumping case. Many governments—both U.S. and foreign—are reluctant to regulate the conduct of private players in the marketplace. Nonintervention is sensible, by and large. But we do need a process by which private respondents can take an antidumping case to the GATT.

We also need a change—some would say a revolution—in the approach to GATT adjudication. We want to build GATT case law on the question whether certain antidumping practices by governments are correct under the GATT standard of making a "fair comparison." Such case-by-case lawmaking requires consistency in the adjudications. But since the GATT, at present, works with ad hoc panels assembled for individual cases, it is not an ideal forum for building case law. Consistency could be improved by increasing the sense of accountability of the GATT panelists, and that is best achieved by having panelists who sit repeatedly on cases rather than when requested, ad hoc.

Countervailing Duty Issues

Countervailing duty issues present a much different picture. The question of which domestic subsidies are countervailable and which ones are not has been a troublesome one under U.S. law. Lawyers in these cases often complain that their clients are hurt by the indecisiveness and shifting nature of the U.S. decisionmaking process. Yet, everyone recognizes that the choice of how much a government will intervene (and under what circumstances) in assisting industries is at the heart of the autonomy or sovereignty of individual countries. It is one of the hardest things to regulate on an international basis.

Perhaps some guidelines will emerge from efforts of the United States and Canada under article 1907 of the Free Trade Agreement, which calls on the two governments to spend five years (extendable by two years) developing a common set of principles to guide the two governments on what is and is not a permissible subsidy. However, little progress has been made on that challenging task in the two years since the agreement was signed. Nonetheless, it is vital for countries that have compatible economic systems to come to a common understanding. In the future, as countries try to achieve greater harmony in their domestic economic practices, there will be more international agreement on what kinds of intervention make sense. Some international rules will undoubtedly evolve.

Another question that will need some attention is how to measure the size of a subsidy when it is part of a complex program with current and long-term consequences for industry. This is probably not an issue that can be adjudicated and clarified under the current GATT, although some progress might be made on a case-by-case basis.

Procedural Fairness Issues

There is some room, however, for dealing with procedural fairness under the current GATT. At least in antidumping cases, one could begin to challenge decisions where evidence indicates they were politicized. Evidence of political influence is sometimes available, thanks to the relative transparency of our government process, and would give the GATT panel an ample basis for ruling that a decision is incompatible with the GATT.

It is harder to challenge a countervailing duty case on the grounds of political influence, because the decisions being made are themselves close to policy decisions. What kind of foreign government practice the U.S. government decides to countervail against is almost a matter of U.S. domestic economic policy.

In antidumping cases, as noted, some of the problems of politically distorted decisionmaking might well be tackled under the GATT if stronger GATT rules were written to make this a nonpolitical process. As other countries begin to adopt and use antidumping laws, which they are doing, the United States will find it all the more important to seek a code of procedural fairness and due process at the international level.

CHAPTER SEVEN

Political Aspects of the Administration of the Trade Remedy Laws

Robert E. Baldwin and Michael O. Moore

Few U.S. industries have sufficient political clout to achieve changes in American trade policy that benefit only their particular sector. The textile and apparel industry has been able to obtain import protection through special quantitative restrictions under the Multifiber Arrangement (MFA), and the steel industry has limited import competition through a series of voluntary export restraint agreements (VERs) negotiated by the government with other countries. But for most industries the only feasible means of gaining favorable changes in trade policy is by joining with other industries in seeking modifications in the way the general trade laws, such as those dealing with foreign dumping and subsidization or fair but injurious import competition, are implemented.

There are four means of influencing the implementation of these laws: (1) change the provisions of the laws themselves, (2) change the agencies administering these laws, (3) change the administrative rules and regulations needed to carry out the provisions of the laws, or (4) change the manner in which the rules and regulations are interpreted by the administering agency.

This chapter explains how these four types of actions have been used to modify the administration of antidumping (AD) and countervailing duty (CVD) laws by the Department of Commerce (DOC)—and earlier by the Treasury Department—over the past twenty-five years or so. It does not cover the role of the International Trade Commission (ITC) in the administration of these laws. The general theme is that Congress, in response to pressures from the business community and because of its dissatisfaction with the executive branch's policies for dealing with problems such as the decline in American international competitiveness and the huge trade deficit, has been the main political force behind all four means of affecting the implementation of these laws. The role of the executive branch has been mainly to dissuade Congress (through the threat of a presidential veto) from enacting provisions that administration officials believed either were inconsistent with U.S. obligations under the General Agreement on Tariffs and Trade (GATT) or would be interpreted as protectionist by our trading partners. Foreign governments seem to have had little direct influence on the administration of the fair trade laws, but instead have exerted their pressures on the executive branch.[1]

The discussion is organized around five main topics: Congress's direct influence on unfair trade laws through changes to the statutes and to the agencies responsible for administering the laws; congressional attempts to shape the rules and regulations formulated by the DOC and to influence the nature of the personnel appointed to the political positions in this agency; the seemingly biased procedures that originated in the DOC itself; results from a regression analysis of DOC final dumping decisions; and the prospects for reform.

Congress "Takes Charge" of the Unfair Trade Laws

U.S. antidumping and countervailing duty legislation over the past twenty-five years illustrates, perhaps better than any other trade issue, the efforts by Congress to regain the dominant role over trade policy it had delegated to the president in the 1930s and the years immediately following World War II.

The Antidumping and Countervailing Duty Laws

Congress first demonstrated renewed interest in antidumping legislation in the late 1960s when the Johnson administration negotiated a new GATT antidumping code as part of the Kennedy Round of multilateral trade negotiations. Key members of Congress, especially Senator Russell Long, the chairman of the Senate Finance Committee, and several of his colleagues on this committee, believed that the code should have been submitted to Congress for approval rather than signed as an executive

---

1. One notable example of successful foreign pressure on U.S. trade remedy law is the introduction of a "material injury" clause into countervailing duty procedures in 1979. The courts have also played an important role in the implementation of U.S. fair trade laws, but this is not discussed here.

agreement. They objected, in particular, to the provision that the imposition of antidumping duties requires dumped imports to be the *principal cause* of material injury, whereas the 1921 antidumping legislation only requires dumping to be causing injury. Congress manifested its displeasure with the executive branch by passing legislation in 1969 directing the International Trade Commission to ignore the code in making its injury determinations.

In the early 1970s Congress became increasingly interested in the role of U.S. unfair trade laws in protecting domestic producers from the rapid rise in imports of industrial products. Many members seemed to accept the claims that dumping by foreign firms and subsidization by foreign governments were damaging firms in their constituencies. At the same time, many tended to agree with Senator Paul J. Fanin's "understanding that your department [Treasury] interprets this statute [on countervailing duties] in such a manner that relief for domestic producers is practically nonexistent."[2] Consequently, Congress began to press for changes that would tighten the enforcement of these laws.

The idea of using the antidumping and countervailing duty laws, rather than the escape clause or safeguard provisions of U.S. trade law, to protect domestic firms facing intense foreign competition had considerable appeal to Congress. Under the safeguard provisions, increased imports had to be "a substantial cause of serious injury" before firms could qualify for protective action, whereas in dumping cases they only had to "be injured" by merchandise sold in the United States at less than fair value.[3] Until 1979, there was no injury requirement at all in countervailing duty cases.

From a congressional viewpoint, the most important disadvantage of seeking protection via the safeguards route is the role played by the president. Although the ITC determines injury by applying technical criteria specified by Congress, all affirmative decisions are sent to the president, who can reject them if he decides that providing import relief "is not in the national economic interest of the United States."[4] This changes the decision from one based on technical factors to one with broader foreign policy implications. The importance of these international

2. *The Trade Reform Act of 1973*, Hearings before the Senate Committee on Finance, 93 Cong. 2 sess. (Government Printing Office, March 1974), pt. 1., p. 197.

3. Trade Act of 1974, P.L. 93-618, sec. 201, 88 Stat. 2012; and Antidumping Act of 1921, chap. 14, title II. The Trade Act of 1979 modified the language so that an industry must be "materially injured."

4. Trade Act of 1974, sec. 202, 88 Stat. 2014.

considerations in moderating protectionist actions is indicated by the fact that the president rejected fifteen of the thirty-three affirmative decisions sent to him by the ITC between 1975 and 1985.

However, the president plays no role in antidumping and countervailing duty determinations. If the DOC finds dumping or subsidization by foreigners and the ITC finds that a domestic industry is materially injured by these actions, offsetting duties are implemented. As Senator Lloyd Bentsen has stated: "Not even the President has the authority to overrule that technical finding, and that is the way we want to keep it."[5] Thus, the determinations are based on considerations that Congress can largely shape through legislation and various pressures on the DOC and the ITC.

Statutory Changes, 1974–88

Between 1974 and 1988 Congress instituted several legislative changes that had a direct effect on dumping and subsidization decisions.

TRADE ACT OF 1974. At the urging of Congress, the administration accepted time limits in the Trade Act of 1974 within which the Treasury must reach its final determinations in antidumping and countervailing duty cases (nine to twelve months for antidumping cases and twelve months for countervailing cases) and specified in detail the deductions and additions permitted in calculating the purchase price or exporter's sales price in antidumping cases. The 1974 act also includes a provision that, in effect, finds dumping if a foreign exporter sells over an extended period at prices below average total costs. This provision, which was included in the act without much discussion, is widely regarded as unfair by foreign producers. It disregards the normal business practice of selling below average total costs but above average variable costs in periods of recession and the need for new producers in industries with high start-up costs and strong learning-curve effects to price initially below total average costs in order to compete with well-established producers. Furthermore, foreign producers argue that, since domestic price competition is not constrained by a fully allocated cost requirement under U.S. antitrust laws, they should not be either.

TRADE ACT OF 1979. Congress continued its efforts to force the executive branch into stricter enforcement of the antidumping and coun-

5. *Nominations of Eric I. Garfinkel, Rufus H. Yerxa, John E. Robson, Robert R. Glauber, and David C. Mulford, Thursday, May 4, 1989*, Senate Committee on Finance (GPO, 1989), p. 2.

tervailing duty laws in the Trade Act of 1979, the main purpose of which was to approve and implement the agreements on nontariff measures negotiated in the Tokyo Round. Still shorter time limits were specified for the final determination of dumping or subsidization (235 days for dumping and 160 days for countervailing duty cases), and annual reviews were required to ensure that antidumping and countervailing duties were maintained at their proper levels. As mentioned, it is alleged that the shortening of the time limits has forced the Department of Commerce to impose requirements that foreign producers find difficult to meet. The grounds on which the DOC can self-initiate antidumping or counter-vailing duty investigations were also broadened in the 1979 act. Another feature encouraging the wider application of U.S. unfair trade statutes was the enumeration in this act of a set of specific government actions that were to be regarded as actionable domestic subsidies.

One manifestation of the influence of Congress in the Tokyo Round negotiations was the exclusion from the new antidumping code of the provision requiring that imports be the principal cause of material injury. At the insistence of the other participants in the Tokyo Round, however, the United States agreed to include a material injury clause in its coun-tervailing duty legislation. Although such a clause is included in article 6 of the GATT, which deals with antidumping and countervailing duties, the United States had been excluded from this requirement, since the U.S. countervailing duty law did not contain such a provision at the time the United States became a GATT member.

The most important accomplishment of Congress in approving the Tokyo Round codes, in terms of enforcing the fair trade laws more vigorously, was that it pressured the president into taking the responsi-bility for the administration of the antidumping and countervailing duty laws away from the Treasury Department.[6] The Treasury had been given responsibility for these matters initially because they involved the col-lection of taxes. However, as the report of the Ways and Means Com-mittee on the 1979 act points out: "The Committee has long been dissatisfied with the administration of the antidumping and countervailing duty stat-utes by the Treasury Department. . . . Given Treasury's performance over the past 10 years, many have questioned whether the dumping and countervail investigations and policy functions should remain in the Trea-sury Department."[7] Many congressional critics of Treasury's adminis-tration would have preferred having a new department created or the

6. *Reorganization Plan No. 3 of 1979*, Message from the President, H. Doc. 96-193, 96 Cong. 1 sess. (GPO, September 1979).

7. *Trade Agreements Act of 1979*, Report of the House Committee on Ways and Means to Accompany H.R. 4537, H. Rept. 317, 96 Cong. 1 sess. (GPO, July 1979), p. 24.

Office of the U.S. Trade Representative enlarged but accepted the shift in responsibility for these matters to the DOC.

Treasury, like the State Department, usually adopts a fairly liberal position in the interagency committees dealing with trade matters. Because of Treasury's statutory concerns with such financial matters as the exchange rate, interest rates, and taxes, the top political appointees in this department must usually be acceptable to the large financial and corporate interests in the country. These interests are heavily involved in international transactions and tend to favor minimum controls over the international movement of goods, services, and capital. Consequently, appointees to the top positions in this department and the bureaucrats who work for these individuals tend to be concerned about the anti-dumping and countervailing duty statutes being used for protectionist purposes.

In contrast, the DOC interacts closely with both large and small businesses in manufacturing and other fields and is greatly concerned with the economic conditions of these businesses. Consequently, the top political appointees, who must be acceptable to this group, and the bureaucracy underneath them tend to become representatives for business interests in their dealings with other government agencies. They are likely to be more sympathetic to claims that U.S. firms are being injured by unfair foreign trade practices than are officials from Treasury. Members of Congress are well aware of the differences in agency positions in interagency deliberations on trade policy matters, and by bringing about this shift in responsibilities on trade matters, they took an important step toward achieving their goal of tightening the enforcement of the fair trade laws.

TRADE AND TARIFF ACT OF 1984. The next significant legislative action on trade issues, the Trade and Tariff Act of 1984, is particularly noteworthy for the provisions that were eliminated. These exclusions—which dealt mainly with targeting, natural resource subsidies, and input dumping—reflected the continued dissatisfaction of the business community and Congress with the administration of the antidumping and countervailing duty laws.[8] In the area of targeting, Congress wanted to impose countervailing duties when a country protected a domestic industry with

---

8. The following discussion draws heavily on Alan F. Holmer and Judith Hippler Bello, "The Trade and Tariff Act of 1984: The Road to Enactment," and Bello and Holmer, "The Trade and Tariff Act of 1984: Principal Antidumping and Countervailing Duty Provisions," in Bello and Holmer, eds., *The Antidumping and Countervailing Duty Laws: Key Legal and Policy Issues* (American Bar Association, 1987), pp. 49–82; 83–117.

the aim of transforming it into a competitive exporter. Under the proposal considered, a targeting subsidy would exist if a government provided coordinated assistance for a specific industry through such actions as the relaxation of antitrust rules, import protection, and restrictions of technology transfer.

The natural resources proposal stemmed from a series of countervailing duty cases involving Mexico and Canada in which the DOC had ruled that subsidies to natural resources used as inputs in exported products were not countervailable because the subsidized inputs (for example, natural gas) were not used just by a specific industry or group of industries. The House passed a bill that permitted countervailing duties even if natural resource subsidies were generally available, provided they constituted a significant proportion of the production costs of exports to the United States.

Input dumping takes place when a product is dumped in the market of a third country and this country uses it as an intermediate input into another product exported to the United States. Both the House and Senate passed bills permitting the application of countervailing duties under these circumstances.

Despite strong support within Congress for all three of these new provisions, none was included in the Trade and Tariff Act of 1984. The targeting measure was finally excluded from the bill reported to the floor by the Ways and Means Committee, and the provisions relating to natural resource subsidies and input dumping were dropped in the House and Senate conference committee. In opposing these measures, the administration and others argued that they were inconsistent with GATT rules, would lead to retaliation against the United States, would be impossible to administer, and would be applied by other countries against the United States.

Although not as significant as the proposals that were rejected, some fairly important changes were included in the 1984 act. One covers so-called upstream subsidies. These are government subsidies to inputs used in manufacturing products that are exported from the subsidizing country to the United States. In the provision adopted, a product can be subject to countervailing duties if subsidized inputs bestow a competitive benefit to the producer—that is, if the price paid for the input is lower than would be paid to another seller in an arm's-length transaction and if this has a significant effect on the cost of manufacturing. As finally drafted, the change merely codified DOC practice.

In response to complaints from small businesses that they were being denied access to the antidumping and countervailing duty laws because of the high costs of hiring the expert legal counsel needed to interpret the legislation, the 1984 act established the Trade Remedy Assistance Office in the ITC to provide information about the procedures involved in filing petitions. The new section also requires all agencies responsible for administering the trade laws to provide small U.S. businesses with technical assistance in preparing petitions and applications for benefits and remedies under these laws. Since similar assistance is not given to foreign small businesses, this provision might be construed as discriminatory.

In other technical changes that benefited U.S. petitioners, the act cut the time and cost of obtaining the confidential business information of respondents and permitted businesses and labor groups to form coalitions in filing antidumping or countervailing duty petitions, thereby reducing the costs to each. Under the act, Commerce is also permitted to establish import monitoring when it believes there is a pattern of persistent and injurious dumping. This would allow the DOC to initiate cases and thus save U.S. producers filing costs.

One change of potential significance involved the use of averages in calculating both the U.S. price and the foreign market value in antidumping cases. Before this change, the DOC could use averaging only in calculating foreign market value. This average price was then compared with individual U.S. prices. If both sets of prices are distributed around the same mean, there is bound to be a finding of dumping, since some of the prices in the United States will be lower than the average of the foreign prices. The new provision permits the use of averages in calculating the U.S. price so that one average can be compared with another. However, most dumping margins are still calculated in the old manner, despite the statutory change.

OMNIBUS TRADE AND COMPETITIVENESS ACT OF 1988. As many others have observed, increased efforts in the 1980s to restrict allegedly dumped and subsidized imports led to increased efforts by foreign producers to circumvent these restrictions. Thus, they began such well-known practices as shipping the parts of a final product subject to an antidumping finding or countervailing duty order into the United States for assembly rather than shipping the final product itself, shipping the parts to a third country not subject to the unfair trade finding for assembly there, or making minor alterations in the product covered by the import restriction.

When the business community complained about these practices, Congress attempted to close these loopholes in the Omnibus Trade and Competitiveness Act of 1988. This act permits the DOC to include imports of the parts of a product in an antidumping or countervailing duty order as well as the product itself. These orders can also be extended to dumped products assembled in third countries and to slightly altered merchandise. Furthermore, the DOC can monitor a downstream product that uses a product subject to antidumping or countervailing duties as an intermediate input if there is reason to believe imports of the downstream product will increase or have increased because of the inputs.

In another effort to broaden the fair trade laws, Congress attempted to discourage dumping by foreign producers in third countries. If such dumping materially injures a U.S. industry (presumably by reducing its exports of the product to the third country), the U.S. trade representative can request the third country to take appropriate action under its own antidumping law on behalf of the United States. If after consultations the country refuses to take action, the trade representative "shall promptly consult with the domestic industry on whether action under any other law of the United States is appropriate."[9]

Two other provisions in the 1988 act relate to the DOC's administration of the fair trade laws. One states that, to be actionable under the countervailing duty law, domestic subsidies must be provided for a specific enterprise or industry or group of enterprises or industries. The 1988 act includes a special rule stating that nominal availability should not be the basis for determining whether a subsidy has been provided for a specific enterprise or industry or group of enterprises and industries. Under pressure from Congress, the Commerce Department had already changed its initial position and adopted this rule, but the act made it binding on the department.

The other provision eliminates drawbacks on antidumping and countervailing duties. Before 1988 an American firm that imported products subject to antidumping or countervailing duties and that used these products as intermediate inputs in a product that was then exported could obtain a rebate of these extra duties, as it could for the regular duties on these products. To the extent that producers in the subsidizing country and in the other exporting countries can purchase these intermediate inputs at subsidized prices, this measure penalizes U.S. exporters, who lose export sales because they are required to pay more for their intermediate inputs.

---

9. *Omnibus Trade and Competitiveness Act of 1988*, Conference Report to Accompany H.R. 3, 100 Cong. 2 sess. (GPO, 1988), sec. 1317.

Another indication of the attitude of Congress toward foreign producers is that it has failed over the years to change the provision in the Antidumping Act of 1921 dealing with cost-of-production calculations. This law requires that not less than 10 percent be included in such calculations for general expenses plus 8 percent for profits. In 1921, when information was difficult to obtain from foreign companies, this rule of thumb made sense. But now that detailed records are available about the profit rates and general expenses of different industries, such a rule no longer makes sense. The DOC should be able to determine average levels of general expenses and profit rates for various industries and use them in cost-of-production calculations. The 8 percent profit rule also ignores the periods of time when it is rational for firms not to cover full costs plus a profit in their prices.

CONCLUSIONS. Understandably, many foreign producers think that certain changes in the antidumping and countervailing duty laws over the past twenty-five years have tilted these laws against them. Most striking perhaps is the rule requiring that foreign market value be above total average costs, which completely overlooks general business conditions and the need for forward pricing in some industries with large initial outlays and strong learning-curve effects. That this rule is not applied to U.S. firms selling within the American market increases the sense of unfairness. As a result of the elimination of drawbacks and the rule on using 8 percent for profit and 10 percent for general expenses in cost-of-production calculations, foreign firms believe that Congress is more interested in providing import protection than in creating conditions of fair trade. Other changes have merely reenforced this view: Congress has tightened the time limits in which foreign firms must respond, while making it easier for U.S. firms to reap the benefits of antidumping and countervailing duty laws by encouraging self-initiation by the DOC, providing technical assistance for small domestic firms, and permitting coalitions of management and labor to file cases.

What needs to be pointed out about these statutory changes, however, is not that they represent a deliberate effort by Congress to tilt the fair trade laws against foreign producers. Rather, they are manifestations of Congress's frustration with flawed laws that are not likely to achieve their intended purpose. When protection is imposed on a country-selective basis, as it is in antidumping and countervailing duty cases, and the products covered are narrowly defined and standardized intermediate inputs used in producing many different products, these duties are not likely to help domestic producers increase production and employment.

Demand may shift not to domestic producers but mainly to producers in other countries not subject to the increase in duties. The producers affected by the antidumping or countervailing orders may themselves shift production facilities to other countries or to the duty-imposing country itself or may assemble the product in these countries. Or they may shift production to a downstream product embodying the affected product, to an upstream product, or to a different item that can be manufactured with the same type of labor and capital. Even if these producers were to withdraw from the U.S. market, U.S. industries might still be injured if they compete in third countries with the alleged subsidizer or dumper.

Most of the antidumping and countervailing duty provisions of 1979, 1984, and 1988 were designed to help mitigate the adverse effects of these duties. Even though some of the simpler means of mitigating the effects of the extra duties have been covered, many more will be difficult to handle without violating GATT rules. The volume and complexity of the statutes and administrative regulations will grow, but the effectiveness of the fair trade laws in protecting domestic output and employment is not likely to improve.

As more methods of circumventing the adverse effects of duty increases are blocked, foreign firms are also likely to change their pricing policies to avoid affirmative dumping determinations, and foreign governments are likely to change their domestic subsidy policies to avoid affirmative countervailing duty determinations. But in many cases foreign producers will still be able to exert strong competitive pressures on U.S. producers. Most of the items covered by antidumping and countervailing duty orders rely on the type of technology and labor and capital requirements in which the United States is losing its comparative advantage. This is a natural consequence of the growth in the global economy, which has helped increase labor skills, the levels of infrastructure investment, and the ability to absorb more advanced technologies. The basic trade problem for the United States is how to adapt to the changing patterns of international trade. At some point in the future, the present use of the unfair trade laws may be attributed to an incorrect perception of the causes of the competitive pressures on U.S. producers.

Pressures on the Department of Commerce

Besides seeking changes in the fair trade laws, protectionist interests may try to influence the administration of existing laws, particularly if those interests have not been organized into effective legislative coalitions. As discussed earlier, the pressure for changing the administration of CVD and AD laws is best routed through Congress. Protection-seeking industries can complain to their representatives and senators, who will subsequently communicate their constituents' concerns to administrators. As expected, the transcripts of congressional hearings show that legislators, especially those on oversight committees, have complained forcefully about the DOC's interpretation of trade law and generally have argued that the DOC should act as an "advocate" for U.S. producer interests. Concerns expressed in private correspondence and contacts may also be important but are beyond the scope of this discussion.

Instead, we concentrate on the DOC practices that have caused the most controversy in Congress: (1) the treatment of small firms in the AD and CVD process, (2) the lack of DOC self-initiated petitions, (3) the handling of "generally available" subsidies, and (4) the DOC's advocacy role in unfair trade cases.[10] Two broad patterns of DOC response emerge. Successful pressure ha˜ not been brought to bear on the DOC in individual cases, with one possible exception. Instead, the DOC has interpreted the law in an essentially evenhanded way in all cases. On the other hand, new regulations seem biased against foreign interests, especially if the statute is open to interpretation. Although the exact source of this bias is impossible to pinpoint, it may be that administrators are reacting to clear and loud "requests" by Congress to act more as an advocate of domestic producer interests in unfair trade cases. Alternatively, the DOC may have an agency-wide bias toward U.S. commercial interests, as discussed earlier in the chapter.

Treatment of Small Firms

Congress has long been concerned with the costs of filing and pursuing CVD and AD petitions. Many on Capitol Hill regard these costs as significant barriers for U.S. firms seeking relief from injurious and unfair

---

10. Congress has also tried to limit the influence of competing executive branch concerns over foreign policy. See, for example, the questions posed to Deputy Assistant Secretary for Import Administration Gary Horlick in *Options to Improve the Trade Remedy Laws*, Hearings before the House Ways and Means Subcommittee on Trade, 98 Cong. 1 sess. (1983), pt. 2, pp. 535–85; and the nomination hearings of Jan Mares for assistant secretary of commerce, *Nomination of W. Allen Moore, Jan W. Mares, and Jill E. Kent*, Hearings before the Senate Finance Committee, 100 Cong. 1 sess. (GPO, 1988), pp. 5–10.

imports, especially small domestic companies. In 1983 Congressman Sam Gibbons (Democrat of Florida), chairman of the House trade subcommittee, pointed out that the costs of CVD and AD petition are especially troublesome to "those that are not extremely large or are not members of huge trade associations."[11] Similarly, Senator Max Baucus (Democrat of Montana), a member of the Senate trade subcommittee, stated in 1984, "I'm a little disturbed by what I perceive to be inadequate representation of small business generally. We in the Congress . . . have a duty . . . to represent the little guy, the person who is not as well heeled, the person who is not able to hire a lobbyist to come to Washington, D.C., and talk to us as frequently as needed. . . . So I suggest that you be more of an advocate for small business."[12]

There have been numerous legislative proposals to reduce the costs to small firms. Some have suggested reimbursing the costs incurred in a successful AD or CVD petition, creating "fast-track" procedures, or having a small business advocate who could initiate petitions and act as an interested party in formal procedures.[13] Although these legislative proposals failed to pass, they do show the importance of this matter for some legislators.

The DOC has been fairly sympathetic to these concerns, at least in its public responses. On numerous occasions, its administrators have commented that they "bend over backward" for small domestic firms at the beginning stages by helping them fill out petitions and assisting in data collection.[14] However, these efforts do not necessarily reflect DOC bias toward small business when calculating dumping and subsidy margins. Indeed, DOC administrators were forceful opponents of the special provisions for small business discussed above. They are quite willing to help small firms at the early stages of the filing process but insist that all completed petitions be treated according to the same rules and regulations. We investigate this issue more formally in the statistical analysis of the next section.

11. *Options to Improve the Trade Remedy Laws*, Hearings, p. 39.

12. *Problems of Access by Small Businesses to Trade Remedies*, Hearings before the Subcommittee on International Trade of the Senate Finance Committee, 98 Cong. 2 sess. (April 1984), p. 54.

13. See, for example, the Small Business and Agricultural Trade Remedies Act of 1983, S. 50, and the Unfair Trade Remedies Simplification Act of 1983, S. 1972.

14. See Deputy Assistant Secretary Gary Horlick's testimony in *Options to Improve the Trade Remedy Laws*, Hearings, pp. 535–85; and Deputy Assistant Secretary Holmer's statement in *Problems of Access*, Hearings, pp. 18–68.

DOC Self-Initiation

Congress has also been concerned about the small number of DOC-initiated AD and CVD petitions. This is perhaps the best example of Commerce's resistance to congressional pressure to change its procedures.

The 1979 Trade Act authorized executive branch self-initiation in an AD or CVD investigation "whenever the administering authority determines, from information available to it, that a formal investigation is warranted."[15] Congressional oversight subcommittee members have repeatedly and pointedly asked DOC administrators about the lack of self-initiated petitions.

The DOC has successfully withstood pressure to increase the number of self-initiated cases. From 1980 to 1985 the only self-initiated petitions involved commitments to file under the trigger-price-mechanism steel program. In spite of congressional complaints, the DOC has stated that it has no incentive to initiate a case for industries that are not injured by imports or are unwilling to bear the substantial costs of a full-blown investigation.[16] Congress, in frustration, has increased the opportunities for petitions by expanding the specific circumstances under which the DOC may self-initiate. Nevertheless, the only self-initiated case in recent years was the 256k semiconductor chip case (ITC case 731-300).

General Availability

Although the DOC has seemingly resisted the pressure for self-initiated petitions, there is evidence that administrators did respond to Congress's clear dissatisfaction with DOC decisions concerning "generally available" subsidies. This is an issue of long-standing controversy in CVD cases and concerns the types of subsidies that may be considered countervailable under U.S. law.

The 1979 Trade Act defines countervailable subsidies as those "provided or required by government action to a *specific* enterprise or industry."[17] The DOC has traditionally ruled that "generally" available government programs such as those connected with education, irrigation projects, and highway construction are not covered by CVD law. However, subsidies that are only "nominally" available to all industries, but

---

15. P.L. 96-39, sec. 702, 93 Stat. 151, and sec. 732, 93 Stat. 162.

16. See the questions posed by Representative Ed Jenkins to Deputy Assistant Secretary Horlick in *Options to Improve the Trade Remedy Laws*, Hearings, pp. 535–85.

17. P.L. 96-39, sec. 771, 93 Stat. 177 (emphasis added).

in fact used by only one, have been considered countervailable by the DOC. As noted earlier, this interpretation was written into the CVD law in 1988.

Controversy has arisen in some cases over what constitutes "nominal" general availability, the most important and politically sensitive cases being those involving Canadian softwood lumber. In 1983 the DOC ruled that the "stumpage" program run by the Canadian government constituted a generally available subsidy. In the related congressional hearings, DOC administrators were aggressively asked to justify their decisions.[18] Subsequently, a number of bills were proposed that would have redefined a countervailable subsidy (see, for example, H.R. 2451 in 1985).

The executive branch successfully fought the passage of these bills, arguing that they would be a violation of U.S. GATT obligations. Nevertheless, when a softwood lumber case was reinitiated in 1986, the DOC ruled in a preliminary decision that the same stumpage program constituted a countervailable subsidy.[19] Many observers believe that this reversal represents one instance at least in which the DOC yielded to intense congressional pressure.

The episode concerning general availability illustrates one way the executive branch has tried to cope with congressional calls for more stringent enforcement of AD and CVD laws. On occasion, the law is interpreted to satisfy Congress and thereby reduce the impact of the more protectionist legislative changes, but the administration resists changing the basic statutes in response to complaints from specific industries.

DOC Advocacy

The advocacy role of the DOC in trade remedy procedures also illustrates how congressional pressure may be applied. The DOC's formal mandate is to determine whether foreign practices violate U.S. law. These

18. See the testimony of Deputy Assistant Secretary Alan F. Holmer, *Proposed Amendments to the Countervailing Duty Law*, Hearings before the Subcommittee on Trade of the House Ways and Means Committee, 98 Cong. 1 sess. (GPO, 1983), pp. 23–39.

19. Asked to comment on a similar reversal involving carbon black feedstock, Deputy Assistant Secretary Gilbert Kaplan stated: "I think some of the thinking in this area has evolved at the Commerce Department and some of the concerns which this committee has which are embodied in this legislation can be dealt with administratively that will work and in a way that is GATT consistent. I would also cite our recent initiation of the lumber case again, and note that there too we are rethinking some of our basic premises." Testimony in *Dual Pricing of Natural Resources*, Hearing before the Subcommittee on International Trade of the Senate Finance Committee, 99 Cong. 2 sess. (GPO, June 1986), pp. 30–31.

decisions should be based on the facts of the case and dispatched in an impartial fashion. For this reason, rules and regulations are published and decisions subjected to judicial review.

Nevertheless, congressional critics have complained repeatedly about the DOC's general approach to domestic and foreign interests. In particular, a number have complained that the DOC is an "adversary" to domestic petitioners.[20] Some members of the House and Senate want DOC administrators to act more as an "advocate" of U.S. domestic producer interests. For example, in nomination hearings for Michael Farren, Senator John C. Danforth (Republican of Missouri) stated, "We count . . . on the Commerce Department in particular to be the advocate for U.S. commercial interests."[21]

To evaluate whether the DOC has responded to these pressures, we consider whether newly adopted DOC rules and regulations, not specifically mandated by statute, reflect an advocacy position. We find that when there is room for interpretation, the DOC has most often chosen procedures that work against the interests of both foreign exporters and domestic consumers. This is consistent with the view that the DOC has acted increasingly as an advocate.

The most important regulatory change that has occurred without statutory prompting concerns the submission of factual information. The law requires only that the DOC base its preliminary and final determinations on "the best information available to it at the time of the determination."[22]

Although legislative requirements remained the same, the amount of information required by the DOC in the conduct of its investigations ballooned in the 1980s. Whereas the regulations issued in 1980 for administration of the AD law contained thirty-seven lines of instructions concerning the submission of information, the regulations implementing the 1984 Trade Act contained forty-nine lines detailing only the format

20. See questions posed by Representative Donald J. Pease to Gary Horlick in *Options to Improve the Trade Remedy Laws*, Hearings, p. 565.

21. Nomination hearings of John Michael Farren for under secretary of Commerce, *Nomination of Kenneth W. Gideon, Bryce L. Harlow, Gerald L. Olson, and John Michael Farren*, Hearings before the Senate Finance Committee, 100 Cong. 1 sess. (GPO, 1989), p. 23. Farren's response provides some insight into recent DOC views on advocacy: "Commerce in the administration of law, particularly the antidumping and countervailing duty law . . . has an opportunity of taking a pro-active role and putting the institution out in front where it has an opportunity to impact on what trade policy is and, frankly, force some decisions in the interagency process" (pp. 23–24).

22. P.L. 96-39, sec. 703, 93 Stat. 153.

of written information submitted to the agency.[23] The DOC has justified this move by pointing to the possibility of judicial review and the statutory deadlines for DOC decisions.

The regulations after 1984 also require that information be submitted on computer media unless the secretary rules that the submitter "does not maintain records in computerized form and cannot supply the requested information . . . without unreasonable additional burden."[24] Furthermore, the exact computer format and method of organizing the data are specified in the DOC questionnaire. Another informational burden is that the submitter must furnish all written documents translated in full into English. Despite complaints by foreign interests, the DOC has rejected the submission of English summaries of individual documents. The DOC can specifically waive this requirement, as it can the computer media requirement, though it has never done so.

These requirements are, of course, particularly onerous for small foreign producers. For a small foreign firm with limited resources, the acquisition of computers and software as well as specially trained personnel capable of translating massive amounts of information on sales and costs into English on short notice is potentially an important impediment to doing business in the United States.[25] Given the congressional concern about the impact of the trade remedy process on small domestic firms, it is ironic how little concern is shown for their potentially "innocent" foreign counterparts.

The significance of the DOC data requirements increases when one considers the potential use of the concept of "best information available" (BIA). U.S. statutes authorize the DOC to use domestic petitioners' allegations concerning dumping or subsidy margins if a foreign firm fails to satisfy all requests for information or fails to submit it by the specified deadlines. The importance of this cannot be underestimated. As the statistics in table 7-1 shows, the average final dumping margin based on the

23. 45 Fed. Reg. no. 26, 8203 (1980); and 54 Fed. Reg. 12781, 12782 (1989).

24. 54 Fed. Reg. at 12782 (1989).

25. This arguably unfair burden on foreigners is even more striking when contrasted with domestic producer requirements in the AD and CVD process. Information is collected by the International Trade Commission in the course of its material injury investigations. The information-gathering burden on the domestic industry has remained substantially unchanged. Furthermore, the questionnaires may be filled in by hand, and, most significant, domestic firms need not submit data using computer media. In a private conversation, an ITC official explained that some small domestic firms did not have the computer resources to handle such requests. Consequently, the requirement was dropped for all domestic producers.

Table 7-1. Descriptive Statistics from DOC Final Dumping Case[a]

		Cases		
Variable[b]	All	Non-BIA[c]	BIA[d]	In regressions
Dumping margin (percent)	34.2 [e]	27.9 [e]	66.7 [e]	31.35 [e]
	(41.2)	(32.9)	(61.1)	(37.85)
Change in exchange rate	7.35	7.92	4.40	9.09
(absolute value)	(15.5)	(16.7)	(4.09)	(18.4)
BIA.DUM	0.16	. . .	. . .	0.16
Number of production	5,129	5,399	3,908	6,346
workers	(12,381)	(12,252)	(4,725)	(15,607)
LDC.DUM	0.18	0.19	0.14	0.23
JAPAN.DUM	0.19	0.19	0.16	0.13
SENATE.DUM	0.67	0.67	0.69	0.83
HOUSE.DUM	0.37	0.36	0.38	0.50
Number of cases	224	188	36	112

Sources: Federal Register and International Trade Commission reports.
a. The numbers in parentheses are standard deviations.
b. See table 7-2 for definition of variables.
c. Cases for which the DOC did not use the "best information available."
d. Cases for which the DOC used the "best information available."
e. Mean of the variable.

questionnaires of foreign firms was 27.9 percent, whereas the average based on BIA was 66.7 percent.

Of course, the use of BIA can be regarded as reasonable, given the obvious incentives of foreign firms to refuse to cooperate in investigations. Indeed, BIA is used quite candidly as a "stick" to induce exporters to provide the requisite information for a complete investigation.[26] Nonetheless, because of the DOC's aggressive information requirements, many firms that would otherwise want to cooperate might be burdened with BIA dumping and subsidy margins.

Biases also appear in the averaging and sampling techniques used to calculate dumping margins. The two most egregious examples involve the use of average foreign market value for dumping margin calculations and the upward bias in the "other firms' " weighted-average dumping margins.

In each antidumping case, the DOC must decide how to compare "the" foreign market value and "the" U.S. value. This is particularly complicated when there are many domestic and foreign sales. In light of this difficulty, the Trade Agreements Act of 1979 authorized the use of "averaging or generally recognized sampling techniques whenever a sig-

26. See the testimony of Gary Horlick, in Options to Improve the Trade Remedy Laws, Hearings, p. 536.

nificant volume of sales is involved" but only when determining *foreign market value*.[27]

The DOC's standard practice has therefore been to compare the average foreign market value with *each* sale in the United States. U.S. sales that occur above or equal to the average foreign value are included in the sample as a zero. (For sales below the foreign value, the margin is calculated as the percentage by which the U.S. price is below the average foreign value.) This obviously yields the absurd result that, as long as prices vary over the sample period, a positive dumping margin can be found even if prices in the two countries are *identical* on every day.[28]

Commerce administrators, recognizing the unfairness of this procedure, asked for legislative authority to use the same averaging technique for calculating the U.S. price. Subsequently, the 1984 Trade Act specifically allowed the use of the average U.S. price for calculating dumping margins. Even so, the DOC has apparently continued with its old practice.

The biased use of averaging techniques also extends to the calculations of the so-called other firms' rate. This dumping margin is applied in cases when only a sample of firms is investigated. The DOC typically investigates a sufficient number of firms to cover at least 60 percent of exports to the United States and usually chooses firms with the largest market shares. Each of these companies receives a firm-specific margin, determined in the investigation.[29] The DOC then orders that the weighted average of all dumping margins be placed on exporters not investigated. However, all negative or de minimis rates are *excluded* in calculating the rate for other firms, while margins based on the best information available, designed to punish uncooperative firms, are *included* in the other firms' rate. Truncating the sample in this fashion clearly biases the other firms' margin upward. It seems especially unfair to burden uninvestigated firms with margins based on punitive rates directed at recalcitrant foreign firms.

27. P.L. 96-39, sec. 773, 93 Stat. 186.

28. Suppose that both the U.S. and foreign prices are $10, $20, and $30 on three separate days, all with the same volume of trade. The average foreign price is $20. The DOC practice would yield a margin of (0% + 0% + 50%)/3 = 16.6%. In contrast, comparing the two average prices would of course result in a dumping margin of zero.

29. A blatantly unfair DOC could use this system to severely bias the other firms' rate upward. For example, since the DOC has access to petitioner claims of unfair sales, administrators could sample only those firms that have the highest alleged dumping margins. The average dumping margins of these firms could then be applied to all other firms. There is no evidence that this has ever occurred.

The Commerce Department's practice has been upheld in a recent Court of International Trade case involving Serampore Industries Pvt. of India (696 F. Supp. [CIT 1988]). Commerce argued in this case that its procedures are fair, since all companies may participate in an antidumping decision by filing voluntary responses. Furthermore, since an administrative review can later establish a firm-specific rate, the firm can later receive a more appropriate margin and be reimbursed with interest for any overcharges. Although the CIT has accepted these arguments and ruled that the practices are not inconsistent with the GATT Antidumping Code, the procedures impose additional burdens on foreign firms. Again the practices are particularly unfair to small exporters. Since participation in the original investigation through voluntary responses and in administrative reviews is costly, these firms must weigh the uncertain gains from a potentially lower rate with the certain costs of providing the vast amount of information necessary for an investigation or review. Furthermore, if one accepts that the 60 percent sample is random and representative, then the other firms' margin should reflect all, including de minimis, rates.

The DOC's treatment of indirect selling expenses, another source of bias in antidumping procedures, has been instituted with little pressure from Congress or other interests. The allowance for indirect selling costs is one of many adjustments made in calculating foreign fair values and U.S. prices. Since the foreign value used in evaluating dumping margins should be ex factory in principle, indirect selling costs should be deducted from the foreign price. This principle also extends to the determination of the U.S. price. U.S. administrators, however, treat indirect selling costs in an asymmetrical fashion. In particular, the allowance for foreign indirect selling costs cannot exceed that for sales in the United States. Consequently, firms whose selling costs are higher at home than in the United States cannot have this fact reflected in AD investigations. If the converse is true, however, the higher U.S. selling costs are fully incorporated, making a positive dumping margin more likely.

This procedure grew out of early resource constraints at the U.S. Treasury Department, the previous administrator of antidumping investigations. Without sufficient resources, the selling cost claims of foreigners could not be verified. Consequently, administrators instituted the present system of capping home market allowances in order to prevent abuse. This procedure has continued, in spite of the enormous amount of data now collected and the resources devoted to verification. As these various examples show, the DOC's procedures are biased against foreign firms. Since these have been formulated without any specific legislative mandate, it appears that the DOC has embraced the advocacy role suggested by Congress.

In summary, Congress has had some success in influencing the day-to-day administration of antidumping and countervailing duty law. Furthermore, the DOC's procedures reflect a tendency toward advocacy rather than impartiality. There is also evidence that the interpretation of general availability in countervailing duty procedures has been successfully changed through direct congressional influence. Both these trends are clearly consistent with congressional wishes for more aggressive administration of these laws.

Empirical Analysis of Final Dumping Margins

In this section we look more closely at the factors affecting DOC calculations of final dumping margins. We determine the presence of bias by controlling for objective economic criteria for each petition as well as for political variables. From the preceding discussion, we expect the detailed published procedures and possibility of judicial review to prevent blatant favoritism or bias in particular cases.

Ideally, these issues should be resolved through case studies on individual petitions evaluating the procedures and evidence collected by the DOC and the consequent margins. The confidential nature of much of the information and the fact that only summaries of particular techniques and procedures are used in the cases make this impossible. Instead, we use regression analysis to explain the calculated dumping margin. Table 7-2 presents the variables used in the analysis and the expected signs on the slope coefficients.

Note that the sample includes only cases that reached the final decision stage at the DOC. Consequently, cases that were ended through voluntary export restraints are not included in the analysis. As many authors have argued, these excluded cases are often more politically sensitive and are perhaps subject to different criteria.[30]

Variable Definitions and Expected Signs

The dependent variable is the final weighted average dumping margin for all firms in a particular case. This margin is calculated according to

30. See, for example, J. Michael Finger and Tracy Murray, *Policing Unfair Imports: The United States Example* (World Bank, 1990).

Table 7-2. *Definition of Variables*

Variable	Definition
Final dumping margin	Weighted average dumping margin calculated by the Department of Commerce (source: *Federal Register*).
Changes in the volume of dumped imports	Percent change in the quantity of allegedly dumped imports for the two most recent periods reported in ITC material injury reports.
Changes in the volume of all imports	Percent change in the quantity of all imports for the two most recent periods reported in ITC material injury reports.
Changes in domestic production	Percent change in the domestic production for the two most recent periods reported in ITC material injury reports.
Changes in exchange rate (absolute value)	(Absolute value of the) percent change in the foreign currency value of the dollar. The base period is the quarterly average one year before the filing of the petition. The second period is the average for the quarter in which the petition was filed (source: *International Financial Statistics*).
Domestic wage	The domestic hourly compensation for production workers in the petitioning industry for the period most recently reported in ITC material injury reports.
Number of production workers	Total number of domestic production workers in the petitioning industry.
BIA.DUM	BIA.DUM takes on a value of 1 if the DOC used best information available in the AD case. BIA.DUM equals 0 otherwise (source: *Federal Register*).
SENATE.DUM	SENATE.DUM takes on a value of 1 if petitioning industry production facilities are located in a state represented on the Senate trade subcommittee.
HOUSE.DUM	HOUSE.DUM takes on a value of 1 if petitioning industry production facilities are located in a congressional district represented on the House trade subcommittee.
JAPAN.DUM	JAPAN.DUM takes on a value of 1 if a case involves imports from Japan.
LDC.DUM	LDC.DUM takes on a value of 1 if a case involves imports from a nonsocialist country from the nonindustrialized world. Newly industrialized countries of the Far East are excluded.

Source: Unless otherwise noted, the data source is International Trade Commission material injury reports.

standard DOC practices; that is, it includes all margins except those deemed de minimis.

The first explanatory is the absolute value of the percentage change in nominal exchange rates for the two quarters before the petition is initiated. This is expected to control for much of the price behavior over the period of investigation, which covers the six months before the initiation of the petition. If the average of foreign prices is compared with each sale in the United States, the greater variability in U.S. prices (because of exchange rate fluctuations) will mean a greater dumping margin, and one can expect a positive sign on the coefficient of this variable.

BIA.DUM takes on a value of 1 if the DOC uses the best information available for any firm in the petition. The expected sign is positive, since the use of BIA often leads the DOC to adopt the petitioner's allegations in calculating the dumping margin.

We also include economic criteria collected by the ITC in determining whether dumping causes material injury to a domestic industry. These may be correlated with the dumping margins, although under the law the determination of dumping margins is not related to the extent of injury. But if greater injury is caused by higher dumping margins, one would expect higher margins to be associated with greater increases in dumped imports and larger decreases in domestic production. Thus, these variables should have positive and negative coefficients, respectively. Changes in overall imports are included to control for general import pressure. A positive coefficient would be indicative of a protectionist bias.

Another set of economic variables helps control for the political economic factors influencing DOC decisions. Some members of Congress clearly want special consideration for small businesses. The number of production workers in the petitioning industry was included. Bias toward these industries would imply a negative coefficient. If the DOC favors low-wage industries for social equity reasons, the wage should have a negative coefficient.

We also investigate whether any bias exists against particular exporting countries. LDC.DUM and JAPAN.DUM take on a value of 1 if the petitions involve less-developed countries or Japan, respectively. Bias would be indicated by a positive-slope coefficient.

A final set of variables controls for direct political influence by congressional oversight subcommittees. SENATE.DUM takes on a value of 1 if the production facilities of the petitioning domestic industry are located in a state represented on the Senate trade subcommittee. HOUSE.DUM is the corresponding variable for production facilities located in the districts of the House trade subcommittee members.[31] If the DOC treats these potentially politically sensitive cases in a biased fashion, the coefficients on SENATE.DUM and HOUSE.DUM should be positive.[32]

Regression Results

The OLS regression results presented in column 1 of table 7-3 indicate that (the absolute value of) changes in exchange rates and the use of the best information available help to explain the final dumping margins. Large movements in exchange rates, either positive or negative, are correlated with high dumping margins. As expected, the use of BIA significantly increases the margins.

The economic indicators of the extent of injury lack explanatory power. Neither falling domestic production nor increases in allegedly dumped imports help explain the dumping margins. There is, however, weak evidence that increasing quantities of overall imports result in high margins.

The variables that control for political pressures are not helpful in predicting DOC decisions. Most important, the slope coefficients on explanatory variables included to control for congressional pressure do not appear to be significant. There is therefore little indication that cases involving Senate or House subcommittee constituencies are favored in any systematic fashion. Similarly, there is no evidence that the DOC finds higher margins in petitions involving small businesses. Nor is there any evidence to indicate that Japan is treated unfairly in the AD process. There is, however, weak evidence that imports from developing countries obtain significantly higher dumping margins.

The high significance level for BIA.DUM indicates that the sample should be separated into two subgroups, one consisting of cases in which

31. The location of production facilities was compiled from ITC reports. This information is available to the DOC before making any final dumping calculations. The locations were matched to congressional districts using the *Almanac of American Politics*.

32. Evidence that these variables help explain material injury decisions by the ITC is found in Wendy L. Hansen, "The International Trade Commission and the Politics of Protectionism," *American Political Science Review*, vol. 84, no. 1 (1990), p. 45; Michael O. Moore, "Rules or Politics? An Empirical Analysis of ITC Antidumping Decisions," Department of Economics Discussion Paper D-9005 (Washington: George Washington University, 1989); and Thomas J. Prusa, "The Selection of Antidumping Cases for ITC Determination," paper presented at the National Bureau of Economic Research conference on Empirical Studies of Commercial Policy, March 16–17, 1990, Cambridge, Mass.

Table 7-3. *Ordinary Least Squares Regression Results*[a]

Variable	Expected sign	Cases		
		All	*Non-BIA*	*BIA*
Constant		28.8*	13.8	137.1*
		(2.35)	(1.12)	(3.4)
Changes in exchange rate (absolute value)	+	0.46**	0.45*	−0.08
		(2.36)	(2.75)	(0.16)
BIA.DUM	+	38.3*		
		(4.19)	. . .	. . .
Changes in volume of dumped imports	+	0.005	−0.27	0.16
		(0.12)	(0.61)	(1.10)
Changes in domestic production	−	−0.02	0.001	0.19
		(0.15)	(0.006)	(0.39)
Changes in volume of all imports	+	0.155***	0.07	0.38
		(1.82)	(0.83)	(1.56)
Number of production workers	−	−0.0001	−0.0001	−0.0002
		(0.74)	(0.79)	(1.29)
Domestic industry wage	−	−0.06	1.03	−2.45
		(0.06)	(1.19)	(0.74)
LDC.DUM	+	19.2**	10.1	34.4
		(2.22)	(1.27)	(0.68)
JAPAN.DUM	+	9.6	9.9	
		(0.95)	(1.13)	. . .[b]
SENATE.DUM	+	−15.3	−4.22	−23.1
		(1.63)	(0.47)	(0.47)
HOUSE.DUM	+	−2.17	2.56	−24.7
		(0.31)	(0.41)	(0.82)
Number of observations		112	94	18
Adjusted *R*-squared		0.23	0.21	0.11
F-statistic		3.9	2.2	2.16
Sum of squared residuals		159,051	85,675	16,510

*Significantly different from zero at a 1 percent level.
**Significantly different from zero at a 5 percent level.
***Significantly different from zero at a 10 percent level.
a. Dependent variable is final dumping margin. The number in parentheses are absolute values of *t*-statistics.
b. No cases involving Japan were included in this data set. Hence this slope coefficient could not be estimated.

BIA was used and the other consisting of decisions based on questionnaire responses. The results of the regression analysis indicate that the most important factor in the non-BIA cases is the movement in the exchange rate. The results for BIA cases indicate that no independent variable offers significant explanatory power.

In sum, the statistical analysis suggests that movements in the exchange rate clearly play an important role in dumping margin decisions. This is not surprising, given the inappropriate method of comparing average U.S.

price to individual foreign sales. The significant impact of the use of BIA on margins also highlights the importance of information requirements and DOC-imposed deadlines. There is also some evidence that developing countries are at a disadvantage in the process.

Prospects for Reform

What are the prospects for eliminating the bias against foreign producers in the DOC's administration of the antidumping and countervailing duty laws? Reform could take place by three possible routes. First, a sufficiently large group in Congress might conclude that the manner in which these laws are being administered is not in the national interest and might therefore press for changes in the fair trade laws. Second, as part of the Uruguay Round negotiations, the administration might agree to changes in the GATT codes on dumping and subsidization that would reduce or eliminate these biases. Since the Uruguay Round package must be accepted or rejected by Congress without the possibility of amending individual parts, these changes may be accepted by a reluctant Congress because members believe that, on balance, the total set of agreements brings benefits to their constituents. Finally, the Department of Commerce could change the administration of existing antidumping and countervailing duty laws.

At present, those in Congress who think the DOC is, if anything, administering the fair trade laws in a way that is too favorable toward foreign firms seem to be in the majority. They have already let it be known to the administration that they oppose any changes in relevant GATT codes that will impose greater discipline over the process of levying antidumping and countervailing duties. Thus, the pressure for reform is unlikely to come from Congress, at least in the short run.

However, two developments might put some political pressure on Congress for changes in existing laws. First, the American economy is becoming increasingly internationalized, and so more U.S. firms are purchasing some of the intermediate inputs they need for their production activities from foreign affiliates or other foreign firms. U.S. firms are beginning to realize that only by combining inputs that can be produced with inexpensive, unskilled foreign labor with other parts of the production process that require skilled U.S. labor will they be able to compete successfully in international markets. Consequently, a growing number of U.S. firms do not want antidumping and countervailing duties imposed on imports used as intermediate inputs, since this raises their production costs.

The second development is that many countries are introducing anti-dumping and countervailing duty laws similar to those in the United States. This raises the possibility that these laws will be administered in a biased manner against U.S. firms. For example, in trying to enter a high-technology market that has been created by another industrial country, American firms may be penalized for the forward-pricing strategy needed to compete in such markets which they have condemned when used by foreign firms attempting to enter the high-technology markets of the United States. As the fear of such outcomes increases, the domestic political constituency in favor of reform is likely to increase gradually. But both this development and the use of foreign-produced goods as intermediate inputs in the United States are unlikely to change the congressional balance of power on trade issues for many years. Industries that benefit from the increased protection resulting from the biased administration of the unfair trade laws still have the political clout to control congressional views on these laws.

The Uruguay Round negotiations are likely to be more successful in promoting changes in the short run. Although the United States is pressing for changes designed to prevent repeat dumping and the evasion of unfair trade penalties by the various means discussed earlier, most other countries are calling for changes that will make it more difficult to impose antidumping and countervailing duties. It is unlikely that the United States will achieve its negotiating objectives in this area without making concessions to those countries. To gain its objectives, the United States may have to accept, among other things, new provisions in the antidumping and subsidies codes aimed at preventing the use of administrative rules to discriminate against foreign countries. This could eventually lead to GATT panel decisions that would prevent the DOC from continuing some of its existing administrative practices.

The outcome is hard to predict. It may well be that both sides will find each other's demands unacceptable and that no significant changes will be made in the dumping and subsidies codes. The chances for this outcome are increased if the United States fails to achieve the better part of its negotiating goals on agricultural trade, trade in services, and the protection of intellectual property rights, and also if the developing countries fail to achieve much of what they are seeking on trade in textiles and apparel, trade in tropical products and agriculture, safeguard rules, and special and differential treatment.

Perhaps the best chance of success lies in changing the Commerce Department's administrative rules covering the unfair trade laws. One theme of this chapter is that many of the DOC's discriminatory practices are not mandated by law. They have apparently been introduced by those charged with the responsibility of administering the unfair trade laws so as to make their task more manageable, to respond to what they think Congress wants, and to implement their own views about how to deal with foreign practices alleged to be unfair.

As mentioned earlier, one administrative practice that is not mandated by law is the DOC's tendency to ignore the information supplied by foreign firms if it does not conform exactly to the required format and instead to use only the information supplied by the firms bringing the dumping and subsidization charges. Many of the format requirements themselves seem to discriminate against foreigners. The practice of comparing the prices of individual U.S. firms with the average price of foreign firms is another biased procedure followed by the DOC, even though Congress modified the law to permit a comparison of averages on both sides.

Most members of the Senate and House want the fair trade laws to be vigorously enforced, but not in ways that themselves are unfair. Consequently, it may well be that the Senate Finance Committee would recommend confirmation of a strong assistant secretary of commerce who believed in the strict enforcement of these laws but who insisted that they be administered fairly. His or her position on administrative rules would be strengthened by emphasizing both the long-run dangers to the United States if such practices spread to other countries and the fact that GATT members are dissatisfied with current U.S. administrative rules in this area.

The current administration—like earlier ones—has shown little interest in making sure that administrative rules in dumping and subsidization cases are not biased against foreigners. But unlike some members of Congress, the top leaders in the administration do not appear to want to deliberately discriminate against foreigners in formulating these rules. The bias has been the result of the interplay of bureaucratic forces within the executive branch and pressures from special interest groups within and outside the government. Consequently, if the top political leaders in the executive branch and in Congress can be made aware of the extent of the bias and the importance of eliminating it from the perspective of long-run self-interest, there may be a reasonable chance of making progress in reducing the bias against foreigners.

Comment

Pietro S. Nivola

The picture of the trade-remedy apparatus that emerges from Baldwin and Moore's discussion seems a far cry from the model that public administration theorists, beginning with Woodrow Wilson, originally had in mind: namely, a framework that would consistently thwart protectionist pressures because legislators would fully delegate responsibility to administrators "capable of looking at the whole economic situation of the country with a dispassionate and disinterested scrutiny," as Wilson put it. Congress may no longer be legislating tariffs or other flagrant trade restrictions, but it still exerts considerable control through more circuitous methods. Among the legislative incursions that have mattered most are provisions enabling antidumping enforcers to impute fair-market values on the basis of average production costs, the transfer of administrative duties from the Treasury to the Commerce Department, and the anticircumvention amendments of the 1988 trade act. In addition, the authors stress that Congress has increasingly insisted that the Department of Commerce act explicitly as an "advocate" for domestic producer interests, and Commerce appears to have responded to congressional pressure by favoring those interests in a number of discretionary gray areas.

The clearest example seems to be the use of so-called best available information (or BIA) in computing dumping margins. The DOC presents alleged foreign offenders with informational requirements so extensive that many fail to supply the necessary data in time or in the proper format. The department then opts for a shortcut—the BIA, which is often drawn from the brief submitted by the domestic petitioner. With this technique, the authors report, the estimated dumping margins tend to be twice as high as those in cases where foreign firms are able to comply with DOC questionnaires.

Another tendentious procedure that seems to stem from the Commerce Department's advocacy role is the way foreign market values are compared to U.S. values in determining dumping margins. For some reason, Commerce compares an average foreign value with each sale in the United States, excluding any sales that occur at or above the average. Not surprisingly, this methodology has generated positive margins.

Examples of seeming methodological biases like these are baffling to anyone who is not a trade policy insider. They beckon for a thorough explanation. My one quibble with Baldwin and Moore is that they don't quite get to the bottom of the problem. Consider the dubious approach to market value comparisons I just mentioned. It turns out that, since 1984, Commerce has had congressional permission to average U.S. sales as well as overseas sales and then juxtapose the two. Yet, department officials continue the old practice of, in effect, comparing what may be apples and oranges.

Baldwin and Moore do not fully explain why, except to suggest that Commerce, like many other federal agencies, engages in a certain amount of anticipatory propitiation of Congress.

Similarly, Baldwin and Moore report that the DOC typically underestimates the indirect selling expenses of foreign firms that may have higher selling costs in their domestic market than in the United States. Curiously, the authors observe that this practice persists "with little pressure from Congress or other interests." If that is the case, what is the explanation? Originally, the procedure may have had to do with administrative-resource constraints, but nowadays, the chapter goes on to say, "those constraints are no longer a factor." So, again, what is going on?

The authors' empirical analysis does not adequately address questions like these but, rather, focuses on final dumping margins as the dependent variable. The principal findings here are two: exchange rates and the use of BIA have significant effects on the margins, and variables purporting to measure congressional pressure (for example, whether a petitioning industry or firm is located in a trade subcommittee member's district) appear to have no influence on how dumping margins are decided.

Three points can be made about this part of their analysis. One is that the results might, conceivably, be somewhat different if the data were disaggregated, differentiating the politically important cases (for example, steel, lumber, and semiconductors) from trivial ones, like those about cut flowers, paint brushes, or 12-volt motorcycle batteries. This, of course, might leave the authors with a collection of case studies rather than an *n* large enough for regression analysis. But the case studies may be where the real answers lie. Certainly, the Canadians suspected in the 1986 anti-subsidy suit against their lumber exports that the activities of the Senate Finance Committee and others on the Hill did not go unnoticed during the Commerce Department's deliberations. It seems implausible that politics, in one form or another and at some level, play no role in other big disputes.

Second, it may not be enough to consider only the influence of the Ways and Means and Finance trade subcommittees. Dozens of congressional panels have a hand in trade policy these days, and agencies like Commerce must worry about several of them, not just the two old standbys.

Third, as I suggested earlier, the size of dumping margins is perhaps less intriguing to investigate than some of the peculiar decision rules that Baldwin and Moore identify elsewhere. Since most, though not all, of these administrative rules do not vary, they are not technically "variables" to be regressed on the determinants that the authors have quantified. But maybe some of them are worth exploring through LOGIT or PROBIT analysis. For example (and I am not sure about this), it might be interesting to model DOC decisions to use constructed values in lieu of direct market prices.

In their comments on the prospects for reform, Baldwin and Moore rightly suggest that a couple of developments on the horizon may dampen some of the demands to expand and stiffen the antidumping and countervailing duty regulations. One is the fact that more and more U.S. multinationals with complex sourcing arrangements fret about AD and CVD actions on intermediate inputs. If these companies weigh into the political process as much as strictly domestic producers have, the current zeal for antidumping and antisubsidy enforcement might ebb. A second development, of course, is that antidumping enforcement is a regulatory program that is being mimicked by a number of other trading partners. So, in a sense, the chickens are coming home to roost. With the European Community and others constructing fair values with at least as much abandon as the U.S. government, American exporters are being subjected to the kinds of regulatory hurdles that foreign firms claim they experience over here. In the long run the result may be greater interest in keeping U.S.- or EC-style trade laws from proliferating further.

That said, Baldwin and Moore are also right to predict (or, at least, to imply) that Congress will not be enthusiastic about ratifying Uruguay Round accords or subsequent multilateral agreements that significantly relax the national antidumping and countervailing duty statutes. This is partly because, as the writers point out, many members of Congress are genuinely convinced that these trade regulations make sense and help level the playing field. It is also partly because plenty of interest groups know that the trade remedies (some of them anyway) can offer an accessible and comfortable shelter from competition.

Comment

I. M. Destler

The opening assertion made by Baldwin and Moore seems correct: Congress has been the branch of government pressing for tighter countervailing duty and antidumping laws, and successive administrations have been trying to limit the changes, and (as many see it) to limit the damage. One of their key prescriptions is also on the mark: the most promising route to reform of the U.S. laws would be a GATT agreement in the Uruguay Round or some other forum that brought enough other benefits for U.S. interests to make it possible to tack changes in these laws onto a general agreement approved through the fast-track procedures. Yet something is lacking in their discussion, as in other discussions in this book. The authors are overlooking some of the broader issues, the badly needed macropolitical perspective.

Consider the political role of the antidumping and countervailing duty laws for members of Congress. These laws seem to be a perfect vehicle for them. They divert specific pressure from legislators to a mechanism that resolves cases through, apparently, clear principles and rules that punish only the definably wicked.

As David Palmeter and others have suggested, support of "unfair trade" laws is an unassailable position, at least rhetorically. It is perfect for a member. It is not so much disguised protectionism as a perfect posture for a member who would like to have it both ways. You can be for free trade and resist various statutory or overt forms of protection and say, at the same time, "I am for free trade, but it has to be fair." And what is more, you can be moral and indignant when somebody suggests that in fact you *are* having it both ways.

So, in this sense, countervailing and antidumping laws are a politician's dream. It is amazing that their postwar rediscovery took so long, that it was more than two decades in coming.

It is hardly surprising that members of Congress would embrace these procedures and tighten them and beat on Treasury Department officials for not enforcing the rights of domestic claimants and insist that the authority be transferred to Commerce. It is hardly surprising that the law gets written so as to give priority to domestic claimants and relatively short shrift to the interests and rights and fairness concerns of foreign claimants. And it is hardly surprising that Commerce officials also may have some tendency to take refuge in elaborate procedures, even procedures that go beyond what the law requires. After all, they, too, feel some need for political protection.

An adroit, skilled, experienced Commerce Department leadership could exploit its statutory leeway on these matters and could probably get away with it, insofar as Congress is concerned. Nevertheless, the safer road is to follow elaborate procedures, to go by the book, particularly when the costs of doing so are paid by interests based outside the United States.

Members of Congress, in pushing for the use of these trade-remedy laws, were urged on, of course, by specific industry interests. One would like to have heard more about which industries have particularly driven the process.

Certainly, in the redrafting of the countervailing duty and antidumping laws in 1979, the concerns and the experience of big steel were central. And that industry was by far the biggest user of those laws in the early 1980s. Ammonia producers were behind the unsuccessful natural resource subsidy campaign of 1983–84, and one can give other examples. It would be useful to have such relationships spelled out—the relationships between members of Congress, who are predisposed to writing tough laws, and industry interests, which have specific purposes and participate in the drafting of the laws that the members of Congress then move forward.

In their support of countervailing duty and antidumping laws, members of Congress are at least as interested in protection for themselves— from having to act directly on specific cases—as they are in achieving maximum protection for their claimants. Evidence for this position might be gleaned from Baldwin and Moore's finding that there appears to be no correlation between the specific interests of influential congressmen and the outcomes of specific dumping-margin cases.

A substantial amount of protection is in fact achieved through various biases in the procedures, at least in the dumping area. One would almost think that all American trade will soon be subject to countervailing duty and antidumping orders. For a while in the early 1980s it looked as though things were going that way, with more and more cases. Many were steel cases, of course, but there was a broader surge in the use of this law.

Lately, something puzzling has been happening. The number of cases seems to be going down despite the enhanced opportunities for anti-dumping petitions in the second half of the 1980s, what with the dollar declining and the prices of imported goods not always passing through that change. The trend, although irregular, seems to be downward and not upward.

Is this apparent decline in cases due to the fact that so much trade is already covered by countervailing duty or antidumping orders or by voluntary export restraint agreements reached under the threat of such orders? Certainly, this has been a factor in cases involving the steel in-dustry. Is part of the reason that these laws offer only partial and inad-equate relief, in only a limited range of import cases, as the administration would argue?

Baldwin and Moore seem to suggest that the latter might be the case, but they don't develop this point. Nor do they or any of the other contributors give a macroanalysis of the unfair trade laws that would assess their total impact on U.S. trade, trade policy, or trade politics. It is not that such an assessment is obligatory (indeed, it would be exceed-ingly difficult to research). Nevertheless, at least asking this question seems to be important for both political analysis and policy prescription.

If the laws are a large, general impediment to trade rather than an unfair nuisance to a limited number of particular trade flows, then reform will presumably be harder to achieve, because the vested interests engaged will be much stronger; but the cause would be more urgent and more worthwhile, and one would, perhaps, want to devote more political en-ergy to it. If the impact of the laws is less central, then reform may be easier, but it might also be a cause that we would choose to defer.

At a minimum, these laws ought to be administered in a more balanced fashion, and when the statute clearly imposes a bias, it should be removed. How would this change come about? Certainly, the political advantage of being able to label your adversary as unfair is important. A few years ago, when John Odell and I studied the role of antiprotection forces in U.S. trade, one of the strongest correlations in our quantitative analysis was between the ability of the proponents of protection to use the un-fairness banner and the *ineffectiveness* of the opponents of protection.

The proponents of reform are going to need to build a counter case that can appropriate and use words like "fairness" in relation to *American* economic actors. Proposals of change need to establish that these pro-cedures are, in concrete ways, unfair to *American* interests, such as U.S. users of imported inputs. The most visible current example is, of course, in the field of semiconductors. All of us who study trade have had to learn that the current U.S.-Japan agreement includes an important ele-ment based on the antidumping laws, the monitoring of prices—product by product and firm by firm—of imports of Japanese semiconductor devices, DRAMs and EPROMs. This has pleased the U.S. producers of these products but angered their U.S. users.

As we approached the expiration of that agreement in mid-1991, the Semiconductor Industry Association realized that getting support for an extension is not easy. Its members concluded that they had to go to the computer makers, to negotiate with that group and develop a common position, if they were to get the U.S. government, let alone the Japanese government, to seek an extension of the arrangement. This led to a joint position that included the dropping of price monitoring in favor of a looser arrangement. This would still involve the antidumping law but would be, arguably, a less distortive mechanism, one that would impose less cost on the users of these products. In exchange, the Semiconductor Industry Association won the computer makers' support for their con-tinued pursuit of their market access goals within Japan.

These U.S. users of semiconductors are the sort of interest on which a reform effort has to be based. It is necessary to have a competing concept of fairness that is endorsed by U.S. business interests, and the arguments for change have to stress giving them a greater voice and a greater role in the evidence-weighing process.

The advocates of change, of course, will still have to show that the U.S. firms which benefit from the antidumping laws will have adequate opportunity to prove real dumping or real subsidies, however defined. And the U.S.-based interests hurt by them will have to demonstrate that they *are* hurt by the existing regime, and that it can be reformed.

CHAPTER EIGHT

Administration of the Antidumping Law: A Different Perspective

Terence P. Stewart

CONTRARY to the assertions of David Palmeter and other analysts, the existing U.S. antidumping law does not constitute a legal or administrative nontariff barrier. U.S. law, like article 6 of the General Agreement on Tariffs and Trade (GATT), has been a necessary predicate for the international trade liberalization that has occurred in the past forty years or so. The promise and the commitment of every Congress and administration in the post–World War II era has been that U.S. companies and their workers would win or lose in the American marketplace against foreign competitors on the basis of their comparative advantage. That is, the winners would be the ones who had the best "mousetrap." U.S. antidumping (AD) and countervailing duty (CVD) laws are designed to offset any artificial advantage that flows from closed foreign markets, cross-subsidization by multiproduct producers, government largesse, or other factors that have nothing to do with comparative advantage. Contrary to the simplistic arguments of many so-called globalists, international trade policy should not be precisely the same as internal competition policy, because it *matters* to nations whether their citizens are unemployed. As Congress has stated in another context, "Unemployed persons are not happy consumers."[1]

If anything, existing U.S. law needs to be *strengthened*. Existing interpretations do not adequately protect the interests of domestic industries, their workers, and communities from the adverse consequences that flow

1. *Trade Reform Act of 1974*, S. Rept. 1298, 93 Cong. 2 sess. (Government Printing Office, 1974), p. 125 (discussion of escape clause relief). See also the remarks by John D. Ong, "The Interface of Trade/Competition Law and Policy: A Businessman's Perspective," *Antitrust Law Journal*, vol. 56 (August 1987) pp. 425–32, especially pp. 429–30.

from the price discrimination and willingness to sell below cost that so frequently characterizes the trade practices of our foreign competitors. Three problems in particular demand attention.

First, although it is widely believed that the intent of the laws is to reestablish a "level playing field," the current interpretation of the U.S. International Trade Commission is that relief is usually not available until a substantial period of injury has been endured, as shown by closed plants, laid-off workers, reduced capital expenditures, reduced research and development, and reduced cash flow. Almost by definition, when the whistle blows and offsetting duties are required, the field is tilted—the domestic industry is *behind* because of reduced capital expenditures and R&D and the loss of capacity and skilled or experienced workers. There is currently no compensation to help injured industries catch up or return to their earlier competitive state. In areas of rapid technological change, such industries may suffer an irreversible loss of competitiveness. For nation-states, such a turn of events—whether intended or not by foreign competitors—is untenable.

If relief is not forthcoming, Congress will be faced with increasing requests for compensation. The large number of bills introduced in recent years seeking "damages" in the context of unfair trade (including requests for treble damages) are an outgrowth of the frustration of domestic users with an unbalanced system.

Second, the circumvention of orders is a widespread problem for domestic industries harmed by dumped products. Companies bring cases to obtain relief. The many methods to circumvent orders substantially reduces the relief available to injured industries and has forced many industries to file repetitive actions. With the increasing presence of multicountry producers, circumvention is likely to become an even greater problem. U.S. efforts to address circumvention in the Uruguay Round negotiations are to be applauded as an important first step.

Third, domestic producers find that a few interpretations of U.S. law by the Department of Commerce bias the results in favor of foreign respondents. These biases are not required by GATT article 6 or the GATT Antidumping Code and are not present in the laws and practices of America's major trading partners. Unless these biases are corrected, existing U.S. law and its administration will create an artificial advantage for foreign producers exporting to the United States.

Before discussing possible ways of strengthening the antidumping duty law, it is important to understand the dumping law and its function and the criticisms of it leveled by Palmeter in chapter 3.

The Antidumping Law and Its Function

In explaining title I of the Trade Agreements Act of 1979, the Senate Finance Committee stated:

> Subsidies and dumping are two of the most pernicious practices which distort international trade to the disadvantage of United States commerce. . . .
>
> Dumping is the general term for selling in another country's market at prices less than "fair value." Fair value is usually determined by the exporter's comparable home market price, though the exporter's price in a third country market, or the constructed value of his merchandise, may be used to determine fair value in appropriate circumstances. Antidumping duties are special duties imposed to offset the amount of the difference between the fair value of the merchandise and the price for which it is sold in the United States, i.e., the dumping margin.[2]

Article 6 of the GATT, the Antidumping Code, and U.S. law (other than the 1916 Antidumping Act) are not concerned with the intent of the dumper. Although companies operating from closed or controlled markets or willing to engage in cross-product subsidization may find merit in dumping, the practice is in fact pernicious—highly injurious or destructive—precisely because it can lead to the misallocation of resources internationally and can divorce exit and entry decisions from an accurate determination of comparative advantage. Because the United States is in general an open market, its producers (in most industries) do not have the option of engaging in the same practices, because arbitrage is likely to undercut their home market prices. Therein lies the rub. Although it may make perfect sense for an individual producer to unload excess capacity at anything above marginal cost *if* basic demand in one's home market can be sold at much higher prices, companies cannot sell their entire output at prices far below full cost on an ongoing basis and remain in business (absent cross-product or government subsidization). In a country like the United States, R&D, capital expenditure, plant closings, employment, and compensation decisions are all based on anticipated returns. Where companies face artificial international competition—that is, competition that does not flow from intrinsic advantages but rather from the artificial advantages identified previously—they can and do respond

---

2. *Trade Agreements Act of 1979*, S. Rept. 249, 96 Cong. 1 sess. (GPO, 1979), p. 37.

to the wrong market signals, since foreign prices suggest adequate returns cannot be earned in the product line being dumped. As a result, countries with comparative advantage in certain products lose the capacity and capability to produce the products in question. For the United States such a result is contrary to the justification for international trade.

This view gave rise to the Antidumping Act of 1921 and remains the fundamental business rationale in 1991. Some of the concerns of Congress were reviewed in the House Ways and Means Committee report on the antidumping provisions in 1919:

In 1903 there were in the United States five manufacturers of salicylic acid. By 1913 three of these had failed. . . . During the latter part of the decade referred to, salicylic acid was selling in Germany at from 26¼ to 30½ cents. During the same period, the German houses were selling it in this country, after paying a duty of 5 cents, at 25 cents or from 6 to 10 cents below what they were getting at home.

Of oxalic acid the report says:

In 1901 where there was no American manufacture it was sold by the Germans at 6 cents. In 1903, when the works of the American Acid & Alkali Co. was started, the price was immediately dropped to 4.7 cents, at about which figure it remained until 1907 when the American factory was shut down for a number of months. During this shutdown the price was instantly raised to 9 cents. When the factory reopened the price was again dropped until in 1908, when the company failed. . . .

The same process was carried on in regard to bicarbonate of potash. In 1900 there was no manufacture and imports ran about 160,000 pounds. In 1901 American manufacture began. This succeeded so well that in 1906 imports had dropped to 45,000 pounds. At this time the American manufacturer's price was 6½ cents, while the import value was given at 4.9 cents. In the following year the Germans made a determined and successful onslaught. Their import value was lowered to 2.2 cents with the result that, instead of 45,000, 310,000 were imported. Accordingly in 1908 the American manufacturer failed. The price was immediately raised to 7½ cents and remained thereabout until the war.[3]

3. *Antidumping Legislation*, H. Rept. 479, 60 Cong. 2 sess. (GPO, 1919), p. 3 (quoting from a report prepared by A. Mitchell Palmer).

Companies unable to make an adequate return on capital employed lose the ability to reinvest, expand, and pay competitive wages. There has never been a need to reduce prices below full cost of production, let alone marginal costs, to drive a competitor from the marketplace.[4] The effect over a number of years is a downward death spiral for a company or industry. The American landscape is littered with the tombstones of companies starved by inadequate returns on capital employed. Many such tombstones have nothing to do with artificial advantages used by foreign competitors. Many—too many—are the direct result of dumping into the U.S. market.

Those who argue that antidumping laws are not necessary either assume that there is no justification for a distinction between internal competition policy and trade policy or that in a perfect world dumping would be self-corrective.[5]

Some—David Palmeter is one—claim that such laws represent a "bar-

4. The Supreme Court and many commentators have tended to examine "predation" in terms of whether the conduct of the actor is "rational" with respect to the particular product on which below-cost pricing is being practiced. See, for example, *Matsushita Electric Industrial Co. Ltd.* v. *Zenith Radio Corporation*, 475 U.S. 574, 588-92 (1986), and sources cited therein. "The alleged predatory scheme makes sense only if petitioners can recoup their losses." 475 U.S. at 592, n. 16. "Nor does the possibility that petitioners have obtained supracompetitive profits in the Japanese market change this calculation. Whether or not petitioners have the *means* to sustain substantial losses in this country over a long period of time, they have not *motive* to sustain such losses absent some strong likelihood that the alleged conspiracy in this country will eventually pay off." 475 U.S. at 593. Unloading excess capacity for whatever can be obtained (above marginal costs) increases the profitability for the foreign producer if arbitrage does not destroy its home market price level—that is, the motive for dumping. In addition, some companies can engage in conduct that appears irrational from a single-product perspective but may be totally rational—even if harmful to domestic producers—when done for multiple products. Stated differently, there are often powerful incentives to engage in cross-product subsidization. For example, in the consumer electronics area, one senior executive of an Asian-based company told me that his particular company has never made money on televisions in the United States but has used television volume to secure distribution outlets for a range of specialty items on which profit margins are very large—a classic example of cross-subsidization. Thus, whether the Supreme Court views such conduct as rational or not, business practices are engaged in which prevent U.S. companies from entering, reentering, or staying in a business area for reasons that have nothing to do with comparative advantage.

5. See, for example, William J. Davey, "Antidumping Laws: A Time for Restriction," *North American and Common Market Antitrust and Trade Laws* (Fordham University School of Law, 1989), pp. 8-10–8-15. Davey concludes: "Whatever the reason, the displacement of one competitor by another is not cause for concern, assuming the behavior of the winner is not predatory."

rier to trade" by their use or threat of use.[6] Such a claim, as is shown in the next section, is without merit. U.S. law attempts to *encourage* the workings of comparative advantage. Unlike some countries, the United States does not want to assess any dumping duties at the end of the day. It is just as happy to see the foreign producer lower home market prices (if above cost) to eliminate the price discrimination as it is to have export prices increased. The law works to permit the company that in fact has the best "mousetrap" to win the game.

Reality versus Theory

Because of arbitrage, perfectly open markets would self-correct at least some of the forms of dumping (they would not cure cross-subsidization based on access to distribution for other products, for example). This is true in theory and tends to be reflected in the real world in countries or sectors that have few formal or informal barriers to trade in both the importing and exporting country. Thus, Hong Kong, which has relatively few barriers, is normally not involved in dumping actions (other than state trading cases involving transshipment through China). Where it is involved, the country receives small or negative dumping margins.[7] Conversely, countries that are generally viewed as closed or subject to various formal and informal barriers, such as Japan, are frequent subjects of antidumping investigations, and in those cases substantial margins of price discrimination are common.[8]

6. See also John H. Jackson, "Dumping in International Trade: Its Meaning and Context," in Jackson and Edwin A. Vermulst, *Antidumping Law and Practice: A Comparative Study* (University of Michigan Press, 1989), pp. 1–22, especially p. 7.

7. See, for example, *Final Determination of Sales at Less Than Fair Value: Sweaters Wholly or in Chief Weight of Man-Made Fiber from Hong Kong*, 55 Fed. Reg. 30733 (1990) (affirmative determination); *Final Determination of Sales at Not Less Than Fair Value; Thermostatically Controlled Appliance Plugs and Internal Probe Thermostats Therefor from Hong Kong*, 53 Fed. Reg. 50064 (1988) (negative determination); and *Photo Albums and Filler Pages from Hong Kong; Final Determination of Sales at Less Than Fair Value*, 50 Fed. Reg. 43751 (1985) (affirmative determination). See also GATT, "Trade Policy Review, Hong Kong," Geneva, November 1990.

8. From July 1980 through June 1989, fifty-one U.S. antidumping investigations were initiated against Japan, twenty-nine of which were decided in the affirmative. See, for example, *Certain High-Capacity Pagers from Japan*, 48 Fed. Reg. 37058-59 (1983) (margins: 70.35, 89.97, and 109.06 percent); *Certain Carbon Steel Butt-Weld Pipe Fittings from Japan*, 52 Fed. Reg. 4167 (1987) (margins: 30.83, 62.79, and 65.81 percent); *Amphorous Silica Filament Fabric from Japan*, 52 Fed. Reg. 35750 (1987) (margin: 193.94 percent); and *Certain Small Business Telephone Systems and Subassemblies Thereof from Japan*, 54 Fed. Reg. 50789-90 (1989) (margins: 136.77, 157.85, and 178.93 percent).

In practice, however, price discrimination is not self-correcting for most of the world. The force of economic logic and the consequences of differential pricing operate in a varying framework of assumptions and imperfect conditions.[9] World trade is open, but only relatively open in some markets. Since the flows of trade are still largely defined by national borders, economic development must still be overseen according to political boundaries. The fact that world trade is open is a matter of trade and competition policies which are based more on a pragmatic political consensus than on the economics of a cost curve that applies to a global economy. The U.S. antidumping laws are defined and implemented in accordance with this political consensus through the GATT. Thus, the economics of antidumping laws, with varying degrees of perfection, are currently embodied in the framework of a domestic political and international consensus.

As explained in the following subsections, the most practical solution to the economic disequilibria under highly competitive market conditions is to acknowledge that (1) dumping occurs and may be injurious at prices above marginal cost and (2) the bridge between economic theory and business practice that inheres in the U.S. antidumping laws and is currently mediated by the GATT is necessary if trade liberalization is to continue.

The Economic Logic of Antidumping Laws

The trend toward the globalization of trade and investment suggests that the principle of comparative advantage has been used to increasing advantage by national companies that desire to expand by increasing sales abroad and by multinational companies seeking new possibilities for sourcing, production, and sales. However, the ability of all interests to participate in this global exercise of comparative advantage is often constrained by host governments that exercise control over domestic economic policy and the flow of goods and services across borders.[10] Host

9. As noted previously, there are (as in consumer electronics) powerful incentives for some companies to heavily cross-subsidize core products, a factor not generally recognized in economic theory.

10. The approach to the concept and movements of comparative advantage adopted here is long term. This approach recognizes that economic progress is inextricably linked with political process. It also recognizes that comparative advantage can be lost and regained by industries that have been injured by internationally recognized unfair trade practices, and that the proper redeployment of resources from developed to developing economies, or among developed economies, is beneficial but must be overseen and stabilized by in-

governments tend to be interested in regulating constraints on perceived comparative advantage, especially where the attendant needs of structural adjustment prove to be disadvantageous to the local economy or government in terms of social, political, and economic costs. Conversely, governments of exporting nations may seek to stimulate the development of comparative advantage through a policy framework, supported by selective resource allocation, such as an export-oriented program of industrial development like those found in the East Asian newly industrialized countries.[11]

WHY FIRMS DUMP PRODUCTS IN OTHER MARKETS. Why companies choose to dump merchandise abroad can vary greatly from case to case or even sale to sale. Many of the reasons (for example, to take advantage of a protected home market to increase profits by unloading excess capacity abroad above marginal costs; and profit maximization through cross-product subsidization) may be acceptable to the business community. Others (for example, market domination and predatory pricing) are obviously not acceptable. The "evil" is not that the conduct is "irrational" but rather that resource allocation is distorted and that companies are weakened and jobs lost for reasons other than comparative advantage.[12]

---

ternational consensus. See C. Michael Aho, "U.S. Labor-Market Adjustment and Import Restrictions," in Ernest H. Preeg, ed., *Hard Bargaining Ahead: U.S. Trade Policy and Developing Countries*, U.S.–Third World Policy Perspectives 4 (New Brunswick: Transaction Books, 1985), chap. 3, especially pp. 87–88.

11. Such constraints include (1) the capital and management resources available to that company, (2) barriers to market entry defined by host governments, culture, or business affiliations (for example, in India and Japan), (3) barriers to market entry created by exporting nations (for example, Japanese *keiretsu*) and the rapid concentration of global producers (for example, consumer electronics, microchips) that can take advantage of massive economies of scale and R&D leverage and that have emerged (on the basis of scale or as a cartel) as pricemakers. The annual National Trade Estimate Report on Foreign Trade Barriers from the USTR's office provides a good overview of government policies on trade.

Recent estimates by the Department of Commerce show that over 70 percent of U.S. manufacturing may now be subject to import competition. See Aho, "U.S. Labor-Market Adjustment," p. 89. This broad front of competition has begun to transform the U.S. economy. For many U.S. industries, especially those that were labor intensive and, recently, those that are capital intensive, structural adjustment has become necessary in response to global competitive pressures.

12. Some have claimed that dumping requires that there be some barrier between the markets so that lower-priced goods are not resold in the higher-priced market by an arbitrageur. Internationally, price discrimination in the form of dumping may occur when demand in the export market is more elastic than in the domestic market, that is, more responsive to lower prices, and when arbitrage is prevented by barriers such as tariffs, transport costs, or any one of a variety of nontariff barriers. Davey, "Antidumping Laws," p. 8-4.

To discriminate successfully, the seller must possess sufficient market power to have some autonomy. In addition to the basic economic circumstances outlined above, there are other conditions under which products may be dumped.

First, the export of goods may be driven by program or policy. Noneconomic forces and influences can have a determining effect on price levels in the marketplace. Industries that produce certain goods solely for export and that may not even have a domestic market for these goods may engage in price discrimination among export markets for a variety of reasons, including differences in trade barriers in different markets, targeting of countries or accounts, the need to generate hard currency, imperfect information, and differences in duty rates.[13]

Price discrimination (or selling below cost) may be supported directly or indirectly by producers' governments in an effort to develop an industrial infrastructure through growth in exported goods. In the case of Japan, in particular, such export development has been tied to industrial policy, and the implementation of this policy has driven Japanese competitiveness up and pushed prices in the targeted markets down.[14]

13. See, for example, Labor-Industry Coalition for International Trade, "Antidumping Reform: An Analysis of Proposed Changes in International Rules to Regulate Injurious Dumping in International Trade," Washington, February 1990, p. 39, n. 74.

14. See, for example, Chikara Higashi, *Japanese Trade Policy Formulation* (Praeger, 1983), p. 22. Higashi says that through MITI's persistent efforts, industrial policies were based on both domestic and international economic considerations. In the late 1950s, priority was placed on four industries—coal, power, steel, and shipbuilding—because these were regarded as essential for recovery from the devastation of World War II. From the late 1950s to the 1960s, the textile industry was strengthened, followed by the electronics, machine, precision tool manufacturing, and automobile industries. Most recently, high-technology industries, such as data processing, telecommunications, and other systems industries, have been marked for rapid development.

The history of antidumping actions in the United States against Japanese products and products from other countries with export-driven growth policies (for example, South Korea) usually reflects and parallels the development policies of the foreign governments. See, for example, *Tuners (of Type Used in Consumer Electric Products) from Japan; Final Determination of Sales at Less Than Fair Value*, 35 Fed. Reg. 11304 (1970); *Synthetic Methionine from Japan; Final Determination of Sales at Less Than Fair Value*, 38 Fed. Reg. 4524 (1973); *Steel Wire Rope from Japan; Final Determination of Sales at Less Than Fair Value*, 38 Fed. Reg. 14972 (1973); *Bicycle Tires and Tubes from the Republic of Korea; Final Determination of Sales at Less Than Fair Value*, 43 Fed. Reg. 61067 (1978); *Stainless Clad Steel Plate from Japan; Final Determination of Sales at Less Than Fair Value*, 47 Fed. Reg. 24379 (1982); *Antidumping, Final Determination of Sales at Less Than Fair Value; Color Television Receivers from Korea*, 49 Fed. Reg. 7620 (1984); *Rectangular Welded Carbon Steel Pipes and Tubes from the Republic of Korea; Final Determination of Sales at Less Than Fair Value*, 49 Fed. Reg. 9936 (1984); and *Final Determination of Sales at Less Than Fair Value: Certain All-Terrain Vehicles from Japan*, 54 Fed. Reg. 4864 (1989).

Second, dumping is used strategically to expand market share. This market-driven strategy is often a corollary to the success of an export-oriented industrial policy, but it may also operate in any competitive market (for example, with a higher price elasticity of demand). The rationale is simple: sell or dump goods . . . gain market share . . . raise prices. The strategy does not have to be drastic or involve monopolistic or oligopolistic arrangements; it is simply an effective and inexpensive way of maximizing returns on long-term investment, especially when the hurdle rate for investment and the short-term expectations of investors are not a great concern. But like many of the reasons given for dumping, this one is based on the assumption that arbitrage cannot undermine the ability of the company to engage in such discrimination and that cross-product subsidization is taking place.

When the antidumping laws were formulated, the industrial structure of many of the more advanced economies was more cartelized (as in steel and chemicals) and was in many instances protected by high tariff barriers.[15] Because these conditions have changed, those who believe the antidumping laws are no longer viable have argued that the laws are therefore an anachronism unsuited to an open world economy.[16] Nevertheless, the logic by which dumping can be used to gain market share is precisely the same regardless of the scale of the industry. The fact that circumstances are different today has not altered the logic of dumping as a tool of market strategy.

Third, it is necessary to dispose of excess domestic production. Although sporadic dumping is probably less likely to produce an antidumping allegation, since price depression is only temporary if structural adjustment in an industrial economy has been delayed by government action or support, dumping conditions may prevail for a longer period. Such delayed structural adjustment and governmental largesse have been behind the world's steel crisis of the past twenty years, making the steel industry the largest user of unfair trade laws, in the United States and elsewhere.

The following example presents a typical scenario of dumping: a heavily subsidized steel producer is in the midst of a prolonged economic downturn and suffers from excess capacity and slow-moving inventories. Neither the government nor the company wants to see production stopped

15. See Alfred E. Eckes, "The Interface of Antitrust and Trade Laws—Conflict or Harmony? An ITC Commissioner's Perspective," *Antitrust Law Journal*, vol. 56 (August 1987), pp. 417–24.
16. Davey, "Antidumping Laws," p. 8-3.

or curtailed, because the social costs would be high and because the host government intends supporting continued steel production as an important part of its industrial infrastructure. Consequently, the firm dumps steel in another market at prices sufficient to cover its variable costs of production, or at whatever price will move the excess inventory.

Such actions can adversely affect the reduced capacity utilization, employment, shutdown costs, start-up costs, maintenance and investment, and any other factors that have bearing on the efficiency and profitability of the domestic industry in the importing country. These costs will be greater if the dumping occurs during a recession. According to one view, such dumping forces the producers in the importing country rather than the exporter to "bear the burden of recession in their own market."[17]

DOES THE ANTIDUMPING LAW HARM CONSUMERS?. Opponents of the concept (rather than the procedures) of the dumping law often claim that antidumping restrictions serve to keep prices higher in the domestic market, thereby depriving consumers of the benefits of competitively produced goods from whatever source and placing domestic users of dumped merchandise at a competitive disadvantage in relation to foreign producers.[18]

First, to the extent that dumping margins are determined on the basis of price comparisons, neutralization of the dumping does not put U.S. purchasers at a disadvantage, since they are merely required to pay a price comparable to that paid by their foreign competitors. U.S. purchasers do lose an artificial advantage that flows from dumped prices. But it would turn the purpose of the Antidumping Code on its head if one could defeat neutralization of one trade distortion to maintain another trade distortion, namely, the artificial advantage to the user.

Although users can be at a competitive disadvantage when foreign producers sell below cost in the home market the same product that is imported, the answer is not to prevent relief to the domestic producer but to provide both domestic market and export remedies for the users who are harmed by such home market pricing tactics. Congress added provisions in the 1988 Omnibus Trade and Competitiveness Act to deal with selected input dumping problems for users.

THE "DYNAMIC EFFECTS" OF DUMPING. Anticompetitive behavior has the effect of redefining comparative advantage on its own terms. An analysis of antidumping reform by the Labor-Industry Coalition for In-

17. Labor-Industry Coalition, "Antidumping Reform," p. 42.
18. See, for example, Jackson and Vermulst, *Antidumping Law and Practice*, p. 28.

ternational Trade indicates that the longer-term effects on the domestic industry have not been properly weighted in studies of the effects of dumping. So-called static analysis assumes that "the import price of the dumped product is the sole causal factor relating to the degree of injury to the domestic industry."[19] Broader implications, such as the effect of current dumping on future investment decisions, are excluded. For example, from an investor's standpoint, if the pricing situation in an industry reduces the likely return on capital employed, it becomes more difficult to justify capital expenditures. As a result, investments are not made or are postponed, and over time the domestic producer loses its competitiveness. This reality is seldom addressed by the critics of injured industries.

These critics fail to recognize that the antidumping law of the United States ensures that the economic opportunities available to U.S. corporations are not destroyed by pricing practices that erode market share and investor confidence on the basis of artificial advantages. Such a law keeps international trade "free but fair."[20] Strong and effective antidumping laws can prevent the unwarranted disruption caused by artificially induced economic restructuring. They do not stifle competitive pricing or create a barrier to market entry. Rather they ensure that the victory goes to the person with the best product, not the company with the deepest pocket, the most protected market, or the greatest government largesse.

Critique of Palmeter's Analysis

The domestic participant would find little to agree with in Palmeter's analysis in chapter 3. Indeed, each of his points can be countered.

Antidumping Amendments Seek Transparency and Fairness

Palmeter's starting premise is that the antidumping (and countervailing duty) investigations done by the Department of Commerce have become increasingly complex. The authority cited for this premise consists of the number of pages in the U.S. Statutes at Large for the Trade Agreements Act of 1979 and subsequent amendments and the number of pages in the current Code of Federal Regulations. While over time the statute and

19. Labor-Industry Coalition, "Antidumping Reform," p. 43.
20. Eric I. Garfinkel and Eleanor C. Shea, "Some Recent Developments in the Administration of the Antidumping and Countervailing Duty Laws," *The Commerce Department Speaks Out* (1989), p. 55.

regulation have been modified to clarify prior ambiguity or to codify agency practice, the core elements of the dumping calculus have remained largely unchanged since at least 1974, and except for the addition of sales below cost, since at least 1958. Indeed, the basic comparison—between the home market price or third-country price and the U.S. price—has changed little since the 1921 Antidumping Act. The same is true for the department's regulations. Only seven of the pages in the current Code of Federal Regulations deal with the calculus of dumping as applied to virtually every case handled by Commerce. The balance of the regulations and a large portion of the statute deal with procedures and procedural rights of the parties. For example, considerable attention is devoted to maintaining a transparent system, recognizing the orderly flow of information, and protecting confidential data.[21]

Contrary to Palmeter's assertions, the burdens of the questionnaires have not increased dramatically. An analysis of agency questionnaires over the years shows that the boilerplate sections (A–F) remain essentially unchanged from case to case.[22] These are followed by appendixes containing glossaries of terms, computer tape format sheets, and the like. Many of these appendixes have expanded over time, but that has not changed the burden on respondents. Rather, the refinement of the questionnaire has made it more understandable and has simplified the process.

There can be substantial differences in the girth of the total questionnaire, depending on whether only home market and export price sections are included, whether data on third-country sales are also sought, whether information on the cost of production or constructed value is necessary, and whether items are imported and further processed before resale. But when a questionnaire has been expanded in a substantive area, it has normally been done to identify specific types of information needed for model comparison or to "customize" the format to obtain data relevant to a particular industry. Such an effort up front reduces the need for supplemental questionnaires later in an investigation or review.

Some cases in recent years have involved significant volumes of trade with unusually large numbers of transactions. Both in investigations and

21. 19 C.F.R. secs. 353.31, 353.33, 353.34.

22. It is true that the questionnaire is only in English, a potential difficulty for members of responding companies. Because the bulk of each questionnaire is boilerplate, it should be possible for at least boilerplate portions to be translated into *major* foreign language by the U.S. government, by the respondent governments, or by one or more of the bar associations. English would be, of course, the official language for purposes of agency action and judicial review.

in compliance, Commerce has attempted to fashion approaches in the unusual case to reduce the reporting burden on respondents.

For example, in the original investigation of *Fresh Cut Flowers from Colombia*, Commerce used sampling techniques to select the respondents to receive dumping questionnaires. It selected twelve growers out of a universe of more than two hundred Colombian growers.[23] These growers were selected through the use of a simple random sample from a list of Colombian growers provided by the Colombian association of flower exporters, Asocolflores. Commerce deleted from the list those growers who did not export to the United States during the period of investigation and those who did not grow any of the flowers subject to the investigation. Commerce then assigned a number to each of the remaining respondents and randomly selected the twelve for the investigation.

Another case involving a large number of transactions was *Antifriction Bearings from Various Countries*.[24] In the investigation stage, Commerce departed from its usual reporting requirements and used what some parties have referred to as "sampling." Normally, Commerce examines at least 60 percent of the exports to the United States in the investigation phase.

23. *Final Determination of Sales at Less Than Fair Value; Certain Fresh Cut Flowers from Colombia*, 52 Fed. Reg. 6842 (1987). Respondents objected to the sampling in this case on grounds that the results were not representative of the Colombian flower industry. The respondents argued that the sample included a disproportionate number of small growers, that the sampled population accounted for only 60 percent of exports to the United States, and that the sample was not selected in a rational manner. 52 Fed. Reg. at 6849.

Commerce stated that the sample was valid because it was selected in accordance with "standard statistical sampling techniques." Commerce noted that since it had no data on which to build stratified populations, it relied on a random sample method which later proved to be effective and legitimate. For instance, Commerce noted that while the sample included a greater number of small growers than large growers, the Colombian industry had more small growers than large growers. Commerce also justified its sample universe on the basis that, given its use of weighted margins for the all-other rate, the company with the largest volume accounted for a greater proportion of the all-other rate. 52 Fed. Reg. at 6849.

Commerce's determination to use a random sample method was upheld on appeal by the Court of International Trade. *Asociacion Colombiana de Exportadores de Flores* v. *United States*, 704 F. Supp. 1114 (Ct. Int'l Trade 1989), *aff'd*, 901 F.2d 1089 (Fed. Cir.), *cert. denied*, 111 S. Ct. 136 (1990). The court found that "plaintiffs desire for one or more types of stratified sampling is not a sufficient basis for objection to ITA's methodology. . . . There is no requirement that a stratified sample be used, particularly when it would require the ITA to conduct a substantial pre-investigation." The court noted that the basis for using a random sample was legally adequate and that the results were not shown to be unrepresentative.

24. *Final Determination of Sales at Less Than Fair Value: Antifriction Bearings (Other Than Tapered Roller Bearings) and Parts Thereof from the Federal Republic of Germany*, 54 Fed. Reg. 18992 (1989). Hereafter *Antifriction Bearings*.

Citing the tremendous number of transactions and different products subject to the investigation, Commerce decided to examine all sales only where identical products were sold at home, or if such sales were less than 33 percent of the total exports for the company to the United States. In doing so, Commerce relied not on its legal authority to sample but on its authority under its "regulation to examine a lower percentage where the circumstances so warrant."[25] In the first *Antifriction Bearings* administrative review, Commerce sampled sales by selecting limited weeks for reporting and by averaging margins for completed bearings to imported parts that are further manufactured.[26]

Although a great deal of information is requested from respondents, much of it (rebates, indirect selling expenses, warranty, advertising, and so on) flows from adjustments to the calculation, often at the request of importers, to explain away price discrimination that appears from a straight price-to-price comparison. Such adjustments require a large number of columns to deal with the "differences" claimed. Insofar as the differences affect price, then the data are necessary to the department's analysis. To the extent that such differences do not affect prices, it is the domestic industry, not the respondents, that is burdened by the data being submitted.

Antidumping Cases Are Investigations, Not Adjudications

Some critics have proposed that the antidumping system would be improved if the decisionmakers in the Department of Commerce were separated from the investigative staff. Proponents of this view argue that the antidumping procedure should be conducted on an adversarial model rather than as an investigation. Palmeter labels Commerce's investigation an "inquisition." Yet, Congress has established that administrative proceedings under title VII of the Tariff Act of 1930 are investigatory and not adjudicatory.[27]

25. *Antifriction Bearings*, 54 Fed. Reg. at 19028.

26. Memorandum from Joseph Spetrini, deputy assistant secretary, Office of Compliance, to Eric Garfinkel, assistant secretary, Import Administration, on sampling technique and methodological approach for administrative reviews of antifriction bearings cases, July 30, 1990.

27. *Budd Co., Ry. Division* v. *United States*, 507 F. Supp. 997 (Ct. Int'l Trade 1980), citing *Trade Agreements Act of 1979*, H. Rept. 317, 96 Cong. 1 sess. (GPO, 1979), p. 61, and S. Rept. 249, p. 248. "The statutory provisions of the Trade Agreements Act of 1979, indeed, clearly express the congressional intent that the Commission will obtain information through its own investigative sources." *Budd Co.*, 507 F. Supp. at 1001.

Such a pejorative term is plainly unwarranted in connection with U.S. trade law and existing Commerce practice.[28] Indeed, the 1980s saw tremendous advances in administrative transparency, access to information, and procedural rights in antidumping cases.

Palmeter neglects to mention that the administrative proceedings are investigations as opposed to adjudications and that an internal review is conducted by people who are not the actual investigators. Three different bodies within the department usually oversee antidumping proceedings: the Office of Policy, the Office of Chief Counsel for Import Administration, and the Office of Compliance and Investigations. Each of these bodies has direct input into the process, and no single body is both investigator and decisionmaker. Finally, of course, department decisions are subject to judicial review (both by the Court of International Trade and the Court of Appeals for the Federal Circuit), which safeguards any concerns about bias or erroneous decisions.

Further moves toward an adjudication standard will significantly increase the already high costs of antidumping cases and delay the proceeding. That is not to anyone's advantage. Because there is no pretrial discovery by interested parties, the government is able to conduct its investigation in a short time, thereby reducing costs, uncertainty, and the burdens on the parties.

Best Information Available

The objective of the statute and the Department of Commerce is to use the respondent's data wherever possible. If companies supply all the data or make a good faith effort to do so and work with the department, their own data will be used. The problem for the department, however, is that the actual data concerning foreign market value and U.S. prices and adjustments are in the control of a foreign company. The domestic interested parties have no access to that data and no rights of independent discovery. Thus, the law is designed so that when a respondent withholds or fails to provide data, there is a resort to "best information" otherwise available. Without such a provision, the targets of an antidumping case could foil the investigation simply by withholding data. What Commerce

28. Congress has stated that "traditional administrative law principles are to be applied in reviewing antidumping . . . duty decisions where by law Congress has entrusted the decision-making authority in a specialized, complex economic situation to administrative agencies." *Trade Agreements Act of 1979*, S. Rept. 249, p. 252. See also *Budd Co., Ry. Division* v. *United States*, 507 F. Supp. at 1000.

has been forced to do over time is try to curb the abuses of respondents and their counsel in manipulating the data submitted.

It has been amply demonstrated that respondents have an interest in presenting data in a light most favorable to themselves. Respondents have hidden, disguised, explained away, or otherwise disavowed the price discrimination that is occurring. Where complete data are presented, it is, of course, the responsibility of the respondent's counsel to make arguments about how the data can be interpreted. When data are not complete, or are "restated," or are otherwise presented in a manner that prevents Commerce from making a decision as to the propriety of the claim made and such action is discovered, the statutory mandate for the use of best information otherwise available becomes operative.

At present, U.S. antidumping duty law provides for the use of information otherwise available whenever a particular respondent will not cooperate or when the data that are submitted cannot be verified or supported. Opponents of this necessary rule of law argue that respondents are increasingly being subjected to the use of best information available (BIA) because the demands for information have been increasing. There is no empirical evidence, however, to support this claim.

Nor do the other facts support Palmeter's critique. First, circumvention has become so prevalent that some respondents appear to take the option of shifting the situs of supply, thus failing to respond to the International Trade Administration's questions and increasing the use of BIA. Second, the claim that BIA is being "increasingly" used ignores the fact that the ITA may find one or two issues not verifiable and use BIA for them (such as ocean freight and imputed interest expense) while using the respondents' data for all other elements. It is not clear that this is at all prejudicial.[29]

Respondents have the ability to determine whether using dumping margins provided in a petition or found for other companies is more favorable than participating in the investigation and having the true margins identified. Although with greater transparency and greater procedural rights, the costs of participating have increased for all parties, BIA

29. Indeed, in *Tapered Roller Bearings from the People's Republic of China*, the domestic industry requested a review because it was believed that the existing dumping margins, less than 1 percent, were too low. 55 Fed. Reg. 41735, 41736 (1990) (preliminary results of antidumping administrative review). The respondent failed to submit an adequate response, and ITA used what was considered to be the best information otherwise available. However, ITA in that case assumed that the existing rate was the "best information" and applied a dumping margin of less than 1 percent. ITA noted the respondents good faith attempt to complete the questionnaire and hardly "punished" the respondent.

remains an important tool that cannot be eliminated. By and large, Commerce has used it appropriately to fill in missing data, to encourage compliance, and to prevent obfuscation.

Moreover, Commerce has taken great strides to improve the process by giving all interested parties an opportunity to identify problems, to identify opportunities, and to get at the actual facts of a case. More participation by domestic parties as a result of earlier and better access has ensured that inadequate or inaccurate responses are identified more often and that corrections are made or, where necessary, best information available is used.

Indeed, *current procedures are adequate to protect the rights of parties.* Even though an original antidumping duty investigation has tight time limits, respondents are given repeated opportunities to submit and supplement their data. During an investigation, the ITA routinely issues deficiency questionnaires to respondents, identifying the areas of deficiency and requesting additional data. During the verification process, foreign respondents, unlike their domestic counterparts, are present and actively advocating their position. Hence, respondents know immediately whether submitted data were supported adequately or are likely to be rejected. Moreover, if minor problems arise during verification, respondents are often permitted to cure those problems on the spot or shortly thereafter through supplemental submissions. For example, in *Oil Country Tubular Goods from Canada*, the department stated that if a questionnaire response was deficient, the respondents would be given an opportunity to respond and clarify the deficiencies.[30] However, if the clarification is not adequate or timely, the department will use BIA. When a respondent submits unresponsive, insufficient, or untimely information, the Court of International Trade has held that the department's use of best information available is justified.[31]

In short, Palmeter protests too much. Commerce is confronted with a wide range of responses from foreign companies. The current practice encourages full and complete reporting. Failure to do so requires the use of best information otherwise available. With the desire of all participants for speedy resolution of the investigation and the lack of subpoena power, the department must be able to pick reasonable data whenever submitted data prove incorrect. It must also be able to assume that margins are at

---

30. 51 Fed. Reg. 15029, 15031 (1986).

31. *Seattle Marine Fishing Supply Co.* v. *United States*, 679 F. Supp. 1119 (Ct. Int'l Trade 1988); *Ansaldo Componenti, S.p.A.* v. *United States*, 628 F. Supp. 198 (Ct. Int'l Trade, 1986); and 19 C.F.R. sec. 353.37.

least as high as the highest alleged when respondents refuse to cooperate or otherwise significantly impede the investigation.

Substantive Issues in the Dumping Calculus

PRICE COMPARISONS (AVERAGING). Palmeter complains that the "present methodology of comparing individual export prices to weighted average home market (or third-country) prices" is unfair to respondents. It is proposed that U.S. law be amended to require that when foreign market value is based on average home market or third-country prices, U.S. prices should also be based on the average of U.S. transactions (rather than on individual transactions) to achieve a more equitable comparison.

This is essentially a red herring issue. U.S. law does permit the averaging of U.S. prices when a large number of sales are involved and when the averaging will not distort the result. The use of average prices was intended to make Commerce's task more manageable, as long as there was no reasonable loss of accuracy in the result. Moreover, under U.S. law, the department will not average home market sales when there is a preponderant price.[32]

U.S. law permits the averaging of sales in certain circumstances. Commerce's history has been to do limited averaging (for example, periodic averaging) when perishable products are involved. For example, in *Fresh Cut Flowers from Columbia*, the agency permitted averaging on a monthly basis. Although the Court of International Trade noted that averaging on a daily or weekly basis would have taken care of the problems of end-of-day sales and the perishability of the product, it nonetheless upheld averaging for a period as long as a month.[33]

Proponents of averaging ignore the fact that, when respondents have demonstrated essentially identical pricing patterns, the United States has not found dumping by averaging in one market and not in the other.[34]

Congress's authorization to use average prices, however, was never intended to permit dumping to be disguised or masked.[35] When the prices

32. 19 U.S.C. sec. 1677f-1; and 19 C.F.R. sec. 353.44(b).

33. *Floral Trade Council of Davis, California* v. *United States*, 704 F. Supp. 233 (Ct. Int'l Trade 1988).

34. *Certain Fresh Winter Vegetables from Mexico*, 45 Fed. Reg. 20512 (1980); and *Southwest Florida Winter Vegetable Growers Assoc.* v. *United States*, 584 F. Supp. 10 (Ct. Int'l Trade 1984).

35. 19 U.S.C.A. sec. 1677f-1. Congress never intended a significant departure from the agency practice of using transaction-specific U.S. price. *Trade Remedies Reform Act of 1989*, H. Rept. 725, 98 Cong. 2 sess. (GPO, 1984), pp. 45–46. To the contrary, the

Table 8-1. *Hypothetical Example of Targeting through Averaging*
U.S. Dollars

Quantity	U.S. price	Average home market price	Actual home market price	Margin (percent)
U.S. method				
100,000	30	25	24	0
100,000	25	25	26	0
100,000	20	25	25	25
Total	. . .	. . .	. . .	6.7
Average method				
300,000	25	25	. . .	0

of an imported product vary over time or among U.S. purchasers, averaging may grossly understate dumping margins. The department has repeatedly rejected average prices on this basis.[36] The limitation on averaging on the U.S. side is necessary to prevent the targeting of certain accounts to be disguised through the averaging of the very low prices at selected accounts with other sales at higher prices. As shown in table 8-1, a foreign producer who targets dumping to one customer or in a particular period could hide sporadic dumping if those prices are averaged with other U.S. prices. Note that the averaging hides targeting and sales below cost.

Targeting has been of great concern to the domestic producer. Where targeting exists, domestic producers can lose sales at particular accounts yet be unable to obtain relief from price discrimination.

Averaging is also terrible policy from an importer's perspective. U.S. law is designed to encourage foreign producers to offer and importers to accept a fair price for the foreign product. Averaging prices frustrates that policy by rewarding those importers able to buy at the deepest discount and penalizing those paying a fair price.

---

statute expressly notes that averaging should not result in the use of U.S. prices which are unrepresentative of the actual transaction prices. In *Rock Salt from Canada*, 50 Fed. Reg. 49741 (1985), the ITA held as follows: "There is no indication that Congress intended Section A to be *a radical departure of our normal methodology of calculating United States prices on a transaction-by-transaction basis. It has always been to ascertain the price of each individual U.S. transaction. . . .* There is no evidence in either the language of the 1984 Act or its legislative history that Congress intended to alter that basic methodology." 50 Fed. Reg. at 49746 (emphasis added).

36. See, for example, *Zenith Radio Corp.* v. *United States*, 606 F. Supp. 695, 703 (Ct. Int'l Trade 1985) (an averaging technique to determine U.S. prices "would clearly be unacceptable" where this could "eliminate dumping margins . . . by averaging in higher prices from a later time").

Table 8-2. *Effect of Averaging on the Importer*[a]

	U.S. price	Amount of dumping	Average duty
Importer A	20	0	2
Importer B	18	2	2
Importer C	16	4	2

a. Home market price average = $20.00.

In table 8-2, the only importer paying "fair" value, Importer A, will nonetheless pay a dumping duty. In effect, Importer A subsidizes Importer C, whose dumping duties are reduced $2.00 by the use of an average U.S. price. This is patently unjustified but is the necessary result of averaging on both sides of the dumping equation.

Not surprisingly, averaging has been opposed by importers. In the antifriction bearing cases, for example, the Department of Commerce considered averaging across foreign manufacturer's prices. But there was an outcry from importers. They feared the department would depart from its traditional methodology and they would become liable for dumping duties owed by other importers.

SALES BELOW COST OF PRODUCTION. Palmeter criticizes the way Commerce deals with sales below cost in an antidumping investigation. He maintains that the antidumping law is not logical, because the cost of production provision is concerned with low-priced sales in a foreign market. But, of course, the purpose of the below-cost investigation is to determine whether home market (or third-country) prices are a valid measure of fair value. If a foreign producer's prices at home are below its cost of production, by definition the comparison price cannot be fair, because no one could remain in business at such prices without cross-product subsidization or government largesse. Hence, that price cannot be used to measure whether export prices reflect comparative advantage or are not discriminating. The provision on sales below cost addresses this factual situation.

Under section 773(b) of the Tariff Act of 1930, if the administering agency determines that home market or third-country sales (a) are below the cost of production "over an extended period of time and in substantial quantities" and (b) "are not at prices which permit recovery of all costs within a reasonable period of time in the normal course of trade," then such sales will be disregarded "in the determination of foreign market value." Congress enacted the cost-of-production provision because it was concerned that sales uniformly at prices below the cost of production, absent a statutory provision, would escape the "purview of the Act, and thereby cause injury to United States industry with impunity."[37]

Palmeter also contends that the cost-test provision is illogical because it is concerned with sales below total cost rather than with sales below variable cost. He mistakes the coverage of the antidumping act. It is not limited to "predatory" conduct. The law is designed to protect businesses and workers from being harmed by conduct that does not flow from comparative advantage. Selling at prices that do not permit the recovery of all costs over a reasonable period of time is an unsustainable business practice (absent some event such as cross-product subsidization). If U.S. companies shut down plants and fire workers because they are competing with prices that do not reflect the commercial reality that companies need to earn an adequate return on capital over time, that is a proper subject of regulation, whether individual businessmen might find such conduct "rational" under conditions of protected market, cross-subsidization, or noncommercial measures.

Congress requires that benchmark prices be sustainable over time: "infrequent sales at less than cost, or sales at prices which will permit recovery of all costs based upon anticipated sales volume over a reasonable time would not be disregarded. However, the practice of systematically selling at prices which will not permit recovery of *all* costs would be covered by this amendment and such sales would accordingly be disregarded."[38]

Palmeter assumes a predatory intent, but that is not the purpose of the antidumping law. Variable costs are used as a benchmark to show predatory intent in the context of the antitrust law. In the remedial context of the antidumping law, however, there are no justifications for such a low threshold. The logic of the antidumping law is unassailable—a price cannot be a comparative advantage price if it does not permit a company to stay in the game over time; since one is comparing export prices to some benchmark, that benchmark must be a price that would exist in the market if the company were attempting to stay in the game for the long term on the basis of its costs and not other factors.

It is not true that the department's approach to sales below cost in the foreign market forces it to resort to constructed value. Even though U.S.

37. *Trade Reform Act of 1974*, S. Rept. 1298, p. 173. The stimulus for a cost of production provision was the Treasury determination in *Elemental Sulfur From Canada*, 37 Fed. Reg. 3933 (1972).

38. *Trade Reform Act of 1974*, S. Rept. 1298, p. 173.

practice is to disregard below-cost sales when there are extensive below-cost sales during the period investigated, the remaining sales are used in determining foreign market value. Only in circumstances in which there are insufficient sales above cost to compare to U.S. sales is constructed value used.[39]

In addition, Palmeter overlooks the fact that U.S. law currently permits below-cost sales to be used as the basis for comparison when the product is in start-up and sales volume is temporarily depressed, or when other extraordinary factors need to be taken into account. Because it is the foreign producer who is in control of the data, U.S. law fairly places the burden on the foreign producer to demonstrate entitlement to the exception.

CONSTRUCTED VALUE. Palmeter recommends that Congress "eliminate the arbitrary and automatic minimums of 10 percent for overhead and 8 percent for profit in constructed value." Such a change is unwarranted. It does not adequately consider, or fails to understand, the situations in which constructed value is invoked, ignores the history of administration in the United States, would substantially increase the burden on parties with no appreciable improvement in process or results, and ignores the experience of companies in other countries. Let us consider these points in turn.

The proposed change is unwarranted. One of the main criticisms of the use of statutory minimums is that they are arbitrary in nature and may give rise to artificially high margins. The experience of the United States demonstrates that these arguments are without merit.

The United States has been using statutory minimums for general, selling, and administrative costs (GS&A) and profit in situations in which the home market prices or third-country prices are unavailable or inadequate ever since the dumping law was enacted. If one were to ask, "How did Customs come up with 8 and 10 percent?" there may be no satisfactory answer (although in fact Customs used similar percentages as reasonable minimums in customs-valuation situations). But seventy years of experience show the 8 percent and 10 percent proxies are more than fair from the perspective of foreign producers. The proxies have proved to be a largely conservative estimate of corporate GS&A and profits. There are many cases in which the agency has found actual GS&A or profit to be far above the statutory minimum for some or all of the companies investigated.[40]

---

39. 19 C.F.R. sec. 353.51. On the use of constructed value, see *Timken Company* vs. *United States*, 673 F. Supp. 495 (Ct. Int'l Trade 1987).

40. See, for example, *Mechanical Transfer Presses from Japan*, 55 Fed. Reg. 335, 337

There are few industries in which GS&A is less than 10 percent of the cost of manufacture. In addition, for virtually every country in the world over time, 8 percent of the cost of manufacture plus GS&A is a conservative estimate of the cost of capital—the "profit" a company must make to stay in the game over time.

The factual situations in which constructed value is used invalidate the proposed change. As stated earlier, constructed value is used as a proxy for the actual home market price when that price is unavailable or inadequate. Such a condition may exist because the producer has a small home market, produces for export only, or has sales in the home market that are below the cost of production. In any of these situations, the company's actual experience in the home market with the merchandise in question (the class or kind) is not usable. Limiting assessments to "actual" profits for the same class or kind for the same company would allow the backdoor use of the very information already identified as unusable.[41] Such a result is clearly unacceptable.

Foreign producers objected strenuously to prior U.S. law, which permitted authorities to use the actual experience of other foreign producers as a basis for comparison in determining normal value for a company with inadequate home market sales. Before 1974, the administering authority was to determine normal value by examining prices in the home market on sales by other producers when sales for the particular company under investigation were unavailable or insufficient. At the urging of many foreign producers and importers, the provision was changed in the Trade Act of 1974. As stated in the Senate report to the act:

Under present law, the Treasury Department is required to resort, for comparison purposes, to sales made by a different company in the

---

(1990); *Certain Small Business Telephone Systems and Subassemblies Thereof from South Korea*, 54 Fed. Reg. 53141, 53144 (1989); and *New Steel Rail, Other Than Light Rail, from Canada*, 54 Fed. Reg. 31984, 31985 (1989).

41. In discussing changes to the law in 1958, the Senate noted that constructed value as used in the antidumping law was intended to have the same interpretation as that used in customs valuation law. *Antidumping Act, 1921*, S. Rept. 1619, 85 Cong. 2 sess. (GPO, 1958), p. 9. The Customs Court and Court of Customs and Patent Appeals (CCPA) have consistently held that "constructed value," as used in the valuation law prior to 1979, was intended to be the value of the imported merchandise, not the value of merchandise sold in another market. See, for example, *United States v. C. J. Tower & Sons of Buffalo*, 470 F. 2d 1393, 1397 (CCPA 1972); *New York Credit Men's Adjustment Bureau, Inc. v. United States*, 314 F. Supp. 1246, 1251 (Cust. Ct. 1970), aff'd, 342 F. Supp. 745 (Cust. Ct. 1972); and *United States v. Dana Perfumes Corp.*, 383 F. Supp. 828, 831 (Cust. Ct. 1974), *modified on other grounds*, 524 F.2d 750 (CCPA 1975).

home market if the company in question makes no sales, or an insignificant number of sales, of such or similar merchandise in the home market. This produces occasional inequities by subjecting companies to dumping findings when their prices to the United States are not lower than their prices in all other markets in which they sell and, further, by rendering them liable to the imposition of dumping duties on the basis of prices which they cannot control and may not even know about. The reverse can also be true and companies may escape liability for dumping duties when—although their prices to third countries, if used as a basis for comparison, would show dumping margins— the Treasury is compelled to use as a comparison basis the home market prices of a different producer which reveals no dumping margins. The amendment will remedy this situation and allow the practices of each producer to stand on their own.[42]

All the problems encountered by the United States when a similar system was used for prices from other producers are also applicable to GS&A and profitability. For many products, moreover, the possibility exists that if the prices of one producer are below cost, prices may likewise be below cost for other producers in the same market. Thus, there is no obvious advantage to using the data from other producers as opposed to statutory minimums in selected cases.

The use of statutory minimums reduces the administration's work load. There is a strong likelihood that much additional effort and expense will be incurred if statutory minimums are prohibited. The attack on U.S. methodology ignores the simplification it provides in many cases. For example, because many respondents with multiple products proclaim that GS&A or profit cannot be determined for a specific product, an overworked agency will routinely resort to the statutory minimums as BIA.

The belief that margins are inflated is contradicted by the experience of other countries and the published profitability figures for many companies in many countries. Proposals that would prohibit the use of a statutory minimum appear to be based on a mistaken perception that margins may be significantly affected by the statutory minimums. First, in countries without statutory minimums, it is not uncommon for the proxy profit and GS&A ratios to be considerably higher than 8 percent and 10 percent, respectively. In a case involving electronic typewriters

42. *Trade Reform Act of 1974,* S. Rept. 1298, p. 177; accord *Trade Reform Act of 1973,* H. Rept. 571, 93 Cong. 1 sess. (GPO, 1973), p. 72.

from Japan, the analysis by the European Community demonstrated home market profit margins in excess of 30 percent.[43] Hence, if an "actual" profit percentage for some product of the same general category had to be used, dumping margins would not be greatly reduced and might even be much higher, since the agency would be forced to find a surrogate.

Moreover, the 8 percent profit margin (as a percentage of the cost of manufacture and GS&A) is objectively conservative. For example, Japan is often held up as a country with slim profit margins. Yet, published financial results for major industries demonstrate that Japanese companies often exceed 8 percent profit margins on the cost of manufacture and GS&A by significant amounts. Similar profit margins have been experienced by companies in other countries as well.

Companies that cannot earn a return equal to or exceeding their cost of capital over the long term are of necessity dying entities. In almost every country of the world, a cost-of-capital figure (when equated to a percentage of the cost of manufacture and GS&A) will exceed the U.S. statutory minimum. Japan might be an exception for some time periods.

Normally, GS&A is also well above 10 percent; in some cases it amounts to 50 percent or more of the cost of manufacture. Although it occasionally falls below 10 percent, that figure is a generally conservative estimate for the proxy required because of inadequate home market sales.

In short, as mentioned, constructed value is used only when there are insufficient home market sales to determine normal value. Consequently, any figure used for GS&A and profit in such a situation is an estimate of what would have been incurred had home market sales been adequate. Although using the 8 percent and 10 percent proxies may not be the only way to handle such a factual situation, if the department was not allowed to use some minimum figure, its administrative effort would increase substantially, with no apparent gain in ensuring a correct result.

The ESP offset and failure to deduct resale profit constitute the bias, not the ESP cap. Palmeter calls for the elimination of the so-called ESP (exporter's sales price) offset cap on the grounds that the cap creates a bias against respondents. It is not the offset cap but the offset that should be eliminated. Existing practice creates a severe bias, but it is against domestic producers, not respondents. Palmeter believes it is unfair to respondents to limit the home market deduction, that is, to cap it by the

---

43. "Council Regulation (EEC) No. 1698/85 . . . Imposing a Definite Anti-dumping Duty on Imports of Electronic Typewriters Originating in Japan," *The European Communities*, no. L163 (June 22, 1985), p. 4.

amount of indirect expenses such as the overhead incurred in the United States. Efforts to uncap the ESP offset would only further skew the results in favor of respondents dealing through related-party importers—which would be quite the opposite of what Congress envisioned in creating the antidumping law.

The ESP offset and its cap arise only when the importer is related to the foreign producer or exporter. Generally that means a subsidiary of the foreign producer in the importing country of the foreign producer. If the foreign producer sells to an unrelated importer in the United States, there is no adjustment either to the U.S. price or to the foreign market value for indirect selling expenses incurred by the foreign producer.

When the Antidumping Act of 1921 was being debated, one option open to Congress in dealing with related-party transactions was to base the export price on the transfer price, at least when such prices approximated arm's-length prices.[44] Congress was concerned, however, about the possible manipulation of the transfer prices and chose instead a methodology that would reduce manipulation and thus protect domestic producers: the construction of an export price by starting with the resale price and deducting all expenses involved in reselling the merchandise in the United States. Commissions were also to be deducted, which practically covered the profit on resale under the prevalent Customs Service usage.

Therefore, a simple test of whether the ESP methodology is working properly is whether the results approximate the transfer price when in fact the transfer price is the same as the arm's-length price (for example, when the foreign producer sells to related and unrelated importers at the same price).[45]

---

44. Foreign producers and related party importers have long sought the ability to have the transfer price used for ordinary customs purposes on the basis that such prices are equivalent to arm's length prices. The amendments to customs valuation made in 1979 (title II of the Trade Agreements Act of 1979) expanded the situations in which the transfer price would be accepted for purposes of determining ordinary customs duties. *Trade Agreements Act of 1979*, S. Rept. 249, p. 121.

45. Stated differently, the purpose of the ESP provision is to approximate the price that would have been charged if the U.S. importer and foreign exporter were not related, that is, a proxy for the f.o.b. origin price. Existing U.S. law and the GATT Antidumping Code require that when the U.S. importer is related to the foreign producer, the U.S. price to be examined is the resale price to the first unrelated purchaser. 19 C.F.R. sec. 353.41(c). Adjustments are made to the resale price to estimate what the sales price to the related importer would have been but for the relationship between producer and importer. Under GATT and U.S. law, all costs incurred in reselling the merchandise in the United States are deducted. See Antidumping Code, article 2:6; 19 U.S.C. sec. 1677a(e); and 19 C.F.R.

In ESP situations, however, to address a perceived unfairness "in the computation of foreign market value," the department allows respondents to offset the ESP-mandated deduction of reselling expenses with a deduction from the foreign market value of the indirect selling expenses incurred in the home market up to the amount of the ESP mandatory deduction.[46] Commerce also does not deduct a reasonable profit on resale. As a result, Commerce methodology does not compare a proxy for this (arm's-length) transfer price with a home market price at the same commercial level.

Whereas the rest of the world correctly constructs an estimated export price between producers and related resellers, the United States, by failing to deduct resale profits and by creating the ESP offset, permits distortions that strongly bias the results in favor of related-party importers.[47] This fact has even been acknowledged by respondents' counsel in law review articles and submissions to Commerce over the years.[48] Eliminating the

---

sec. 353.41(e). The GATT code and all our trading partners also deduct reasonable profits in the resales. See, for example, "Regulation (EEC) no. 459/68 of the Council of 5 April 1968 . . .," *Official Journal of the European Communities*, no. L93/1, article 3, para. 4(b); An Act Respecting the Imposition of Anti-Dumping Duty (Canada), 10(c)(ii) (December 18, 1968); Australia Customs Tariff (Anti-Dumping) Act of 1975 (no. 76 of 1975), 4A(iii), as amended by the Customs Tariff Amendment Act of 1981 (no. 66 of 1981). See also "Council Regulation (EEC) No. 1698/85," p. 6; and *Notice of Final Determination of Dumping . . . Plate Coils, Fully or Partially Manufactured, Originating in or Exported from the United States of America, Canada Gazette*, vol. 118 (July 14, 1984), pt. 1, p. 5641.

46. The agency's discretion to create the "offset" was approved in *Smith-Corona Group* v. *United States*, 713 F.2d 1568, 1577 (Fed. Cir. 1983), *cert. denied* 465 U.S. 1022 (1984). The "cap" was approved in *Consumer Products Division, SCM Corporation* v. *Silver Reed America*, 753 F.2d 1033, 1040 (Fed. Cir. 1985) (recognizing that an increased allowance would distort the dumping computation in favor of foreign producers).

47. In contrast, the GATT Antidumping Code specifically provides that when the export price is "unreliable" because of being between related parties, the export price may be constructed on the basis of the price at which the imported products are "first resold to an independent buyer. . . . Allowance for costs, including duties and taxes, incurred between importation and resale, and for profits accruing, should also be made." Antidumping Code, article 2, secs. 5, 6. This provision is implemented by all our major trading partners with active antidumping rules. For example, in some cases the EC determined the amount of profit to be deducted by looking at the profit earned by unrelated importers on their sale of identical merchandise; this profit was used as the reasonable profit on resale for the related party importer. See, for example, "Council Regulation (EEC) No. 1698/85."

48. See, for example, Noel Hemmendinger and William H. Barringer, "The Defense of Antidumping and Countervailing Duty Investigations under the Trade Agreements Act of 1979," *North Carolina Journal of International Law and Commercial Regulation*, vol. 6 (Summer 1981), pp. 433–34. ("The exporter's sales price often is a more favorable basis of calculating fair value because, unlike purchase price, the profit of the U.S. importer is included in the net adjusted price, resulting in a higher United States price"); and Memorandum from Wender Murase & White, attorneys for Sumitomo Metal Industries, Ltd.,

cap would simply further the interests of the foreign respondents. It is difficult to imagine any result more contrary to the congressional purpose.

Nonmarket economies should not be excluded from the antidumping laws. Palmeter argues that the United States should not apply the antidumping law to nonmarket economies. Although many would agree that nonmarket economy calculations, at least as they are handled at present, do not accurately reflect constructed value, the problem is that the state-controlled economy exporters would be favored. Under the 1988 statutory revisions, as implemented, many state-controlled companies have been given an export preference by the United States, with benchmarks far below any price in any market economy (including many developing country markets) in the world.

Although situations involving state-controlled economies are problematic, the proposal that such countries be freed from the antidumping laws makes no sense. Because factors of production in a state-controlled country do not respond to market forces and internal prices are not market-driven, exports are likely to violate comparative advantage principles. The only options available to safeguard trade liberalization based on comparative advantage is either to have managed trade with state-controlled countries or to have a reasonable surrogate price for the countries involved. The uncertainty that flowed from the price-based system which existed before 1988 was not inherent in the system and could have been dealt with in a way that should have been agreeable to all (for example, the ITA could issue an annual list of countries found to be state-controlled; with surrogate countries for each).

The cases since 1988 have become bogged down in a factors-of-production approach. Large portions of the factors are estimated in ways that to date have resulted in simply shocking findings. In short, reform is needed, but not that envisioned by Palmeter.

Duty deposits encourage exporters to reform their pricing. Palmeter states that duty deposits impose an unlimited contingent liability on importers. Yet, the U.S. system is objectively the fairest in the world. Although actual liability is not known until the administrative reviews are completed, this contingency is neither novel nor unreasonable. In fact, rather than simply assume duties, the U.S. system encourages ex-

---

July 26, 1984, p. 12 ("It has been our experience as trade lawyers that exporter's sales price frequently [but not always] operates to the advantage of foreign respondents. In the case of SMI steel sold to the U.S. through a trading company, there is no question but that the use of exporter's sales price would benefit the respondent, for the trading company's selling price includes a profit which would elevate the U.S. price by an equal amount").

porters to reform their pricing—to lower their home market prices, increase their export prices, or to use some combination of the two. The necessary corollary is that if dumping increases, liability also increases. Price discrimination cannot be neutralized on any other basis.

Although delays in completing reviews are harmful to both sides,[49] Palmeter's description of Commerce practice is simply inaccurate in most cases. It is true that in older cases, abdication of responsibility to respondents and their counsel was corrected through judicial review and ultimately changed the results (for the better). But the general methodology remains relatively constant, subject of course to changes in the statute or regulation, which are relatively rare events. Greater cooperation between parties and other changes mentioned later in the chapter, coupled with the substantial effort of the Commerce Department to deal with its backlog, can help keep the administrative review process up to date.[50]

The de minimis standard is acceptable. Palmeter proposes that the current de minimis standard of dumping should be raised from 0.5 percent to 5 percent. Although the Department of Commerce is responsible for calculating the margins, it is the International Trade Commission that determines whether a U.S. industry has been injured by dumping. And the commission has found injury in many cases where antidumping duties of less than 5 percent have been imposed on imported merchandise.[51] The proposal to set an arbitrarily high standard would permit foreign producers to continue to dump even though the commission found material injury.

49. In one case, entries of tapered roller bearings from certain Japanese producers were imported for sixteen years without even an estimated antidumping duty deposit because the Commerce Department had not completed its first annual review of an antidumping order under 19 U.S.C. sec. 1675 until June 1, 1990. Consequently, the domestic industry secured no relief since the dumping finding in 1976.

50. Other problems in the assessment and collection of duties have also made it difficult for domestic industries facing unfair trade competition to procure timely and effective relief. Congressional concern over the inability of administrative agencies to assess and collect duties as intended by Congress is self-apparent. See the report issued by the House Subcommittee on Oversight, "Abuses and Mismanagement in U.S. Customs Service Commercial Operations," February 1990 ("Customs has done a poor job of enforcing antidumping and countervailing duty (AD/CVD) laws, due mainly to an inaccurate and archaic system for collecting key information"); see also *Import Duties: Assessment of Duties and Unfairly Priced Imports Not Reviewed*, GAO Report GGD-89-124 (September 1989), p. 6 (concluding that "assessment of [antidumping duties] is not being fully administered").

51. See, for example, *Certain Malleable Cast-Iron Pipe Fittings from Thailand*, 52 Fed. Reg. 31095 (1987) (ITC final determination that margins of 1.70 percent materially injure the domestic industry); and *Frozen Concentrated Orange Juice from Brazil*, 52 Fed. Reg. 15566 (1987) (ITC final determination that margins of 1.96 percent materially injure the domestic industry).

Palmeter and other proponents of raising the de minimis standard ignore commercial realities. A de minimis standard of 2 percent would permit foreign producers to depress the profit margin in the United States by two percentage points. Yet, a reduction in the average sales price of 2 percent would reduce U.S. corporate profitability in the manufacturing sector (before taxes) by 26 percent.[52] Such a reduction is significant and cannot possibly qualify as de minimis.

The anticircumvention amendments are not disguised rules for determining origin. Contrary to Palmeter's contentions, there is no surreptitious process underfoot to use rules-of-origin determinations to further protectionist ends. The newly enacted anticircumvention provisions in the 1984 and 1988 amendments to the antidumping law are not disguised rules for the determination of origin. The issues involved in the Customs Service's determination of the country of origin of goods that enter into U.S. customs territory are distinct from the issues encountered by the Commerce Department in enforcing the antidumping law.

It is hornbook law that remedial legislation is to be broadly construed to suppress a perceived evil and thereby foster the remedial purpose.[53] Not surprisingly, as increasing instances of circumvention have been identified, Congress has acted to effectuate the remedial purpose of the antidumping law and cut off anticircumvention routes. Specifically, Congress in 1984 and 1988 granted the department express authority to prevent evasion of an antidumping order through the importation of parts for assembly in the United States, the assembly of parts of a dumped product in a third country, the minor modification of an article in order to evade the scope of an order, the transshipment of articles through third countries, and other similar tactics.

That Palmeter does not agree with the congressional choice does not render it "protectionist." The focus of the department's inquiry when addressing the problem of circumvention of antidumping duty orders is not whether goods originating in Country A have undergone substantial transformation in Country B so as to establish Country B as the "country of origin" for customs purposes. The function of Customs in the antidumping context is purely ministerial.[54] Rather, the department is inter-

---

52. Bureau of the Census, *Quarterly Financial Report for Manufacturing, Mining and Trade Corporations* (Department of Commerce, third quarter, 1989).

53. *Badger-Powhatan, a Division of Figgie International Inc., v. United States*, 608 F. Supp. 653, 656 (Ct. Int'l Trade 1985).

54. *Trade Agreements Act of 1980*, 19 U.S.C. secs. 1673e(a), 1673h. See also *Reorganizing the Government's International Trade and Investment Functions*, Hearings before

ested in whether the conduct of a foreign producer on its face represents an intended effort, through modest steps, to avoid the reach of an anti-dumping order.

Palmeter makes no effort to deal with the frustration of the remedial purpose that occurs through circumvention. Repetitious cases seem to be his avenue of obtaining effective relief—even though relief is not retro-active, no compensation is paid to injured industries, and circumvention largely involves related companies. Stated differently, Palmeter would promote the congressionally identified evil and suppress the remedy.

Issues Raised by Other Authors

Another issue that has been raised concerns standing: who has the stand-ing to file an antidumping petition "on behalf of an industry" in the United States.[55] Some complain that petitions are brought by individual U.S. firms and that those opposing a petition have the burden of showing that the petition is not brought on behalf of the domestic industry. They call this approach prejudicial and argue that the party bringing an action should have the burden of proving its allegations, as in U.S. civil litigation in general.

It has been suggested that the petitioner be required to show affirmative support of 50 percent or more of the industry before an investigation is initiated and that the administering agency be required to provide reasons for initiating an investigation. These proposals are cures for an unknown problem. In the history of the antidumping law, there are only two instances in which any bona fide concern was raised about a petitioner's standing. Both cases involved steel imports, where bilateral agreements restricting exports to the United States were viewed by the U.S. industry as a more desirable outcome than dumping investigations or ad valorem duties. In both cases, those in opposition had no problem coming forward to express their concern. In virtually every other case, those concerned with standing are those engaged in dumping, their related-party import-ers, or those liable for the dumping duties (importers, whether related

---

the Senate Committee on Governmental Affairs, 96 Cong. 1 sess. (GPO, 1979); Report of the Senate Governmental Affairs Committee to accompany S. Res. 245, 96 Cong. 1 sess. (GPO, 1979), p. 29; and *Royal Business Machines, Inc.* v. *United States*, 507 F. Supp. 1007 (Ct. Int'l Trade 1980).

55. See Tracy Murray's chapter in this volume, p. 27.

or not).[56] Interestingly, not a single country in the Uruguay Round negotiations has taken the position that parties related to foreign producers or importers could block antidumping investigations. Indeed, it is widely agreed that all such companies must be excluded from any head count to determine domestic support for a petition.

What additional standing requirements would do is increase the cost of bringing cases in some instances, make cases impossible to bring simply because of the fragmented nature of the industry, or enable large commercial users to intimidate selected domestic suppliers.

Current U.S. law and practice on standing appropriately effectuate congressional objectives. It would be illogical to reverse the rebuttable presumption that a domestic manufacturer's efforts to neutralize unfair trade practices are on behalf of the domestic industry. Furthermore, creating a "polling requirement" on the administering authority is unwarranted, since no significant problem or abuse has ever been demonstrated to exist.

Under U.S. law, a petition is filed by an interested party "on behalf of" a domestic industry. The purpose of this language is to prevent the filing of petitions by persons with no actual interest in the outcome.[57] Petitions are almost always filed by one or more domestic producers or labor unions. Despite this fact, enormous resources have been spent in many investigations in the past six years by respondents and related-party importers trying to demonstrate that some portion or all of the investigation should be dismissed because it was not filed "on behalf of the industry." These challenges have been repeatedly denied both by the agency and the reviewing court.

The proposal is also not logical in its allocation of burdens. Currently, it is the burden of those opposing the petition to demonstrate that a majority of the industry does not support the petition.[58] Present practice

56. *Oregon Steel Mills Inc.* v. *United States*, 862 F.2d 1541 (Fed. Cir. 1988); *Gilmore Steel Corporation* v. *United States*, 585 F. Supp. 670 (Ct. Int'l Trade 1984). See also *Antifriction Bearings*, 54 Fed. Reg. at 19005; *Citrosuco Paulista S.A.* v. *United States*, 704 F. Supp. 1075 (Ct. Int'l Trade 1988); and *Comeau Seafoods Ltd.* v. *United States*, 724 F. Supp. 1407 (Ct. Int'l Trade 1989).

57. *Trade Agreements Act of 1979*, S. Rept. 249, p. 47.

58. See, for example, *Mechanical Transfer Presses from Japan*, 55 Fed. Reg. 335 (1990); *Antifriction Bearings*, 54 Fed. Reg. at 19,005; *3.5" Microdisks and Coated Media Thereof from Japan*, 54 Fed. Reg. 6433 (1989); and *Frozen Concentrated Orange Juice from Brazil*, 52 Fed. Reg. 8324 (1987).

The Court of International Trade has upheld the ITA's interpretation of the statutory standing requirements. See *Citrosuco Paulista S.A.* v. *United States, Comeau Seafoods Ltd.* v. *United States, Vitro Flex, S.A. and Cristales Inastillables de Mexico, S.A.* v. *United States,*

properly allocates the burden of proof, since it should not be presumed that other members of the domestic industry would be opposed to restoring conditions of fair trade. Moreover, a petitioner will not know whether its U.S. competitors support a petition, without polling—a needless step for the invocation of a remedial statute. Under existing law and practice, those producers are able to state their own position once the petition has been filed. Indeed, in more fragmented industries (such as apparel, agriculture, and floralculture) a petitioner may not even know the full extent of the U.S. industry or of its domestic competitors.[59]

Finally, suggestions that additional explanation be provided in initiating investigations are unjustified. An unnecessary burden on the administering agency is the likely by-product of any requirement that the agency provide reasons for initiation beyond those already provided. Decisions to initiate investigations are not judicially reviewable. Nor is there a history of "frivolous" cases being filed. Of the hundreds of cases filed, few have resulted in a finding of no dumping or subsidization. To require a statement of reasons for initiation is a meaningless procedural formality that will add to the burden of the Commerce Department without any real benefits to the parties.

Cost-Saving Measures

The costs incurred by interested parties who participate in the administration of antidumping and countervailing duty proceedings have received wide attention. The extent of such costs is often cited as grounds for making substantive changes to the antidumping and countervailing duties statutes.[60] As mentioned earlier, Palmeter's proposed changes would, among other things, not decrease the costs associated with antidumping

714 F. Supp. 1229 (Ct. Int'l Trade 1989); *accord, Sandvik AB v. United States,* 721 F. Supp. 1322 (1989), *aff'd,* 904 F.2d 46 (Fed. Cir. 1990). But see also *Suramerica de Aleaciones Laminadas, C.A. v. United States,* 746 F. Supp. 139 (1990), *consolidated appeal pending,* Court nos. 91-1015, 91-1050, 91-1055 (November 19, 1990).

59. *Frozen Concentrated Orange Juice from Brazil,* 52 Fed. Reg. 8324 (1987); *Certain Fresh Atlantic Groundfish from Canada,* 51 Fed. Reg. 10041 (1986); *Certain Carbon Steel Butt-Weld Pipe Fittings from Brazil,* 52 Fed. Reg. 8324 (1987); *Certain Stainless Steel Hollow Products from Sweden,* 52 Fed. Reg. 5794 (1987); *Certain Textile Mill Products and Apparel from Malaysia,* 50 Fed. Reg. 9852 (1985); and *Certain Fresh Cut Flowers from Mexico,* 52 Fed. Reg. 6361 (1987).

60. See, for example, GAO, *International Trade: Pursuit of Trade Law Remedies by Small Business,* GAO/NSIAD-89-69BR (December 1988), pp. 8–9.

proceedings. There are, however, ways to streamline the proceedings so as to reduce the overall costs incurred by the interested parties and ease the administrative burden without changing the statute.

ADMINISTRATIVE PROTECTIVE ORDER APPLICATIONS. The ITA should provide law firms with a standard form for gaining access to administrative protective orders (APOs) and, when relevant, should make the forms available to outside consultants or computer firms so that the APO applications can be filed simply and reviewed quickly. The data to be released under protective order should be served at the time of submission. Otherwise, the submitter should indicate whether the information should be returned if an exception to that procedure is requested but not granted. Finally, to prevent delay through agency inaction, there should be a short time limit (say, forty-eight hours) in which nonaction would presumptively result in the release of the information under the APO.

MODIFICATIONS TO THE QUESTIONNAIRE. When the ITA is soliciting or considering views concerning changes to the questionnaire, it should hear comments from all interested parties. This would reduce the problems that arise after submission when changes have been agreed to informally without input from all the parties.

PUBLIC VERSIONS. Substantial costs are incurred because public versions of submissions are inadequate. Problems seem to flow from several sources: (1) case analysts differ in the extent to which they adhere to the regulations; (2) opponents may try to delay comments on the merits; (3) no guidelines are available on what, if anything, must be summarized from public, confidential, and APO material.

Commerce should follow the example of the International Trade Commission (ITC), which has put a small group in charge of APO applications, and have a small group checking the incoming public versions for compliance with department regulations. All nonconforming responses (including the APO version) should be rejected within forty-eight hours of submission, and the burden should be on the submitter to justify within an equally short period why a revised public version should be accepted. After one rejection per company, a revised submission should be accepted only with good cause. Second, this same group should handle subsequent violations of the regulation (for example, data varying by more than the stated percentage) within a short time (say, forty-eight hours). To implement this approach, the ITA should establish clear guidelines explaining how, if at all, it expects parties to summarize combinations of public, confidential, and APO material. The language of the APO prohibits the mention of anything not known from the public version. Over the years, it has become clear that counsels have different interpretations of their obligations and rights with regard to the use of APO material. To date there has been little guidance and much controversy. The ITA and the ITC should issue guidelines on the most common issues and should provide some mechanism for quick and binding decisions by the respective general counsel's offices.

COMPUTER PROGRAM DEBUGGING. The parties expend a great deal of effort in debugging computer programs after a preliminary or final determination just to determine why their program has failed to execute what the ITA has indicated is being done. Several steps could be taken to make reviews much simpler for all parties.

—Programs should always be put in the public record (with confidential information deleted or public ranged numbers included) of an investigation or administrative review. The record should also show the alleged problems with the program used in the investigation or review.

—Programs from the original investigation or the most recently completed review should be placed in the record of the new review at the beginning of the review.

—Once the questionnaire responses are filed and comments are received from domestic parties, Commerce should provide the parties with a draft program for comment before the program is run. The department should also provide a written description of the steps the program is intended to execute and any intended deviations from the programming steps used in the original investigation or the most recently completed administrative review. Interested parties should not be allowed to comment on the merits of adjustments or other substantive issues in this exercise, merely on whether there appear to be programming problems that will prevent the program from doing what the agency has indicated it is trying to do.

—The previous step would not eliminate the right of the parties to full disclosure after the preliminary or final review or the need for further examination of clerical or other errors.

EARLY EXAMINATION OF ADJUSTMENT QUESTIONS. Commerce should allow issues relating to entitlement to adjustments to be resolved tentatively (that is, subject to verification) at a relatively early stage in the investigation or review, before the agency generates its computer program. To permit earlier substantive consideration of the claims, respondents should be required to fully justify their claims on the record, with at least sample documentation and all work sheets included as exhibits to the questionnaire responses. Thus the propriety of claimed adjustments could be fully argued earlier in the case. This would obviously not prevent the authorities from reexamining issues on the basis of the verification.

PREDISCLOSURE OF DISCLOSURE DOCUMENTS. Commerce should make uniform its apparent practice in some cases of making disclosure materials available before the disclosure conference so that the conference can be more meaningful.

DEALING WITH ISSUES APPEARING IN FINAL DETERMINATIONS. In cases where Commerce intends to adopt a new methodology or position in the final determination, the parties should be permitted to review the computer program language to be used, and the parties should be permitted to submit written comments in a timely manner if they have not yet been briefed on the issue.

ESTABLISHING SCHEDULES. Although some change may be necessary during the processing of an administrative review, Commerce should establish schedules for the main events of a review or investigation, similar to the ITC schedules for each case (for example, questionnaire responses, cost allegations, verification, and hearing). This should allow better planning by everyone concerned.

SCOPE REVIEWS. The ITA is continually asked to determine whether a particular product is within the scope of an AD and CVD proceeding, or within the scope of an existing AD or CVD order. The ITA usually deals with these requests in a piecemeal fashion. As a result, parties are forced to participate in several "minireviews" at different stages of the proceedings, at greater cost to the parties involved.

The ITA should not conduct any scope reviews during an investigation. Instead, it should collect all requests for a scope determination and conduct a single scope review during the first and, if necessary, subsequent administrative review. By deciding issues that are similar in law and fact in a single setting, it can conserve the resources of the parties and ease the administrative burden.

STATE-CONTROLLED ECONOMIES. In antidumping cases involving state-controlled economies, the ITA usually bases foreign market value on surrogate countries at a level of economic development similar to that of the market being compared. Although the same countries are invariably chosen as surrogates for respective state-controlled economies, considerable resources are expended in each case involving state-controlled economies over the selection of the surrogate country.

The ITA could greatly reduce the costs incurred by the parties, and ease its administrative burden, by using the same surrogate countries for given state-controlled economies, and it should announce this early in the proceeding—for example, when the notice of initiation gives out. Any party that objects to the surrogate that was selected can state why at an early stage of the proceedings, and the issue can therefore be resolved before the preliminary determination. Given the ITA's past consistency in its selection of surrogates, an early determination would eliminate the need to submit information in support of the selection of a particular surrogate and to rebut the selections of other parties.

Suggested Reforms

Existing U.S. law or practice might be reformed in several ways to address the practical problems injured industries face under the existing interpretations—namely, that relief does not restore the status quo ante (that is, it does not level the playing field) and that relief is often not effective because of the myriad circumvention options still available and the costs inherent in having to bring multiple rounds of cases. One option would be to change the injury standard as administered by the International Trade Commission to make relief available earlier. Although the current statutory language should be adequate (including "threat of material injury"), in practice industries generally must be injured for some period of time before there is a reasonable likelihood of an affirmative determination from the commission. In addition, the U.S. antidumping statute should be revised to incorporate a number of the changes proposed by the United States in the context of the Uruguay Round (such as the so-called country hopping by multinational companies found to be dumping in one country) to deal with a range of circumvention issues not specifically covered by the statute at present.

Earlier Relief

When companies have reduced their research and development spending, laid off skilled workers, and eliminated or postponed capital expenditures in response to unfairly traded imports, the mere neutralization of price discrimination or government subsidies does not ensure that the outcome will be driven by comparative advantage. Stated differently, the playing field is not leveled, for the domestic industry is behind where it would have been but for the unfair trade practices. Under current law and practice, there is no compensation for the injured industries. Companies are not returned to their earlier status. For relief to be effective it must permit in fact a level playing field. This can be achieved by seeing that relief is consistently available in a "threat" context or that injured firms are compensated for past harm. At present, neither situation exists.

A comparison of two antidumping cases brought on behalf of high-technology industries demonstrates that early relief can be crucial to industry survival. In 1985, antidumping investigations were initiated for *64K Dynamic Random Access Memory Components from Japan* and *Erasable Programmable Read Only Memories from Japan*, alleging aggressive pricing below the cost of production by Japanese producers. The 64K DRAM investigation resulted in an affirmative determination and anti-dumping order, whereas the EPROM investigation was suspended without the imposition of duties as a result of an overall settlement with individual Japanese exporters.[61] In 1986, spending by U.S. firms on plant and equipment fell by an unprecedented 45 percent, the lowest annual spending level since 1979.[62]

Japanese exporters of DRAMs were dumping in the U.S. market in 1985–86, at which time six of eight U.S. producers of DRAMs, but no Japanese producers, exited the market. The high investment requirements and substantial lead time necessary to design and market a new generation of DRAMs make it highly unlikely that a DRAM producer will reenter the market once it exits. U.S. market share in DRAMs has substantially declined despite the affirmative determinations. This is an example of relief arriving too late.

61. The suspension agreement mandated a commitment from these Japanese companies not to sell EPROMs at prices below the cost of production in the U.S. markets. Under this agreement, the ITA calculates quarterly fair market values to govern the U.S. sales of DRAMs and EPROMs of each producer. GAO, *International Trade*, pp. 8–9.

The semiconductor design and technology has continually evolved since the introduction of the 1K DRAM in 1970 and DRAM capacity has quadrupled every several years. See *Certain Dynamic Random Access Memories, Components Thereof and Products Containing Same*, USITC Pub. 2034, inv. no. 337-TA-242 (Final) (November 1987), p. 14. Within the industry, each succeeding capacity DRAM is known as a "generation." The time between successive DRAM generations or the product life cycles has become increasingly compressed. Thus the ability of a DRAM manufacturer to compete involves substantial R&D in DRAM design and large investments in production technology to develop and market new generation DRAMS. *Ibid.*, p. 15. To enter the high volume DRAM market as a major competitor would require an initial investment of approximately $500 million to $1 billion, with a 1MB DRAM fabrication facility estimated at $300 million and a 4MB DRAM facility estimated at $500 million. Dewey, Ballantine, Bushby, Palmer & Wood, "*Antidumping Law Reform and the Semiconductor Industry: A Discussion of the Issues*," Washington, February 1990, p. 7, n. 7.

62. Thomas J. Howell and others, *The Microelectronics Race: The Impact of Government Policy on International Competition* (Boulder, Colo.; Westview Press, 1988), p. 26.

The EPROM case had a somewhat happier ending, since all the major U.S. EPROM producers remained in the market despite large losses. The preliminary duties were imposed on Japanese exporters of EPROMs when U.S. producers still maintained about 40 percent share of the world market. In an industry in which product life is measured in quarters, the ability to get the government to act quickly can mean the difference between survival and irreparable injury. The debilitating consequences that can flow from even relatively short periods of dumping point as well to the urgent need to consider compensation to domestic producers who have been injured.

However, the need for early relief is not limited to high-technology industries. When dumping occurs over time, many industries may be seriously prejudiced in their long-term prospects. The steel industry is a good example.

Relief must be timely or compensation must be provided so that companies are not penalized in the long term because of artificial advantages used by foreign competitors in the short term. The history of the steel industry demonstrates that without some method of returning an injured party to its original status, the industry may never fully recover from dumped imports.

The International Trade Commission has built up an elaborate set of criteria for finding injury early, including the threat of injury. It is inconceivable that additional or different criteria need to be added to the analysis. What is needed is a review by the individual commissioners of whether the criteria are being applied in a manner that fulfills the congressional objective of providing relief before injury has occurred. If there is no change in the injury standard applied, Congress should consider mandating the payment of compensation, perhaps from dumping duties collected by the Customs Service.

Anticircumvention Measures

The circumvention of antidumping orders has become a serious problem that has led the United States not only to amend its domestic rules but also to try to strengthen existing international disciplines. In 1988, U.S. law was amended to more effectively deal with the myriad forms of circumvention that frustrate the remedial effect of the statute. Further reform is needed, however.

Antidumping duty orders focus on imports from a specific country and are limited to products identified by a petitioner as the source of material injury to the domestic industry. As a result, foreign manufacturers found to be dumping can readily avoid the dumping duty by shifting their source of supply to a manufacturing plant in a third country. They can also avoid paying duties by exporting parts and components of the covered merchandise to be assembled into the finished product in the United States or in a third country.

To try to reduce the efforts to circumvent antidumping duty orders, Congress has acted repeatedly and consistently to close loopholes in the law. In 1974, for example, Congress added provisions to prevent foreign manufacturers from citing sales below cost in the home market as a basis for avoiding liability, and to prevent multinational corporations from circumventing the law by setting up export-only operations in third countries, thereby offering no home market prices for comparison.

In 1979, Congress added the requirements for the verification of information, and provided for retroactive suspension of liquidation in cases of "critical circumstances," that is, cases in which a surge in imports occurred following the filing of the petition but before the suspension of liquidation, so as to evade any antidumping duties imposed.

In 1984, Congress amended the statute to address the transshipment of dumped goods through third countries. Congress also strengthened the provisions for the collection of interest on unpaid duties.

In the most recent amendments, Congress clearly intended that U.S. antidumping and countervailing duty laws should be administered by the Commerce Department so as to more effectively prevent circumvention through minor changes in the production of merchandise already the subject of a dumping order. The law was amended to include a section entitled "Prevention of Circumvention of Antidumping and Countervailing Duty Orders." The new anticircumvention provision enumerates several circumstances of circumvention that are specifically subject to the department's authority to prevent. The importation of parts and components used to complete or assemble, in the United States, the merchandise subject to an order is potentially covered if the operations in the United States add only a small value. The department has identical authority in treating merchandise from a third country when the third country's role has been the addition of a small amount of value added to parts exported from a country covered by the order. Congress also confirmed the department's authority to clarify orders with regard to slightly altered or later-developed merchandise.

The Senate Finance Committee has expressed strong sentiment in favor of closing any loopholes in the antidumping law. Despite the efforts of the administration and Congress to close loopholes, a few important ones remain, including country hopping. Closing such loopholes should be covered in any revisions to U.S. law. Similarly, Commerce and the ITC expedited or abbreviated procedures for follow-on investigations of products already covered by existing antidumping or countervailing duty orders.

Conclusion

The U.S. antidumping law has been in existence for seventy years. It has received substantial scrutiny from domestic users, importers, and other interested parties. Administrative practice since 1979 has been the subject of hundreds of judicial challenges. The result of all of the scrutiny and review is a system that is fundamentally fair. Both the Commerce Department and the International Trade Commission have worked hard to improve the operation of their procedures and the correctness of their decisions. They deserve much credit for the enormous efforts that have been made to date.

Although additional fine tuning is always possible and a few differences of interpretation still need to be settled, the claims of bias, "inquisition," and procedural unfairness elsewhere in this volume are unfair and unfounded. If anything, the existing system favors respondents, for the reasons outlined in this chapter. This is not the result of intentional actions on the part of the agencies, but merely the result of many years of decisionmaking that has made reexamination of selected issues difficult in a bureaucratic environment.

Domestic users are frustrated with the existing antidumping law because of the expenses involved, because relief often comes too late, and because the playing field does not become level. These are problems that can be corrected by changes in interpretations or modifications to the law to strengthen them, not weaken them. Dumping over time is a "crime" that reduces the ability of the domestic producers (who may start out with the best product) to stay in the game. Economic theorists claim that countries with an open market will actually benefit when others choose to dump in their market. The business reality, however, is quite different. Companies that can hide behind closed markets, that have the breadth of product to afford deep cross-product subsidization, or that can sustain themselves from government largesse can take away from U.S. companies the one tool they need to survive—competitiveness. This has happened with alarming and increasing frequency. The antidumping law, imperfect though it may be, allows companies in an open economy to stay the course. It would be tragic if the law was damaged or destroyed.

General Discussion

As NOTED in the foreword, drafts of each paper and the formal discussant's comment were presented by their authors at the conference on unfair trade held at Brookings on November 27, 1990, which was attended by approximately 100 economists, attorneys, and other interested persons knowledgeable about the issues examined in the papers. Following the presentation of each paper and related formal discussion, general comments were made by many of those in attendance. Since the subject matters of the papers and of the related comments often overlapped, the summary of the general discussion here is organized by topic rather than by the particular paper to which the comments may have been addressed. The persons whose comments are summarized, together with their institutional affiliations, are listed below.

Administration of the Antidumping Law

The participants were divided over the extent to which, if any, the Department of Commerce has administered the antidumping law with a

Participants: Keith B. Anderson (U.S. International Trade Commission); Robert E. Baldwin (University of Wisconsin); David L. Binder (U.S. Department of Commerce); Richard D. Boltuck (Office of Management and Budget); Richard Boyce (private consultant); Richard Diamond (Georgetown University School of Law); Joseph W. Dorn (Kilpatrick & Cody); Noel Hemmendinger (Willkie, Farr & Gallagher); Gary Horlick (O'Melveny & Myers); Seth Kaplan (U.S. International Trade Commission); Daniel W. Klett (ICF Consulting Associates, Inc.); Robert E. Litan (Brookings Institution); Patrick Macrory (Akin, Gump, Hauer & Feld); Robert J. Martin (Canadian International Trade Tribunal, in Ottawa); N. David Palmeter (Mudge, Rose, Guthrie, Alexander & Ferdon and the University of Maryland); Leonard M. Shambon (private practitioner); Terence P. Stewart (Stewart & Stewart); Daniel K. Tarullo (Shearman & Sterling); and Andrew R. Wechsler (Law and Economics Consulting Group).

bias toward petitioners. Many of the comments agreed with the thrust of those papers which argued that such a bias exists. However, Terence Stewart and Joseph Dorn, among others, asserted that if any bias is present, it favors importers.

The first criticism of a particular practice was voiced by David Palmeter, who argued that the computer requirements placed by Commerce on the respondents are unduly burdensome. According to Palmeter, few producers have access to the computer hardware and software that are required for the responses to the department's questionnaires, yet it is Commerce's position that as long as some independent agency offers the necessary computer facilities, respondents must put the data into a system that is readable by the department. This procedure is complicated by the lack of communication among the various divisions within the DOC involved in administering the procedure. David Binder, of the Department of Commerce, defended its policy by explaining that it entertains requests for tape or disk submissions but that they are rarely made.

A number of discussants recommended using average prices of both domestic and foreign producers to avoid finding margins due purely to normal price fluctuations. Keith Anderson also suggested using a sample of prices from both sides rather than analyzing every transaction. Stewart disagreed that there would be substantial benefits from using averages, because, in his view, the absence of dual-sided averages adds at most 2 percentage points to the margin of dumping, and most margins found are in the 70 to 100 percent range.

Regarding the adjustments made in situations using third-country comparisons, Binder emphasized that no shortcuts are taken in adjusting for such circumstances as differences in quantity and quality or for the cost of shipping. Stewart commented that adjustments, which are usually given to the respondents, do not create margins of dumping where they do not exist. In addition, he remarked that few petitioners ask that third-country sales be examined.

Robert Martin contended that since the present system is based on a one-year cycle and is basically designed for production-line manufacturing, producers of goods with longer base periods are often found guilty of dumping. Dorn countered that when there are large price fluctuations, the department used month-to-month comparisons to eliminate any distortions from the changing prices.

Several participants focused on the use of "best information available." Most of the papers presented referred to BIA as a procedure tending to favor the petitioner. Yet a number of discussants cited BIA as a balancing mechanism helpful in dealing with uncooperative respondents. Len Shambon said the practice provides an incentive for parties that do not want to be regulated to produce the requested information. Indeed, Dorn asserted that in the absence of BIA respondents can present selective information to minimize the dumping margin. Stewart and Andrew Wechsler both commented that a respondent chooses BIA when it feels this method will produce a more favorable outcome than its own numbers will.

Administration of the Countervailing Duty Law

The negative effects of predatory pricing were not disputed, but many participants disagreed on the effect of subsidies. Thus, whereas the discussion concerning antidumping focused on the methodologies and procedure used by Commerce, the debate about subsidies centered more on the purposes of countervailing duty law.

Seth Kaplan believes the purpose of the CVD law should be to offset the negative effects felt by U.S. firms. Yet he argued that Commerce concentrates instead on simply punishing foreign firms found to have benefited from subsidies.

Both Robert Baldwin and Richard Boltuck described situations in which the levying of CVDs is not a desirable response to foreign subsidies. As Baldwin explained, some subsidies are used as a positive offset to an externality, and others benefit more than just one country. A distinction should be made between subsidies that help to increase world efficiency and those that just benefit a single nation. Boltuck commented that subsidies which lower the price of goods purchased by U.S. citizens are beneficial to U.S. consumers.

At the same time, however, CVDs protect domestic producers from the effect of artificially low-priced goods. Gary Horlick suggested that only Congress, after considering the various possibilities of capture by different interests, can decide this consumer-producer trade-off. Though Horlick concluded that the best option would be to enact a global agreement to end inefficient subsidies, he argued that empirical evidence shows that CVD law reduces some countries' export subsidies, which in turn contributes both to world economic efficiency and domestic producers' welfare.

Procedural Issues Common to Both Antidumping and CVD

Daniel Tarullo initiated discussion about how well the AD and CVD laws are administered since the changes in the amount of discretion allowed the department. In particular, he wondered if Commerce administered unfair trade laws more intelligently when given increased discretion. He made a comparison to the Sherman Antitrust Act of 1890, which, he asserted, originated with no consistent principles but which became an important regulatory instrument because of changes in judicial interpretations of the law. Palmeter argued that only when judges applied economic reasoning were they able to bring coherence to the Sherman Act. But there is one big difference between the Sherman Act and CVD law: in 1890 each side of the antitrust question had a strong domestic constituency, whereas in international trade disputes, domestic pressure is usually only in one direction.

Richard Diamond stated that antidumping law has been administered more intelligently as interpretations of the statutes have improved, but the same is not true of CVD law, which is not based on coherent principles. Horlick commented that dumping lends itself to a more streamlined method of investigation than subsidies do. Palmeter did not believe Congress would allow the DOC much leeway in interpreting CVD law, and he stressed that there is nothing resembling "the rule of reason" in the trade statutes.

Binder directly answered a number of other criticisms of Commerce's procedures advanced by several participants. He responded to Palmeter's statement that questionnaires have been increasing in length by explaining that many of the added pages are explanatory, to aid the respondents in understanding the new statutes enacted in 1974. He made it clear that preliminary determinations are made on day 160 of any investigation, not day 110. In addition, Binder offered the department's public records for inspection in response to the suggestion that some respondents intentionally do not complete the questionnaires, a practice he denies being aware of. Palmeter claimed these situations do exist.

Binder stressed the objectivity of both the analysts and the verifiers. In answer to Patrick Macrory's questions about the ability of verifiers to understand the bookkeeping of foreign companies, he explained that the verification staff not only has years of experience but is backed by a staff of accountants, all of whom are CPAs. Binder completed his comments by saying that it is clear in the department's report whether the respondents' numbers have passed verification.

The Politics of Unfair Trade

Though most of the discussion concentrated on methodological and economic issues connected with antidumping and CVD law and procedures, some of it focused on the political influences affecting the administration of the unfair trade laws. From an economic perspective, protectionist policies are certain to decrease overall efficiency in trade, but, as Horlick pointed out, some strong interests in the United States support protection. The negative effects of protectionist policies are dispersed among consumers, but the benefits are concentrated among producers, providing the impetus for political pressure away from freer trade.

Noel Hemmendinger observed that multinational companies are gradually becoming more involved in debates about unfair trade laws, both as consumers and exporters. These corporations are affected by the price of foreign components and by the retaliatory use of unfair trade laws by trade partners. Yet though these corporations are helping to balance protectionist forces, politicians remain strongly influenced by the powerful domestic industries that are now protected; they do not want to stray from the politically appealing stance and support "fair trade." And allied domestic industry groups, such as LICIT (Labor-Industry Coalition for International Trade), are able to get immediate large support from members of Congress any time it seems their interests are threatened. Hemmindinger concluded that any changes removing the domestic industry bias in the administration of the unfair trade laws will be best achieved through the education of committee members, but he recognized the uphill nature of the task.

Although the papers and the conference focused on the administration of unfair trade laws by the Department of Commerce, several discussants voiced comments about the International Trade Commission's role in the investigation process.[1] Wechsler countered the notion that ITC members are unduly influenced in individual cases by congressional subcommittee members. At the same time, however, he suggested that industries with large trade problems certainly have strong interests in getting their elected representatives on the trade subcommittee. Anderson followed by suggesting that the relationship between congressional committee members and ITC decisions is best explained by subtle changes in the statutes, put

---

1. In the cases where the Commerce Department finds that imports have been dumped or unfairly subsidized, the ITC is charged with determining whether those imports have been the cause of "material injury" to a domestic industry.

in at the behest of specific industries. These changes are not captured in statistical analyses purporting to explain the outcomes of ITC decisions.

Wechsler claimed there is no need for a settlement procedure if there is a consistent set of principles applied to unfair trade law, particularly because a settlement mechanism makes the process more susceptible to political influence. In addition, if there are consistent principles, the domestic side of the debate should not oppose the "unitary" method of injury calculation (explained in the next section).

There was discussion about how to redirect the goals of Congress and the Department of Commerce in interpreting unfair trade law. Tarullo, using the progression of the interpretations of the Sherman Act as a model, suggested developing laws from general principles, such as "do not price discriminate." Martin proposed that the United States consider implementing a policy like Canada's, where in addition to the initial investigation, the general good of the public is evaluated and considered as a factor in any injury decision.

Economic Issues

Richard Boyce started the dialogue about the economics involved in unfair trade law by discussing the differences between "fair value" and "foreign market value." There is more flexibility in defining fair value, so regulators are able to consider the economics of the industry they are investigating. But in a section 751 review, where the goal is to determine the amount of duties to be reimbursed, foreign market value is strictly defined. Boyce recommended that one look to the administrators of unfair trade regulations, not Congress or the GATT, for improvements.

Stewart remarked that the ITC is not capable of making accurate appraisals of industries during periods of high growth. Thus fewer petitions were filed in the last five years of the 1980s, when the U.S. economy was expanding strongly. Dorn suggested that fewer cases had been filed because of a feeling in the business community that, owing to the free trade orientation of the present administration, the unfair trade process has become politicized in favor of respondents. Kaplan agreed that more firms file petitions during economic downturns, but suggested that this is the period when the economy is most injured by affirmative finds.

Though Wechsler agreed with Stewart's comments about the difficulties the ITC has in dealing with growth industries, he believed they could be resolved if the ITC adopted the so-called unitary method of determining injury. Under this approach, even an industry that is preforming well by some objective standard could still obtain an affirmative injury finding if it could demonstrate that "but for" the unfair trade practice (dumping or subsidization) it would have done significantly better. Wechsler also discussed the belief among some economists that no harmful price discrimination exists in international trade. He claimed that the finding of consistent margins of dumping by certain countries points to barriers to entry, not biases in the methodology. These barriers prevent arbitrage, which in a united market eliminates dumping.

Binder tackled the complicated issue of exchange rates discussed in Palmeter's paper. He pointed out that the DOC enforces a three-month lag period, a grace period during which exporters may respond to currency swings. He said analysts are careful when studying currency jumps beyond the 5 percent band to make sure they are not the sole determinant in the finding of dumping. Boltuck added that controversy about exchange rate dumping dates from the 1920s, when Gottfried Haberler classified exchange dumping as "not real dumping."

Anderson raised the point that in the debate concerning price versus cost adjustments, one must consider more than just the change in the cost of producing in one market versus another, and that as a rule the higher cost does not get fully passed through to the price. In situations in which analysts must consider differences in service or quality, adjustments become increasingly complicated because of shifts along the demand curve. Though the department can standardize its assumptions about whether costs have been passed through into prices in the home market, Robert Litan felt the best method is to use costs rather than price adjustments, to avoid both the complications and expense of making more specified determinations.

Horlick expressed his support for the cash flow approach in determining the presence of subsidies. Boltuck wondered if Congress is mandated to adopt the effects approach rather than the benefits approach, or if this reform requires statutory changes. He also added that if Commerce adopted an approach covering export subsidies affecting exports to countries other than the United States, there would be a reinterpretation of the mathematics involved in his equations.

Diamond noted that, though there is currently more concentration on antidumping, countervailing cases will increase as more countries make the transition to free market economies. At another point in the discussion, Diamond voiced confidence that the DOC could use economic principles to bring coherence to countervailing law.

Finally, Daniel Klett commented on the risks that exporters face because of the unfair trade laws. Specifically, exporters must consider not only the variability between the deposit rate and the assessment rate but also which rate will exceed the other. Though changes in exchange rates and market prices are beyond the control of the exporter, it does have control over pricing decisions. Klett also remarked that Boltuck, Francois, and Kaplan's paper seemed to imply that fair market value is often based on a share of the home market sales, not the total universe, which means the results can be affected by technical differences between markets.

Contributors

JEFFREY C. ANSPACHER
*U.S. International Trade
Commission*

ROBERT E. BALDWIN
University of Wisconsin

RICHARD BOLTUCK
*Office of Management
and Budget*

RONALD A. CASS
*Boston University School
of Law*

MICHAEL COURSEY
Vinson & Elkins

I. M. DESTLER
University of Maryland

RICHARD DIAMOND
*Georgetown University School
of Law*

TOM EMRICH
Trade Resources, Inc.

ROBERT M. FEINBERG
American University

JOSEPH F. FRANCOIS
*U.S. International Trade
Commission*

NOEL HEMMENDINGER
Willkie, Farr & Gallagher

ROBERT HERZSTEIN
Shearman & Sterling

BRIAN HINDLEY
London School of Economics

GARY HORLICK
O'Melveny & Myers

SETH KAPLAN
*U.S. International Trade
Commission*

ROBERT E. LITAN
Brookings Institution

PATRICK MACRORY
Akin, Gump, Hauer & Feld

MICHAEL O. MOORE
George Washington University

TRACY MURRAY
University of Arkansas

STEPHEN J. NARKIN
Asia Pacific Investors Company

PIETRO S. NIVOLA
Brookings Institution

N. DAVID PALMETER
*Mudge, Rose, Guthrie,
Alexander & Ferdon*

TERENCE P. STEWART
Stewart & Stewart

Index